I0820794

HOLKHAM

HOLKHAM

AN ENGLISH TREASURE HOUSE AND ITS LANDSCAPE

Edited by
Leo Schmidt and Elizabeth Angelicoussis

Foreword by
The Earl of Leicester

Contributions by
Peter Burman, Polly Feversham, Anne Glenconner,
Katherine Hardwick-Kulpa, John Hardy, Uta Hassler, Gerard M-F Hill,
Christine Hiskey, Markus Joachim, Christian Keller, Axel Klausmeier,
Werner Koch, Silke Langenberg, Tom Leicester, Laura Nuvoloni,
Bernhard Ritter, Christoph Martin Vogtherr and Tom Williamson

Photographs by
Pete Huggins

HIRMER

HIRMER AUGMENTED REALITY APP

The **HIRMER** AUGMENTED REALITY APP is a virtual extension of the printed book, bringing selected pictures to life as videos.

1. Search for the **HIRMER** AUGMENTED REALITY APP in the App Store or Play Store and install the app on your smartphone or tablet.
2. Open the app and point your device at images marked with the ►■◄ symbol. These images can be found on pages 9, 10, 40, 82, 88, 98, 158, 168, 213 and 223.

TABLE OF CONTENTS

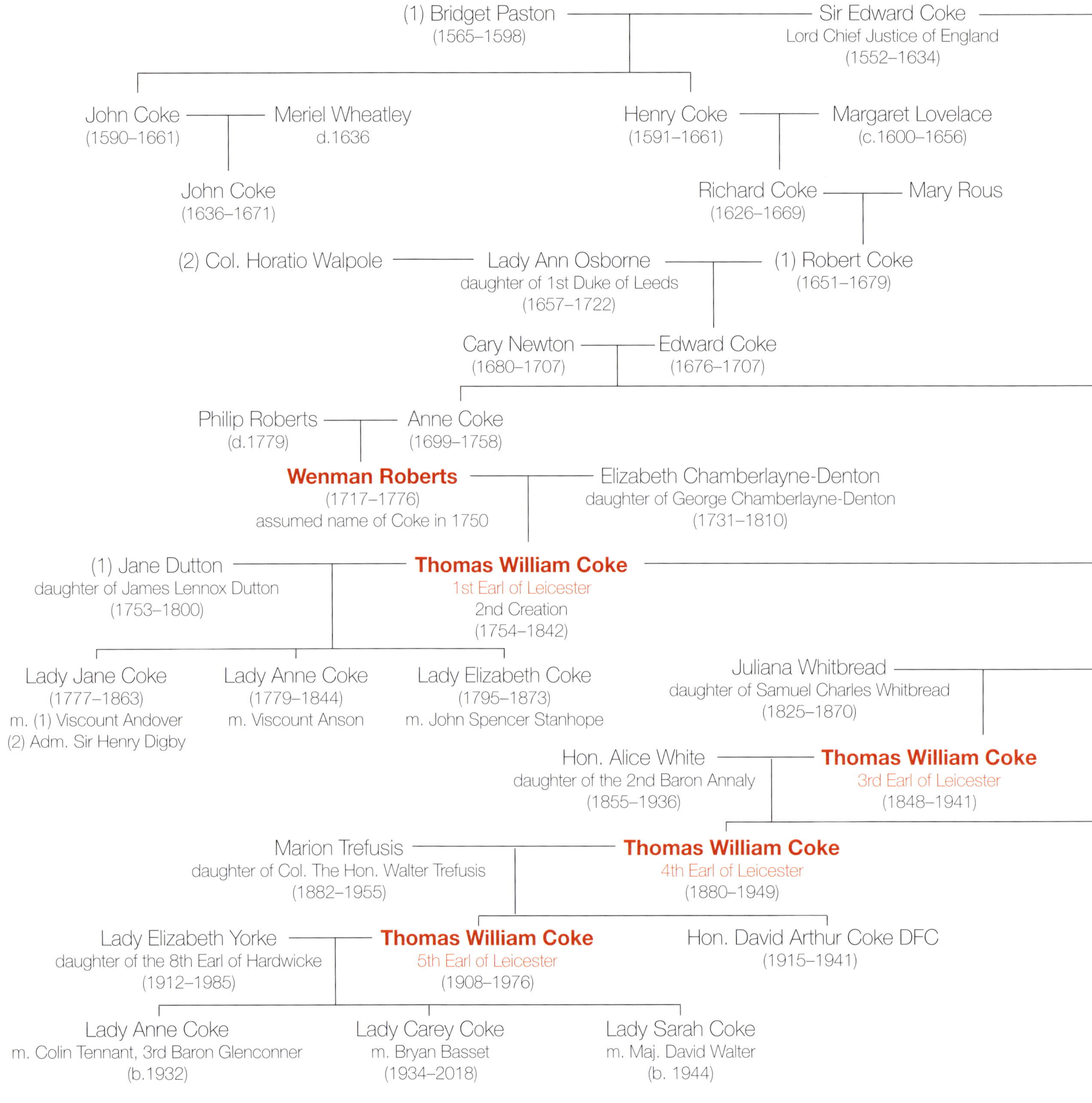

(1) Bridget Paston
(1565–1598)
Sir Edward Coke
Lord Chief Justice of England
(1552–1634)
John Coke
(1590–1661)
Meriel Wheatley
d.1636
Henry Coke
(1591–1661)
Margaret Lovelace
(c.1600–1656)
John Coke
(1636–1671)
Richard Coke
(1626–1669)
Mary Rous
(2) Col. Horatio Walpole
Lady Ann Osborne
daughter of 1st Duke of Leeds
(1657–1722)
(1) Robert Coke
(1651–1679)
Cary Newton
(1680–1707)
Edward Coke
(1676–1707)
Philip Roberts
(d.1779)
Anne Coke
(1699–1758)
Wenman Roberts
(1717–1776)
assumed name of Coke in 1750
Elizabeth Chamberlayne-Denton
daughter of George Chamberlayne-Denton
(1731–1810)
(1) Jane Dutton
daughter of James Lennox Dutton
(1753–1800)
Thomas William Coke
1st Earl of Leicester
2nd Creation
(1754–1842)
Lady Jane Coke
(1777–1863)
m. (1) Viscount Andover
(2) Adm. Sir Henry Digby
Lady Anne Coke
(1779–1844)
m. Viscount Anson
Lady Elizabeth Coke
(1795–1873)
m. John Spencer Stanhope
Juliana Whitbread
daughter of Samuel Charles Whitbread
(1825–1870)
Hon. Alice White
daughter of the 2nd Baron Annaly
(1855–1936)
Thomas William Coke
3rd Earl of Leicester
(1848–1941)
Marion Trefusis
daughter of Col. The Hon. Walter Trefusis
(1882–1955)
Thomas William Coke
4th Earl of Leicester
(1880–1949)
Lady Elizabeth Yorke
daughter of the 8th Earl of Hardwicke
(1912–1985)
Thomas William Coke
5th Earl of Leicester
(1908–1976)
Hon. David Arthur Coke DFC
(1915–1941)
Lady Anne Coke
m. Colin Tennant, 3rd Baron Glenconner
(b.1932)
Lady Carey Coke
m. Bryan Basset
(1934–2018)
Lady Sarah Coke
m. Maj. David Walter
(b. 1944)

(2) Lady Elizabeth Hatton
née Cecil, daughter of the 1st Earl of Exeter
(1578–1646)

The Coke Family

and the owners of Holkham Hall

Thomas Coke
1st Earl of Leicester
1st Creation
(1697–1759)

Lady Margaret Tufton
Countess of Leicester and 19th Baroness de Clifford
daughter of the 6th Earl of Thanet
(1700–1775)

Edward, Viscount Coke
(1719–1753)

Lady Mary Campbell
daughter of the 2nd Duke of Argyll and Greenwich
(1727–1811)

(2) Lady Anne Keppel
daughter of the 4th Earl of Albemarle
(1803–1844)

Thomas William Coke
2nd Earl of Leicester
(1822–1909)

(2) Hon. Georgiana Cavendish
daughter of the 2nd Baron Chesham
(1852–1937)

Hon. Arthur George Coke
(1882–1915)

Phyllis Hermione Drury
daughter of Francis Saxham Elmer Drury
(1885–1976)

(1) Moyra Crossley
daughter of Douglas Crossley
(1906–1987)

Anthony Louis Lovel Coke
6th Earl of Leicester
(1909–1994)

(2) Vera Haigh
(3) Elizabeth Johnstone

(1) Valeria Potter
daughter of Leonard A. Potter

Edward Douglas Coke
7th Earl of Leicester
(1936–2015)

(2) Sarah de Chair
daughter of Noel Henry Boys Forde

Polly Whateley
daughter of Thomas Whateley

Thomas Edward Coke
8th Earl of Leicester
(b. 1965)

Lady Laura Coke
m. Jonathan Paul

Hon. Rupert Coke
m. Ranil Sanatinia PhD

Lady Hermione Coke

Lady Juno Coke

Edward, Viscount Coke

Lady Elizabeth Coke

FOREWORD

Holkham Hall is a treasure house and an architectural masterpiece which Sir Nicholas Pevsner called 'the most classically correct house in England'. It was conceived and built nearly three hundred years ago by one man: Thomas Coke, first Earl of Leicester. During the long years of planning and building he consulted many people, but Holkham is ultimately the product of his own ideas, his refined taste and sense of quality, his admiration for ancient Rome and his personal and political ambitions.

He filled its splendid rooms with wonderful paintings and Roman sculptures collected on his extended Grand Tour of Europe. With its hundreds of illuminated medieval manuscripts, his library is regarded as the finest in private hands in the country.

The Hall, its treasures and the surrounding estate have survived essentially intact into the twenty-first century thanks to the efforts of successive generations of the family. In his turn, the builder's great-nephew Thomas William Coke, first Earl of Leicester of the second creation, again bought works of art on his Grand Tour and also added a significant collection of political portraiture. He started the process of consolidating the family's land holdings in Norfolk whilst at the same time playing a key part in the Agricultural Revolution. The second earl built the Victorian terraces around the house, mercifully in classical rather than gothic style, along with a vast array of buildings such as the stables and offices to the east of the Hall as well as a large number of barns and workers' cottages. The third earl bought the parishes of Burnham Overy and Thorpe in 1922, on account of the 'excellent partridge shooting'.

Inheriting in 1941, the fourth earl faced very difficult times indeed, and that same year he also lost his younger son, David, killed in action in North Africa. His elder son Tommy, the fifth earl, had to deal with the war's aftermath. Punitive post-war taxes reduced the estate from 42,000 acres to 25,000 and at one stage the Hall and half its land were nearly given to the National Trust, the result of post-war gloom that we can now barely contemplate. Tommy steered the estate through the 1950s and 1960s whilst hundreds of other country houses foundered and were demolished.

Thanks to the (many would say) archaic system of primogeniture whereby the estate is entailed in the male line, my father, Eddy, later to become the seventh earl, was summoned from southern Africa to take on the estate. He introduced modern management practices and through Herculean efforts managed to put the estate on an even keel. This has allowed me to move forward with new confidence. Whilst agriculture and conservation are still the core of Holkham, now we have tourism and leisure activities like events and concerts in the park and weddings and Christmas displays in the Hall, supported by cafés, car parks, a hotel and a caravan holiday park.

In my father's time we had fifty employees, but I suspect that Holkham has never employed as many staff as it does now: 450 in the summer months, along with 90 volunteers. Indeed, it is our wonderful team who are responsible for so many of the good things that happen here. One of our proudest achievements came in 2023, when we won the award for 'best large employer in the East of England'.

Fig. 1. The Earl of Leicester in the Long Library.

►■◄

The estate is an economic driver within the community, as an historic place but also as a working country estate. The architecture and works of art would not be there without the land and its use, and without the long-term ambition and ideas of the people who have shaped it.

I am most grateful to all who have contributed to this book, but my especial thanks go to the two editors. Leo Schmidt has been the driving force behind the project. Twenty years after he produced the first edition of *Holkham*, he has returned to it, but this time without the pressure of changing the nappies of two young children whilst hastily preparing lectures for his students. Now in retirement, with the benefit of a few grey hairs, he has produced a master tome – jointly with Elizabeth Angelicoussis. The new book owes very much to Elizabeth's deep commitment to the cultural values of Holkham and particularly to its outstanding collection of classical sculpture – a commitment that led her to produce a much-acclaimed book on the topic in 2001, a book that she is currently reworking for a new and updated edition.

Our family have owned land and lived at Holkham for four hundred years. I very much hope and expect we will continue to do so for the next four hundred. I trust you will enjoy this excellent book and hope that, if you have never done so, you will visit us at Holkham, where I can promise you a warm welcome.

The Earl of Leicester
2024

Fig. 2. The Triumphal Arch, erected 1745–48, marks the southern entrance to Holkham Park and the beginning of the long approach to the Hall.

INTRODUCTION

If there has ever been a place that deserves to be hailed as a treasure house, that place is Holkham. It is full of remarkable, even unique, treasures: the grand rooms and interiors contain the foremost private collection of ancient sculptures in Britain, there is a beautiful library full of rare books as well as illuminated manuscripts, there are exquisite paintings and old master drawings, and the superbly designed and richly decorated rooms with their classical ceilings and friezes and their original textile hangings and original furniture make a perfect setting for these works of art.

But this is not all. The works of art are contained within a building of extraordinary qualities. It is itself the centre-piece of a much wider setting in a park, in a designed land-scape that forms the core of a vast estate. That whole land-scape is shaped and used for agriculture and forestry and gamekeeping, but also for sport and pleasure. As if that were not enough, this man-made landscape, populated by sheep, deer and pheasants, interacts directly with the immediately adjoining marshlands and wide sandy beaches of the North Sea with their teeming wildlife.

Within this unique complex of landscape, architecture and works of art, all elements are designed to interact with each other – they form one harmonious entity. Although many artists and craftsmen were involved in the creation of this ensemble, a single man was the driving force and guid-ing spirit who conceived the whole huge complex and made it happen over a period of roughly four decades. This man was Thomas Coke (1697–1759). In his creation of Holkham he was inspired by two ambitions. One source was his love and admiration for ancient Rome, its culture, architecture and art. Ancient Rome was the ideal that he aimed to emu-late and recreate in the Norfolk countryside. His other driv-ing force was a more worldly ambition. The ensemble was conceived to be the seat of a noble dynasty, and Mr Coke did not rest until he had gained the earldom that he felt was due to him. Both ambitions did of course go hand in hand: at the time, creating a great country seat was a very usual entry ticket to membership of the House of Lords.

Because of his central rôle in the creation of the place we know today, this book focuses on Thomas Coke and his achievements. Therefore the first chapter is dedicated to this man as a person. We look at his family background and his formative years, which included a truly Grand Tour on the Continent: nearly six years of travelling, first in France and then in Italy, bringing him into intensive contact with contemporary culture and art, and a phase during which he bought many of the treasures that adorn Holkham today.

To understand what Holkham is about, one needs to un-derstand the personality, qualities and ambitions of its crea-tor – a highly gifted man, erudite and creative as well as am-bitious. Characterised by his contemporaries as a patron both of the arts and of cockfighting, he was also passionate and impulsive, capable of stout friendship yet also engender-ing strong dislike, for instance from Horace Walpole, who misjudged him as 'a very cunning man but not a deep one'.[1]

Coke had a loyal wife, Lady Margaret, who supported him during their married life and completed the house after his death. They shared and enjoyed ambitions and successes as well as setbacks and personal tragedies. She was to bear him several children, of whom only one, Edward, survived childhood. But Edward died at the age of thirty-four, thus leaving Thomas Coke without an heir to the seat he had been building and the earldom of Leicester he had acquired.

The second chapter looks at the landscape as the foundation and setting of the treasure house that Coke was to build there. What was the situation he found there, at the edge of the North Sea? How was the site transformed from a typical segment of medieval rural Norfolk, with scattered houses, hedgerows, small fields and winding roads, to a grand and monumental landscape combining large new elements, such as a long straight approach designed to impress any visitor, with smaller-scale and picturesque elements, a fair semblance of Arcadia? What purposes was this designed landscape expected to serve? Of course the land, of which the park was the core, was supposed to provide the economic basis of the estate through agriculture, mostly carried out by tenants. But its woodlands and fields were also designed for sport and entertainment such as hunting and shooting, whilst the pond and the seats of the pleasure ground next to the house offered opportunities for enjoying gentler and more leisurely activities. Landscape, largely made up of living plants, tends to change much more quickly than architecture, so the setting of the house that we see is the product of several phases in the eighteenth and nineteenth centuries of adapting the landscape to new tastes and interests.

The central structure of the whole estate is of course the great house, Holkham Hall. How did the architecture come into being? Why does it look the way it does? This is discussed in the third chapter. Though Coke was immensely rich in land, he was always strapped for cash: no doubt he would have preferred to move more quickly, but he had to wait many years before he could actually start building. On the bright side, this time was used for planning and designing, producing a far deeper concept, both artistically and functionally, than would have been possible had the whole process been rushed through. So the question is: What happened during the decade or so of planning and thinking before the first spade was put in the ground? What concepts were brought up and discarded, to whom did Coke look for inspiration and support, and how did his ideals and priorities change during this time when other people were also designing and building great country houses?

A better understanding of Holkham's planning process is also crucial for the narrative of British architectural history in the first half of the eighteenth century. When exactly were its decisive features conceived? And by whom? These are questions hotly debated by architectural historians. This book lays out the argument for Holkham's claim to an even more important place in architectural history than hitherto accepted.

Coke's financial difficulties were far from over when building actually began, and they were to plague him for the rest of his life, which meant that building did not progress as quickly as he would no doubt have preferred. As with the long-drawn-out planning, this slow progress had a silver lining, not for Coke (who died before he could see his great house finished) but for later historians: it has made the story more transparent, because we can see Coke's priorities quite clearly. A closer look at the building as a physical historical source allows many insights into the tricks of the trade, but also into the mistakes that were made during execution, the difficulties that were encountered, and the sometimes quite ingenious ways of overcoming those problems.

Within the house itself, close study of the building fabric and of the available plans and documents allows us to identify corrections and improvements to the appearance and the functional qualities that had been thought out at different times in the building process. At times we can almost look over Thomas Coke's shoulder as he eyed the progress of the building and decided to do things differently after all. Thomas Coke died before he could see the house finished, but his widow completed the task for him, not without some significant design decisions of her own.

The fourth chapter discusses how the house works as a unique ensemble where the sequence of the rooms, their shape, interior decoration and contents are designed to interact on many levels with each other and with the architecture. Again the dominant theme is ancient Rome. The temple-like Marble Hall sets the tone and, like the Hall's columns, friezes and ceilings, all the architectural decoration in the staterooms is painstakingly copied from the most prominent ancient buildings in Rome: the sources are proudly given in a splendid tome of engravings published shortly after the completion of the house. The Roman theme was clearly the one that was closest to Coke's heart, but there is a competing layer in the design.

A house of this size had to be fit for the sovereign, should he or she ever deign to visit, so it needed a proper state apartment featuring a sequence of rooms, leading from the saloon through at least two ante-chambers to a state bedroom, rounded off by a cabinet and the compulsory back stairs: an arrangement that can be found in hundreds of palaces and great houses in Europe at the time, all wanting to emulate the Sun King's Château de Versailles.

The state apartment and indeed the whole body of the house was meant to be one vast exhibition space, presenting the wonderful works of art carefully chosen and arranged by the owner and builder so that his guests, and he himself, might enjoy them. It was also to become a lasting monument to himself, his taste, erudition and wit – in short, his claim to be one of the élite who were entitled to rule the country because they felt they were simply the best. Within this scheme, the ancient sculptures and busts that Coke had brought from Rome no doubt ranked first, with the paintings a very close second, and the masterpieces of both collections were arranged according to a carefully conceived concept that ran far deeper than a placement based merely on formal or aesthetic aspects.

The fifth chapter looks at the functions and purposes of the house – at the ways Holkham has been used. Architecture and splendid interiors are not an end in themselves, but a means. Their purpose is to provide the setting for what is supposed to happen in this place. The house had separate living and working areas for the family and for the servants, and it provided the stage for the gatherings and social events that were its ultimate *raison d'être*. In the understanding of the time, a great house had to be *convenient*.

What did this term mean in the eighteenth century? What did life in the house look like, for the family and their guests, and also for the fifty-odd servants who ran the place? And what of the changes that became necessary in the course of two and a half centuries? How has the house been maintained and adapted to the needs and ideas of successive generations and to the changes in societal values?

Following up that last question of changes, the sixth chapter explores in greater detail how Holkham has made it into the present day, and where it is headed. Who were the people – the successive owners – who brought it forward through the ages, what did they see in the place and how did they see their own rôle in relation to it? What different challenges did they face and how did they deal with them? At some points in its history, Holkham might well have lost its feasibility and become a 'hulk stranded from the past',[2] like many great houses that are preserved as museums, but it is far more than that. It is a vibrant country estate with an ambitious vision to carry on with time-honoured values and even to revive them: going back to the roots as the basis of a policy of sustainable management of the land, with the treasure house as the pinnacle of a thriving country estate – to be enjoyed not just by a select few but by all those who want to come and take part, and even useful as a beacon of an approach that could and should be emulated by many others who have responsibilities for land.

* * *

This book builds upon an earlier publication of 2005 that was the joint achievement of a number of experts in such diverse fields as landscape archaeology, garden history, architectural history, building archaeology, classical archaeology, paintings, interior decoration, furniture and social history as well as heritage management. Lavishly illustrated, that book was aimed at the wider audience who visit great houses and delight in the wealth of aesthetic qualities they have to offer and who also want to gain a better understanding of what they represent, of what brought them into being. Such visitors and readers also want to understand what happened to the great house over time and what it means to be running such a place today: a house and park open to the public, not as a museum but as the centre of a living and working estate that has to make money to survive and to support the great house and the cultural asset it represents.

Knowledge, points of view and interests have changed and progressed over two decades, so that two thirds of this text is new – incorporating new research, filling some gaps and deepening the focus with contributions from new collaborators intimately involved with the place today. Not only have there been many new publications on Holkham – sometimes responding to the 2005 book – but this new book is also reacting to the fact that today's audience has become more interested in people than in things. They want to know more about the personalities behind the things, about their values, motivations and challenges. What will of course be immediately obvious is that the illustrations have been completely reviewed and largely replaced so as to do even better justice to the visual qualities of the landscape, the house, the interiors and the works of art, all equally extraordinary.

Fig. 3. Emulating the architecture of ancient Rome, the Marble Hall is designed to welcome and to impress the visitor.

CHAPTER 1

THOMAS COKE, EARL OF LEICESTER – THE BUILDER OF HOLKHAM

OVERLEAF
Detail from Jonathan Richardson's portrait of Thomas Coke in his robes as Knight of the Bath.

The Coke family have been at Holkham since 1609, when the founder of the family's fortunes, Chief Justice Sir Edward Coke (fig. 4), acquired Neales, one of the three manors of the Holkham parish. He was enormously influential as a jurist and his legal commentaries and judgements are still referred to today.[3] Sir Edward also became one of the greatest landowners far and wide, with properties in Norfolk and in many other counties.

In time the properties acquired by the Chief Justice descended to his great-great-grandson, another Edward – the builder's father (fig. 5). Through his maternal grandfather, the first Duke of Leeds, and other relatives Edward was well connected to the aristocracy. At the age of twenty, in 1696, he married Cary Newton, daughter of Sir John Newton Bt and an heiress (fig. 6). Although they both died quite young in 1707, aged thirty-one and twenty-seven respectively, they had managed to get themselves into considerable financial difficulties. They left five small children behind: Thomas, the eldest, born on 17 June 1697 at No. 5 St James's Square in London and christened in Wren's Church of St James Piccadilly close by, and his siblings Cary (b. 1698), Anne (b. 1699), Edward (b. 1702) and Robert (b. 1704). Thomas's childhood was partly spent in the metropolis, but the family's country residence was the comparatively modest Elizabethan manor house of Wheatley or Hill Hall at Holkham.[4]

TWO FIRST EARLS OF LEICESTER AT HOLKHAM

It has always been the cause of some confusion that the history of Holkham in the eighteenth and nineteenth centuries is dominated by two figures who are both known as the first Earl of Leicester: Thomas Coke, the builder of the house (1697–1759) (fig. 7) and Thomas William Coke, his grand-nephew (1754–1842) (fig. 8).

The earldom of Leicester had been (re-)created in 1744 for Thomas Coke, who clearly regarded this high aristocratic rank as an important part of his achievements. However, as his only son Edward predeceased him, it became extinct again with Thomas's death in 1759. Holkham Hall and all his property first passed to his widow, Lady Margaret, and then to his nephew Wenman Roberts, son of his sister Anne, who had married Philip Roberts (figs. 9 and 10). Upon inheriting Longford in Derbyshire, the Coke family's lesser great house, from Thomas's younger brother Robert in 1750, Wenman changed his surname to Coke.

Wenman Coke enjoyed possession of Holkham only for a year between 1775 and 1776. His son Thomas William Coke, born in 1754, grew up at Longford in the knowledge that he would eventually inherit Holkham.[5] His achievements as an agricultural reformer and politician earned him not only the lasting sobriquet of 'Coke of Norfolk' but also – in 1837 – an earldom for which he chose his predecessor's title, Leicester. Coke of Norfolk's life and achievement have been the subject of many studies[6] and cannot adequately be dealt with here, but his contributions to the house, its collections and its setting are discussed in their proper contexts.

Fig. 4. Sir Edward Coke (1551/52–1634), the founder of the family's fortunes, was Attorney General under Queen Elizabeth and Chief Justice of the Common Pleas under King James I. Painting at Holkham by Marcus Gheeraerts.

THE GRAND TOUR

Born in 1697, Thomas Coke inherited at the tender age of ten, and guardians administered his affairs until his majority. Even during his adolescence, his tutors and his relations recognised in him an abundance of talent and a great interest in classical authors, but also noted a somewhat disturbing addiction to cockfighting. An extended Grand Tour of the Continent seemed a good way of developing the gentler side of Thomas's character, and for the next six years he travelled extensively in France, Italy and the German Empire.[7]

Exposure to the cultural treasures of Old Europe quickly bore fruit. In a letter from Rome, Thomas wrote to his guardian: 'I am become since my stay in Rome, a perfect virtuoso, and a great lover of pictures, even so far as to encroach on the kindness of my Guardians as to buy some few.'[8] He also developed an interest in books, commenting that 'certainly one of the greatest ornaments to a Gentleman and his family is a fine Library.'[9] Under the guidance of

Figs. 5 and 6. Edward Coke (1676–1707) and his wife Cary (1680–1707) both died quite young but left five small children behind – among them Thomas, the eldest, who was to build Holkham Hall. Paintings at Holkham by Michael Dahl.

his tutor, Dr Hobart, as well as increasingly following his own tastes, Thomas amassed the core of the vast collections that are on display at Holkham today.

Architecture, however, seems to have fascinated the young man more than the other arts. In 1714, Thomas, then aged seventeen, was instructed in the rudiments of the art of building by a Signor Giacomo – the Roman architect Giacomo Mariari.[10] He received instruction in architecture for two months on one occasion and two and a half months on another. This took the form of direct experience of existing buildings, both ancient and contemporary – 'goeing about the town' – and in a more theoretical form through the study of books and drawings. He was also shown the principles of architectural draughtsmanship ('drawing cornissh', as his servant noted in his account book).

Coke's first-hand knowledge of Continental buildings was extensive. The list of places he visited is impressive to say the least, including the palaces of Versailles, Marly and Fontainebleau, the *châteaux* of the Loire and the castle and town of Richelieu. Many *palazzi* in Rome, Florence and northern Italy, villas in the Veneto, the Belvedere in Vienna and the palaces of Dresden, Potsdam and Charlottenburg in Berlin were also visited by the young man. Coke was particularly interested in ancient ruins and contemporary fortifications: Greek and Roman sites near Naples and on Sicily were part of his itinerary, as were Vauban's fortresses in Neuf-Brisach and Kehl on the Rhine.

THE MAN ON THE MAKE

This enviable, extended time of well-subsidised travelling, studying and shopping came to an end with Thomas Coke's return to England on 18 May 1718. Four weeks later, on

Fig. 7. Thomas Coke (1697–1759), the builder of Holkham, was raised to the peerage in 1728 as Baron Lovell of Minster Lovell and became Earl of Leicester in 1744. As he had no male heir, his titles lapsed with his death. Painting at Holkham by Francesco Trevisani.

17 June, he came of age and took possession of his inheritance, and by 2 July he was a married man. His bride was eighteen-year-old Lady Margaret Tufton (fig. 11) – a good match both financially and socially, arranged of course by his guardians. Born on 16 June 1700, Lady Margaret was a daughter of the 6th Earl of Thanet. In 1734, she became the nineteenth Baroness of Clifford, inheriting a title that can descend through both male and female lines.

Their honeymoon took them via Windsor, Reading and Oxford to Blenheim Palace, where the Duchess of Marlborough reputedly refused to let them see the house.[11] Nevertheless, nineteen shillings greasing the palms of 'y.e serv.ts at Bleinham ho.s'[12] opened the doors of the great palace to the sightseeing couple.

A son, Edward, was born on 21 June 1719 (fig. 12). The parents moved on to Holkham, leaving the baby at their London residence, Thanet House,[13] in the care of a wet nurse and under the eye of the eminent physician Dr Hans Sloane.[14] Further children were born (little Thomas in 1721, and an unnamed child in 1723), but they died almost instantly, so that Edward was the only child to reach maturity.

In financial terms, however, things must have looked very bright for young Mr Coke and his wife. The guardians had administered his property in an exemplary way: rents alone

Fig. 8. Thomas William Coke (1754–1842), grandson of Thomas's sister Ann, inherited Holkham in 1776. He gained fame as a politician and agricultural reformer and is widely known as 'Coke of Norfolk'. In 1837 the earldom of Leicester was recreated for him. Painting at Holkham by Pompeo Batoni.

yielded an annual income of about ten thousand pounds, equalling roughly £1.8 million in 2023 terms.[15] This placed Mr Coke amongst the richest landowners in the three kingdoms and the young man must have felt the world was his oyster. However, 'a spirited burst of extravagance'[16] led him to overspending by about £15,000 in the first two years. Some of his expenses may be seen as expressions of gratitude and generosity, such as a present of a precious ring (fifty guineas) to his tutor, Dr Hobart, who also received a gift of 200 guineas 'for his faithfull services'; or of his far-ranging scholarly interests, such as £10.15s.0d paid 'To Mr Simon Oakley Arabick professor at Cambridge for translating & copying an Arabick Mss.' Others speak of his delight in precious objects; £620 was paid for two large diamond rings, and he bought £261 worth of jewels as well as 'a Gold picture case & Chrystall for Lady Margaretts picture' (a mere £7.10s.0d). £2,210 (£400,000 today) went to Paul de Lamerie, one of the most renowned silversmiths of the day, for a splendid set of plate.[17] Substantial losses at gambling and cockfighting did nothing to help the situation.

But this prodigal life was to change dramatically. In 1720, Mr Coke made the disastrous mistake of joining the gullible souls who were hoping to make money quickly by investing in South Sea stock. He invested heavily, largely on credit. Between April and September 1720, Coke laid out at least £58,000. All in all, he lost £37,928.14s.8d in the South Sea Bubble,[18] equalling nearly £7,000,000 today, a sum which even he, with all his property and secure annual income, found hard to stomach.

The resulting debts made the following years very difficult for Coke, but that does not necessarily mean that he and his wife lived frugally. Although the Old House at Holkham, known as Hill Hall, was not very large, it housed a considerable retinue of thirteen male and seven female servants. A large variety of payments, including several subscriptions to the Royal Academy of Music at £10 each as well as a guinea for 'a Poor Man who had his Tongue cut out', suggest that the Cokes were still living according to their status. Mr Coke's health, however, seems to have given occasional trouble: early in 1723 a surgeon, Mr Tubbing, was paid the remarkably generous sum of five guineas 'for Dressing & looking to my Masters Shoulder having been turn'd over in ye Coach at Holkham' and in 1724 Mr Coke wrote letters from Bath complaining about his ill health.

Figs. 9 and 10. Anne Coke, Thomas Coke's sister, and Philip Roberts. Much to the family's distress, in 1715 sixteen-year-old Ann eloped with Philip, then a young cornet of the Life Guards. But all the earls of Leicester of the second creation descend from her and Philip through their son Wenman Roberts (who changed his name to Coke in 1750) and their grandson Thomas William.

Though he had a taste for the fast life and for all kinds of sport, Coke found great pleasure during these years in studying the valuable manuscripts he had bought on the Continent. Scholarly works such as Thomas Dempster's *De Etruria Regali* (printed in Florence in 1724 and edited by Coke) owed much to his patronage (fig. 204). Edward Spelman, whose translation of Xenophon appeared in 1742, addressed Lord Lovell in an affectionate dedication, recalling, in a vivid sketch of Coke's widely divergent interests:

> when we were Fox-hunters, and a long Day's Sport had rather tir'd than satisfied us, we often pass'd the evening in reading the Ancient Authors; and when the Beauty of their Language, the Strength, and Justness of their Thoughts for ever glowing with a noble Spirit of Liberty, made us forget not only the Pains, but the Pleasures of the Day.[19]

On his return from the Continent, Coke had entered politics under the guidance of his neighbour and distant relative,

Fig. 11. Lady Margaret Tufton (1700–1775), daughter of the sixth Earl of Thanet, married Thomas Coke on his return from his Grand Tour in 1718. Following his death in 1759, she completed the building of the house. As their only son Edward had predeceased his parents, the estate then passed to Thomas's nephew Wenman Roberts Coke. Painting at Holkham by Sir Godfrey Kneller.

Fig. 12. Edward Coke (1719–1753) with his mother, Lady Margaret. Painting at Holkham by Jonathan Richardson.

Robert Walpole, who was about to become the first Prime Minister and was in the process of building his new seat at Houghton. An important first step in Coke's political career was his election to the House of Commons as member for the county of Norfolk in 1721, at the age of twenty-four. His loyal, though by no means disinterested, support of Walpole and his ministry soon began to pay dividends in the form of various coveted honours. Coke was frequently at the court of George I, Kensington Palace, where his painter friend William Kent was providing spectacular decoration for a suite of grand rooms. Remarkably, Kent even managed to include Coke's most treasured ancient sculpture in the decoration of the palace, the statue of Diana, which was brought to England on board HMS *Superb* in January 1720 and then put on display at Coke's London residence, Thanet House (fig. 13).[20] The top of the King's Stair, where Kent was working in 1725–27, features *trompe-l'œil* niches with Roman statues, and Kent's *Diana* (a rather softer depiction than the keen huntress of the actual sculpture) is on display next to the Farnese *Hercules* (figs. 144 and 148): a clever way of making the King and court aware of this ambitious and cultured young man.

Fig. 13. The married couple's London residence, Thanet House in Great Russell Street, as it looked in Thomas Coke's time. The sculptures, paintings and other treasures bought by Coke on his Grand Tour were kept here for many years before at least some of them could be moved to the new house at Holkham.

In 1725, around the time Kent was busy with this royal commission, Coke became one of the first thirty-eight knights of the newly revived Order of the Bath (fig. 14), spending considerable amounts on robes and fees, as we know from his personal accounts.[21] It is to the credit of the young knight that the first payment mentioning his new title was for an act of charity: ten guineas given to 'Lemon a poor man by Sr Tho.s Cokes order' – a generous sum, considering that this was equal to about £1,800 in today's terms.

MATURITY AND SUCCESS

In 1728, Sir Thomas was raised to the peerage by George II, taking the title of Baron Lovell of Minster Lovell (after his property at Minster Lovell in Oxfordshire, now a ruin but at that time still a manor house in good order). Membership of

Fig. 14. Sir Thomas Coke KB in his robes as Knight of the Bath. He was one of the first knights of this order established by George I in 1725. Painting at Holkham by Jonathan Richardson.

this highly exclusive group must have bolstered his ego considerably and, like Oliver, he lost no time in asking for more. Before an important vote in Parliament in 1730, Lord Lovell, in conversation with the Earl of Chesterfield, made out that he did not know how to vote, at length letting it slip, however, that he expected to be rewarded for voting with the government: his property was suitable for an earl or a viscount, he explained, and he wanted one of these titles. Chesterfield tried to deflect Lovell's advances by making a joke of it, saying his ambition was hopeless due to that famous maxim of English law, 'the King can do no wrong'.[22] Although the system of patronage, involving constant struggle for positions both for oneself and for one's clients and family, was hardly considered dishonourable in the eighteenth century, it is interesting to note the nonchalance with which people like Coke expected to profit from their political commitment.

In June 1733, a valuable position came his way when he became Postmaster General of England, a seat he was to fill for the rest of his life, either alone or with a partner. His acquaintances, rightly or wrongly, assumed that Lovell read any mail that might be of interest to him. Indeed, the Post Office was also a rudimentary intelligence service, and although this was not under the control of the Postmasters General[23] they would have been well aware of its existence. The salary Lord Lovell received as Postmaster General – roughly £1,000 per annum – represented a welcome boost to his income and may well have encouraged him to seize the nettle and actually start building his new house at Holkham in 1734. The new appointment also meant that, as Lord Lovell could now appoint his favourites to lucrative positions in the mail service, he became a far more serious player in the patronage system. Yet the position as Postmaster General also held unexpected dangers, as we see from a somewhat disturbing letter that arrived at Holkham in October 1753:

> My lord,
> I find that it was by your orders that Mr Stockdale was hung in chains; now, if you don't order him to be taken down, I will set fire to your house, and blow your brains out the first opportunity.[24]

John Stockdale had been executed on 3 July 1753 for murdering a postman,[25] and Coke, as Postmaster General, must have pressed for draconian measures. An award (initially of £100 and rising to £500 after a second, equally charming missive) was offered for information on the author of the anonymous letter, but the matter remained unresolved.

A significant link between influential men at the time was their common interest in Freemasonry. The earliest public indication of Lord Lovell's Masonic connections was his election to the exalted post of Grand Master of the English Freemasons for the year 1731 – proof of an already long-standing and unusually deep involvement with the brotherhood and its mysterious ideas. One wonders who introduced him to this group; Robert Walpole might well have initiated Coke – his 'creature', in the words of Lord Egmont. His election as a Fellow of the Royal Society (a largely Masonic body at the time) on 27 March 1735 may be seen as a further indication of his integration into the most influential circles of the time.

In view of Coke's direct involvement with Walpole (and his close friendship with Walpole's successors Pelham and Newcastle), it is remarkable that he has been suspected of

Jacobite leanings.[26] The young man abroad might have been full of immature ideas in 1715 or 1717, but after his return from the Continent he was and remained a staunch Whig. It may well be true that, as Robert Walpole himself argued, 'your right Jacobite . . . disguises his true sentiment . . . These are the men we have most reason to be afraid of.'[27] In the year of rebellion in 1745, Coke donated the enormous sum of £1,000 to a Norfolk anti-Jacobite fund, with his son Edward adding £500 more.[28] Together they even surpassed the donations made by Robert Walpole and his son, who gave £1,400. If people like Thomas Coke were crypto-Jacobites, the Stuarts hardly needed enemies.[29]

Images and elements at Holkham hitherto interpreted as pro-Jacobite are, in fact, based on Masonic ideas. In 1731, 'Grand Master Lovell summoned a private Lodge at Houghton Hall, in Norfolk, and advanced the Duke of Newcastle, and Francis Grand Duke of Tuscany, to the High Degree of Master Masons.'[30] How he must have cursed his luck in losing so much money in the South Sea Bubble; otherwise the ceremony might have been held at Holkham, a building destined to be full of Masonic significance. At least he was able to show his fellow Masons what he was planning there. A letter written around this time, on 16 July 1731, from Lord Hervey to the Prince of Wales, gives an impression of an august group of gentlemen travelling from one great East Anglian house to the next. Lord Lovell's old house was characterised as 'a most unpleasant place; but he comforts himself with a park in embryo, and a Burlington house with four pavilions on paper.'[31] Indeed, an engraving exists from the 1730s (fig. 83) that may well have enabled him to display the impressive project to his friends. Owning a great and fashionable house, or at least showing that such a house was in the offing, demonstrated a determination to seize a modicum of political power and to play an appropriate rôle in society.

Architecture in eighteenth-century Britain had a large and aristocratic following, and the country-house topics of agriculture, horticulture, hunting, shooting and political intriguing provided endless amusement for this happy band. There is no reason to imagine that Lord Lovell was alone on his many extended and well-documented country house tours; apart from the personal retinue he would have taken for granted, more often than not he was surrounded by like-minded friends. The excuse he gave to Lord Hardwicke in September 1744 for neglecting him is entirely credible – he had not had one moment to himself, he wrote, having been 'constantly on the road with a Party of Friends in seeing places'.[32]

His own residence at Holkham was regularly invaded by similar bands of travelling connoisseurs. In a letter he wrote to his people at Holkham from London in 1739 or 1740, he announced, 'I shall be at Holkham wth 12 more gentlemen at Fryday senight, for 3 or 4 days'[33] – at a time when the first wing of his new house was only just being finished and old Hill Hall was still needed to help in accommodating larger groups of guests.

Lord Lovell was a gregarious and colourful creature with a rather coarse sense of humour. Not everybody warmed to him; Charles Hanbury Williams, for example, portrayed him as:

Lovel, – the oddest character in town;
A lover, statesman, connoisseur, buffoon:
Extract him well, this is his quintessence,

Much folly, but more cunning, and some sense;
To neither party is his heart inclin'd,
He steer'd twixt both with politics refin'd
Voted with Walpole, and with Pulteney din'd.[34]

Or even more vividly, after his elevation to the earldom of Leicester:

Unless perchance Earl Leicester comes,
As noisy as a dozen drums,
And makes a horrid pother;
Else might we quiet sit and quaff
And Gently chat, and gayly laugh
At this, at that, and t'other.[35]

It is not surprising that Lovell's full-blooded nature did not find fulfilment in politics and art alone. For one thing, he competed very publicly with his fellow Freemason Lord Chesterfield for the charms of one Lady Fanny. Their rivalry was reflected in various letters, such as this one from Lord Lovell to the Earl of Essex in October 1735:

> You have open'd my wounds by speaking of Lady Fanny, she is quite lost to me, that foul fiend Chesterfield has bewitch't her, & under pretence of serving me, has intirely defeated me & is in full possession of the Ladys soul, as for her body that is so glorifyed that I presume none of our grosser mortal substance can ever think of that.[36]

Since he was, during his thirties and early forties, a well-known figure in the salons and drawing rooms of the metropolis, his involvement with the beautiful Lady Fanny and his comical rivalry with Chesterfield could not fail to be the subject of gossip and were even immortalised in various satirical and suggestive poems, with Lady Fanny lightly camouflaged as 'Flavia'. To quote from *An Epistle from Lord L--l to Lord C---d:*

I.
O Hol---m! blest, belov'd abode!
Productive of an Annual Ode,
If C---d inspire:
Clio and I will club for wit,
Beneath the spreading Oak we'll sit,
And thrumb the Lyrick Lyre.

II.
How beauteous is this rural scene!
With constant Verdure ever green,
How healthy, gay and pleasant!
A clean, tho' an ungrateful Soil,
Rewarding well the Sportsman's Toil,
With Partridges and Pheasant.

III.
To you, my Lord, I send my Lays,
Fondly conceiv'd in *Flavia's* Praise,
Flavia can make a Poet.
Happy the Man, of choicest Taste,
Who sees whate'er's above the Waist,
Much happier, what's below it.[37]

Many years later Coke's public persona was characterised by Horace Walpole in a way that seems tainted by personal dislike, describing him as

> a very cunning man but not a deep one. He affected frankness and a noisy kind of buffoonery, both to disguise his art, and his superficial understanding.

Figs. 15 and 16. Thomas and Margaret with their robes and coronets after Thomas had been granted the earldom of Leicester in 1744. Thomas is also wearing the chain of his Order of the Bath and is shown in front of his proudest possession, the figure of Diana in his as yet unbuilt sculpture gallery. Paintings at Holkham by Andrea Casali.

> He owed all his preferments to Sir Robert Walpole, who patronized him for his great estate and for being a near neighbour in Norfolk, and a sort of relation, his grandmother having married Sir Robert's uncle.[38]

According to Horace Walpole, the coveted earldom of Leicester came to Lord Lovell in 1744 'on an old promise which my father had obtained for him'. By then forty-seven years old, this was the pinnacle of his career, and a pair of portraits of Lord and Lady Leicester were commissioned to mark the event (figs. 15 and 16). Lady Leicester, graceful in her gorgeous gown, had been raised to the peerage in her own right in 1734 as 19th Baroness de Clifford, inheriting one of the few English titles that could be passed through the female line. Not very much is known about her activities and everyday life at Holkham before her husband's death, though we may assume that she looked after the teeming household. She certainly had control of the domestic accounts; many volumes are filled in her distinctive hand, enumerating the petty expenses for the household.

Lord Leicester was represented wearing his peer's robe, his finger pointing discreetly to the earl's coronet in the foreground. In the background is the figure of Diana, in his own opinion the best amongst the many sculptures in his remarkable collection. Coronet and sculpture are symbols of his dual ambitions and achievements. The image also represents him as a 'fine figure of a man', tall and, as we know from another source, more than a little overweight. On one of his country-house tours he was weighed at the Duke of Montagu's house at Ditton near Windsor. Leicester

Figs. 17 and 18. In 1746, Thomas and Margaret's only surviving son Edward, Viscount Coke, married Lady Mary Campbell, daughter of the Duke of Argyll. The marriage was a disaster and did not produce the heir Lord Leicester must have hoped for. Pastels at Holkham by Rosalba Carriera.

tipped the scales at a remarkable 19 stone 8 lbs,[39] effortlessly surpassing the Duke of Rutland (16 stone 9 lbs) and the Earl of Cardigan (a mere 11 stone 5 lbs).[40]

The image of confidence, craftiness and boisterous masculinity emanating from various poems and letters does not sit easily with that of the sensitive and earnest youth who had devoted himself to art and culture during his Grand Tour, nor with the thoughtful and erudite builder of Holkham and Fellow of the Royal Society,[41] and yet they were combined within the one corpulent person.

DISILLUSIONMENT

For all his successes and his close proximity to the court and to the most influential politicians of his time, such as Robert Walpole and the Duke of Newcastle, Lord Leicester never entered the nation's inner circle of power. Certainly one great ambition was unfulfilled by the mid-1740s: his dynastic visions. They naturally depended on the successful marriage of his heir. In this he was to be disappointed due to the dissolute life, ill-starred marriage and early death of his only son, Edward (fig. 17).

Edward Coke had spent some time at Oxford University, 'one of those Schools of Vices',[42] as his mother commented bitterly much later, before embarking on his Grand Tour in 1737. On the Continent he made a favourable impression. Joseph Spence, who met him in Blois in December 1737, wrote to his mother: 'a very pretty young gentleman came to the house where we were, son of the great Coke of Norfolk, now Lord Lovel. He had a gentleman with him, of a weather-beaten aspect, a rough air, and a rougher voice.' The weather-beaten gentleman was Edward's then thirty-five-year-old 'bear-leader' George Shelvocke, an extremely experienced traveller, who had already been on a spectacular voyage on board his father's ship, the twenty-two-gun privateer *Speedwell*.[43]

Marrying Edward took rather longer than his father had anticipated. In 1746 a bride was found at last in the person of eighteen-year-old Lady Mary Campbell, daughter of the late Duke of Argyll (fig. 18). The Duchess, her mother, was not too keen on Lord Leicester, 'on account of [his] notoriously bad, dissolute, and violent character', but she formed a favourable opinion of the young bridegroom, who no doubt put himself out to be agreeable to the Dowager. Lady Mary herself had fewer illusions; as Horace Walpole commented, she objected 'to his loving none of her sex but the 4 Queens in a pack of cards, but he promises to abandon Whites, and both Clubs for her sake'.[44]

So Lady Mary went to the altar with Lord Coke, a step she saw as little less than a personal sacrifice:

> But rumour whispered that the sacrifice remained incomplete … the bridegroom, who conceived he had a long score of insolence to pay off, who was predetermined to mortify the fair bride by every means in his power, did not scruple entertaining his bottle-companions with a ludicrous detail of particulars. He found her ladyship, he said, in the mood of King Solomon's Egyptian captive, 'Darting scorn and sorrow from her eyes', prepared to become the wretched victim of abhorred compulsion. Therefore, coolly assuring her she was quite mistaken in apprehending any violence from him, he begged she would make herself easy, and wished her a very good night.[45]

Lord Leicester must have been the last to realise that his son led an even more dissolute life than he himself and that no heir was to be expected from this unconsummated marriage. There would be no direct descendants to inherit the rural palace Lord Leicester was building and the titles for which he had laboured so long.

Two years into her marriage, Lady Mary decided to sue for divorce; the case was opened on 17 November 1749. The publicity of the divorce case was enormous; people went to it as to a play and were not disappointed by the sight of Lady Mary arriving theatrically ill-dressed, almost in tatters. The mob pressed forward to gain a sight of her and broke the glass of her sedan chair. 'Take care!', said her tender husband as he handed her out of it. 'My dearest love! Take care and do not hurt yourself.'[46]

Lady Mary was a poor witness, proving unable to detail any of the cruelties she had allegedly suffered at the hands of her husband. In the end, the case was dismissed and the couple went their separate ways, Lady Mary agreeing to live quietly in Sudbury, avoiding society life in the metropolis.

Lord Coke, however, was declining in health, and he was not to succeed to his father's titles and properties (fig. 19). He died at Greenwich on 30 August 1753, aged thirty-four years. His father wrote to the Duke of Devonshire, thanking him for his condolences:

> We had but too much preparation to fortify ourselves against the last [misfortune], yet it could not but be very shocking when it came, besides the great grief of my Wife, who has always behaved in so good and tender a manner to me, I own it gives me so great concern that I cannot think of recovering my spirits, till she does in some manner hers.[47]

Fig. 19. Edward Viscount Coke in front of the great house he was never to inherit. He was a good-looking and gifted young man, representing Norfolk and later Harwich in the House of Commons from 1741 onwards, but he appears to have led a dissolute life that led to his early death in 1753. Painting at Holkham by Andrea Casali.

THE FREEDOM OF OLD AGE

There can be little doubt that his son's inauspicious marriage affected Lord Leicester deeply. Not only was his long-term vision for Holkham dashed, but the notoriety of the family name must also have been a source of great shame to him. He seems to have dropped out of smart society for a while, feeling more at home with friends who shared his taste for country activities, such as shooting and landscaping. These included the Duke of Newcastle, who was creating his landscape garden at Claremont at the time, and the Duke of Grafton, Coke's particular friend and East Anglian neighbour, who had the grounds at Euston remodelled by William Kent and his house rebuilt by Matthew Brettingham. Leicester called him Baldassar, whereas Grafton referred to his friend as Trot. Once, in October 1754, a letter addressed by the Duke simply to 'My Angell Trott'[48] and containing an invitation to join Grafton and the Duke of Cumberland at Euston arrived, astonishingly, on the desk of the Postmaster General, causing Lord Leicester to comment: 'one of our clerks being with me at Holkham found out that "Trott" . . . meant me, else I had missed the journey thither.'[49]

After his son's death in 1753, Lord Leicester tried to renew his old successes in the London drawing rooms, but eventually realised that he had lost touch with the fast-moving metropolis. Once more, Horace Walpole casts a pitiless light on Leicester's personal affairs:

> but ah! Madam, the nonsense of one age is not the nonsense of another age! I remember the late Lord Leicester, who had formed a galimatias that was much to the taste of his contemporaries: he retired to Holkham for a few years, returned to town and to White's; a new generation was come forth, who stared and concluded he was superannuated; and he was forced to pack up his obsolete Phrases and antiquated humour and decamp again, to rail at the dullness of the young men.[50]

Leicester's transformation of Holkham brought him far greater rewards than his abortive attempts to rejoin fashionable society in London, and there are clear indications that he threw himself into the task with great energy and determination.

A glimpse of life at Holkham is provided by a letter of Admiral Edward Boscawen, who stayed at Holkham in October 1757, together with Lords Egremont, Thomond and Waldegrave. He had a 'very kind reception from the fat, laughing, joking peer of this house, whose taste for building is so elegant that it is far beyond conception or description' and described the house in some detail:

> the house ... is not finished or furnished, but the room, or Chambre d'Assembly, 105 feet long, we live in, elegant to a degree, and when lighted up, quite scenery; a library at each end, the middle a gallery ornamented with perfect antique statues, all over the house the ceilings are finished, and the finest furniture preparing that can be purchased; Pickford the person recommended to us by Lord Duncannon to make our chimney peices does that business here, and is now at this place making the pillars for the Hall at the Grand Entrance. ... The Appartments are elegant, and very convenient, a dressing room to every bed-chamber, with servants room to each, and Water closets to most of them;
>
> ... (I had forgot to tell you that Lord Leicester has a very fine collection of pictures, Lord Egremont who knows the hands and seems to understand them, says at least ten thousand pounds worth, all I know of them is they appear very fine and pleasing).[51]

The Admiral, as a sea dog and naval hero, could, of course, afford to confess to his ignorance of paintings and simply enjoy them for their beauty, unlike the polished connoisseurs who made up the rest of the party. He included a brief reference to Lady Leicester, characterising her as a 'good sort of a Pyning kind of woman,[52] I conclude clever in her family', but the guests never saw her except at meals.

Without such visitors, life could be lonely at Holkham. One of his last letters to the younger Brettingham sounds quite sad:

> It is a melancholy thing to stand alone in one's own Country. I look around, not a house to be seen but my own. I am Giant, of Giant Castle, and I have ate up all my neighbours – my nearest neighbour is the King of Denmark.[53]

Lord Leicester's final months saw him embroiled in a dispute with his Norfolk neighbour, young Colonel (later Marquis) Townshend of Raynham. The bone of contention was the militia that was raised at the time: an amateurish military body that caused Lord Leicester much merriment and made him either quote or perhaps even invent a derisive doggerel:

> The country rings around with loud alarms
> And Raw in fields the Rude militia Swarms;
> Mouths without hands maintained at vast expence,
> In peace a charge, in War of no defence.
> Stout once a month, they march a blustring Band,
> And ever, but in times of need, at hand.
> Of seeming Arms they make a short Essay,
> Then hasten to be drunk, the business of the day.[54]

As Colonel of the Militia, Townshend was not amused, sensing his military honour impugned. He sent Leicester an abusive letter, in effect a challenge, calling him a 'malignant, pensioned, renegade peer' and ending sneeringly 'with ye

Fig. 20. Marble bust of Lord Leicester on a large funerary monument in the church of St Mary in Tittleshall, opposite the monument for Sir Edward the Chief Justice. Lord Leicester's bust is by Louis-François Roubiliac.

utmost contempt for the Right Honourable ye Postmaster Generall'.[55] Lord Leicester knew better than to take up the gauntlet; his reply was both dignified and mildly self-deprecating:

> It would be ridiculous and rash for an old fellow retired from the world, who cannot even without great fatigue visit his neighbours, to begin duelling with an officer of your rank in his prime ... you would get no Honour by vanquishing a man older than your Father, and grown quite unwieldy and unfit for such encounters by a long, lazy and inactive life and entire disuse of sword and file, not having this twenty years wore a sword that could be of any use and for a pistol I never could hit a barn-door with a gun, so it would be very difficult for me to chuse weapons, and I think to turn duellist in my grand climacterick would be a great proof of indiscreet rashness rather than true courage.[56]

With this apology of sorts, Leicester was able to defuse the situation, and Townshend was somewhat mollified. But only six weeks later, Lord Leicester was dead, giving rise to a rumour that a duel had indeed been fought in which he had received mortal wounds. No corroborating evidence can be found, however. A small but poignant reminder of Lord Leicester's sudden death may be seen in the accounts documenting the daily progress of work in the Marble Hall. They show all the marble masons busily employed on 17, 18, and 19 April – just as they had been on every workday over the last two years. On 20 April 1759, however, no work was done in the Hall, nor on any of the following days, for his Lordship had died in the early hours of the morning.

Fig. 21. Marble bust of Lady Leicester in the church of St Mary in Tittleshall, by William Atkinson.

Lord Leicester was buried in Tittleshall Church, alongside many of his ancestors, including the Chief Justice, in the vault that had already received the body of his son, Edward. The expenses for burial (£525.18s.0d altogether, nearly £90,000 today) provide some idea of the splendour of the occasion. Two mourning coaches and their coachmen were hired for three days: one day winding their slow way along the road to Tittleshall, twenty miles south of Holkham, one day for the funeral, and one day for the return journey. The carpenter James Lillie, hitherto occupied with the wooden structures in the house, made two wainscot coffins (presumably one to put inside the other) and fixed the hatchment on Holkham's façade; John Bullin, another craftsman busy at Holkham, made a lead coffin. Shroud, winding pillow and gloves cost £2.12s.6d. Nine 'under-bearers' did their duty whilst two constables and thirteen assistants kept order at the church door. A representation of the house servants attended, clad from head to foot in new mourning clothes: seventeen hats, seventeen pairs of black hose, seventeen suits of mourning and seventeen frocks were made for them, with £80 worth of mourning cloth, shalloon, buttons and silk garters adding to the sombre splendour of the occasion. The poor of Tittleshall profited from Lord Leicester's largesse to the tune of ten guineas distributed amongst them.

For the remaining sixteen years of her life, Lady Leicester became the sole mistress of Holkham. Having been a loyal wife, she was a dutiful and conscientious co-executrix of Lord Leicester's will, dedicated to completing his life's work at Holkham. Her interest is clear from entries in the new books of building accounts. 'Paid to Mathew Brettingham Surveyor of the Buildings a Quarters salary to Midsummer 1759 then discharged'[57] is the brusque line in the accounts recording the termination of his contract of more than thirty years' standing. For the remaining five years, the craftsman James Miller took over the supervision of the building activities, at £50 per annum – half of Brettingham's salary.

In 1760, the Dowager commissioned Messrs. Atkinson of London to execute a splendid monument for herself, her husband and their son, Viscount Coke. Its architectural ensemble – a pedimental niche supported by Corinthian columns – includes a sarcophagus of Sienna marble, fancifully decorated with elaborate pumpkin segments and raised on a pedestal. Above it, the Leicester coat of arms is prominently displayed in the central panel of black marble, and the pedestal bears three dedicatory inscriptions. Busts of the earl and the countess flank the monument (figs. 20 and 21), the countess's facing the church nave while her husband's seems hidden behind the far column. Nevertheless, the earl's bust, by the eminent sculptor Louis François Roubiliac, presents an imposing image, bewigged and in contemporary dress with a masterful display of drapery for which the sculptor was justly famous. He proudly sports the star of the Order of the Bath, his first step up the ladder of aristocratic rank. In an age-old pose, his head is sharply twisted to his left to convey a dynamic, superior personality. He has a high forehead, robust features including a strong nose together with a prominent chin and inquisitive eyes. A plaster version of this portrait was later placed over the door from the Marble Hall to the Saloon. The countess's bust stood on the mantelpiece of the State Bedroom before it was integrated into the monument at Tittleshall.[58] Simply dressed in attire that would befit a Roman matron, the countess, sculpted by Atkinson, coldly stares straight ahead. Her regular, handsome features show a determined mien which she manifested by deed: after all, it was she who completed Holkham to her husband's specifications and who commissioned this memorial according to her own wishes.

COKE ARCHITECTUS?

A large engraving based on a picture by Christian Friedrich Zincke presents Thomas Coke bewigged and in formal attire, wearing the star and sash of the Bath and a sword at his side (fig. 22). He is leaning on a classical pedestal onto which all his titles are inscribed. In the background we see most of Holkham's splendid south front, with the backdrop of a tree-topped hill where there should simply be sky above the endless expanse of the North Sea. His right arm rests lightly on a scroll of a plan of a room with columns on which he appears to indicate something with a pair of dividers, the archetypal attribute of an architect. He has taken it from the open *etui* in his left hand: a professional-looking pocket magazine case of a type very common with architects and engineers at the time, containing their essential instruments (fig. 23).[59]

The image portrays Coke both as an aristocrat and as an architect, together with his greatest achievement, Holkham Hall. Is it justified to call Coke an architect – however we define this term in the context of his time? In his *Plans of Holkham*, Brettingham says about Lord Leicester that 'the Study of Architecture became his chief Amusement and

Fig. 22. Thomas Coke, Earl of Leicester, in an engraving after Christian Friedrich Zincke. Thomas's formal attire, wearing a nobleman's sword as well as the sash and star of his Order of the Bath, contrasts with the fact that he is also characterised as an architect, with a pair of dividers in one hand and a case for drawing instruments in the other.

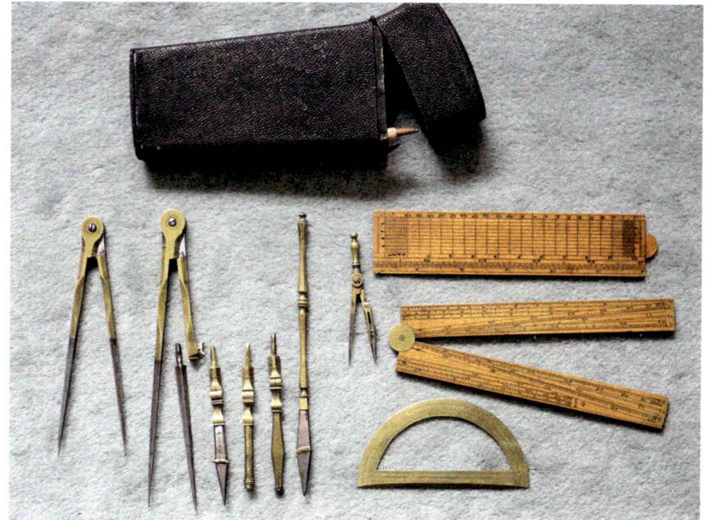

Fig. 23. An example of an *etui* of drawing instruments as shown in Coke's hand in fig. 22.

Delight, during the greatest Part of his Life'.[60] The extent of his architectural qualifications and activities has often been debated.[61] As we have seen, Coke received a significant amount of architectural training in Rome, at the hands of Signor Giacomo. Added to that, his familiarity with the architectural tomes of Palladio, Desgodetz and others and his first-hand experience of many of the greatest works of architecture on the Continent certainly meant that he knew a great deal about great buildings and about architectural design: probably rather more than most of the practitioners active in England at the time, in the first half of the eighteenth century, when those who commissioned great houses usually were far better educated and thus more knowledgeable in architectural principles than the builders they employed.[62]

He was certainly able to express his architectural views quite forcefully. In January 1738/39, William Kent wrote a letter to Burlington mentioning that:

> - my Ld Lovell desirs his service to you, and this day goes to Chiswick with Marchese Sacchette, my Ld told him Mich: Angello was an Ignorante in Arche.tr come nostro M Angello - nove non chi niente che value - [63]

It takes some confidence to denigrate Michelangelo's architectural ability (or rather his non-adherence to classical rules) to a visiting Italian nobleman, although Lord Lovell must have done it in fluent Italian and in the knowledge that Burlington shared his views.[64]

Coke undoubtedly provided far more input into the conception of his own house at Holkham than the average patron, as will be discussed in the Architecture chapter. Whilst everybody who has a house designed and built for them becomes, to some degree, a designing architect themselves, this reaches a different plane when such a person produces architectural concepts for other places, or simply for the sake of designing. In this respect the final paragraph in the preface to the older Brettingham's *Plans of Holkham*, published in 1761, provides an important clue:

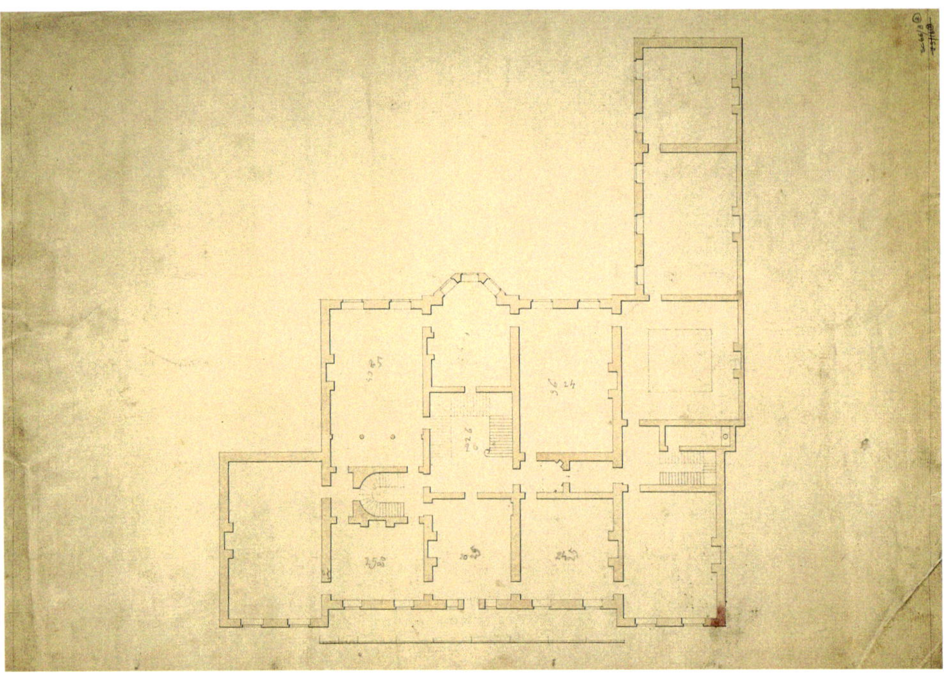

Fig. 24. One plan from a set of drawings by Matthew Brettingham for the new house on Berkeley Square that Lord Leicester was planning for himself in the 1750s. Leicester died before he could execute his plans; the design was passed on to the new owners of the site and used in modified form by their architect, Robert Adam. RIBA Drawings Collection in the Victoria & Albert Museum.

> The EARL of LEICESTER's delight and passsion for architecture was such, that he frequently concerted with me the publication of a book of plans of houses, from ten, to fifty thousand pounds expence, and some others of less value. This was our joint study and amusement in the country, and the drawings for this work have been made by me near twenty years; but they were not to appear in print, till after the publication of Holkham: if leasure permits, they may possible be engraved next year, together with the EARL of LEICESTER's intended plans for a new house in town.

Apparently 'leasure' did not permit, sadly, so this book was never realised, but the RIBA Drawings Collection holds a number of architectural drawings by Brettingham, doubtlessly with Coke's guidance, that seem to have been made in preparation of the planned publication. Most of them, it must be said, seem rather lacking in inspiration, but one project sticks out: Coke's project of building his own house in London. Since his marriage to Lady Margaret, the Earl of Thanet's daughter, Coke had had the use of Thanet House in Great Russell Street, but the lease for the house was going to be up in 1759; therefore, he needed to look for an alternative. In the early 1750s he bought a large building site at the southern end of Berkeley Square. Brettingham's drawings show several different design schemes for the site, both in plans and elevations. It is possible to follow the evolution of the plan from something fairly simple, resembling the grid plan of the pavilions at Holkham, to a rather more complex and grander arrangement, characterised by a wing projecting along the northern border and containing a sequence of three rooms (figs. 24 and 25).

Coke never got the chance to build his house in Berkeley Square as he died in 1759, but the concept did not join the zillions of unbuilt designs architects have produced over centuries. The site was sold by Coke's executors to Lord Bute in 1762, and the new owner must have acquired a set of Coke's and Brettingham's architectural plans along with the title for the land. Bute clearly wished to use those plans and charged his own architect with adapting them to his requirements. This architect was one of the most fashionable and prolific at the time: Robert Adam. No architect of that calibre is happy if he has to work with someone else's design, but it may have mollified Adam to know that the originator of the project was a figure of some architectural authority: in 1756, when Coke was still alive, Adam had been told by Sir William Stanhope that:

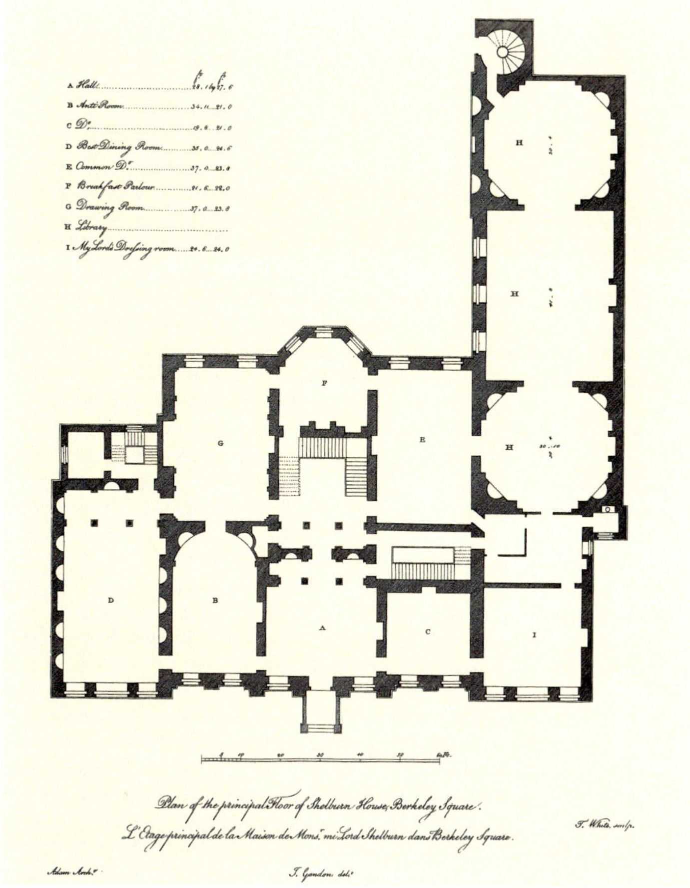

Fig. 25. Ground-floor plan of Robert Adam's Lansdowne House, built from 1762 onwards on the basis of the plans developed by Lord Leicester with the assistance of Matthew Brettingham. Published in *Vitruvius Britannicus*, vol. V, 1771.

> Lord Leicester is the Burlington of the times; that his condemnation or approbation is sufficient either to raise a man in my way or knock him in the head.[65]

It is interesting to see that Adam had no qualms to publish the plans eventually under his own name. But no one who puts the plans for Lansdowne House next to Coke's and Brettingham's plan will deny that the one is directly derived from the other. It is worth noting that the northern wing in Adam's executed version bears an uncanny resemblance to Holkham's tripartite Statue Gallery, possibly preconfigured in the fully developed set of plans by Coke and Brettingham that Bute acquired together with the site.

These observations are not intended to accuse Adam of plagiarism – within the frame of reference of the times he felt just as entitled to put his name to it as William Kent did when he had a print published showing his alternative façade for Holkham (cf. fig. 83).

With all his lifelong, passionate involvement with architecture, why did Coke never put himself forward and claim his birthright as the one who conceived Holkham, as an architect in his own right? Lord Burlington did so, but his peers found this somewhat disconcerting. Members of the élite were of course expected to understand architecture, but only up to a point, as Lord Chesterfield warned his son in 1749:

> for the minute and mechanical parts of it, leave them to masons, bricklayers, and Lord Burlington, who has, to a certain degree, lessened himself, by knowing them too well. … All these things I would have you know, but remember, that they must only be amusement, not business, to a man of parts.

Richard Boyle, third Earl of Burlington and fourth Earl of Cork, KG, could afford to ignore snide remarks of this kind, since his position in the aristocracy was unassailable. Mr Thomas Coke, even after becoming a Knight of the Bath in 1725, was in a rather different position for most of his life. As we have seen, an important part of his life's ambition was founding a dynasty based on a great seat and on a peerage – at least a viscountcy or an earldom, as he explained to Lord Chesterfield in 1730. Therefore, all through the 1720s, when he was patiently developing architectural schemes, and at least until 1744 when he finally gained his earl's coronet, Coke would not have wanted to risk his advance up the aristocratic ladder by appearing to be suspiciously close to the professional classes. It may not be by accident that the engraving representing him as an architect was only created after 1744, when there was no longer any risk involved in such a display.[66]

LANDSCAPE

Pl. 1

►■◄

Pls. 2, 3

Pl. 4

Pl. 5

Pl. 6

Pl. 7

CHAPTER 2

THE HOLKHAM LANDSCAPE

OVERLEAF
Aerial view of Holkham from Obelisk Wood towards the North Sea.

A country house is defined by the land that surrounds it. There is a symbiotic relationship between the house and its landscape – one makes no sense without the other. Of course the land at Holkham existed long before the house, and it was farmed and inhabited for many centuries. But conceiving and building a house as the centre of an estate and as the residence of a landowner and his family had consequences for the surrounding land.

One of the first defining elements laid out was the long, straight axis of an approach from the south, pointing towards an empty space that would be filled, much later, by the centre of the classical portico, and beyond it to the North Sea. Older structures such as dwellings and roads were erased – woodlands were planted, avenues and vistas created.

Aerial views give a good impression of how Holkham's park contrasts against the surrounding small-scale fields as a grandiose shape defined by woodlands with sinuous edges and of course the long central axis of the approach flanked by massive clumps of ilex oaks.

The parkland combines several important functions such as agriculture and sport, beauty and entertainment.

Agriculture and forestry are interlaced with the interest in sport and aesthetics – sport meaning, of course, game shooting. The sinuous edges of the woodlands are not merely an aesthetically pleasing feature in the landscape typical for an eighteenth-century English country park; they also serve to increase the opportunities for shooting birds emerging from the woods and flying up into the sky (fig. 26).

To provide for entertainment and beauty, the house was initially set within a very decorative pleasure ground. Sadly, this pleasing setting, which must have done much to alleviate the stern aspect of the Hall's architecture, was swept away before the century was out and replaced with an unbroken expanse of grass up to the south front. A later generation had the house surrounded by a massive terrace. The nineteenth century also saw the addition of an arboretum containing exotic tree species.

Apart from eminently practical purposes, the designed landscape also speaks of philosophical and political notions and aims. Transforming the previously open countryside by enclosing and reordering a large part of it was a very public demonstration of the ambition and power of the landlord. An aristocratic family would be expected to have a large country estate as a matter of course; conversely, owning a country estate was a nearly infallible entry ticket to the aristocracy.

What entitled this landowning class to wealth and political power, and how could their possession be justified? Legitimation is an ever-present and overarching topic both in landscape design and in the architecture and interior decoration of the great houses. In essence, legitimation is claimed through tradition and history, by saying, 'we have always been here'. Thus the English royal family traced their ancestry back to Noah and thence to Adam. The Cokes of Holkham and many other landowning families of the era used a different approach: they saw and presented themselves as the legitimate successors, at least in spirit and culture, of the landowning patricians ruling ancient Rome. To demonstrate this connection, their landscapes emulated the beautiful wilderness of Arcadia as pictured by their favourite painters, Claude and Poussin – in stark contrast to the parks around the palaces of absolutist rulers on the Continent, such as Versailles.

The main function of the land was to generate the income that paid for the lifestyle and the cultural assets of the country estate. Both first earls – Thomas Coke the builder as well as Coke of Norfolk – were very active farmers and agricultural reformers, and although increasing profits were their driving force for doing so, this should not diminish their lasting achievements in improving the soil through marling and the introduction of four-crop rotation, laying the basis for approaches that are still valuable in the twenty-first century.

THE PREDECESSOR: WHEATLEY MANOR

Ideally, Thomas Coke's transformation of Holkham in the eighteenth century needed a blank canvas, but the site he had chosen was occupied by the houses, gardens, roads and fields of Holkham village. The success of his venture, integrating hall, park and landscape, gradually destroyed most visible signs of the earlier history of Holkham and nurtured the myth that they had scarcely existed. The territorial and financial foundations for his creation had been laid back in the seventeenth century, when the Coke family, new to the parish, rising by means of a fortune earned in the law, judicious marriages and patient acquisition of land and status, focused its attention on this flourishing agricultural community.

Holkham 'Town' spread along the road slightly inland from the coast and lay almost central to the parish, which covered about 4,000 acres and included three manors (fig. 27). One manor house had disappeared by 1600, but

Fig. 26. An aerial view of Holkham Park, looking north to the sea, shows the long and straight avenue from the southern entrance to the park, culminating in the Obelisk at the highest point of the axis and then the mansion next to the artificial lake. Note the sinuous edges of the woodlands, pleasing to the eye but at the same time useful for the sport of shooting.

the Neales manor house, set in about fourteen acres of land, still stood at the western end of the village and the larger house of Wheatley or Hill Hall, surrounded by more extensive grounds, lay further to the east. A mile to the north, another cluster of houses at the staithe had ceded its former activity as a port to silting channels and shifting coastline. The parish church of St Withburga stood alone, on a high point equidistant from the two settlements of Town and Staithe (fig. 28).[67]

Beyond the village houses and their closes stretched the open fields: Church Field to the north-west, Staithe Field to the north-east, and South Field. Here, the influence of the manors extended far beyond manor house and court, for the manorial lords controlled the system of husbandry, unique to Norfolk and parts of Suffolk, based on the fold course or sheep walk.[68] In winter, when the fold courses included the stubble or shack of the unenclosed arable fields, the country around Holkham appeared to support little but

Fig. 27. A map of Holkham, dated 1590. Of all the many buildings, roads and other features shown, only Holkham Church (in the top left quarter) survives.

Fig. 28. The Church of St Withburga, sole survivor among the medieval structures of Holkham. Retaining some elements dating back to the thirteenth century, it is mostly the result of a major restoration in the second earl's time, from 1869 onwards.

Fig. 29. Detail of the 1590 map of Holkham. The Elizabethan manor house of Wheatley near the centre of the map, surrounded by an orchard, remained the main residence of the Coke family and was only demolished in 1757, when the new mansion (to which it was connected by a wooden passage) was nearing completion.

sheep. In the growing season, however, when the sheep were confined to their summer pastures and the arable fields were returned to the owners or tenants of the individual strips, the light soil, so thoroughly manured and trampled during the winter by the lord's sheep, yielded crops of barley, wheat, rye, vetches (peas and beans) and oats. In the 1640s, for example, between thirty-three and thirty-nine farmers were each cultivating from half an acre to 250 acres, continuing a system of successful sheep–corn husbandry that had existed at Holkham since at least the thirteenth century.[69]

Some sixteen miles to the south, Sir Edward Coke, a wealthy and eminent lawyer, had a country house at Godwick, near Tittleshall. In 1600, he was Attorney General to Elizabeth I, and was to rise still higher under James I. His roots were in Norfolk, but his success in the law had already enabled him to buy properties in several counties: his 'Great Book of Conveyances' eventually recorded over 100 purchases, in sixty-six manors, at a total cost of £80,000.[70] He had no land in or near Holkham, though distant links with the owners of all three manors gave him every opportunity to be aware of potential openings there.

One of these openings was the death of the lord of the manor of Wheatley in 1600. He left only a daughter: Meriel, aged three. The profitable right to her 'custody, wardship and marriage' was granted by the Court of Wards to one George Knightley.

A note in Sir Edward Coke's hand, on the back of the grant, reveals the real situation: 'I took the wardshippe in my uncle Knightley's name and payed the fine for it, and it is only to my b[usines]s'.[71] A few years later, in 1609, Sir Edward bought the neighbouring manor of Neales from Meriel's uncle, William Armiger. This was an investment property for Sir Edward and he immediately let it to a tenant at £140 p.a. Believing that 'a good man leaveth an inheritance to his sonnes and to theire children', his acquisition of numerous individual manors enabled him to settle land on each of his four surviving younger sons without damaging the inheritance of his eldest, and this manor was settled to pass, after his death, to his fourth son, John.[72]

It was clearly the culmination of several years of planning when, in 1612, John married his father's ward, Meriel Wheatley. The Wheatley manor land, extending to about

200 acres plus a fold course, was sufficient to establish John Coke at the lower end of the gentry. The manor house (fig. 29) became their family home: ever since, the Coke family have lived at Holkham.

Twenty-two years later, upon his father's death in 1634, John inherited the neighbouring Neales manor, his father's original purchase at Holkham, giving him a rental income in addition to the home farm. In the same year, he took steps to acquire the third Holkham manor, Burgh Hall, which had two particularly valuable fold courses. A widow's life interest in the manor delayed John Coke's financial gain, but this purchase was a crucial long-term contribution to the Holkham estate.

John had even greater expectations, as heir presumptive to most of 'the great estate' created by his father. Its present head, his elder brother, Sir Robert Coke of Huntingfield (Suffolk), had no living children. He did, however, have a tendency to 'improvident and excessive expense' and royalist sympathies which, during the Civil War, led to the sequestration of some of his estates. For nearly twenty years, John exercised constant vigilance where the interests of his branch of the family were concerned, vigorously opposing his brother's efforts to vary the family settlement.[73] Finally, in 1653, upon the death of Sir Robert, the great estate passed to John, and henceforth Holkham was its centre.

Just as John Coke benefited from the failure of heirs in the senior branches of the family, the line of succession in his own family was becoming precarious. The death of his eldest son in 1655 left only the youngest of his six sons still living. This son, also named John, refused to join in a resettlement of the whole estate, the normal practice to secure the line of succession. He went off to France for three years and was still alienated from his father when the latter died in 1661.

Meanwhile, concerns about his immediate heir did nothing to lessen the father's ambitions for Holkham. When Coke finally gained possession of the Burgh Hall manor in 1659, he immediately began a programme of embanking and draining its western marshes. In the same year, he added to his three manors the extensive estate of Edmund Newgate, whose family had been accumulating lands in the north of the parish long before Sir Edward Coke first cast an eye on Holkham. It included his house at the staithe, which was sufficiently important to survive the rebuilding of the village more than two centuries later and still stands as 'The Ancient House'; arable land, which increased John Coke's by more than a third, bringing it to over 1,100 acres; and, although Newgate was not a manorial lord, an extensive fold course in the Staithe Field and eastern marshes.

THE OLD MANOR HOUSE

Around this time, John Coke extended and altered his house. When his future wife had inherited Wheatley, also known as Hill Hall, in 1600, it was the principal house in the village, a typical Tudor manor house, with a central hall, great and little parlours, study, long gallery and five bedchambers.[74] By the late 1650s, however, John Coke had a household of twenty-three servants and a sizeable family. His wife and five sons had died, but his six surviving married daughters either still lived in the house or visited frequently. His household, income and status had long since outgrown

Fig. 30. The central part of a large map on vellum that was used in the 1720s. On this palimpsest, older structures, such as property borders and roads, have been erased and are overlaid by the new elements of Thomas Coke's designed landscape, such as Obelisk Wood with its vistas. The features of the landscape define the axis of the future mansion, which is not yet shown. The E-shaped Elizabethan house, the Hall, stands west of the axis, and further west the outline of the future lake is already visible.

the old house. It was occasionally known as Holkham Hall as early as 1634 and it is unlikely that he delayed improvements until his old age, but no account book survives from before the late 1650s. A flurry of building work in 1659–60 is insufficiently itemised to give accurate totals but, at over £400, it suggests considerable extension and improvement, possibly including a long wing projecting at right angles from the eastern end of the original house.[75]

When John Coke died in 1661, the central hall still functioned as the servants' eating room, but there were now spacious old and new dining rooms, capable together of seating forty-five people. This was now the sort of house at which, fifteen years later, Robert Coke could host a gathering of the Court or royalist party of the county.[76] There were new and old parlours, a porter's lodge, at least eight principal chambers and twelve servants' chambers.

Even the vicar was accommodated. Not listed in the inventory but often mentioned in the accounts was a porch closet, which at times contained well over £2,000 of estate receipts. A few years later, the house was assessed for hearth tax on 35 hearths: it was now far larger than its neighbours at Holkham (the next largest had five hearths), larger than the Walpole family's old house at Houghton (about 21 hearths), roughly the same size as Thomas Bedingfield's Oxburgh (34 hearths) but smaller than John Hobart's Blickling (58 hearths).[77]

Although by the mid-seventeenth century very much a gentleman's residence, it was still a working farm. Near the yard and porter's lodge there were nine more chambers for the steward, farm bailiff, groom, husbandmen and harvestmen, and a horse mill for grinding corn. John Coke's three flocks totalled over 2,000 sheep, including some raised on the salt marshes, which were particularly 'fit for the butcher', but bullocks and steers were also regularly bought and sold, or killed for the table. The farmyard provided turkeys, geese, capons, chickens, pigs and honey; while fish, rabbits, pigeons and other birds came from the estate. The farm sent turnips and other roots to the house, wheat and rye to the mill, oats and barley to the dairymaid, and oats and beans to the stables. Beer was brewed at the house from home-produced malt and hops, and butter and cheese were made in the dairy. More barley was sold to maltsters at Wells-next-the-Sea; wool, hides, skins, rye and timber were also regularly sold. Saffron was grown, probably for export from Wells; when John Coke died, his 'sweet meat closet' contained a painted box holding 28 pounds of saffron. Loading marl, spreading muck and looking after ditches and hedges were regular features of the farm year, and marshes and meadows were drained.[78] Farming at Holkham, so celebrated in later centuries, had long been vital for supplying the considerable consumption of a large household, and a significant source of income.

The remainder of the seventeenth century, after John Coke's death, saw three short-lived successors and a long minority. The size and profitability of the great estate enabled it to survive mortalities, mistakes and extravagances.

Those years, however, also saw positive contributions to the future of the estate. John Coke the younger, stigmatised by the family biographer as a 'poor, foolish man', embroiled the estate in legal problems and financial losses.[79]

Nevertheless, although he had refused to cooperate in a family settlement in his father's lifetime and had therefore

Brick Kill Close
14:1:35
Kitchen Garden
CVII
CVIII.
15:3:00
CIX.
63:3:06
CIV. in 4 Pieces
Eight Acre Close
CXVI. Part of the two Ten Acre Closes
CLOSES
CXVIII.
CXVII. in 4 Pieces
The Five Acre Close
Fourteen Acre Close
14:3:23
CXX. in 2 Pieces
CXXXIV. in 3 Pieces
4:4:13

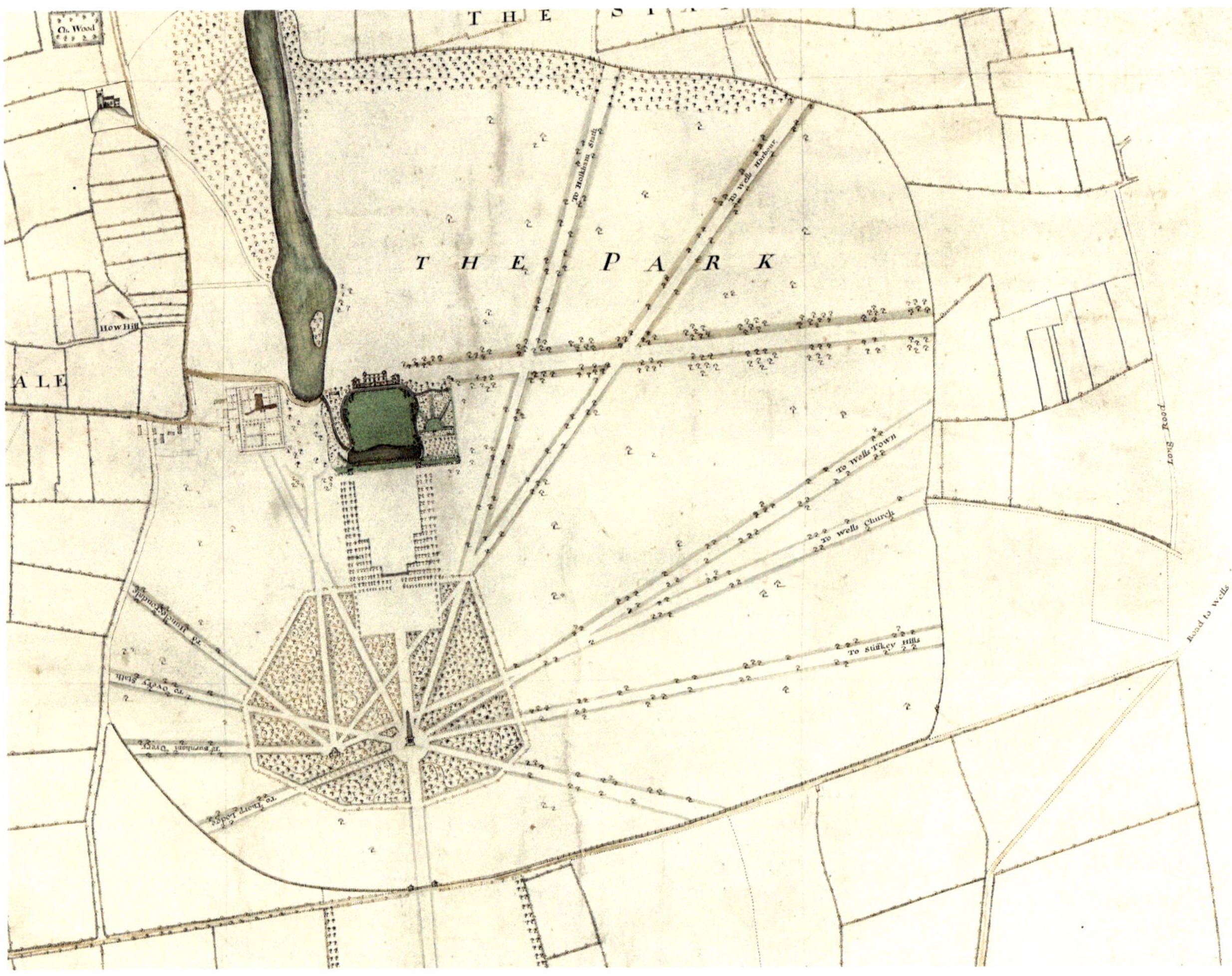

Fig. 31. A map from c. 1750 shows how the central features of the new designed landscape have replaced the older structures.

inherited the estate with absolute ownership, he protected its future by resettling it 'in his owne and the name family and bloud of Sir Edward Coke late lord Chieffe Justice his grandfather.' Furthermore, he used a new and effective legal device to do so.[80]

When he died unmarried in 1671, the estate passed under his settlement to Robert, a descendant of his father's younger brother. Although three generations of Robert's family had lived at Thorington, in Suffolk, there was now no question of anywhere but Holkham being the centre of the great estate. Robert was snapped up as a son-in-law by the great Thomas Osborne, Earl of Danby, and became the first occupant of Holkham to enter Parliament, but he died after only eight years as head of the estate. His heir, Edward, came of age in 1697 but died ten years later.

Thus, Edward's son, Thomas, inherited Holkham. The estate accumulated and preserved through the seventeenth century gave Thomas scope in the coming decades to remove most of the village, carve out a park while maintaining a home farm, enclose open fields into tenanted farms beyond the park, and increase his rental by draining marshes.[81]

THE DEVELOPMENT OF HOLKHAM PARK

The history of the designed Holkham landscape effectively begins in the 1720s. Thomas Coke returned from the Grand Tour in 1718 and soon afterwards began work on the landscape which was to form the setting for his new hall, even though the latter's construction was not to commence for more than a decade and a half. At this time, the existing manor house – Hill Hall – stood in relatively modest grounds, bounded on three sides by public roads and with the houses of Holkham village lying immediately to the

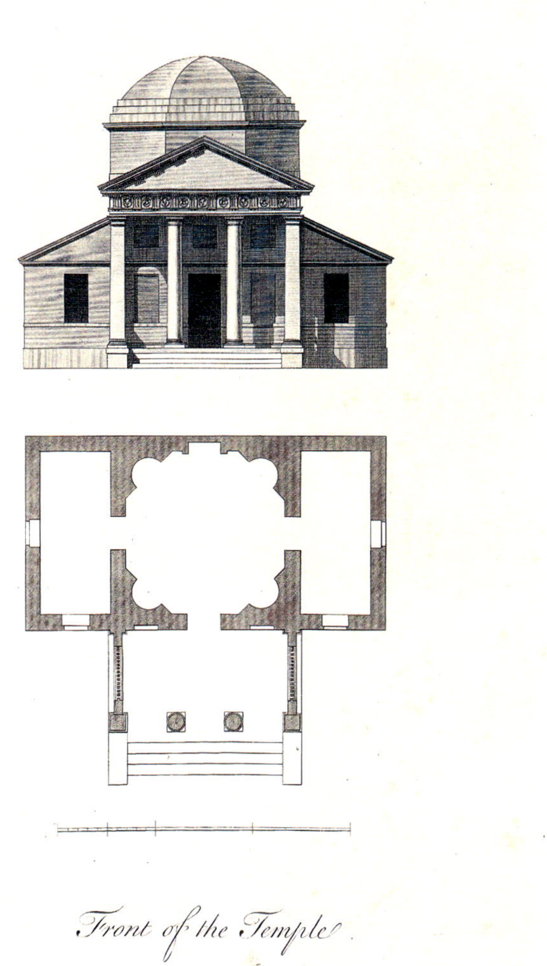

Fig. 32. The Temple in Obelisk Wood, built from 1730 onwards.

west.[82] In 1722, a writ of *ad quod damnum* closed the Burnham Market to Wighton road, which ran just to the south, and between 1724 and 1729 the South Lawn, the area extending up the hill to the south of the house, was systematically levelled and seeded. Formal lines of trees, probably cut into box-like shape, were planted in 1726 and 1727 – their shape echoing the layout of the forecourt of the Palace of Versailles – framing a vista towards Obelisk Wood, which was itself planted on the summit of the hill between 1726 and 1730 (figs. 30 and 31). The kitchen garden was constructed a little to the west of the Hall between 1726 and 1728; the Clint, a natural water course to the north-west of the Hall, was dammed to form a lake between 1725 and 1731; and a geometric basin to the south of the Hall was excavated between 1730 and 1734. The Obelisk itself and the Temple (fig. 32) were built from 1730 onwards, and a complex pattern of *allées* or straight paths or rides laid out within it.

The creation of this new landscape involved the systematic destruction of the old working countryside. The village of Holkham was demolished and its site levelled in work which began in 1728 and continued for several years. Field boundaries lying within view of the Hall were stubbed and flattened, although some hedgerow trees were incorporated into the new design.[83] Today, the late seventeenth-century icehouse to the south-west of the Hall is the only obvious survivor from the old landscape.

A vast amount of work was thus carried out in the 1720s and early 1730s, and by 1734, when the construction of the new hall finally commenced, a large, geometric landscape, organised around a great north–south vista, was taking shape. The formality of the design – and the central, articulating function of the main axis, which also formed the central axis of the new hall – was further emphasised by the planting of the great south avenue in 1735. This was evidently a landscape which, in many ways, looked back to the great geometric designs of the seventeenth century, rather than forward to the more informal and naturalistic layouts of the second half of the eighteenth century created by Capability Brown and his contemporaries. Even the new lake was, to judge from the cartographic evidence, a fairly formal feature. By good fortune, the configuration of the natural topography ensured that it was long, relatively thin and remarkably straight-sided, more like a broad artificial canal than the more serpentine lakes of the later landscape tradition.

Fig. 33. The charming pleasure ground framing the mansion on the south and south-west was designed by William Kent to evoke an Italian or even Arcadian landscape.

Holkham is, indeed, a salutary reminder of how we should not underestimate the idea of geometry in the gardens of eighteenth-century England. Although fussy parterres and topiary declined in popularity, the great gardens of the 1720s and 1730s were still dominated by straight lines and symmetry. It is noteworthy that in 1728, at an early stage in the development of the new landscape, the head gardener at Holkham, John Aram, was paid 19s.7d 'for travelling . . . to Chatsworth', the great baroque garden in Derbyshire, presumably to glean ideas about the creation of an extensive formal design.

A NEW APPROACH: WILLIAM KENT

Nevertheless, by the time construction of the house had begun in earnest, new ideas were beginning to affect the design of the gardens in England – ideas closely associated with William Kent. Until the 1730s, Kent had worked primarily as a painter and interior designer. At Holkham, he was responsible for designing at least some of the garden buildings – the porches, Obelisk and south lodge – which adorned the new geometric landscape here. But he began to turn his ideas to the design of the gardens and landscapes within which such buildings were placed, and Holkham was one of the first places where he tried out his new ideas.

The estate accounts make it clear that a new phase of activity began in 1737. A number of existing features, only just completed, were removed or extensively altered and a number of entirely new elements were added to the grounds. Such wholesale revision of an only partially completed design is superficially surprising, but we should remember that work on building the house was still, at this time, in its very early stages. The new works were in Kent's innovative style – irregular and 'naturalistic' in layout, and inspired by and imitating both idealised Italian scenery and its depiction in the paintings of Lorrain and Poussin, which Thomas Coke admired and of which he possessed quite a few.

The most important changes were in the area immediately to the south and west of the Hall, which was now laid out as a piece of Italy in miniature. The main feature of the design was an artificial hillock, the New Mount, created in 1742; and the Seat on the Mount, constructed in the following year (figs. 33, 34 and 35). The lake was connected to the basin – now made more irregular in shape – by a serpentine river, crossed by a stone bridge carrying the main drive to the Hall. The old 'porches' at either end of the basin remained, but otherwise the view was radically transformed (fig. 36).

There were no straight lines here: the trees were scattered irregularly. The whole scene was like a picture postcard in three dimensions, a little slice of Arcadia somewhat improbably recreated on the cold Norfolk coast. It was the perfect complement to the studied Palladianism of the Hall's south façade, then under construction.[84]

A somewhat grating component within this elaborate pleasure ground was the old manor house which, however outdated, was still being used and inhabited and kept in good repair. A new servants' hall was built as late as 1729, and its Tudor great hall hosted the twice-yearly audits or rent days. Its position in relation to the new house and to the nineteenth-century terraces can be assessed on the basis of the various maps (fig. 37). Eventually linked by a passage to the first wing of the new house, it continued in use until it was demolished in 1757. It had gradually lost its walled gardens, bowling green, gravel walks, kennels, stew ponds and wooded grounds to Thomas Coke's new landscape.

Fig. 34. The Seat on the Mount was the central feature of the artificial hillock south-west of the house. It survived later reshaping of this part of the park until the late nineteenth century.

Fig. 35. The heads of the four figures of the Seat on the Mount, by the sculptor Peter Scheemakers, preserved outside a house in the nearby village of Burnham Overy.

Fig. 36. A drawing by William Kent showing the view from the house towards the south across the pond, with the classical 'porches' framing the formal lines of trees defining the space between the house and Obelisk Wood.

Thus it was not until two years before his death that Coke, his wife, household and visitors were at last able to view Holkham's great south front without the old house in the foreground.

Kent's innovative piece of landscape, the pleasure ground, was not the sole or even the primary setting for the Hall. It existed within what was still a highly structured and geometric framework, featuring not only the great south avenue (its impact increased by the construction at its southern end of Kent's Triumphal Arch in 1745–48) but also the formal lines of trees flanking the South Lawn, extending up to Obelisk Wood, as well as the pattern of straight rides that dissected the wood itself. Nevertheless, serpentine and irregular features were now being introduced into the wider landscape. The shore of the lake nearest the Hall was made more sinuous and an island was created within it (fig. 38). The late 1730s, 1740s and 1750s saw much planting both within this park (especially at its northern end) and on the rising ground outside it, taking

Fig. 37. The contours of the Elizabethan manor house of Wheatley shown in relation to Holkham's south-west pavilion or Family Wing. The old house remained in use until its demolition in 1757.

Fig. 38. Detail of an undated map of Holkham showing the completed transformation of the designed landscape around 1760. Note that the somewhat outmoded formal lines of trees south of the pond have vanished.

the form both of large blocks of woodland and of small skyline clumps of trees. Kent died in 1748, but the landscape continued to unfold according to the agenda he had set. Between 1750 and 1755, the North Lawn – the area extending to the north of the Hall – was systematically levelled and planted with a regular pattern of clumps framing the north lodge, also designed by Kent and erected between 1753 and 1755 (fig. 39).

Thomas Coke died in 1759, with the design of the great Palladian house almost completed. The landscape at this point in time was, in many ways, typical of the great designs created in the 1730s and 1740s.[85] Stripped-down geometry was combined with serpentine, Italianate elements, and with a variety of buildings and ornaments in a broadly Palladian style. Particularly striking was – and, indeed, still is – the great southern approach, nearly three kilometres in length, which constitutes a classic piece of early eighteenth-century landscape theatre, the subtlety of which can only be experienced on the ground, rather than on a map. The Hall cannot be seen from the start of the avenue, just to the south of Kent's Triumphal Arch, for it is hidden by Obelisk Hill and the visitor passes along what seems an interminable route to reach it (fig. 2 and pl. 1). Indeed, it is the Obelisk on the skyline that appears to be the destination of the drive, and its distant presence seems to accentuate the length of the approach. The Hall remains hidden, even when the summit of the hill is reached, by the bulk of the Obelisk; only when the drive sweeps round the latter is it revealed, framed by the vista, settled comfortably below.

Whenever we examine designed landscapes, we need to consider how they would have been experienced on the ground. Only then can we begin to explore some of the ways they were used, understood and experienced by contemporaries. Obelisk Wood, with its Temple, Obelisk and complex network of straight rides, is a case in point. This was clearly in the tradition of seventeenth- and early eighteenth-century 'wildernesses' – that is, ornamental woods cut by geometric paths – but while these had usually been planted close to

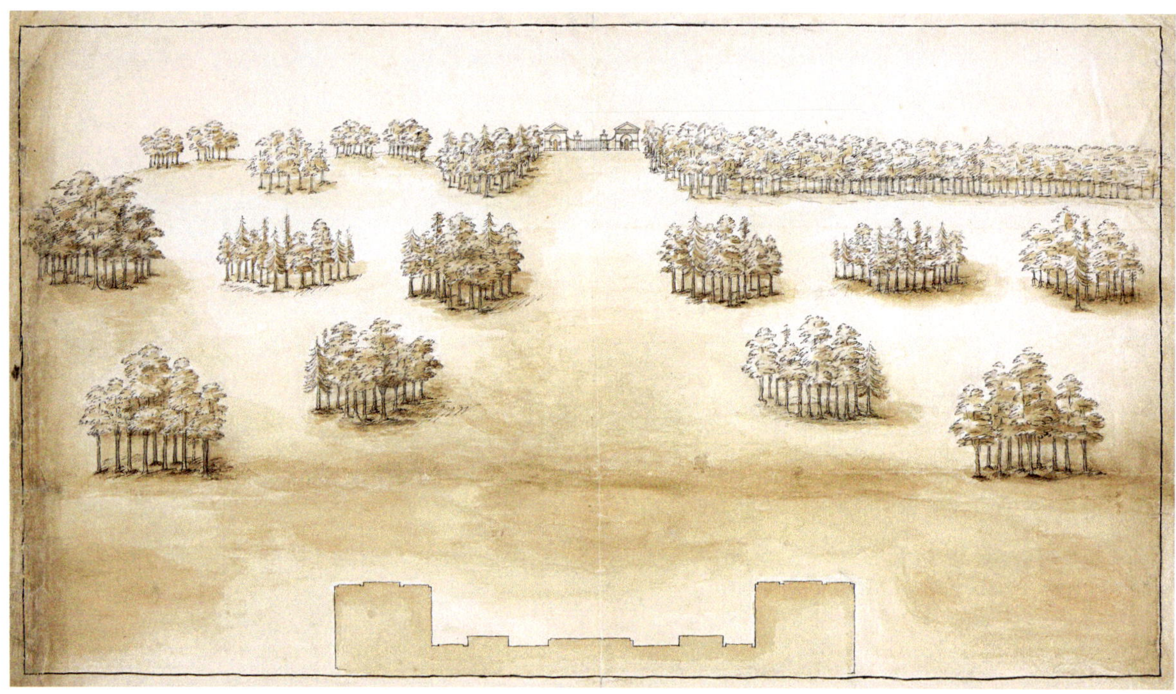

Fig. 39. William Kent's design for the area north from the mansion, with clumps of trees and the north lodges also built to his design but demolished in 1845.

the Hall, Obelisk Wood was set some way away, effectively detached from the main area of gardens. From the windows of the Hall, the Obelisk on the skyline must have seemed like an invitation to drive or ride up to the wood, to explore; once there, the 'temple in the Wood' provided a suitable place for rest and relaxation. The straight paths all focused on one or other of these features, but their actual orientation was decided by what lay well outside the wood. The mid-eighteenth-century plan mentioned earlier (fig. 31) thus shows that they were directed towards a number of distant 'targets', each of which is distinctly labelled: 'Holkham Church', 'Stiffkey Hills', 'Wells Town', etc.[86] The pattern of rides no longer survives, but a somewhat cryptic entry in the diary of a visitor, Sylas Neville, in 1778 may allude to the effect that they created:

> The lake with its hanging woods and Holkham church on the hill by much the finest objects seen from the house or grounds. Look back from a high bank to Holt. View of Cley and the sea between two banks on the right. View of Wells and the sea.[87]

Just as the immediate setting for the house was laid out in imitation of a landscape painting, so the views from the wood into the surrounding landscape were presented as a series of carefully framed prospects. The structured, indeed contrived, character of the landscape – the coexistence of Kent's serpentine and Italianate features with rigidly geometric elements in the old, formal tradition of gardening – and the fact that, while a park pale was constructed between 1730 and 1742, the land within it, covering some 360 acres, was still to a significant extent subdivided by hedges, all marked out the landscape of Holkham as very much a product of the pre-1750 period – and so, rather different in character from the simple, open, naturalistic landscape parks that became fashionable in the 1750s and 1760s.

COKE OF NORFOLK: UPDATING THE PARK

Yet in spite of the fact that, at the time of Thomas Coke's death, the Holkham landscape must already have seemed old-fashioned, relatively little was done to improve it in the 1760s and 1770s. Lady Margaret, Coke's widow, employed Capability Brown, or more probably one of his 'assistants', at Holkham in 1762–64 but as far as the evidence goes, this work was restricted to the pleasure grounds in the immediate vicinity of the Hall. Under Lady Margaret, or possibly under Wenman Coke, the remaining field boundaries within the park pale were finally removed, and the park thus

Fig. 40. As this mid-nineteenth century watercolour by George Hayter shows, all the decorative park elements of the pleasure ground were swept away around 1780 and the grassland was extended right up to the house.

obtained a more open and typically 'park-like' appearance. The park was also expanded slightly to the west. But when Thomas William Coke inherited the estate in 1776, some of the features created around the Hall in the 1720s, 1730s and 1740s were apparently still in place, including the Seat on the Mount, Kent's elaborate Italianate garden, and the network of *allées* in Obelisk Wood. The kitchen garden lay in full view of the western façade – a very unfashionable arrangement in an age in which overt signs of domestic production were increasingly being hidden from polite eyes. All in all, this was a landscape ripe for improvement.

Not surprisingly, then, the accession of Thomas William Coke in 1776 heralded another period of radical change. No man of wealth or taste could possibly be happy with so old-fashioned a setting for his home. Some time around 1780, the basin to the south of the Hall and the serpentine river were duly filled in (fig. 40). Only the Seat on the Mount survived until the late nineteenth century; the heads of the terms by Peter Scheemakers now adorn the front of a house in the nearby village of Burnham Overy (fig. 35).[88] The old kitchen garden was demolished and a replacement, located some 600 metres to the west of the Hall, was constructed, together with a new orangery to its south. They were designed by the architect Samuel Wyatt and cost around £10,000 to build. Between 1782 and 1786 the lake, now considered too stiff and formal in shape, was given a serpentine 'twist' at its northern end by William Emes, an important designer with a national practice based in the east Midlands, and Kent's island removed. Between 1801 and 1803 the lake's southern end was given a similar treatment

Fig. 41. Detail of a map of Holkham dated 1843. The lake was given serpentine twists at both ends and the kitchen garden was replaced with a much larger one further to the west. Kent's stables on the far side of the lake were demolished a few years after this map was made.

by Emes's former pupil, John Webb. The Hall thus gained a more open and naturalistic prospect, in line with contemporary taste.

But Thomas William Coke evidently desired a landscape that was not only more up to date, but also more extensive, in character (fig. 41). In 1780, a major Road Order diverted roads to the west, south and south-east of the park. Further orders followed in 1782, this time diverting roads on the northern boundary. The park was then massively expanded, mainly to the south but to some extent in all directions, so that by 1800 it extended over an area of no less than 1,200 hectares. New lodges were built, to designs by Samuel Wyatt, in part to replace the existing ones, which were now marooned within the park. Kent's south lodge was demolished in 1781; his north lodge remained for a while, but new uses were found for it.[89]

Perhaps the most striking features in the landscape, however, were the numerous new areas of woodland which were created as a result of a sustained planting campaign, beginning in 1781 and continuing well into the nineteenth century. All in all, well over two million trees were planted. The park was surrounded by a continuous perimeter belt, while the newly emparked land to the south was embellished with a number of large clumps. These new areas of woodland were very varied in their composition.[90] For the most part, they were dominated by deciduous forest trees, principally oak, ash, sycamore and beech; to a lesser extent by chestnut and elm. Most also contained a substantial conifer component, especially larch, spruce and Scots pine; and most also contained small numbers of more ornamental species, such as spindle, Lombardy poplar, weeping willow, Weymouth pine, plane, wild service, etc. These were often

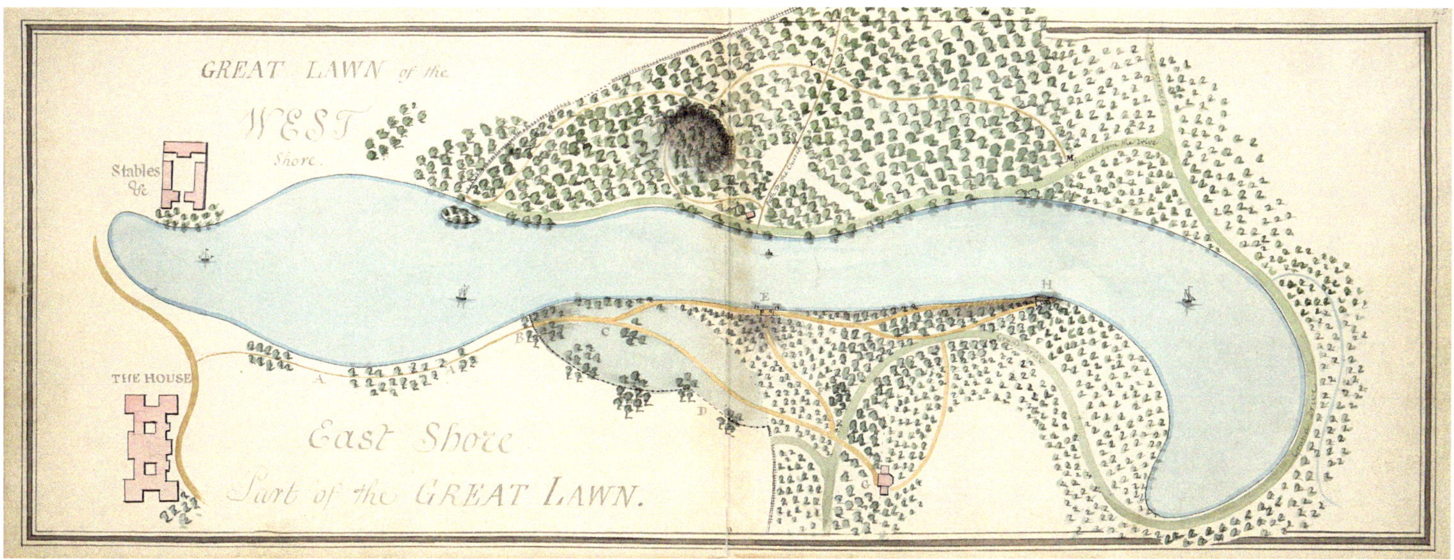

Fig. 42. Humphry Repton's fashionable improvements of the lake and its surroundings in his Red Book for Holkham, 1789.

present only in very small quantities, to judge from the surviving planting accounts – a hundred, fifty or even a mere twenty in plantations containing hundreds or even thousands of other trees. These more ornamental varieties were probably used to line rides or walks within the belts, part of the 'circuit' described in nineteenth-century guides to Holkham.

The designer of all this new planting was one John Sandys, possibly the son of the head gardener who had succeeded William Emes at Kedleston in Derbyshire. He certainly seems to have come to Holkham on Emes's recommendation, for he first appears in the estate accounts around the time that Emes himself came to alter the lake. He was employed as head gardener until 1805, when he left Holkham, married 'Elizabeth Bryan, Widow of Wells', and apparently set himself up as an adviser on forestry matters.

HUMPHRY REPTON'S CONTRIBUTION

While Sandys's vast plantations were spreading across the Holkham landscape, another, much more famous, individual was commissioned to advise on the grounds. Humphry Repton, Brown's successor as the most important landscape designer in England, began his professional career in 1788 (his first commission was Catton, just to the north of Norwich) and produced a 'Red Book' – an illustrated design proposal – for Holkham in the following year (fig. 42).[91] Repton was specifically asked to suggest improvements to the area around the lake, and he clearly saw his work as a contribution to a much wider on-going scheme of improvement, at one point emphasising how he endeavoured 'to avoid anything that may interfere with his [i.e. Coke's] plans'. The Red Book's key proposal was for an elaborate walk leading to a pleasure ground located on the eastern shore of the lake. A number of paths were to be threaded through the woods, taking in various points of interest; the latter included 'a Room ... reserved for a sea view', apparently created by converting Kent's old north lodge; and a new boathouse and fishing pavilion, which was to be designed by Samuel Wyatt. Repton also wanted to extend walks into the woods on the western shore of the lake, which he considered 'the most beautiful ground in Holkham Park', but was faced with the problem that a 'vast circuit must be made by land around either end of the lake' in order to reach it. He argued that:

> A bridge, however elegant for the sake of magnificence, or however simple for the sake of convenience, would be intolerable, because it would destroy the effect of the lake, and make it a river.

He therefore proposed that the two shores should be linked by a 'ferry-boat of peculiar construction', a chain ferry which would run from Wyatt's new boathouse to 'a snug thatched cottage ... picturesquely embosomed in trees' on the far shore.[92] This should be permanently inhabited by an individual described as 'a sort of acquatic game keeper', and

Fig. 43. The Great Barn, built in 1790 to designs by Samuel Wyatt, was the central place for Coke of Norfolk's famous 'sheep shearings' – annual gatherings of farmers and landowners.

would form an interesting element in the view from the Hall, for chimney smoke 'is always a most interesting object when fleecy folds are revealed, as in the present instance, by a rich background of hanging woods.' Other proposals included converting a small chalk pit, which still survives on the western shore, into a picturesque feature with a small cave – the whole described by Repton, not implausibly, as a 'picturesque and awful spot'.

AGRICULTURE IN THE PARK

Whatever the precise character of Repton's contribution to the landscape at Holkham, there is no doubt that it formed only a minor element in the vast scheme of planting and expansion which continued throughout the 1780s and 1790s and into the early nineteenth century, and which resulted in Holkham becoming the largest park in Norfolk and one of the largest in eastern England. Yet it is important to note that not all the land within the perimeter belts ever lay under pasture. In fact, most of the newly emparked land, to the south of Obelisk Wood, continued to be farmed as arable. Holkham was not entirely unusual in this – in many other very large parks, some land lying at a distance from the house might be cultivated, and there was no clear line between the 'park' and the 'home farm'.

But at Holkham the arable area of the park was both particularly extensive and proudly displayed on either side of the main approach to the Hall, an arrangement that clearly reflects Thomas William Coke's deep interest in agricultural improvement. Indeed, the new southern area of parkland contained only a single 'garden building' – the Great Barn, built in 1790 to designs by Samuel Wyatt (fig. 43). It also served as the venue for the 'sheep shearings', annual gatherings of farmers and landowners at which the ideas of the 'new husbandry' could be propagated. Visitors were delighted by the appearance of this carefully ornamented farmland, J. C. Curwen in 1809 proclaiming: 'What can be more beautiful than the diversified scenery that there presents itself? … The effects of order and industry, combined with abundance, must be gratifying to every spectator.'[93]

In the prominence of farmed land within the belt, Holkham was unusual, but for the most part the great changes carried out by Wyatt, Emes, Webb, Repton and above all by John Sandys ensured that by the early nineteenth century the Holkham landscape had lost its rather old-fashioned appearance and was, for the most part, a classic landscape park in the Capability Brown tradition. The house stood 'free of

Fig. 44. A design for the capital of William Donthorne's monument for Coke of Norfolk, built 1845–50 on the site of Kent's north lodge.

walls', looking out to north and south across open parkland ornamented with woods and clumps. Most of the more prominent geometric elements had been softened or removed, although – to the south of Obelisk Wood, and thus out of sight of the Hall – the south avenue remained in place, as did many of the *allées* in Obelisk Wood. Evidently satisfied with what had been achieved, Coke seems to have done relatively little to the landscape in his later years. A new west drive was created around 1830, the planting was embellished in a number of areas and, most strikingly, between 1833 and 1839 a brick wall was constructed all around the perimeter of the park. This was a particularly formidable undertaking, as it can have served no very serious practical purpose, given its height, in terms of keeping game within the park, or unwelcome visitors out. It remains the longest park wall in East Anglia.

By the time of Thomas William Coke's death in 1842, fashions had again moved on. Landscape parks remained the quintessential symbol of status, but their planting became more complex and diverse. More importantly, gardens returned to prominence in the country-house landscape, and by the 1840s and 1850s designers were laying out particularly extensive examples which included many of the features – terraces, topiary, parterres – which had been fashionable in gardens of the seventeenth and early eighteenth centuries, before the vogue for 'nature' and informality.

Bedding-out schemes were increasingly popular, with plants like geraniums and pelargoniums used to create colourful and complex displays. William Andrews Nesfield was the most important and most successful of mid-nineteenth-century gardeners. Together with the architect William Burn (with whom he often cooperated), he laid out the present terraces and box parterres around the Hall.

The 1840s and 1850s also saw numerous changes in the wider landscape of the park. In 1845, Kent's north lodge was finally demolished and a tall monument to Thomas William Coke, designed by the Norfolk architect William Donthorne and with reliefs by John Henning depicting Coke's activities as England's leading agricultural improver, was erected on its site between 1845 and 1850. Opinion has always been divided about this immense structure, Coke's own daughter declaring that it was 'much too near and frightful, the wheat sheaf looking like a vulgar evergreen flower stuck on the top' (fig.44). In 1847, new south lodges designed by S. S. Teulon were built, and shortly afterwards the central section of the long southern approach was embellished with the distinctive clumps of evergreen oaks which today form such an impressive sight. In spite of these changes, the importance of the southern approach to the Hall was clearly declining. Its somewhat sombre, monumental, exclusive character was out of keeping with the times. Great landowners now preferred to signal their active, paternalistic involvement with the local community, and the north entrance, through the village of Holkham Staithe, became the principal approach. A new gateway and gothic screen were erected here, again to designs by Teulon. They linked the two almshouses built by Thomas Coke's widow, Lady Margaret (fig. 228), and these, with the rest of the village, still seem to cluster deferentially at the entrance to the park, echoing the words of the Victorian hymn, 'the rich man in his castle, the poor man at his gate'.

A LANDSCAPE OF MANY LAYERS

Little survives in the Holkham landscape from the period before the eighteenth century – the earthworks of a few old road and field boundaries, some ancient hedgerow trees and the old ice house to the south-west of the Hall.

But there are numerous traces of the first earl's great gardens. The magnificent south avenue is still in place (fig. 26), with Kent's Triumphal Arch at its southern end (figs. 2 and 45). Obelisk Wood still dominates the skyline: a few of the original trees still remain among later replanting, and while the layout of straight rides has largely vanished, the Obelisk and the Temple survive in good condition. The main body of the lake remains much as Kent left it, and the woods around its southern end still contain numerous trees planted in the first half of the eighteenth century. More prominent, however, are the great works carried out by Thomas William Coke in the last decades of the eighteenth and the first decades of the nineteenth century. The great perimeter belt, the clumps in the south of the park and the fashionable 'twists' at each end of the lake all serve to give the landscape its peculiarly monumental yet naturalistic appearance.

The most important changes carried out in the nineteenth century are close to the Hall, where Nesfield's great terraces have entirely altered its relationship with the surrounding parkland, although much of the planting in the park is also from this period, and Donthorne's immense monument is visible from far and wide.

What we see today is thus a complex palimpsest: the woods and plantations, in particular, vary greatly in age. Yet, as noted at the start of this chapter, few visitors probably realise this. Most additions have been influenced by existing forms and structures, and in each phase of its development the landscape incorporated many features of previous designs, often used and interpreted in new ways. Donthorne's monument to Thomas William Coke, for example, was built on the site of Kent's north lodge and thus perpetuates the great central axis of the landscape, first established in the 1720s. There are continuities, too – especially the idiosyncrasies of the planting – which give the whole design an overall coherence. Holm oaks (*Quercus ilex*) were planted at Holkham in the first half of the eighteenth century, and

Fig. 45. The Triumphal Arch was built to mark the beginning of the main approach to the park from the south. Drawing by William Kent, c. 1730. The scrawl on the tablet below the pediment reads 'W Kent and Lord Lovell'.

some examples survive, but the tree became something of a Holkham speciality and most of the remaining examples date from the nineteenth century. As a result, there is little in the Holkham landscape that seems out of place or intrusive. It is a richly textured, vast and awe-inspiring creation, and the perfect setting for the monumental architecture of the Hall itself.

THOMAS COKE'S KITCHEN GARDEN

Today's visitors will find no evidence of Holkham's first kitchen gardens, once laid out immediately to the south-west of the house (fig. 31). These great gardens were already in existence when Thomas Coke was planning the new house, and although still in perfect condition, they were removed in the mid-1770s by Coke's successor, Thomas William Coke, for aesthetic and economic reasons.

Though the gardens have disappeared, we know a great deal about their original layout and contents as the surviving inventory[94] from 1748 in the Holkham archives contains detailed information on their development. The kitchen gardens played a vital rôle in Coke's building project, as they provided fresh food for the household. Work on the gardens, which were entirely surrounded by brick walls, started in 1727, seven years before the new house was begun.[95] The six-acre site was fully integrated into the geometric layout of the park and was connected by pathways to other garden features, including the Obelisk. The gardens were situated close to the head of the lake. As high winds from the North Sea are a permanent feature at Holkham, shelter had to be provided for plants, fruits and vegetables. Thus the rectangular gardens were divided by brick walls fourteen feet high, enclosing approximately twenty areas of land. Bricks for the walls were produced on the estate; during 1727 alone, 297,000 bricks were fired for the kitchen gardens and were

Kitchen Garden.

Reine Duke Turkey 3 B:heart 2 Duke B:heart Duke
Claudes Cherry Apricock Cherrys Cherrys Cherry Cherry

Roman Portugall Green Bellows Rumbullion Catharine
Apricock peach Gage peach peach plumb

Fruit Garden

Fig. 46. A detail from the plant catalogue of Thomas Coke's kitchen garden in the 1730s.

probably all used in the same year.[96] Some of the walls could be heated (known as 'firewalls') and provided excellent frost protection.

From 1723, the kitchen garden was the domain of Nottinghamshire-born head gardener John Aram (or Oram). In 1728, John Aram directed work on soil improvement, and the first vegetables were produced in vegetable patches. Small ponds in the northern areas of the kitchen gardens were used for the water supply, and a heated glasshouse can be dated to 1729.[97] Work on the kitchen gardens went hand in hand with the embellishment of the park, where numerous trees from throughout England were planted. Well-known visitors and neighbours, such as Sir Robert Walpole of Houghton, England's first Prime Minister, and his younger brother, Horatio of Wolterton, donated trees, contributing to the improvement of the park.

It is interesting to record that the experienced head gardener John Aram and his 'under gardiner', William Aram, his nephew, as well as senior gardener John Hastings, constantly exchanged and widened their knowledge of production methods, botanical species and modern technology by visiting other estates and meeting other gardeners. They visited the Blickling, Wolterton, Houghton and Raynham estates on a regular basis and, after 1745, travelled to London and even across the Channel to Holland, where they bought new plants, seeds and planting equipment. Similarly, many estate gardeners visited Holkham and contributed to its high standard of gardening and fruit production. Experts on certain sensitive species, such as orange or lemon trees, gave practical help during times of plant disease and introduced new cutting methods. Vegetable plants were regularly exchanged, enabling the range of species to be broadened.[98] Seeds, plants and equipment were brought to Holkham from all over the kingdom, mostly by ship via the port of Wells-next-the-Sea, but an intensive trade was also developed with the firms Stavely and Cross, John Maldrich of Norwich and William Towell of London.[99]

By 1732, a wide range of traditional fruits and vegetables was being produced, but exotic plants such as bergamots and citrus trees were also grown at Holkham in large quantities. These plants were much sought after and brought to Holkham by boat via Wells; they were cultivated in wooden containers placed on linen cloths in the parterre on the south side of the Hall.[100] Another large glasshouse was built in 1733, facilitating the survival of these species (fig. 46).

So great was Thomas Coke's enthusiasm for luxurious orange trees that the valuable stock was continually enlarged during the following years. In 1736, a Mr Luceras received £6.16s.0d for an unknown quantity of 'Burgamots, Cedratas, Limes, Sweet lemons etc.' In 1738, Mr Costa supplied '20 large Orange Trees of different sorts £8.0s.0d; 6 Nutmeg Oranges 0.15s.0d; 6 Olives £0.12s.0d; 4 Caper plants £0.6s.0d; 4 bunches of spanish Jessamins; 6 Figg Trees; 20 Cenes of the Pignoli; 100 Tuby Roses £0.8s.0d'.[101] All in all, a small fortune was spent on these plants, which were, apart from their usefulness and beauty, a symbol of wealth and good taste. An 'Anninus House'[102] was erected in 1735/36, the plants for which were supplied by Mr Scott, Lord Burlington's head gardener at Chiswick. Scott stayed at Holkham for nearly a year and taught the local gardeners to handle these delicate trees. Thomas Coke's enthusiasm for his 'Anninus' must have been considerable, since in 1737 the money spent on pineapple trees surpassed the total expenditure for the kitchen garden by a quarter.[103] The kitchen garden and its fruit clearly gave Coke great pleasure; in a letter to Brettingham in 1738/39 he writes:

> I am very glad to hear the kitchen garden is in such good order & that the apricocks my favourite fruit have escaped so well.[104]

Until their amalgamation in 1743, the kitchen garden and the orangery were two separate departments. Coke must certainly have been satisfied with his head gardener's work, as John Aram received a gift of ten guineas in January 1738, a sum equal to his monthly income.[105]

The formal layout of Holkham's first kitchen gardens corresponded to the fashion of the day, but the extraordinary variety of species grown there – as we know from a survey in 1748 – was quite remarkable. Figs, peaches, cherries, plums, nectarines, pears, grapes, various apples, mulberries, quinces, filberts, almonds, greengages, medlars and soft fruit are all listed. Moreover, Coke had most of these trees in a wide range of varieties, partly to secure the longest possible availability of produce: there were, for example, nine fig trees in at least five varieties and forty peach trees in twenty-three varieties. Added to which, melons and strawberries were cultivated in vegetable patches, often under glass bells.

The gardens were maintained at this extraordinary pitch until Thomas Coke died in 1759. But his successor, Thomas William Coke, had no scruples about demolishing the walled gardens in the 1770s to make way for the 'curl' added to the south end of the lake. It was his great aim to encourage agricultural production on his tenant farms through new leases and buildings, including the fashionable farmhouses designed by Samuel Wyatt. In the next decades he created the Home Farm, a showpiece within the newly expanded deer park perimeter, and the massive Great Barn designed by Wyatt as a venue for agricultural shows. He also carried out an extensive campaign of planting under the direction of John Sandys, and further to the west of the original garden he spared no cost on creating a new kitchen garden and improving the lake and pleasure grounds. As we have seen, the lake was altered, cleared of an island created by William Kent, and given a serpentine twist. The slopes around were planted with many different species to provide a variety of views.[106] And so the first kitchen gardens disappeared for good.

VICTORIAN EXTENSIONS: THE TERRACES

As we have seen, William Kent's picturesque and private pleasure ground on the south and west side of the house was largely swept away around 1780, soon after Thomas William Coke took over Holkham, and throughout the latter's tenure the greensward swept right up to the house itself. In the mid-nineteenth century, however, the pendulum swung back again when the second earl had the house enclosed in formal terracing (fig. 47).

> It seems as if a fairy wand had waved over the well-remembered scene,' commented *The Gardener's Chronicle* in 1858: 'There stands that Hall – the same, yet changed. The long green slope which gradually descended into the richly turfed undulation is now fairy land. Terrace upon terrace rises, broad and noble

Fig. 47. An aerial view of the house in its parkland, with the sea in the background. The mansion is framed by the terraces built for the second Earl of Leicester between 1849 and 1855.

> as are the walks – sloping banks of velvety green intervene, while on the broader verdant surface small beds of flowers, whose distinct forms are brought out by their contrast of colour as well as by their varied shapes, the different coloured pebbles which fill the intervening spaces, and their white borders give the surface a gay beauty, which heightens the general effect. In front is a magnificent fountain, the centre representing St George in the act of striking the dragon, from whose open upturned jaws spouts a continuous flood.

What prompted the second Earl of Leicester to change the appearance of one of the most classically correct houses in Britain? As far as many of the ancillary buildings were concerned, the reasons would have been predominantly economic. No longer did aristocratic landowners have never-ending streams of money. Increased trade and the Industrial Revolution meant that the burgeoning middle classes were now competing against them. No longer could large houses afford to have vast servant populations; activities had to be streamlined and made efficient. The introduction of an Agent's Lodge and Steward's Office illustrates how the estate was in the process of being made economically viable. But one cannot ignore the fact that the income from the Coke family estates was fairly large – large enough to cope with such an ambitious project. Perhaps it was the mere presence of such an amount of money that prompted the second earl to think of ways of spending it.

But why construct the terraces as well? Was it that he was merely carried away with the idea of 'improvement', so prevalent in the Victorian era? The earl and his family, as was increasingly the Victorian fashion, exhibited a keen interest in gardening. He subscribed to *The Gardener's Chronicle*, his mother had introduced a flower garden to the east of the Hall, and in 1838 a well-stocked vinery, 'the finest perhaps in England and well-deserving the attention of strangers', had been erected to the west of the house, on the other side of the lake adjacent to the kitchen gardens.

It is also suggested that one of the second earl's daughters had her own flower garden between the Chapel and Kitchen Wings on the east side of the house. All this interest in gardening and botany had its natural culmination in the terraces, with their parterres of box and bedding plants, and in the new conservatory put up by William Burn, as well as in the pleasure grounds which had been elaborated to include separate little gardens, each with its own specialities – artistic or botanical. In the arboretum, for example, the fernery, with its many species of fern, its shell-house and its grotesque statuary set in lava caves, exuded the strange atmosphere of a secluded grotto. The shell-house in the fernery had actually been erected in about 1832 by the head gardener, Mr Girwan. Its exterior walls are cobbled with Norfolk flints, while the interior is patterned with shells both local and foreign. The large clam shells lying on the Corinthian capital were brought from the Indian Ocean by Admiral Sir Henry Keppel, Coke of Norfolk's brother-in-law (figs. 48 and 49).

However, no matter how great the current interest in gardening, that alone could not have prompted such huge changes. There was another reason – that of privacy. The mere presence of guidebooks to the Hall in the nineteenth century is an indication of this. They inform us that the house was open to general visitors on Tuesdays, whilst during the rest of the week people might walk around the exterior of the house and peer in through the windows.

Fig. 48. A view of the arboretum east of the house, laid out in the early nineteenth century to provide a private area for the family.

Fig. 49. The central feature of the pond in the Fernery from 1832 is an ancient Corinthian capital bearing clam shells brought from the Indian Ocean by Admiral Sir Henry Keppel.

Fig. 50. A design by the architect S. S. Teulon for the terraces on the west side of the house, 1846/47.

The 1857 guide even mentions 'Those numerous parties of Summer Excursionists ... who inspect the Gardens and Grounds.' Locked iron gates and a virtually unassailable terrace put paid to this, preserving the family's privacy even today. Visitors are now invited to walk around the terraces, keeping to the gravelled paths, but not to press their noses to the windows.

Social practices and requirements of deportment in the mid-nineteenth century may also have been important in the realisation of the terraces. Victorian morals required that life be carried out in a genteel manner. Women could no longer stroll at leisure through the countryside, nor even through a well-ordered parkland, but were restricted to the ordered and man-made walkways of gravel (they could not walk on grass, for fear it would wet their shoes and dirty the hems of their dresses). These gravel walkways were to be found within the terrace walls, each different terrace joined across sloping grass areas by stone steps. In the pleasure grounds the walkways were protected from the 'wild countryside' by six-foot-high iron deer fences. When there were large house parties at the Hall, a fair proportion of the time would have been spent wandering around outside in the fashion described above (fig. 225). One might be entertained by the various small fountains in the pleasure ground or the large one of St George and the Dragon, where the tinkling sound of water would play on the ears of the house guests, no doubt impressing them greatly. The massive conservatory built by Burn to separate the domestic buildings and offices from the new terraces emphasised both the social distinctions and the desire for privacy so characteristic of the Victorian era.

However, perhaps the main reason for building the terraces was that the second earl succumbed to the Victorian mania for 'improvement'. In this age of expansion, when the British Empire was painting much of the globe pink, many aristocrats, industrialists and country squires made their own improvements by adding extensions to their existing country houses or by building new ones. It was almost an anomaly if any structure remained untouched. Luckily, the additions to the Hall were inspired by the Victorian classical movement and not the far more popular Gothic revival. In 1846–47, the architect S. S. Teu-

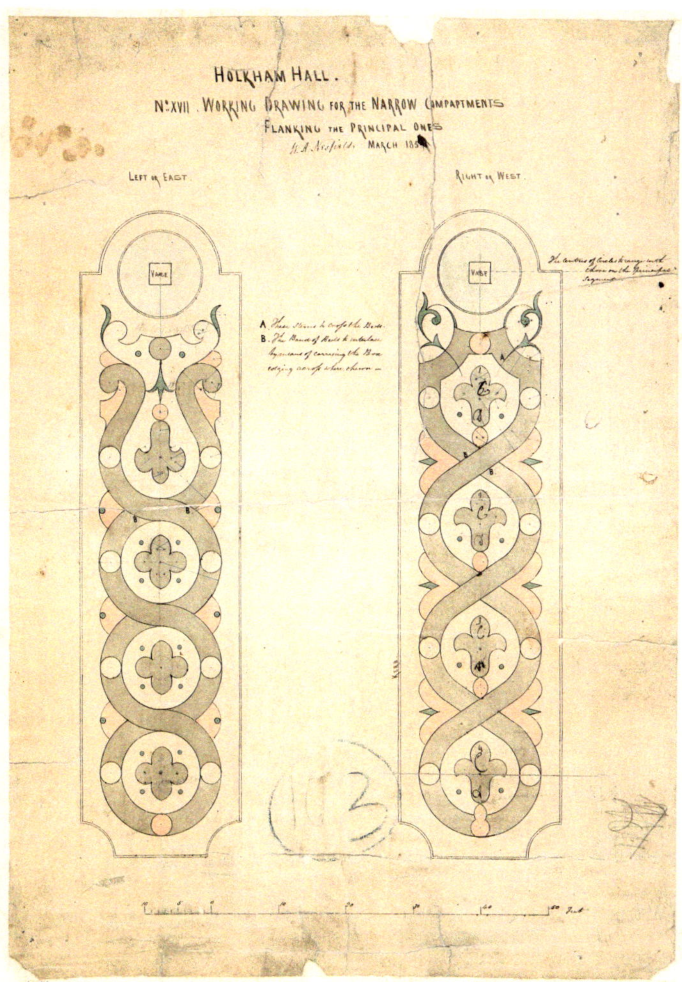

Fig. 51. A working drawing for the planting of the box compartments on the south terrace, by the landscape architect W. A. Nesfield.

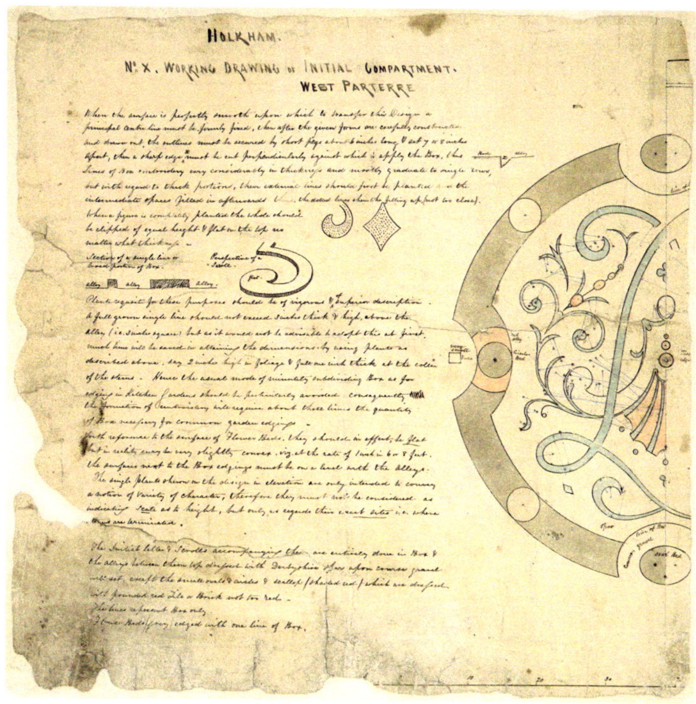

Fig. 52. A working drawing for the 'initial' compartment on the west terrace showing the Leicester 'L', by W. A. Nesfield.

lon was building the north and south lodges, and, although he submitted plans for the terraces (fig. 50), it was the landscape architect W. A. Nesfield (1793–1881) whose designs were accepted.

Nesfield's gardens were intended to reflect the period in which the house was built and the style in which it was designed. He favoured a learned approach when laying out his parterres: at Worsley Hall, Lincolnshire, for instance, he used a design taken from a seventeenth-century French source. Similarly, for a parterre at Kew Gardens in 1845 he attempted to emulate those in front of the Palace at Versailles. Nesfield, whose work remained very popular from about 1840 to 1865, was so caught up in the wave of Victorian 'improvement' that his obituary in *The Gardener's Chronicle* read: 'There are few of the large parks and gardens of this country that do not owe something to his taste and skill.'

Work on the construction of the terraces started in 1849 and went on until 1855 (figs. 51 and 52). Planting started with the shrubs and evergreens in 1854 and the less robust plants in the spring of 1855. The massive sculpture of St George and the Dragon, designed by Charles Raymond Smith, was finally erected in 1856.

In 1850, Nesfield left Holkham to work for Queen Victoria at St James's Park, London and at Buckingham Palace. He then went on to design and lay out the Royal Horticultural Society's new gardens at Kensington Gore, seen by many as his ultimate achievement. Here, in 1861, he created a parterre composed solely of box hedges, coloured gravels and glasses in the shapes of the emblematic plants of England, Ireland, Scotland and Wales: the rose, the shamrock, the thistle and the leek, surrounded by canals and a maze.

Fig. 53. Vertical view of the box compartments on the south terrace.

The terraces have changed considerably since they were planted 150 years ago. Many shrubs became oversized and were then taken out, and the box has obviously exceeded its original height of three inches (fig. 53). Planting fashions have changed and the colours of the parterre bedding plants have become more muted. The coloured aggregates that filled the beds – more evident during the winter months when there was no plant covering – have, over the years, become mixed in with the earth and gradually disappeared.

The vast expanse of gravel that covered the whole of the top terrace was replaced with grass by the fifth Earl of Leicester after World War II – making a considerable change to the appearance of the whole. However, during this time, the eastern part of the north terrace was neglected, with the result that this upper walkway has remained untouched since its creation. It is important to remember that Nesfield intended the terraces to be dominated by the Hall; the vast expanse of gravel would, he believed, clash less with the similarly coloured yellow brick of the Hall.

On the western terrace, four levels of terracing are employed. The 'initial' compartment occupies the lowest of these levels (fig. 54). There appear to be two reasons why there are more terraces on this side of the house than on the others. The most obvious of these is that here there was a steeper gradient (from the house down to the lake) than on the other sides. More levels could accommodate this

Fig. 54. View of the 'initial' compartment on the west terrace with the lake in the background.

gradient and thus not interfere with the planned shape of the terrace wall. The second reason is that by lowering the initial compartment to a fourth terrace, it increased the angle of view from the State Wing and made the pattern easier to distinguish. This pattern is made up of intricate arabesques in box, supplemented with bedding plants and a variety of coloured gravels and stones to fill in the spaces between the low topiary. The main feature amongst the arabesque is a pair of initials: two Leicester 'L's intertwined.

Nesfield's popularity was short-lived; the gardening press virtually passed over his death in March 1881, in contrast to the long eulogies they had written on the death of the younger but more famous gardener Joseph Paxton fifteen years previously. Paxton had been responsible for polychrome parterres as well, but had died whilst they were still popular. However, the terraced gardens remained true to their original plans until the fifth Earl of Leicester inherited Holkham in 1949, when they assumed their present appearance. Considering what could have been built by the Victorians, the terraces at Holkham have complemented the Hall in a wonderfully understated way. Maintaining their rôle vis-à-vis privacy and security, to the impartial observer, they look as though they were always intended to be part of the original design.

MARBLE HALL

Pl. 8

Pls. 9, 10, 11

THIS SEAT, on an open barren Estate
Was planned, planted, built, decorated,
And inhabited the middle of the XVIII Century
By THO.S COKE EARL of LEICESTER

SALOON

Pl. 12

►■◄

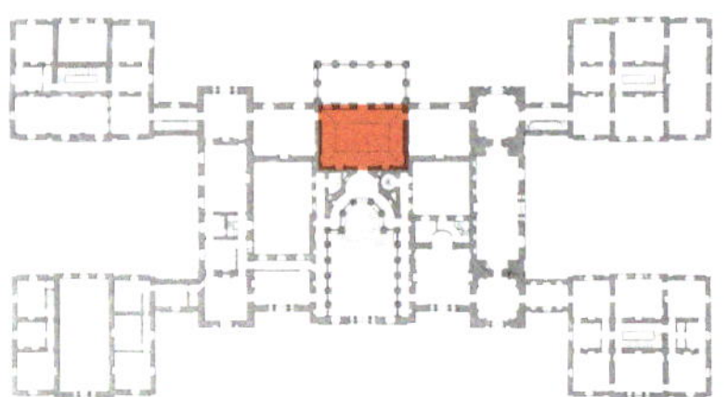

Pl. 13

Pl. 14

Pl. 15

Pl. 16

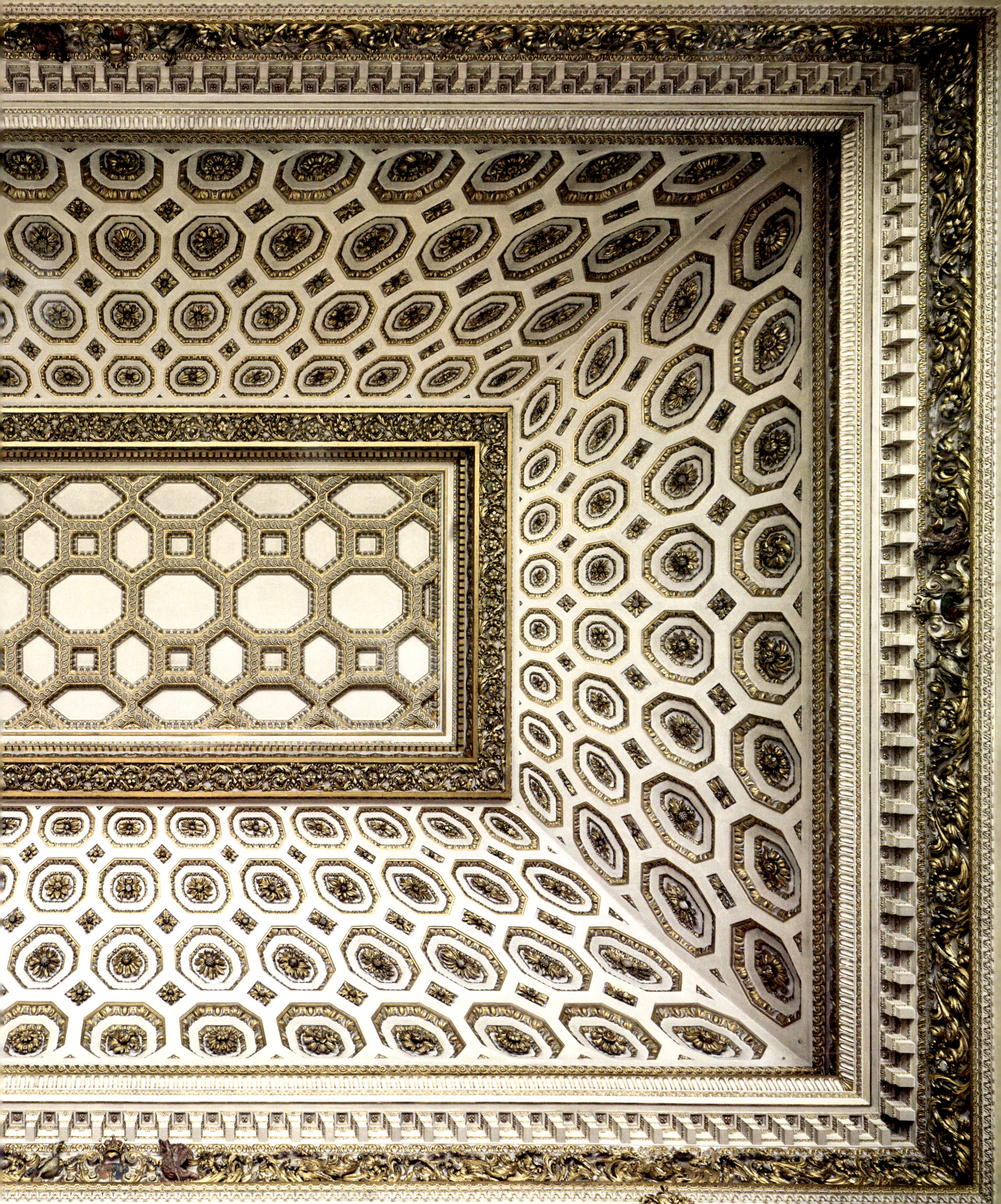

Pl. 17

STATE DINING ROOM

Pl. 18

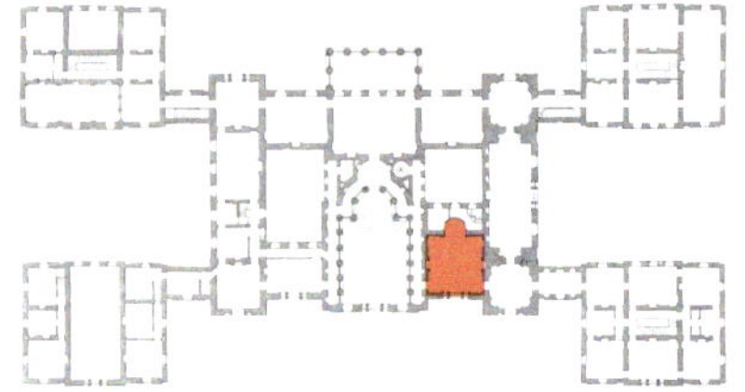

Pl. 19

STATUE GALLERY

Pl. 20

►■◄

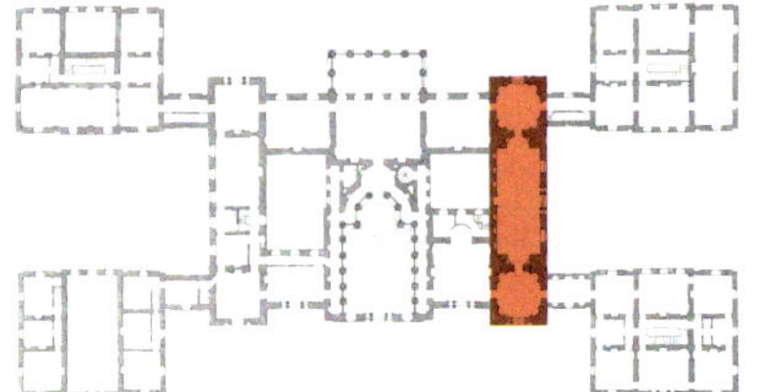

Pl. 21

Pl. 22

Pl. 23

Pls. 24, 25

Pl. 26

Pl. 27

CHAPTER 3

THE ARCHITECTURE

OVERLEAF
Detail of the south elevation of the house, from Matthew Brettingham's *Plans of Holkham*, 1761.

Throughout the seventeenth century, none of the Chief Justice's descendants attempted to build a great house commensurate with the family's property – perhaps because they all tended to die within a decade of inheriting.

When Thomas Coke inherited the extensive estate in 1718, his magnificent collections acquired on his Grand Tour were crying out for an appropriate architectural setting, and he must have been raring to create a building worthy of his passion for the arts and for the grandeur of ancient Rome. However, his South Sea losses threatened his plans even before they were formulated.

More than a decade was to pass before building work started on the grand new house at Holkham. Though doubtlessly trying the young man's patience, this period from the early 1720s to 1734 was valuable in providing ample time for gradually developing the architectural features of the house in a design process that allowed for reflection and improvement.

As the purest and grandest surviving example of neo-Palladian country house architecture, Holkham holds a special place in British architectural history.[107] But who can be credited with the design of Holkham? It has always been accepted that four men were involved in the building's concept and its execution – Thomas Coke, Lord Burlington, William Kent and Matthew Brettingham (figs. 55 to 58) – whereas the rôle and independent contribution of Thomas Coke's widow, Lady Margaret (fig. 59), has rarely earned more than a footnote.

However, there has been much debate about their respective contributions. Most textbooks name William Kent as Holkham's architect and assume that he produced the designs for the house only a couple of years before work began in 1734. Without detracting from Holkham as an architectural and artistic achievement, this date would place it firmly in the wake of Lord Burlington's seminal creation at Chiswick, which shows a number of novel features that we also find at Holkham. It turns out that things are not quite as simple as that.

In view of a nearly total absence of straightforward archival documentation, the decisive development phases of Holkham must be researched and interpreted on the basis of the available plans and drawings. Luckily, there are quite a few of these. Many of them have survived at Holkham, but some of the earliest designs were only discovered fairly recently in other places.

Fig. 55. Thomas Coke, Lord Lovell and Earl of Leicester (1697–1759). Detail of a painting at Holkham by Jonathan Richardson, 1725.

HOLKHAM I

Until the late 1970s, a portfolio at Holkham loosely known as 'the Kent drawings' contained all the known designs for the house and grounds. But since then, several other important sources have come to light. The most significant new find was a remarkably well-drawn and detailed set of seven plans and elevations preserved in the British Library (figs. 60 to 65)[108] as part of King George III's Topographical Collection. Exactly how and when the drawings got there is unclear, but the King's librarians clearly felt justified in cataloguing them under the name 'Holkham' even though the design lacks the four pavilions so characteristic of the Norfolk building.

The drawings are not signed, but their draughtsmanship and the handwriting of the inscribed measurements leave no doubt that they were made by Matthew Brettingham, Holkham's executive architect.

It is more than tempting to connect these drawings (which we may refer to as Holkham I) to a payment recorded in the Holkham accounts in the year 1726 when ten guineas were paid 'To Mr Breckingham by Sr Thomas's order for drawing a Plan of a New House':[109] the sum is appropriate for such a group of drawings, and the expense represents the only recorded payment to Brettingham before he was charged with overseeing the building activities at Holkham from 1734 onwards.

Let us look more closely at these drawings and compare them to Holkham as it was built. Outwardly the design conforms to the body of the house as it was planned and built later, with its four corner towers, the temple front, the rusticated ground floor and the smooth surfaces of the upper façades. The most significant difference is Holkham I's 'Attick storey' lit by windows all along the west, south and east fronts (though not on the north or entrance front where they would have interfered with the Burlingtonian relieving arches over the Venetian windows).

In the plan of the principal floor, we recognise Holkham's iconic features – the columnar hall in the centre and the tripartite gallery in the west. In the eastern side of the house we find two symmetrically arranged apartments, each consisting of ante-chamber, dressing room and bedroom, connected by a joint cabinet and the backstairs in the approved manner of baroque state apartments.

Although similar in general outline, the gallery of Holkham I differs in significant detail from the Statue Gallery that is Holkham's most splendid feature today. Its octagonal end rooms were clearly not intended for sculptures, instead showing cupboards, fireplaces and access to

Fig. 56. Richard Boyle, third Earl of Burlington (1694–1753). Painting at Chatsworth House by George Knapton, 1743.

Fig. 57. William Kent (1685–1748). Portrait by William Aikman, c. 1720.

newel stairs where there are now niches for statuary. Even the long centre room offers only four niches for sculptures in the apses. At some later stage, however, someone pencilled in six more niches along the room's interior long wall in the places where they are now – a detail indicating that this plan was at some point used to illustrate what changes needed to be made.

In view of the fact that Thomas Coke had bought a large number of valuable manuscripts and books on his Grand Tour, he would obviously need a library in his house. The most likely room for this in Holkham I would be one on the north side between the Gallery and the entrance hall, later to become the State Dining Room. Unusually, this room has no false doors mirroring the real ones for symmetry: might this indicate that the walls would have been covered by bookshelves and presses?

The mezzanine storey deserves a closer look. Its layout is planned and drawn in remarkable detail. The outlines of beds show that there were to be eight apartments, mostly consisting of a bedchamber and a dressing room each; the two bedrooms in the western towers would have shared the long room above the Gallery, perhaps as a kind of sitting room. Clearly, these rooms were meant for family members and guests. They would have been far too large and too grand for servants, who would have been housed on the ground floor or in the adjoining buildings that the house would have needed anyway.

The interior arrangements in these plans seem plausible enough; it is only at a second glance that one doubts whether they would really have worked. Access would have been a problem. Four staircases lead up to the mezzanine: two narrow circular stairs accessible from the octagonal end rooms of the Gallery, the backstairs servicing the two grand apartments on the main floor, and a queerly shaped triangular staircase in a corner behind the Hall apse. None of them would have been acceptable for a gentleman or a lady, as they

Fig. 58. Matthew Brettingham (1699–1769), Thomas Coke's amanuensis and executive architect. The portrait shows him holding an elevation of the Triumphal Arch, which was in fact designed mostly by William Kent. Portrait by John Theodore Heins, 1749.

Fig. 59. Margaret, Countess of Leicester (1700–1775), who completed the building of the house and its interior decoration after her husband's death.

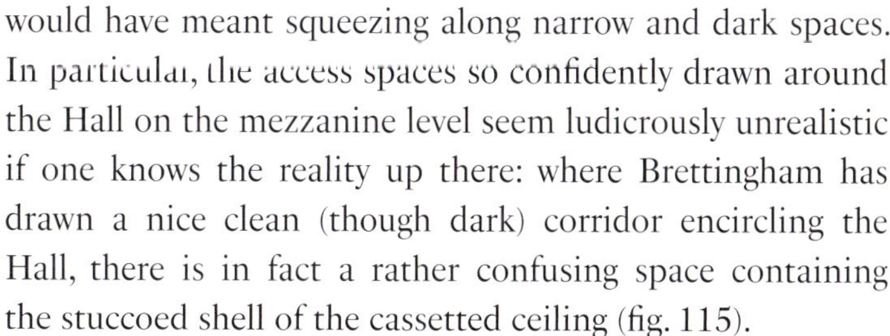

would have meant squeezing along narrow and dark spaces. In particular, the access spaces so confidently drawn around the Hall on the mezzanine level seem ludicrously unrealistic if one knows the reality up there: where Brettingham has drawn a nice clean (though dark) corridor encircling the Hall, there is in fact a rather confusing space containing the stuccoed shell of the cassetted ceiling (fig. 115).

Other problems can be spotted on the main floor. The lack of service access would have made daily life difficult: for example, footmen would have had to rub shoulders with the gentry on their way to serving food in the dining room between the Hall and the Gallery. It should also be noted that the existence of a mezzanine floor would impact on the octagonal end rooms of the Gallery: there would have been no space for the high vaulted ceilings that make them so impressive today (fig. 73).

To sum up: the Holkham I designs are the earliest documented step on the way to the building that we now know. It is in the nature of the design process for a large and complex house that there must have been earlier, tentative steps leading up to these fair drawn plans – a range of alternative ideas that were considered and largely rejected, but which gradually focused on one avenue. They document a stage that must have seemed pretty definite at the time, and yet they contain quite a few imperfections.

But before we turn to the next phase in Holkham's development we should look at the context of Holkham I. Who were the people involved with the planning at this stage in the early and mid-1720s, and what were their backgrounds? What may have been their contributions? The drawings themselves were made by Matthew Brettingham (1699–1769), Thomas Coke's architectural amanuensis for the next few decades (fig. 58). The young Norwich bricklayer was a competent draughtsman who would later develop into a moderately successful builder of great houses, but it seems fair to say that he never had an original architectural idea in

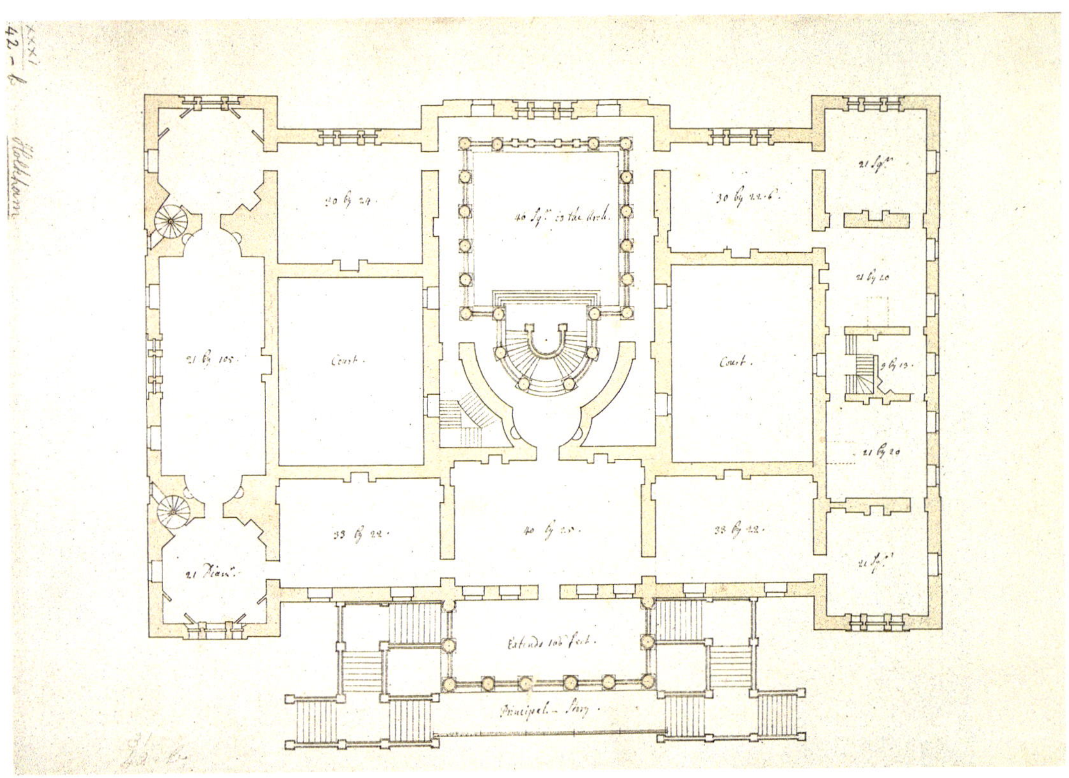

Fig. 60. Holkham I (1726), plan of the main floor. In the first designs, the house was planned without pavilions. The hall is already well developed, even if the gallery does not yet have much space for sculptures (although six niches are pencilled into its eastern wall). Note the two symmetrical apartments in the eastern (right-hand) part of the house. Drawn by Matthew Brettingham.

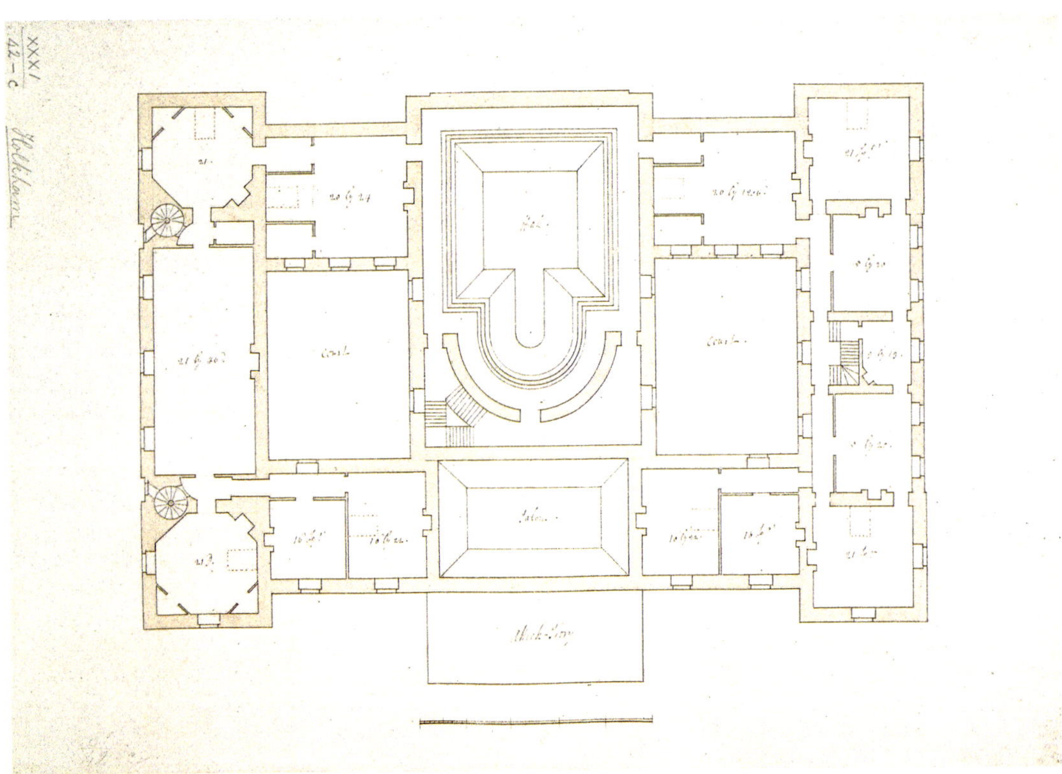

Fig. 61. Holkham I (1726), plan of the 'attick' or mezzanine floor, containing eight bedrooms and their dressing rooms, presumably for family members and visitors. Drawn by Matthew Brettingham.

Fig. 62. Holkham I (1726), south elevation, with stairs to the portico (an alternative version without stairs is also part of the set of drawings). Apart from the windows of the mezzanine storey, the elevation conforms to that of the executed building. Drawn by Matthew Brettingham.

Fig. 63. Holkham I (1726), north elevation. Note the very small entrance door. The elevation conforms to that of the executed building. Drawn by Matthew Brettingham.

Fig. 64. Holkham I (1726), west elevation or gallery front. Note the narrow windows in the recesses next to the towers which provide some light for the newel stairs connecting the three storeys. As the mezzanine was abolished, the newels were never executed, but the 'ghosts' of the windows can still be seen on the façade today. Drawn by Matthew Brettingham.

Fig. 65. Holkham I (1726), east elevation. On the east side of the house, the mezzanine storey was in fact executed (see fig. 108). Drawn by Matthew Brettingham.

Fig. 66. Elevation of Wanstead I, Essex, by Colen Campbell as published in his *Vitruvius Britannicus*, vol. I (1715). Built 1713–17 (and demolished 1824), this first neo-Palladian country house in England was hugely influential.

his life: Howard Colvin justly calls him an 'orthodox but unenterprising Palladian'.

Coke's own architectural training was far superior, and on the basis of his extensive visual experience he may well have had some very original ideas about the house he wanted to build; but for all his impressive store of theoretical knowledge of architecture, he had virtually no practical experience in designing a building. Therefore, as architectural historian Robert Tavernor has pointed out, it would be unreasonable to assume that these two men could have designed Holkham between themselves: 'such maturity is not easily won.'[110] This must be particularly true for a design like Holkham I that is, for its time, at the absolute forefront of stylistic development.

It seems therefore reasonable to surmise that Brettingham's 1726 drawings – although the earliest plans for Holkham we have – must be based on some design input from some other, shadowy figure. But who can it have been?

Tradition links Lord Burlington and William Kent with Holkham, but William Kent had not acquired any practical experience in architecture by 1726 – his contribution came later, and mostly in other fields than the architecture proper. Coke's relationship with Lord Burlington will be addressed anon. But in the early 1720s Thomas Coke was in contact with some of the few first-rate architects of the time, and one of them could have been involved in the first designs for Holkham.

James Gibbs is certainly a contender: in 1719, he was employed to modernise the family's London residence, Thanet House, and Coke might well have consulted him about his country house project. Another prominent name cropped up in Coke's account books in 1722: 'Mr Tallman' (presumably John Talman, son of William Talman, who had died in 1719) received ten guineas for a drawing, but the subject is unknown – it may have been one of the Palladio originals he had inherited from his father. Rather more germane is a payment recorded in 1725–26, when 'Mr Colin Campbell Surveyor' was paid sixteen guineas under the heading of 'Sundry Expences which seem to belong to Sir Thomas's Personal Expence.' As the author of *Vitruvius Britannicus* and as the architect who had made the first designs for neighbouring Houghton Hall, Colen Campbell (1676–1729) would have been an obvious candidate for collaboration with Thomas Coke, and this fee represented a considerable amount of money, quite appropriate for a set of architectural plans at the time.

The connection went back several years: Coke had bought the first two volumes of *Vitruvius Britannicus* in March 1720, and shortly afterwards Campbell visited Coke's properties at Stoke Poges in Buckinghamshire and Holkham, possibly to view some of the sites Coke was considering for his new seat. This journey predates a letter of 18 November 1721 written by Thomas Coke's uncle Michael Newton in which he wrote that Holkham

> is as healthfull as most other places, it stands in a very clear Air, & no Fenns within Twenty miles of it ... Mr Coke likes this place so well now that I believe if ever he builds it will be here, & he will find it necessary to add something, for there is not convenient Room for the company he usually has with him.[111]

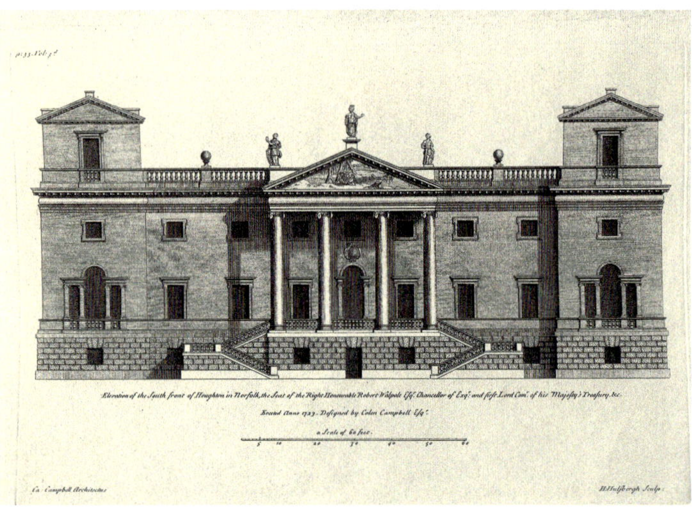

Fig. 67. Elevation of Houghton Hall, Norfolk, by Colen Campbell as published in his *Vitruvius Britannicus*, vol. III (1725). Built for Robert Walpole, Thomas Coke's near neighbour and political patron, the Houghton design was an obvious starting point for Coke's concept.

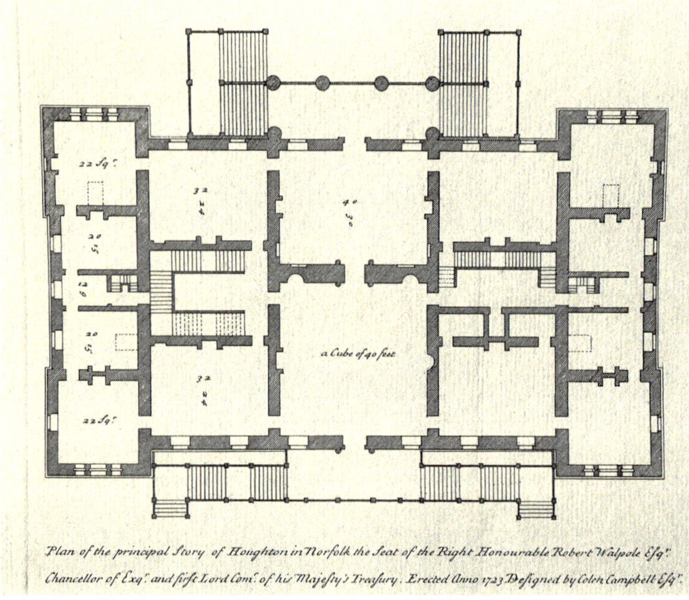

Fig. 68. Main floor plan of Houghton Hall, Norfolk, by Colen Campbell as published in his *Vitruvius Britannicus*, vol. III (1725). Although generally similar to the plan of Holkham I (fig. 60), the arrangement at Houghton seems focussed on providing living space in the shape of four apartments on the main floor and more in the mezzanine. Its large staircases are rather more functional than the narrow ones of Holkham I.

A comparison between Brettingham's 1726 drawings and Campbell's œuvre is enlightening. The first two volumes of *Vitruvius Britannicus* contained numerous engravings of unexciting buildings no doubt included by Campbell in the hope of currying favour with their owners, but there is one gem amongst them that must have appealed to Coke's feeling for ancient Rome: Campbell's Wanstead House in Essex (fig. 66). There are obvious affinities to the Holkham I concept: Holkham's portico might even have been directly modelled on Wanstead. As Campbell commented proudly, Wanstead's portico is 'a just Hexastyle, the first yet practised in this manner in the Kingdom',[112] and since the hall featured pilasters of nearly the same size as the portico, the 'temple idea was pretty forcibly implanted'[113] there.

Other features at Holkham that correspond to those at Wanstead and at Campbell's other great house, Houghton Hall, designed for Robert Walpole in 1722, are the rusticated ground floor and the roof balustrade. Although Campbell did not publish the Houghton designs until 1725, in the third volume of *Vitruvius Britannicus* (figs. 67 and 68), Thomas Coke would have known them even before their publication, since Walpole was his neighbour, kinsman and political patron. Whilst we find Holkham's portico and classical grandeur presaged by Wanstead, Houghton provided the model for the four corner towers[114] – a feature that Coke would have appreciated for its classical allusions: not only was Scamozzi's reconstruction of the Roman *villa rustica* characterised by such corner towers (fig. 69), but Serlio had built his own version at Ancy-le-Franc in the 1540s. However, unlike Houghton, Holkham I possesses spacious interior courtyards which in effect turn it into

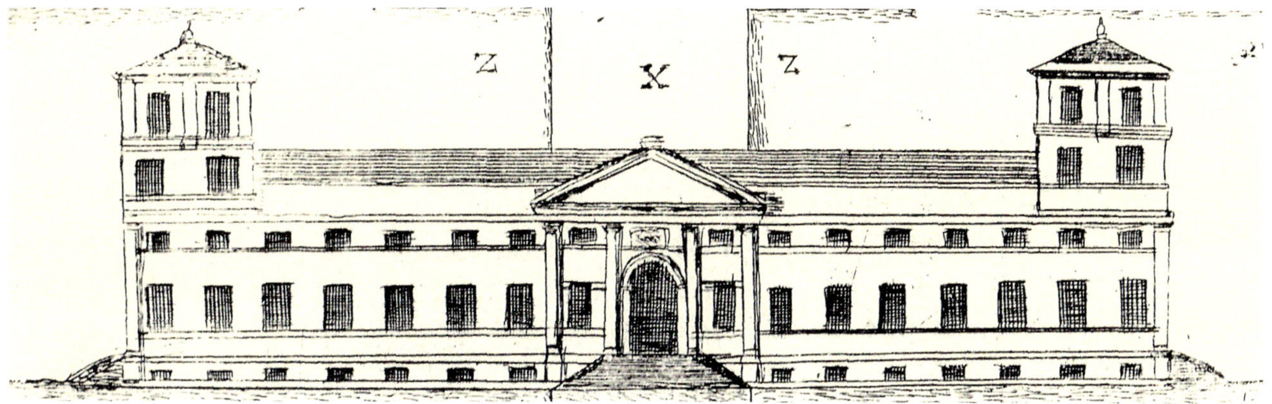

Fig. 69. With its corner towers, the classical Villa Rustica, as reconstructed by Vincenzo Scamozzi (1548–1616), provided the inspiration for many neo-Palladian country houses.

a more ambitious, even somewhat palatial, version of its Norfolk neighbour.

In view of the similarities between Holkham I and Campbell's œuvre it seems reasonable to assume that Colen Campbell did, indeed, produce a country house design for Thomas Coke for a fee of sixteen guineas and that this became the basis of the 1726 plans.

And yet Brettingham's drawings for Holkham I contain some elements that we might call un-Campbellesque – elements that have been interpreted as indications of Lord Burlington's influence. Lord Burlington's villa at Chiswick – a much smaller building, more a demonstration of a new architectural style than a house to live in – shares several characteristics with Holkham: uncanny similarities even, hitherto easily explained by the understanding that Holkham was conceived a number of years after Chiswick (fig. 70). With Chiswick being built from 1727 onwards, however, the date of 1726 for the Holkham I drawings suggests that the two designs were developed in tandem, in a fascinating interchange of ideas between Burlington and Coke that leaves us wondering who had come up with which idea first. We will never know how this collaboration worked in detail, but we may assume from later letters that Coke tended to defer to Burlington as the resident arbiter of taste.

As for the similarities between Chiswick and Holkham, both buildings share the same artistic approach regarding their exteriors, both composed of smooth and sharp-edged shapes and both lacking ornaments or other softening features. In both buildings, Venetian windows recessed under a relieving arch dominate one of the main fronts.[115] Even more significantly, both buildings feature a tripartite

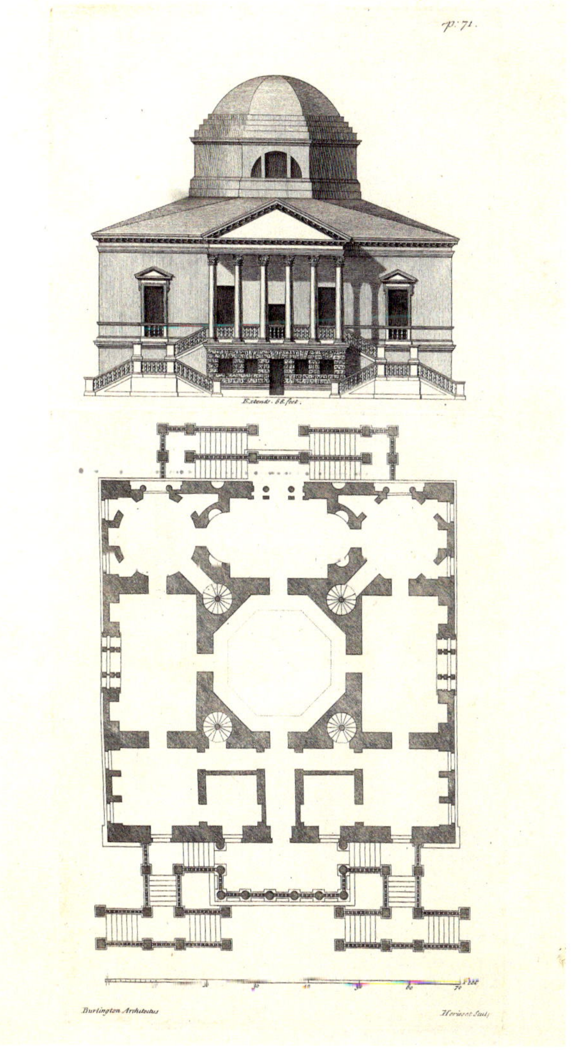

Fig. 70. Elevation and main floor plan of Chiswick House, designed by Lord Burlington at roughly the same time as Holkham I and built from 1727 onwards. Engraving from William Kent's book *The Designs of Inigo Jones*, 1727.

Fig. 71. Elevation of Tottenham House, designed by Lord Burlington and built in the 1720s – clearly one of the inspirations for Holkham I. Drawing by Henry Flitcroft, dated 1721.

gallery, with octagonal end rooms flanking an oblong space that is defined by apsed ends (see plans in figs. 60 and 70). As observed earlier, Holkham I's mezzanine meant that the three gallery rooms would have been of the same height, just as they are in Chiswick. Compared to the highly ornamented gallery at Chiswick, Holkham's Statue Gallery is austere and sober, or – in the words of Pope's epistle to Burlington – 'glorious, not profuse': a quality that was to become more marked by the time of Holkham's execution and that even transcends Campbell's grandest creations such as Wanstead.

Another Burlingtonian feature at Holkham is the low pyramidal roofs of the towers, recalling those at Tottenham Park, Wiltshire.[116] In a façade that is deliberately reduced to what its designers must have regarded as the pure ideal of ancient Rome, only one small element recalls Campbell's less rigid stance: the portico's central intercolumnium is slightly wider than the others – in Burlingtonian terms an outdated feature by the mid-1720s.[117]

To sum up, the Holkham I concept formulated some very exciting ideas and novel features, created and developed through a great deal of interchange with Colen Campbell and Lord Burlington, and its most characteristic features had already reached a definite form that would henceforth remain unchanged. Clearly, a great deal of creativity had gone into what we may perhaps call the demonstrative elements of the building, the parts that were meant to overwhelm the viewers and impress them with a grand architectural vision. This gives us a feeling for the priorities of its originator – Thomas Coke, the patron.

By contrast, at this stage far less brainpower had gone into the functional aspects, into imagining the ways the house would work and fulfil the many practical purposes of a country seat. This was about to change.

HOLKHAM II: THE FOUR-PAVILION SOLUTION

With the Holkham I drawings fairly drawn in 1726 defining the *status quo*, the second half of the 1720s may be seen as a kind of fermentation period for the building project. Coke was still unable to put his ideas into action due to his straitened circumstances (although the landscape setting was being prepared during this time – a sensible thing to do, since trees need time to grow). No doubt Coke made use of the time by handling the plans, reflecting on them and considering how they would work in practice – gradually realising their inherent weaknesses. It must have become glaringly obvious that there was no decent way of accessing the mezzanine storey, particularly its western part. The decision to omit the two bedroom suites originally planned there may not have been easy, but it had its advantages: losing the mezzanine opened the way to upgrading the rooms on the main floor. Thus, the (North) State Dining Room gained a high domed ceiling, but the consequences

Fig. 72. Chiswick, section through the gallery. Drawing by Henry Flitcroft.

Fig. 73. Holkham II, section through the gallery. From Brettingham's *Plans*, 1773.

for the Gallery's octagonal end rooms were even more significant. At Chiswick, as in the Holkham I concept, all three rooms of the gallery were of the same height (fig. 72). In Holkham II, the end rooms could now fill all the space formerly taken up by bedrooms above, allowing them to become dramatically higher than those at Chiswick (fig. 73).

THE STATUE GALLERY

In spite of some differences in character and scale, it has always been obvious that the tripartite galleries of Chiswick and Holkham are closely related. With Chiswick being built from 1727 onwards and Holkham being started as late as 1734, it seemed equally obvious that the Norfolk version was modelled on the London original. The discovery of the Holkham I concept – which already contains the tripartite gallery – and particularly its dating to the year 1726 has challenged and upset this traditional view. Instead, the available evidence now suggests that both galleries sprang from one architectural concept invented jointly by two very erudite and enthusiastic amateurs, Lord Burlington and Thomas Coke, who were in close contact during those formative years, the 1720s, and even later. Starting out from the same architectural idea of a double-apsed oblong space with octagonal end rooms, each developed it further according to his own aims and needs. Though similar in type, the two executed galleries are markedly different in character, with the one at Holkham standing out as a much more adult and serious sibling of the smaller and rather playful version at Chiswick.

How did Burlington and Coke develop this unique concept, and what were their sources? In his 1773 edition of the *Plans of Holkham*, the younger Brettingham commented:

> The Statue Gallery, a capital part of the plan, and the completest in this kingdom, for the manner and style of furnishing, bears a near analogy to that in the Earl of Burlington's elegant little villa at Chiswick; confessedly taken, though with many deviations, from the Marchese Capri's, built by Andrea Palladio, near the town of Vicenza. The gallery of Chiswick, which is that of Holkham in miniature, is not indeed to be found in Palladio's plan just named; but its resemblance may be traced in the plans of a town-house, constructed by that architect, for the Counts Thieni, within the walls of the same city.[118]

Although Brettingham junior was clearly very knowledgeable about Holkham in its completed and furnished form, his text does not seem to contain much first-hand knowledge about Holkham's gestation period – knowledge that might have been handed down to him from his father (who had died in 1769). Instead, the younger Brettingham seems to have worked more like a modern art historian, using the evidence available to him at the time to piece together a somewhat speculative model of the sources and inspirations for the house and its characteristic and original rooms. Of course he knew his Palladio and, as he says, some elements in the plan of the Palazzo Thiene, published in Palladio's *Quattro Libri*,[119] clearly resemble those in the galleries of Holkham and Chiswick – notably the octagonal corner rooms, but also the oblong space with rounded ends, all of them clearly featuring niches for sculptures. Both Coke and

Fig. 74. Octagonal room in Palladio's Palazzo Thiene in Vicenza, inspiration for the gallery end rooms at Chiswick and Holkham.

Fig. 75. One of several drawings by Palladio in Burlington's possession showing a gallery layout with a double-apsed room in the middle.

Burlington had been to Vicenza and had doubtless seen the Palazzo with their own eyes: its corner rooms must have left a lasting impression (fig. 74). But there were other inspirations, even for the octagonal end rooms. The hint is in the name: at Holkham, the Gallery's octagonal end rooms have always been known as the Tribunes (whereas Burlington called his octagonal central hall at Chiswick the tribunal) – a reference to the famous *Tribuna* of the Uffizi in Florence, which Coke had of course seen for himself: the *Tribuna* was the domed octagonal exhibition hall built in the late sixteenth century to house the most important antiquities and artworks of the Medici collection.

Brettingham may not have been aware that Burlington had also brought a treasure trove of original Palladio drawings back to England. Amongst those drawings were several that seem to have provided further inspiration as to the shape of the Gallery's middle room. Palladio used this double-apsed room type, which he knew from his studies of Roman baths and other monuments, in a number of unexecuted designs (figs. 75 and 89),[120] and we can see their influence at Chiswick and Holkham but also in other places such as Adam's Osterley (see below).

Solving one problem – in this case, getting rid of the problematic mezzanine storey – often creates a new one. Without the rooms in the mezzanine, Coke's grand new house would now be too small to fulfil its primary function: providing living space not only for the family, but particularly for the groups of visitors that needed to be accommodated. No doubt Coke was loath to share the experiences of his friend, Lord Burlington, whose exciting new house at Chiswick had become an easy target for wits such as the Earl of Chesterfield:

Possessed of one great hall of state
Without a place to sleep or eat
How well you build let flattery tell
And all mankind how ill you dwell.

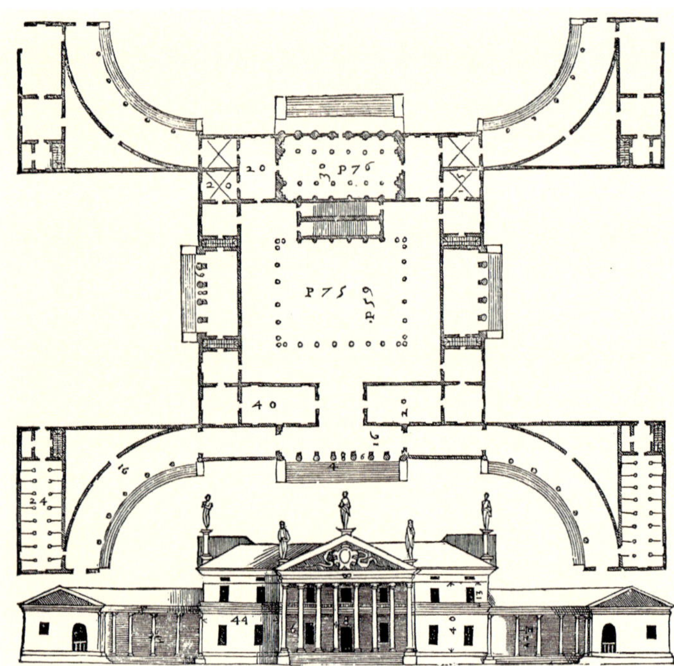

Fig. 76. The Villa Mocenigo, as published by Andrea Palladio in his *Quattro Libri dell'Architettura* (1570), vol. II, 66, both inspired and authorised the novel four-pavilion concept elaborated for Holkham II.

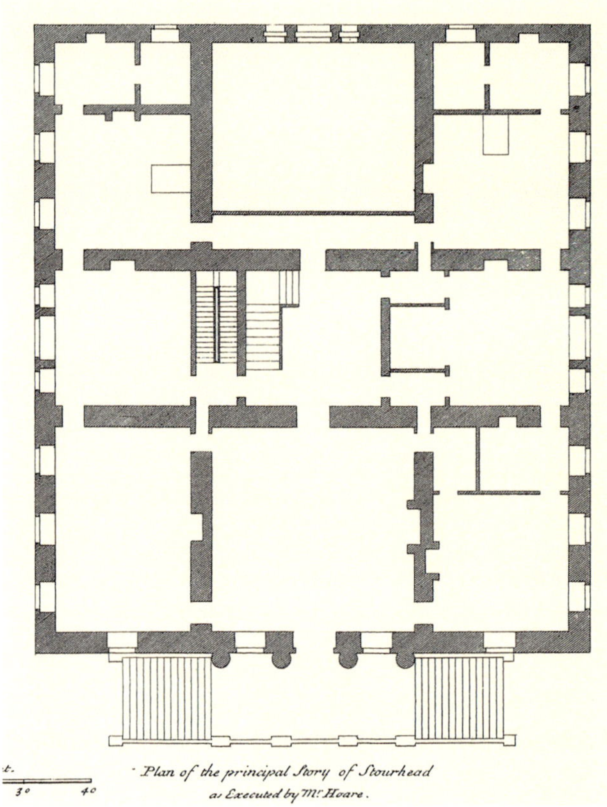

Fig. 77. The layout of villas like Colen Campbell's Stourhead, published in his *Vitruvius Britannicus*, vol. III (1725), may have been the starting point for developing the modular grid plan perfected for the pavilions of Holkham II.

Although this would inevitably boost the building cost, Coke bravely took the decision to make the house considerably larger than originally intended. Rather than replanning from scratch, he decided to use the existing concept as a point of departure and look for a way of enlarging or extending it. In keeping with the approach that had led to Holkham I – that of adding together individually designed elements based on models from antiquity and out of Palladio's *Quattro Libri* – Coke appears to have looked for inspiration in his architectural books. Palladio's design for the Villa Mocenigo (fig. 76) gave him the idea of adding structures at each corner tower: four pavilions to house all the required functions.

For once we have a date for this stage in the planning. In a letter written in 1731, Lord Hervey comments on a 'Burlington house with four pavilions on paper' that he had seen at Lord Lovell's. For 'Burlington' read 'Burlingtonian', because the *cognoscenti* would have immediately recognised the design's specific architectural flavour.

The four-pavilion layout that Lord Hervey saw in 1731 may have been just a sketch, however – it would have taken time to work out both the interior structure and the appearance of these additions. That the pavilions had to be identical on the outside was a given, in view of the Palladians' insistence on symmetry. And yet they would have to house widely different functions. What kind of façade would be equally appropriate for all these functions – smart enough for the family's and the guests' quarters without being out of place for the kitchen and the laundry? And what kind of interior structure would be adaptable enough for this range of uses?

Again, inspiration was found amongst the works of Coke's authorities, in this case Campbell: the grid plan used for Newby Park and Stourhead (fig. 77) may well have been the starting point for a design process that eventually produced a strikingly original and deeply rational solution. Deceptively simple, it consisted essentially of a box, divided twice crosswise and twice lengthwise: this produced nine compartments

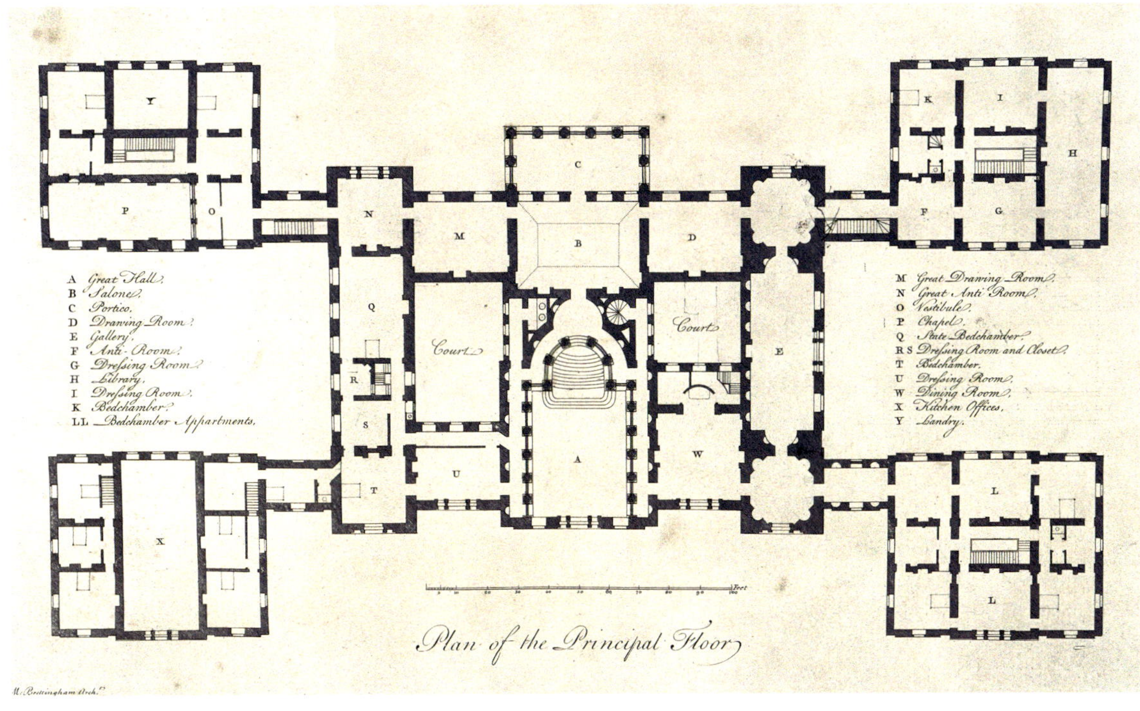

Fig. 78. Main floor plan of Holkham II as published by Matthew Brettingham in his *Plans of Holkham* (1761), showing the fully developed four-pavilion concept with its flexible layout for the wings.

Fig. 79. Holkham II, north elevation and northern half of the main floor plan, drawn by Matthew Brettingham, c. 1733. This earliest Holkham II plan of at least part of the body of the house is still closely based on Holkham I, as one can see in the design for the gallery, but shows some development in the dining room area. The façades of the pavilions are probably based on designs by William Kent (figs. 83, 84 and 85). Note that the central windows of Kitchen and Strangers' Wings in Brettingham's and Kent's drawings are not yet upgraded to Venetian windows.

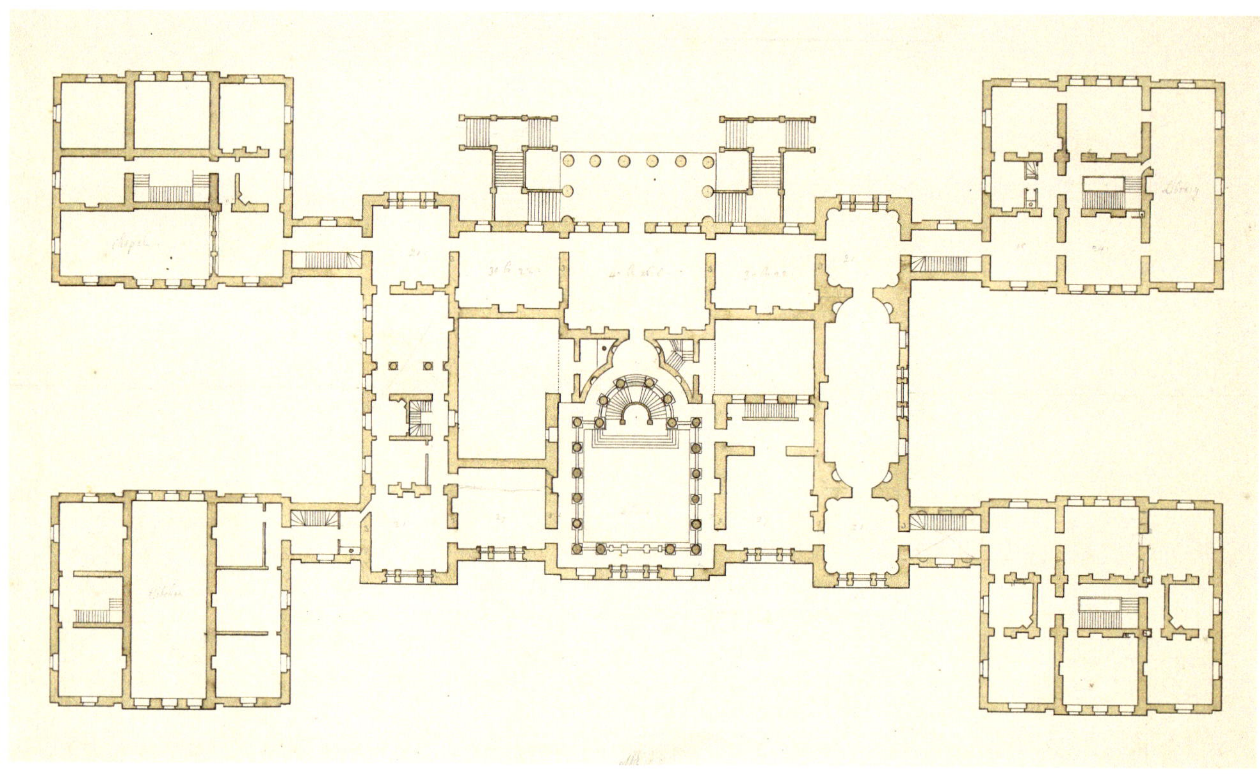

Fig. 80. The earliest complete main floor plan of Holkham II, drawn by Matthew Brettingham, c. 1733. Compared to the earlier drawing, fig. 79, the dining room area has been developed further, providing better service access from the rear. The gallery has nearly reached its final form, except that its eastern wall does not have niches for sculptures. Note the state bedroom in the eastern part of the house showing two columns forming a screen for a state bed. The great stairs to the portico were never executed.

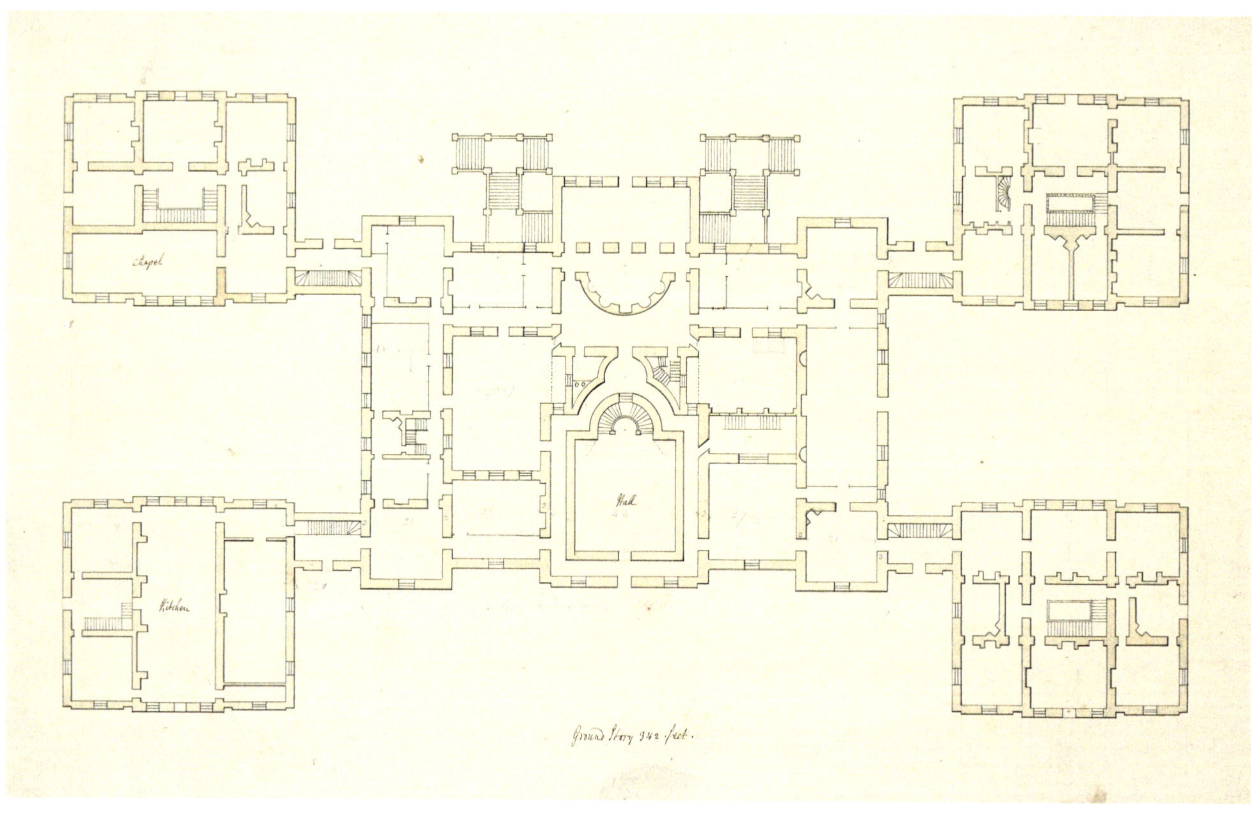

Fig. 81. Ground floor plan of Holkham II, drawn by Matthew Brettingham, c. 1733.

Fig. 82. Letter written by Thomas Coke to Matthew Brettingham at the end of March 1733, beginning 'It is wth pleasure I can inform you our whole design is vastly approved of by Ld. Burlington'.

on each level. The central compartment became the staircase hall, allowing direct access to most of the rooms, but the rooms could also be connected to each other. The ingenious thing about this structure was its modular character, the result of an approach far ahead of its time. Within its strict geometric structure, one could simply leave out the odd wall or ceiling and thus produce the Long Library, the Chapel, the kitchen or the laundry – rooms vastly different in their spatial and functional character (fig. 78).[121]

The result was a novel amalgamation of the grand and formal country house, or house of parade, as defined by the four-towered body of the house or *corps de logis*, with its antithesis, the compact and more private villa.

Two drawings by Brettingham show the earliest surviving floor plan of the Holkham II configuration. One drawing (fig. 79) combines the northern half of the main floor plan with the corresponding elevation showing Strangers' Wing and Kitchen Wing. (This is how all the pavilions are referred to at Holkham, without 'the'.) These two wings are not yet adorned with Venetian windows on their façades, but their respective interiors are already well developed and will later be executed with only very minor changes. The interior of the body of the house, however, has not yet reached its final shape at this time. The Gallery plan is quite close to the Holkham I concept, with the North Tribune still featuring a fireplace and also cupboards rather than niches for sculptures.

Two changes in the plan are remarkable, however: the Dining Room has now gained an urgently needed service access from the courtyard side, and the backstairs/cabinet combination on the eastern side has been moved northwards by one bay. The reason for this move is revealed in the second drawing (fig. 80), the earliest representation of the whole main floor plan: no longer are there two apartments in the eastern half of the house equal in size. One has been extended, at the cost of the other, to become a highly prestigious state apartment. This consists of a grand sequence of rooms, beginning with the Saloon and culminating in a State Bedroom where two columns are clearly meant to frame a gorgeous state bed. By contrast, the northern apartment has been truncated, the bedroom having moved to the corner room in the tower. A pencilled line in the dressing room indicates the intention to introduce a service corridor, much needed in practice but further diminishing the size of the northern apartment. The second drawing also shows a further (though not yet the final) stage in the gradual development of the service access and staircase to the Dining Room.

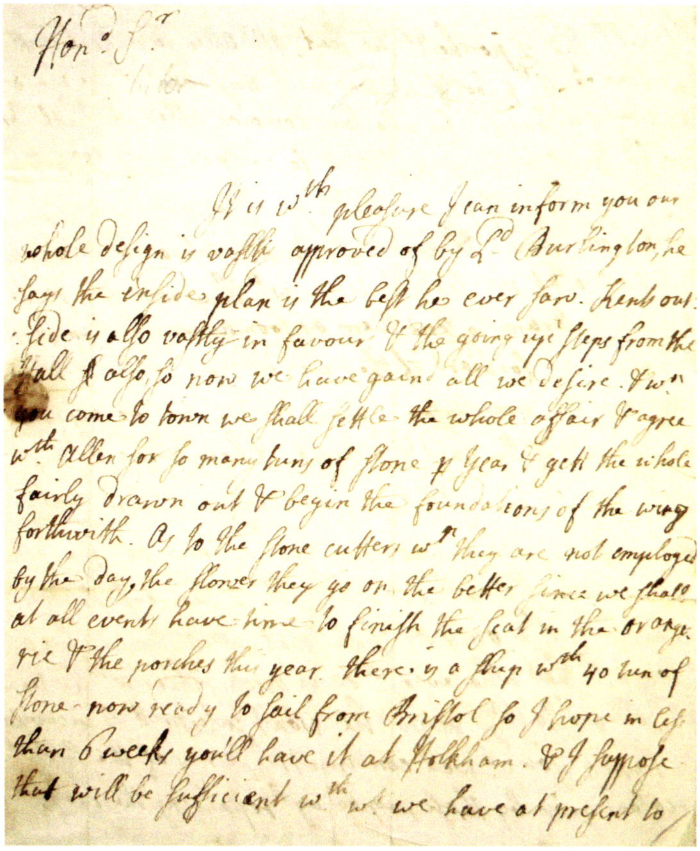

Having finalised the concept for the pavilions over the winter of 1733/34, and determined to start building at last,

Coke still rather touchingly felt the need to seek the blessing of Lord Burlington for his project. To his credit, Burlington immediately recognised the qualities and potential of the grid plan. A letter from Coke to Brettingham from London written in March 1734 (fig. 82) radiates both relief and a great eagerness to get going:

> It is wth pleasure I can inform you our whole design is vastly approved of by Ld. Burlington, he says the insides plan is the best he ever saw. Kents outside is also vastly in favour & the going up steps from the hall also, so now we have gain'd all we desire & wn you come to town we shall ... gett the whole fairly drawn out & begin the foundations of the wing forthwith.[122]

And begin they did: in the Holkham accounts, the expenses relating to the 'New House' start on 4 May 1734, with £3.11s.0d paid 'To Labour:s diging Earth out of ye foundation'.

WILLIAM KENT'S CONTRIBUTION

Coke's letter also mentions a new hand in the game, one who had been making his presence felt for a couple of years: this was William Kent (1685–1748), who originally trained as a sign and coach painter (fig. 57).[123] Kent had lived in Italy from 1709 to 1719, studying painting and looking for useful contacts amongst the English Grand Tourists. There he met not only Lord Burlington, who eventually took him under his wing, brought him back to England and helped him start a stellar career, but also young Thomas Coke. Coke clearly took a liking to the artist, who was twelve years older, as they twice travelled together around northern Italy for several months – once in 1714 and again in 1716. The following year, Kent and Coke had quite an adventure together, involving Coke's most treasured sculpture, the Diana. In a letter from Rome written on 15 June 1717, Kent told Burrell Massingberd, one of his patrons at the time, about

> an imbroglio I have had about a fine Antique Statue Mr. Coke bought, got it safe away to Leghorn when it was discovered here. They sent a Corrier and had it sequestered and would have confined Mr. Coke and was to have been sent away from Rome, but at last all was ajusted and he has got ye statue.[124]

In Italy, both Burlington and Coke befriended Kent, whom they referred to as the *signor*. Burlington brought him back to England, installed him at Burlington House and helped him to get commissions such as the decoration of Kensington Palace.

Kent was an enormously creative personality, always overflowing with ideas. In the late nineteenth century, the architect and writer Sir Reginald Blomfield dismissed him as 'one of those generally accomplished persons who can do everything up to a certain point – and nothing well'.[125] Initially ambitious and quite prolific – though famously and scathingly ridiculed by William Hogarth[126] – as a painter, he eventually excelled in designing interior decorations, furniture and also gardens, including garden architecture.

Although Kent was often the butt of their patronising jokes,[127] Burlington and Coke clearly found his talents useful. Having more or less given up painting in the later 1720s, Kent had graduated to garden designs for Lord Burlington's Chiswick. Apparently Coke liked them so much that he

Fig. 83. The south front of Holkham II, showing William Kent's suggestion for more elaborate decoration on the main-floor façade, c. 1733. Note the oval windows as remnants of Holkham I's mezzanine storey; note also the niches filling the outer bays behind the portico – they recur in the drawings shown in figs. 84 and 86 and indicate an alternative design for the Saloon. Engraving inscribed (bottom left) 'Gulielmus Kent Archit. et Pict. Invenit et Delin.'

brought him to Holkham for more of the same. Thus Kent designed, as his first contribution to the place, the Obelisk on the highest point of Holkham's long north–south axis and approach. Executed in 1730, this was followed by the nearby Temple. Apart from the fairly straight-laced Obelisk Wood, Kent also designed the charming pleasure ground that would eventually frame the Hall on its south and west sides, but execution of this part would have to wait until the 1740s.

With Kent working for Coke and Holkham in the early 1730s, it was perhaps inevitable that he offered advice, or was asked to do so, about the house project that was being developed at the time, thus becoming part of the 'ill-assorted committee'[128] that conceived the Hall. Indeed, the earliest extant representations of Holkham II were produced by Kent. They show two slightly different stages of development. The earlier stage is represented by an engraving of which only a single copy is known (fig. 83),[129] whereas the other is documented in two drawings, also by Kent, showing the south and north elevations of the house respectively (figs. 84 and 85).

Clearly Kent had brought a new and very different attitude to bear. One can practically feel the dismay he must have felt looking at Holkham I's austere and cool, nearly featureless façades representing Coke's cerebral vision of a Roman house. In the engraving and the drawings, Kent gave the façades of the main body a thorough makeover, extending the basement's rustication to cover the fronts up to the entablature and around the windows,[130] adding garlands and shields on the frieze as well as statues to the pediment. Coke seems to have remained unconvinced, however. From Kent's versions, only the muscular window surrounds survive in the elevations precisely drawn by Brettingham a little later (fig. 86), but even those were subsequently dropped.

A rather more lasting contribution by Kent seems have been the external design of the new wings, or pavilions: 'Kent's outside is also vastly in favour' with Lord Burlington, according to Coke's letter quoted earlier. The characteristic tripartite staccato fronts may well be an element derived from garden architecture. Not all architectural historians agree with Burlington's praise,[131] but it could be said that the design works equally well for the exterior of the family's

Fig. 84. Holkham II, south elevation, drawing by William Kent based on his engraving and suggesting more decoration (fig. 83) but now without any remnants of the mezzanine floor.

Fig. 85. Holkham II, north elevation, drawing by William Kent showing his ideas for more rustication.

Fig. 86. Holkham II, south elevation, drawing by Matthew Brettingham integrating a small part of the more elaborate ornamentation suggested by William Kent.

and the visitors' accommodation as for the rather more mundane Kitchen Wing. Undeniably, however, the designer's attention appears to have been focused exclusively on the frontal view, neglecting the lateral aspect (fig. 87).

Kent's involvement with Family Wing was to continue over several years. In a letter dated 21 September 1734, Coke informed Brettingham that 'Kent has the plans & will draw the elevations of the 2 sides of the wing east & west. he approves of the rusticks on the corners of the smooth piers' – one of many examples in Coke's letters of his remarkable attention to detail. And when the shell of the pavilion was built and roofed, Coke wrote to Burlington on 26 November 1736: 'I shall ... wait on you with my Port feuill, & make the Signor scold, for now we must think of the inside of the rooms'.[132] (For Kent's contribution to the interiors of Holkham, see Chapter 4.)

As an aside, it is curious that hardly any payments to Kent can be traced in the Holkham accounts[133] – one wonders: did he ever get paid for his trouble, and if so, how? Perhaps he saw his involvement with Holkham as a way to qualify for commissions from other patrons. Indeed, it may well have been Kent who had the engraving made that so proudly names him as architect, intended as advertisement for his services elsewhere.

Fig. 87. The gallery flank of the house and the pavilions suggests that the designers of Holkham II were not giving the lateral aspect as much attention as they gave to the two main fronts.

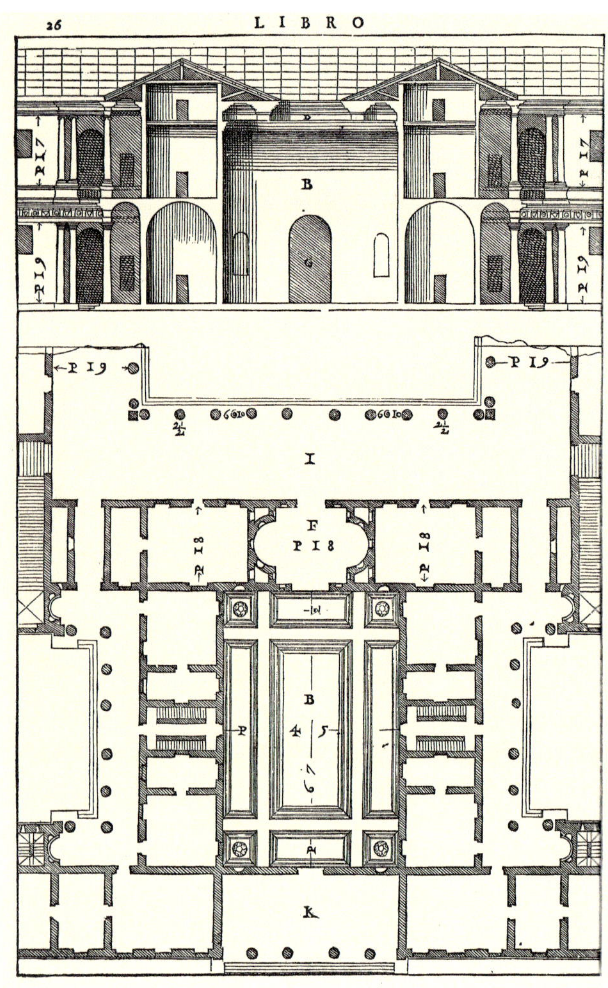

Fig. 88. The double-apsed room frequently occurring in Roman houses, here shown in the centre of Andrea Palladio's design *Atrio di Quattro Colonne,* published in his *Quattro Libri dell'Architettura* (1570), vol. II, 26, inspired Coke to conceive his own version at Holkham.

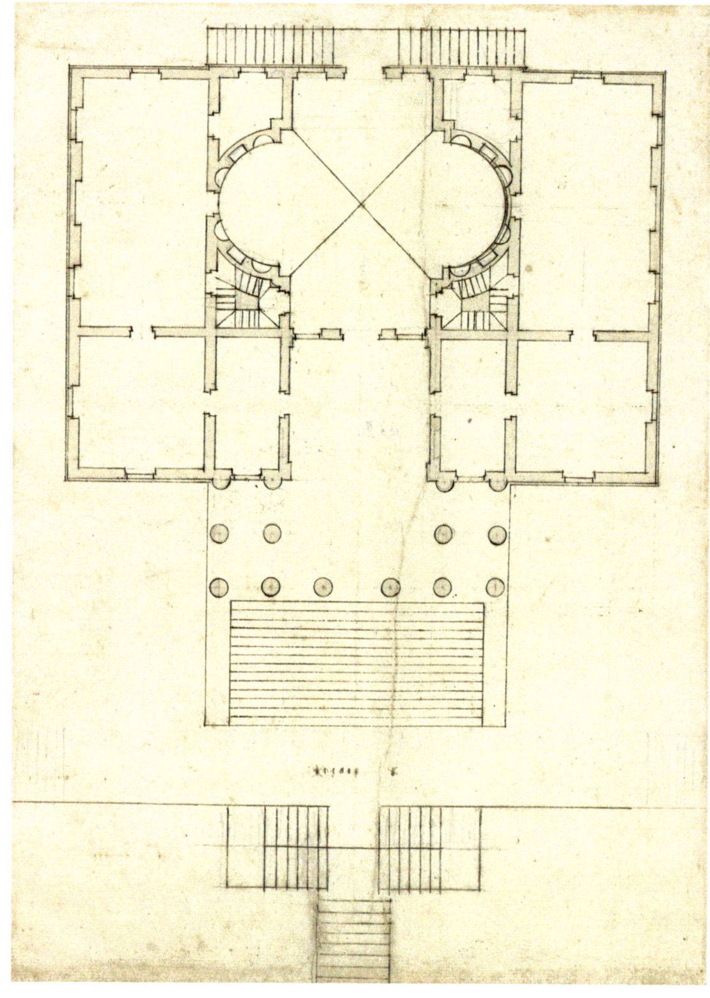

Fig. 89. An unexecuted design by Palladio for the Villa Chiericati, Vancimuglio di Grumolo delle Abbadesse, showing his use of the double-apsed room.

THE ROMAN SALOON

Kent's engraving and his slightly later drawing of the south elevation offer a surprising insight into ideas pursued at this stage of planning in the early 1730s. There are only three windows behind the portico, not five – the portico's outer intercolumnia are filled by niches, no doubt intended for statues. No floor plans survive that fit these elevations. So what does this mean for the plan of the room behind the portico, the Saloon? Without the outer windows, it cannot have been the rectangular space shown in Holkham I and executed when the body of the house was built during the 1740s. Once again, Coke had sought and found inspiration from his authorities, in this case Palladio's *Quattro Libri.* The central room in his reconstruction of an ancient Roman house, the *Atrio di Quattro Colonne*[134] (fig. 88), features apsed ends – not unlike the middle room of Holkham's Statue Gallery. A similar double-apsed room can also be found in Scamozzi's *House of the Ancients*, published in 1615. One drawing in Lord Burlington's possession shows how Palladio himself used the double-apsed room in an unexecuted design (fig. 89).

These sources allow us to attempt a hypothetical reconstruction of the plan of the Roman Saloon (fig. 90). Although the room itself was never executed at Holkham, a remarkably similar one was created many years later by none other

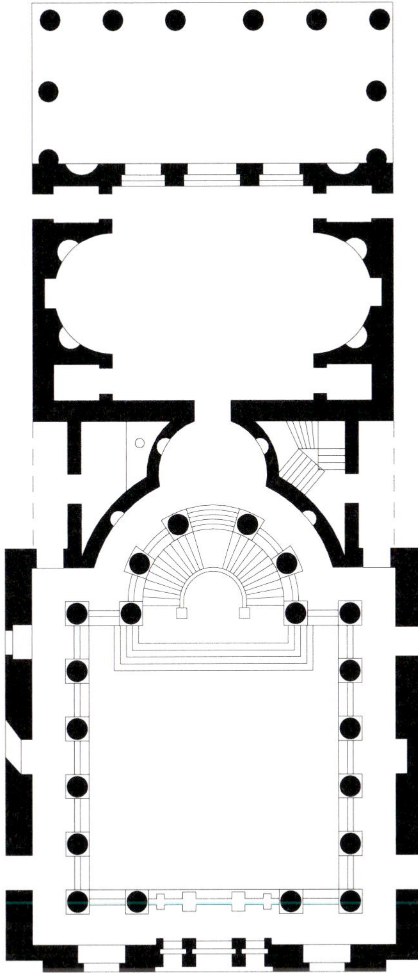

Fig. 90. The elevations shown in figs. 83, 84 and 86 suggest that the room behind the portico was at this stage planned as a double-apsed Roman saloon, as hypothetically reconstructed in this plan.

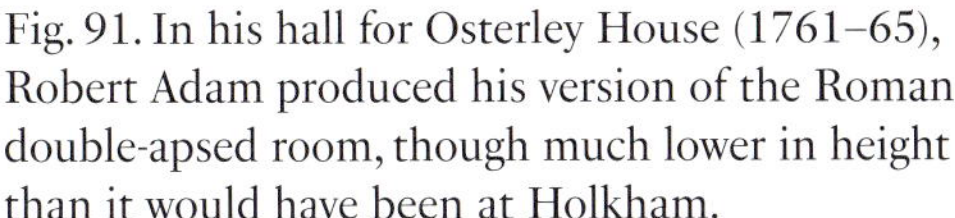

Fig. 91. In his hall for Osterley House (1761–65), Robert Adam produced his version of the Roman double-apsed room, though much lower in height than it would have been at Holkham.

Fig. 92. The double-apsed room for the Cottonian library in William Kent's design for the Houses of Parliament, drawn c. 1733, seems inspired by Kent's experiences at Holkham just around this time. Its coffered barrel vault may well be a version of what was planned for the Roman Saloon at Holkham.

Fig. 93. Hypothetical visualisation of the Roman Saloon considered at Holkham in the mid-1730s.

than Robert Adam, at Osterley Park (fig. 91). The proportions are necessarily different, as the situation at Osterley provides no overhead space, but all the essential features of the Roman Saloon are present.

Whether the room at Osterley was an independent creation or in some way based on the idea considered at Holkham is impossible to say. A much closer link exists to several designs attributed to William Kent[135] and dated to just about the time, around 1733, when the Roman Saloon was being considered at Holkham. Kent's proposal for the Houses of Parliament contains a room for the Cottonian Library (fig. 92) that allows us to speculate that the Saloon at Holkham may have been conceived with a cassetted barrel vault (fig. 93).

Thus, at this stage of the planning for Holkham, not only were the Marble Hall, the Statue Gallery and the State Dining Room to present the austere and cool appearance of an ancient Roman *villa rustica*, but so were the Saloon and necessarily the West Drawing Room – filling two thirds of the main floor of the body of the house, with just a few rooms left in the eastern part to be used as more conventional apartments. In intellectual and artistic terms, Coke would have found the idea extremely tempting, but doubts must have crept in: wasn't he overdoing the Roman thing? And the Roman rooms could only house sculpture – where would he hang the many paintings he had bought and commissioned? In the end, pragmatism prevailed and the learned but ultimately unworkable idea of the Roman Saloon was dropped in favour of a more conventionally baroque solution.

THE MARBLE HALL

Having passed through an entrance that is misleadingly small and undistinguished, virtually every visitor to Holkham is struck by the unexpected splendour of Holkham's most spectacular feature, the Marble Hall (fig. 94 and pls. 8 to 12). We may speculate that Coke wanted to make the most of the somewhat theatrical contrast between the austere and restrained exterior and the overwhelmingly monumental interior.

Holkham's Marble Hall is a unique spatial achievement, blending concepts and elements from a wide range of sources, mostly selected from ancient buildings that Coke had visited in Rome and whose architectural details had been published.

The room's essential features were already worked out by 1726, as the Holkham I plans show. When Kent arrived at Holkham a few years later, he took a hand in elaborating the room as a volume, as a three-dimensional space (fig. 95). Kent's powers of spatial imagination seem to have surpassed those of Coke and Brettingham, enabling him to correct a serious fault in the inner north front of the Hall. The Holkham I plan seems to suggest that the entablature on the north side should span the distance over the large Venetian window without any support: whilst technically or structurally feasible, such a length of unsupported entablature would go against all Vitruvian rules. Kent solved the problem by having the entablature double back to the inner north wall, and he sketched the resulting ceiling structure.

Annotated measurements in Kent's drawing (given in either Coke's or Brettingham's hand – their handwriting is

Fig. 94. Holkham, the Marble Hall as executed.

eerily similar) underline the idea that the original concept involved two cubes, one within the other. By the mid-1720s, cube halls had a long tradition in England; though many of them were decorated to resemble exterior architecture, they were seen and used as habitable spaces.[136]

The Marble Hall's most striking features, the free-standing columns and the apse, had no country-house precedent at the time but, in a design for Robert Walpole published in *Vitruvius Britannicus*, Colen Campbell 'endeavoured to introduce the Temple beauties in a private Building',[137] and the monumental pilasters in his hall at Wanstead carried the idea further. Other contemporary architects were toying with similar ideas, such as James Gibbs at Sudbrooke and Giacomo Leoni at Carshalton. In his English edition of Leon Battista Alberti's *Ten Books*, published in 1726 (Coke bought a copy that is still in Holkham's library, alongside Alberti's original 1565 edition), Leoni wrote:

> exactly answering the middle of your Court-yard place your entrance, with a handsome vestibule, neither narrow, difficult nor obscure. Let the first room that offers itself be a chapel dedicated to God; with its Altar, where Strangers and Guests may offer their

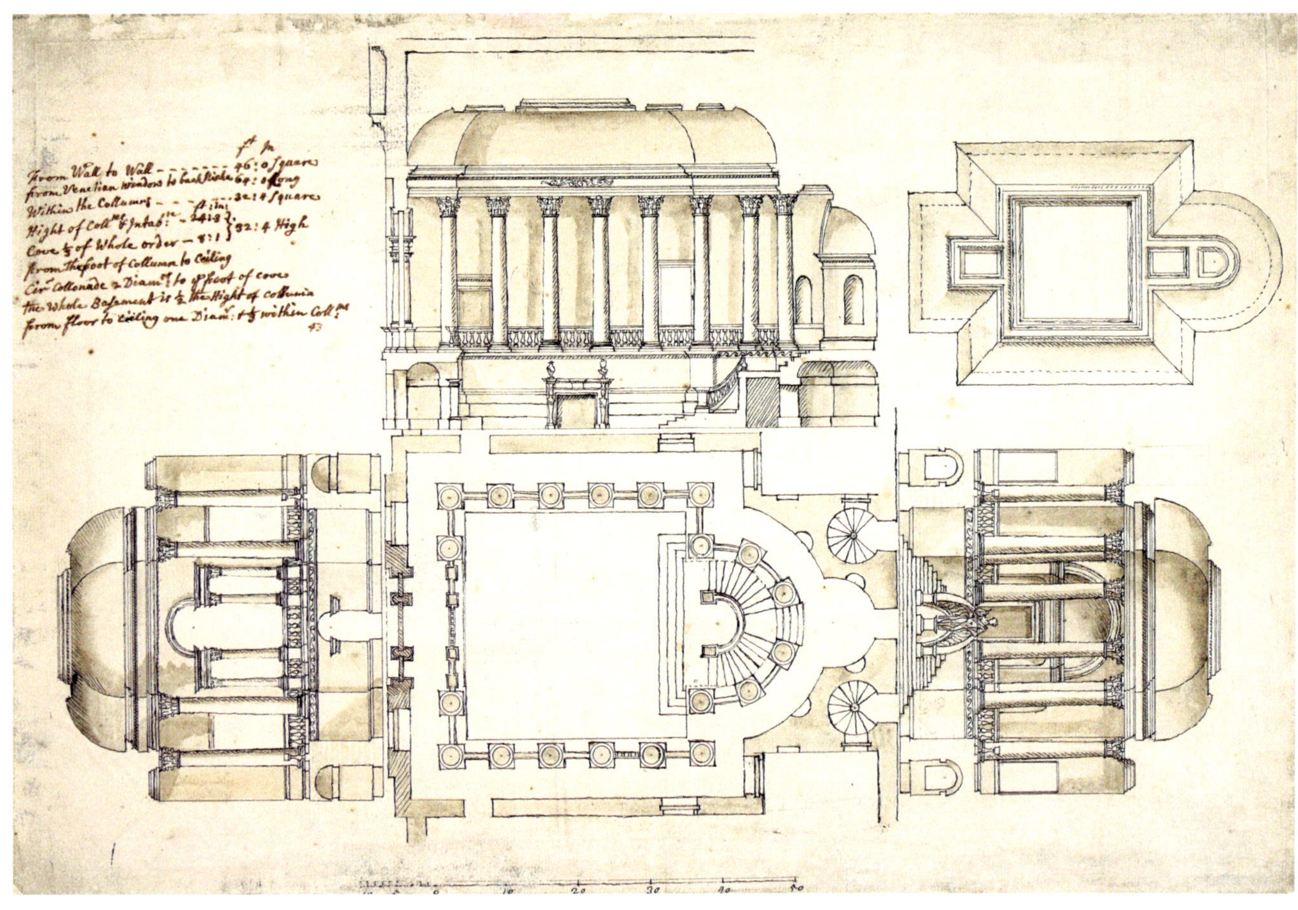

Fig. 95. Holkham, the Marble Hall in a drawing by William Kent, c. 1733, based on the Holkham I concept of 1726. Note the fireplace in the lateral wall of the ground level; note also the two circular staircases opening into the Saloon.

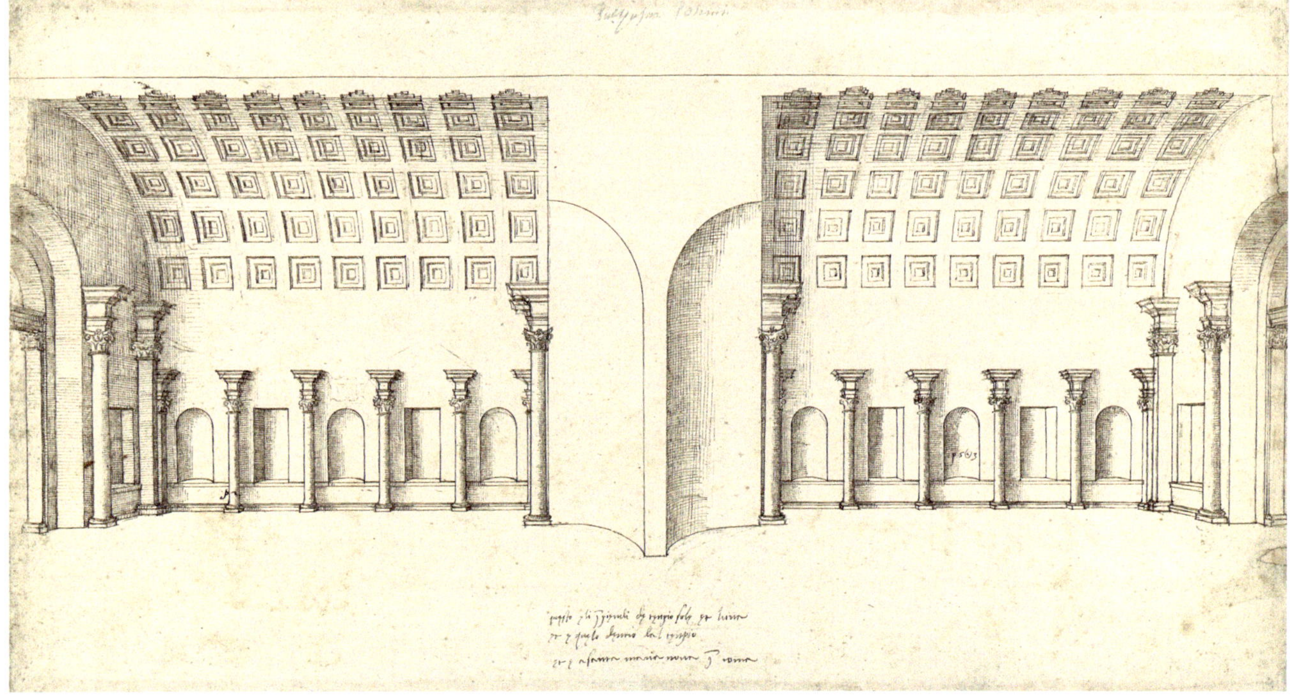

Fig. 96. The Temple of Venus and Roma – here shown in a drawing by Andrea Palladio – was one of the sources for the Marble Hall.

> devotions, beginning their Friendship by Religion; and where the Father of the family may put up his prayers for the peace of his house and the welfare of his relations. Here let him embrace those who come to visit him, and if any cause be referred to him by his friends, or he has any other serious business of that nature to transact, let him do it in this place.[138]

Like Holkham, Alberti's vestibule, or hall, combines the functions of temple and basilica. The overtones of a court of justice would have appealed to Coke as a reference to the Chief Justice, the founder of the family's fortunes. Several famous buildings, all well known to the widely travelled Thomas Coke, inspired the hall developed at Holkham. The choir of Palladio's Redentore church in Venice clearly influenced the arrangement of the apse. The palace chapel at Versailles also displays some striking similarities: compare, for example, the apse, the gallery with its columns and the arrangement of the elevation. Furthermore, there are echoes of the opera stage at Holkham – possibly more than coincidental, considering that Thomas Coke loved opera and had enjoyed ample opportunities to attend performances in Rome.

A particularly close affinity exists to the Temple of Venus and Roma, also known as the Temple of the Sun and Moon, whose extensive ruins are preserved next to the Colosseum in Rome. Palladio published a reconstruction in his *Quattro Libri* and drew a perspective (fig. 96). There are similarities in the proportions of the space, in the columns framing niches with sculptures, in the coffered vault and in the apse featuring the lozenge pattern that was actually copied at Holkham for the apses in the Statue Gallery.

Fig. 97. The tabernacle in Solomon's Temple, as reconstructed by Juan Bautista Villalpando and published in 1605, was another of the sources used for the Marble Hall, indicating the Masonic significance of the room in particular and the house in general.

Fig. 98. Detail of Kent's drawing of the Marble Hall (fig. 95) showing the figure of a lion: in this position a further Masonic reference.

Fig. 99. The palms shown in Villalpando's engraving (fig. 97) recur in a design for a bedroom of Charles II at Greenwich attributed to Inigo Jones and published by John Vardy and William Kent in 1744.

Fig. 100. The Palm Room in Spencer House in London, designed by John Vardy, 1756.

Tradition had it (and Thomas Coke with his classical education must have been aware of this) that the Temple of Venus and Roma was designed by that august amateur architect, Emperor Hadrian himself – an emperor who had particular interest for Coke, as he not only had British connections but had also been involved with the other Temple that must have loomed large in Coke's mind: Solomon's Temple, the central edifice of Freemasonry. In AD 70, Hadrian built a splendid new structure on its ruins, thus fulfilling the great ambition of later Freemasons: the rebuilding of the Temple. We may surmise that Thomas Coke, one-time Grand Master of English Freemasons, took the task of recreating the Temple very much to heart. As it happens, Holkham's façade is 200 royal cubits in length, thus conforming to the frontage of the central building in Solomon's Temple;[139] and Holkham's centrepiece, the Marble Hall, encompasses the dimensions and proportions of the Tabernacle, the inner sanctum in Solomon's Temple. Villalpando's representation of this room, published in the most authoritative tome on the Temple known in the early eighteenth century, must surely be interpreted as a source of inspiration for the hall at Holkham (fig. 97). Columns, coves and cofferings, as well as the proportions of the room, all show a number of similarities, and even the statues in the hall at Holkham may be echoes of the cherubim in Villalpando's Tabernacle.

According to the Bible, the Tabernacle was a cube twenty royal cubits in length, width and height.[140] Twenty royal cubits equal roughly 34.5 ft or 10.50 metres; the square defined by the centre points of the hall's columns is 34.8 ft or 10.57 metres each side. The Tabernacle is frequently adorned with twelve columns, six on each side of the room, possibly represented by the Marble Hall's two outer rows of six columns each. The two columns framing the hall's apse could be interpreted as Jachin and Boaz,[141] the two most prominent Temple columns that have become an icon of Masonic lore. Time and again we find Jachin and Boaz paired with lions. Can it be coincidence that William Kent, in his drawing for the hall, pencilled a lion on the dado just below the right-hand column (fig. 98)?[142]

Villalpando's engraving of the Tabernacle had a strong and hitherto unrecognised influence on Palladian interior architecture in England. In 1744, William Kent and John Vardy published a design for the bedroom of King Charles II at Greenwich (fig. 99), ascribed by them to Inigo Jones:[143] a direct transformation of Villalpando's holiest of holies into secular architecture. In view of its sacred source, the King's bedroom was obviously interpreted as the dwelling place of an almost godlike being – the divine right of kings is clearly an issue here. The fact that Vardy used the same design for the Palm Room in Spencer House in 1755 (fig. 100) underlines the continuing significance of these references to the Temple throughout the eighteenth century.

The architectural imagery of Holkham can be read in two ways. On the one hand, we can see Holkham as rational, Vitruvian architecture, a learned reconstruction of a Roman *villa rustica*, telling us that its builder saw himself and his peers in the tradition of Roman patricians – he even had himself portrayed in this rôle, in a bust executed by Francis Leggatt Chantrey on the basis of an original by Louis-François Roubiliac (fig. 101).

Of course, the Roman patriciate could be seen as a simile for the Whig oligarchs of the time. On the other hand, we can read Holkham as a revival of Solomon's Temple, full of concealed allusions to a mythical building that only made sense to the members of a secret society. Both readings are equally valid and we may be sure that Thomas Coke, the mastermind behind this concept, not only revelled in the ambiguity of his building, but probably recognised the truth of both approaches. The Roman interpretation is the far more obvious and public one; indeed, Brettingham in his book makes sure we are familiar with every ancient source for the various ideas and details of the house. By contrast, the Masonic content was never even hinted at in print; to Coke, no doubt, the reference to Solomon's Temple represented the deeper, truer meaning behind the obvious references to classical Rome – a meaning fully accessible only to the initiated.

Fig. 101. Bust of Thomas Coke, Earl of Leicester, as a Roman patrician, executed by Francis Leggatt Chantrey on the basis of an original by Louis-François Roubiliac.

TRADITION AND CONTROVERSY

In 1761, two years after Lord Leicester's death, Matthew Brettingham published a large and impressive volume:

THE
PLANS,
Elevations and Sections,
of
HOLKHAM in NORFOLK,
The SEAT of the late
EARL of LEICESTER.
BY
MATTHEW BRETTINGHAM.

Apart from the beautifully engraved illustrations, it contained only two pages of text: a dedication to HRH The Duke of Cumberland and a preface. In the preface, Brettingham bows to Leicester as the driving force in the creation of the house, but subsequently stakes out his own claim to fame by inscribing many of the plates with the words 'M. Brettingham Arch.t'. As we have seen, such easy claims to authorship were no more than par for the course at the time, but in this case a very influential person, the writer Horace Walpole, youngest son of Robert Walpole at nearby Houghton, was provoked into furious comment and rebuttal:

> How the designs of that house [Holkham], which I have seen an hundred times in Kent's original drawings, came to be published under another name, and without the slightest mention of the real architect, is beyond my comprehension.[144]

What Walpole had seen at Holkham may well have been the very same portfolio of so-called Kent drawings that was later studied by twentieth-century architectural historians, without realising that only some of them were actually by Kent whereas all the properly executed plans and elevations it contained were in fact drawn by Matthew Brettingham.

In his own much extended version of the *Plans of Holkham* published in 1773, Brettingham's son, Matthew junior, tried to limit the damage to his (by then deceased) father's reputation by explaining that

> The general ideas of the Plans, Elevations, and Sections, of Holkham Hall, in the county of Norfolk, were first struck out by the Earls of Leicester and Burlington, assisted by Mr. William Kent[145]

and that Brettingham senior had after all been responsible for all the stages of actually executing the building.

However, both Walpole (born in 1717) and Brettingham junior (born in 1725) were too young to have witnessed the decisive years when Holkham was conceived, and it is quite obvious that neither of them had ever heard of the pre-Kent planning stage of Holkham I, conceived nearly half a century before Walpole's outburst. Having been hidden in King George III's Topographical Collection, the Holkham I plans only came to light in 1980.

To some architectural historians, their discovery and publication came as a shock. They realised that there were wide-reaching consequences if these plans had in fact been produced in 1726, as the payment to Brettingham in that year suggested: not to put too fine a point on it, the story of English neo-Palladian architecture would need rewriting. Frank Salmon spells it out for us:

were 'Holkham I' really to date from 1726, that would make the Norfolk building the fraternal (indeed perhaps first-out) twin of Chiswick rather than its part progeny, and consequently a building of seminal importance for the history of British architecture rather than a stellar and much developed example of an idiom already initiated elsewhere.[146]

Rather than accepting such a momentous change in the overall narrative of the era, Salmon published an article rejecting the idea that Matthew Brettingham's 'Holkham I' drawings in the British Library could possibly be as early as 1726, and even denying that they showed a design for Holkham. Instead he suggested that the drawings represented most likely 'a *reduction* of the Holkham design, produced later in life by Brettingham ... in the hope of attracting a client wishing to build a similar but smaller house.'[147]

No doubt Brettingham, on the lookout for clients, always had a few architectural drawings at hand that he could use to advertise his services. He did so at Lowther in Westmorland in 1759, having just been dismissed at Holkham after Lord Leicester's death. Although Salmon stops short of claiming that the plans in the British Library were in fact made for Lowther, he makes much of the fact that one of Brettingham's drawings at Lowther is nearly identical to the west elevation of the 'Holkham I' set. But any attempt at dating the 'Holkham I' drawings to the late 1750s or at suggesting they might be for some other project than Thomas Coke's house does not stand up to close study of the drawings themselves, corroborated by observations of its built fabric.[148]

Amongst the many arguments supporting the claim that 'Holkham I' is in fact the earliest extant design for Coke's country house and that it cannot possibly have been produced decades later, one aspect stands out: 'Holkham I' has a number of grave imperfections and functional defects which are typical of an early design stage – defects which, as we have seen, were in fact addressed and corrected at Holkham over several stages in the further planning and building process. How could Brettingham – with the rich experience of actually having built Holkham over a quarter of a century – have produced a '*reduction* of the Holkham design' (Salmon) that is full of beginners' errors?

Instead, Salmon revives the traditional view that Holkham was in all essentials – four-pavilion configuration, façades and interiors – designed by William Kent not long before building commenced in 1734. In his view, the engraving (fig. 83) represents the earliest design and shows what Kent wanted to build at Holkham. And indeed the proud inscription 'Gulielmus Kent Archit. et Pict. Invenit et Delin.' ('William Kent architect and painter invented and drew it') seems to authenticate this claim. But we should consider the context of the engraving and its inscription. We do not know who commissioned it. It may well have been Kent himself, trying to establish himself as an architect and to get proper architectural commissions. And he may well have felt within his rights to assert his authorship since the highly decorated elevation displayed by the engraving was undoubtedly of his invention, albeit overlaid on the earlier concept of Holkham I.

In support of his claim that Kent played the dominant rôle in the conception of Holkham, Frank Salmon also mentions that Coke himself frequently praised 'our Great Master Kent'[149] or 'our great Master the gran Signor'.[150] Not only does the invariably bantering tone make it difficult to take such laudatory remarks literally: it should also be noted that they exclusively refer to Kent's rôle in landscape designing – at Holkham, but also at the Duke of Grafton's place at Euston and the Duke of Newcastle's at Claremont.

As far as the conceptual design of the architecture was concerned – as opposed to decorating external and internal surfaces – no essential input from William Kent can be identified at Holkham. If one looks at his Horse Guards in London, which he was commissioned to design in 1745, it is, however, obvious that his experience at Holkham proved useful for him for other projects, not unlike Brettingham, who also used ideas from Holkham for designs elsewhere.[151]

What Kent brought to Holkham was his unique instinct for ornament and playfulness: a sense of gaiety diametrically opposed to the cool, classical and ultimately cerebral nature of Coke's architectural vision. Sadly, Kent's pleasure ground has been lost and replaced by later features, but Holkham's interiors, particularly in the Family Wing, owe their outstanding quality to his designs and his influence, which continued after his death. As for the architecture of the house, he should be credited with the tripartite façades of the pavilions, but his well-meant suggestions for upgrading the external appearance of the body of the house were ultimately disregarded.

And yet the belief that Kent designed Holkham is deeply ingrained in public perception, and there is no doubt that this will not easily change, whatever a closer look at the available evidence suggests. People take it for granted that Kent must have designed Holkham because of his reputation as a great architect – not realising that this reputation is ultimately based on the endlessly repeated assertion that he designed Holkham.

THE BUILDING PROCESS

Planning a big house is one thing; getting it built is quite another matter. The building accounts – fairly laconic during the early years but far more detailed and descriptive after 1753 – allow us to follow the construction through the expenses paid first to bricklayers and carpenters for the construction of the great house, then to the various craftsmen who saw to the interior decoration. A graph of the expenses between 1730 and 1765, distinguishing between costs for bricklayers (black), carpenters and other structural workers (grey) and finishing trades such as stonemasons, plasterers, painters, joiners and gilders (yellow), shows the progress on the construction site over the years (fig. 102). It also illustrates, perhaps unsurprisingly, that the best part of the money went to pay for the elaborate decoration in the staterooms of the body of the house, followed by the apartments for the family and guests.

The accounts allow us to understand how a large eighteenth-century construction site was organised. Building a huge empty brick shell and getting it covered was clearly a priority; only then, protected from the weather, could the shell be filled in with interior structures such as floors and walls. This was a tricky business, since every detail in the brick structure, every niche, opening or flue for the fireplaces, had to be planned ahead. As we shall see, this did

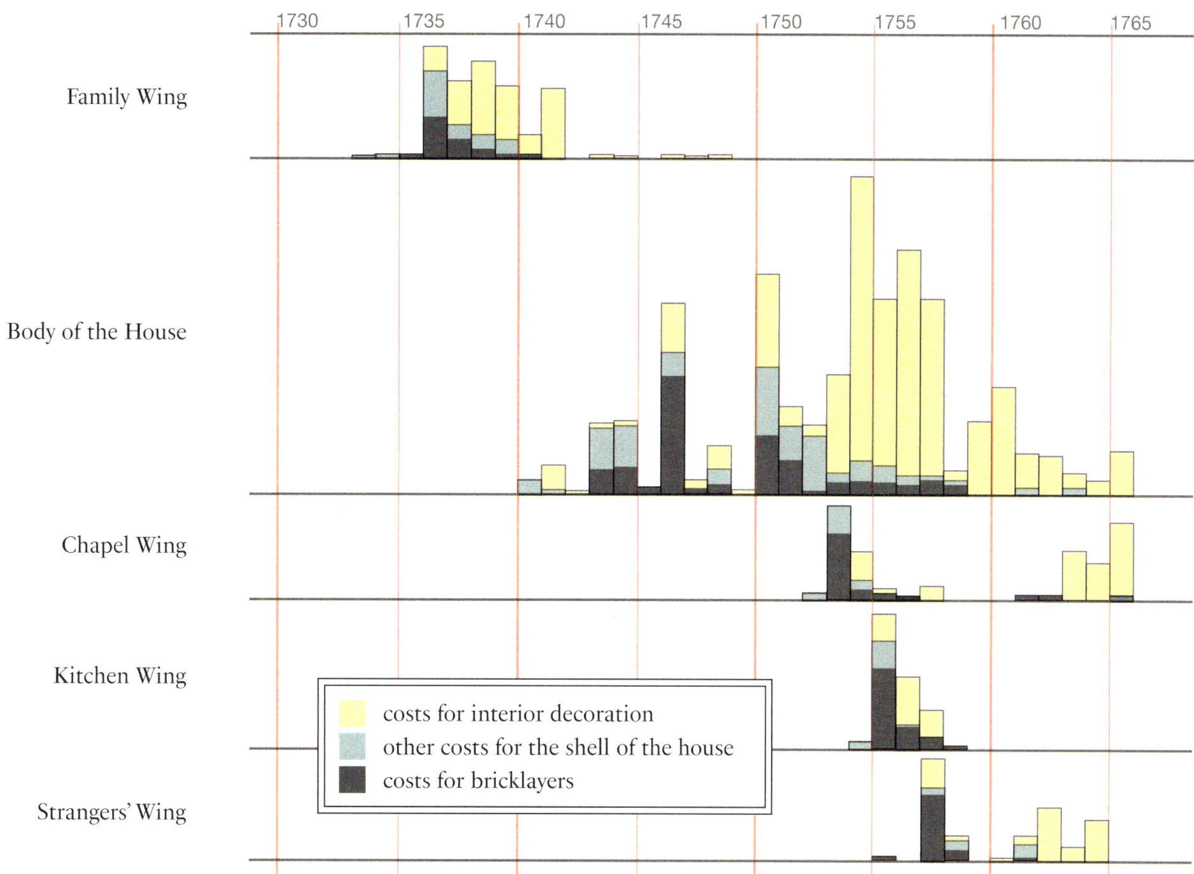

Fig. 102. A graph showing the expenses for building the various parts of the house between 1734 and 1765 and differentiating between costs for bricklayers (black), other costs for the shell of the house (grey) and the massive amounts spent on the interior decoration (yellow).

not always work out as planned, and we also see some of the tricks of the trade when it came to working out solutions for bodged situations.

The huge task of building Holkham Hall was very sensibly split into distinct phases, a process facilitated by the articulated design of the building, with its four pavilions attached to a central pile (figs. 103 to 106). Building started in the spring of 1734, and activities concentrated initially on the construction of the south-west pavilion, Family Wing, a pragmatic decision motivated by the lack of decent living space in the old house. Family Wing was roofed in 1736; work on the interior, however, went on for several years, involving marble masons for the fireplaces, stucco workers, joiners and woodcarvers. Glazing, painting and gilding were recorded in 1739 and pictures were hung. In 1740, the family moved into the new wing.[152]

Lord Lovell must have been delighted to be able to move into the new pavilion in 1740–41, but he was less than happy about the general impression of the construction site. In a letter written in or before 1742, Brettingham found himself admonished:

> As to the execution of a building I will do you the justice to say no body understands that better, & scarce any one so well, but as for the nice laying up of materials etc. I ever thought your honary high genius overlook't it, and that they lay slovenly about there-fore as the building is adjourned they sd be taken an account of, & better lay'd up.[153]

For a good number of years, until the mid-1750s, the slowly growing construction must have looked somewhat out of proportion: much higher than today, since the basement storey stood on top of the ground rather than being sunk into it. In a clever move, the builders – Thomas Coke and his man on the spot, Matthew Brettingham – had decided not to dig deeply into the soil for the basements, but to erect the whole building on top of the existing ground level.

Figs. 103 to 106. Visualisation of the progress of the structure, with the Family Wing attached to the Old House by a wooden passage. The southern aspect of the house was externally completed by 1749, the body of the house and Chapel Wing finished by 1755 and Strangers' Wing just being started on in 1757. Note that the basement was built, in red brick, on top of the existing ground level and the earth filled around the southern, western and northern sides of the house from the mid-1750s onwards.

This had several advantages. It limited excavation work (carried out by Thomas Coke's own labourers from the home farm) to relatively shallow foundation trenches,[154] thus saving an immense amount of digging and hauling and avoiding the risk of getting into trouble with the groundwater. In addition, this unconventional approach helped to raise the house to a higher level – no bad thing in the predominantly flat country of East Anglia.

Only one eighteenth-century visitor remarked on this feature: the Hanoverian court director of buildings and gardens, Friedrich Carl von Hardenberg, who travelled widely in England in 1744–45. Arriving at Holkham from Wolterton on 23 October 1744, he enjoyed Lord Leicester's hospitality for several days. He sketched the grounds (fig. 107) and Lord Leicester apparently told him it was 'all by Kent'. He also noted:

> Mylord Leicester's new building will be one of the most magnificent in England, it is a large corps de logis, with 4 wings that are connected to it as pavilions. One pavilion is finished, and the rustic story of the house. … These pavilions are vaulted throughout, but not deeply sunk into the ground.[155]

Following the erection of the whole shell of the house in this way, many cartloads of soil were moved from digging out the lake and other construction sites and were used to raise the grounds around the house to their proper level – at least on the three sides that are visible to the public.[156] The eastern side, which always remained hidden from view, retained the natural ground level – anyone approaching the house through the walled yards walks straight into the basement (fig. 108).

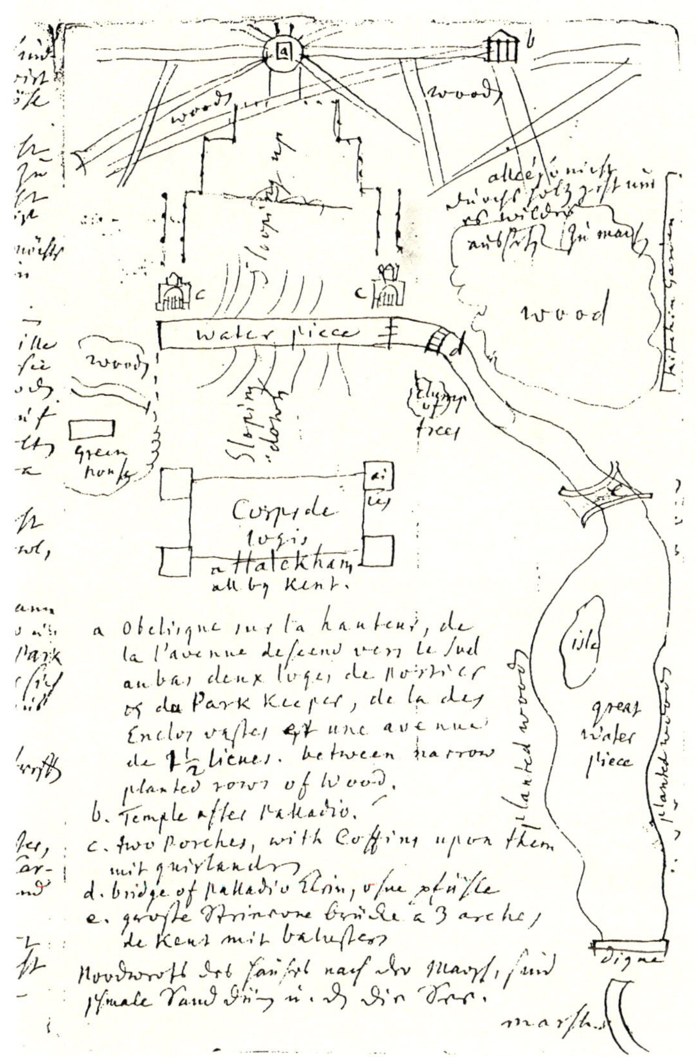

Fig. 107. A sketch by Friedrich Carl von Hardenberg who visited Holkham in 1744. As the Hanoverian court director of buildings and gardens, he was mostly interested in the designed landscape, but he also noted that the family wing was 'not deeply sunk into the ground'.

Fig. 108. In the courtyard formed by the east façade of the house and the adjoining wings, one can see how the basement was built on top of the natural ground level.

With Family Wing completed, work began on the body of the house. It is interesting to note that work on the central block initially focused on the southern half of the great new building, indicating that the erection of the south façade (the prospect greeting visitors arriving from London) was regarded as a priority. The first tower on the south façade was completed in 1748, with John Neals receiving eighteen shillings for 'Gilding the Fane on the Tower' and the workmen were entertained royally to the tune of four guineas. The second tower was finished in 1749 (ten shillings' worth of drinks all round) and the portico and the roof over the southern half were completed in 1750.[157] Let us hope all this cheered up Thomas Coke at a difficult time in his life, overshadowed as it was by William Kent's death in 1748 and particularly by the scandal over Lord Coke's divorce in 1749.

The exterior shell of the *corps de logis* was complete by 1752 and we can imagine its inside as an echoing brick box with roof, windows and rough floorboards laid over the floor beams; timber-framed partition walls were added from 1753 onwards. The bricklayers immediately started work on the erection of the south-east wing so that the south façade would be completed as soon as possible. Work on the north-east wing, or Kitchen Wing, was started in 1755 and on the north-west wing, or Strangers' Wing, in 1757.

Fig. 110. Holkham II, section through the Hall and Saloon, drawn by Matthew Brettingham, c. 1753. The Hall has been redesigned using the Ionic order. Compared to the section published by Brettingham in 1761 (fig. 112) and the measured drawing (fig. 113), the proportions of the Saloon appear incorrectly drawn.

A SECOND WIND

An indication that the whole building process of Holkham had reached a turning point in the early 1750s may be seen in the row that flared up in 1752 over the work carried out by the bricklayers and carpenters. Two surveyors, J. Sanderson and G. Bascube, were called in to check and measure their work 'in the Body of the Main house', and they found that John Elliott the bricklayer and James Lillie the carpenter had grossly overcharged, Lillie by £250 and Elliott by £315.8s.4d.

Until then, throughout the 1730s and 1740s, construction had progressed in a fairly leisurely way. An apparently easy-going supervisor, Brettingham managed the building site on behalf of an absentee patron whose attention was largely focused on his political and private affairs in London and who was always somewhat strapped for cash. Things were to change dramatically. The death of his son and heir in 1753, although emotionally shattering, ended a long period of uncharacteristic indecision for Lord Leicester. His dream of founding a dynasty of lasting rank and wealth at Holkham might have evaporated, but his own path now stretched clearly before him. There was now little to be gained by politicking in London; and by the same token, thriftiness was no longer a priority. Only one task was left to him: the completion of Holkham Hall.

The effects were immediate. Until 1753, when the Statue Gallery was nearing completion, annual expenditure on the building had been very moderate, averaging £1,400 during the building of the first wing and rising to about £2,300 during the 1740s: sums that could easily be channelled out of Leicester's income. The effect of Edward Coke's death was like the breaking of a dam. Expenditure on the building rocketed, peaking at £7,100 in 1755 and averaging around £4,000 during the final years of Leicester's life. As Leicester himself commented on the sale of some land in a letter in 1754: 'my present income, which is what, having no son, I am chiefly to consider, will be much increased.'[158]

There were also changes in the organisation of the building work. After the rumpus over the fraudulent bills, the building accounts became far more detailed than before. It also seems that Brettingham's activities at Holkham were

Fig. 110. Holkham II, section along the northern enfilade of the body of the house, looking south (towards the rooms), drawn by Matthew Brettingham, c. 1753. The Dining Room details conform to the version executed in 1753–4.

Fig. 111. Holkham II, section along the northern enfilade of the body of the house, looking north (towards the windows), drawn by Matthew Brettingham, c. 1753.

Fig. 112. Holkham II, section through the Hall and Saloon, published by Matthew Brettingham in his *Plans of Holkham*, 1761.

scrutinised by Lord Leicester and found wanting. As he complained to Brettingham junior in a letter of 6 January 1755:

> your father ... has built me a house to look at, not to live in, as the Chimneys smoke so intolerably, & Mr Elliots Quackery can't yet cure them, tho' he has tried many tricks, they are full as bad as before.[159]

Not only was the building process speeded up, but the six years left to Lord Leicester before his own death in 1759 were to be the most intense in the creation of Holkham. Everything now rested on the patron himself. For the decoration of Family Wing, Coke had had the invaluable support not only of William Kent, who had designed most of the rooms and the furniture, and also of Lord Burlington, whom Coke had consulted about 'the inside of the rooms' of Family Wing in 1736. But neither was available when the time came for detailed decisions about the body of the house, Kent having died in 1748 and Lord Burlington in 1753. All changes to the design made in his last years must therefore be attributed to Lord Leicester alone.

Three detailed sections of the body of the house can be dated to this phase, the early 1750s (figs. 109 to 111). The first of the changes Coke introduced at this stage was comparatively modest. Elliott the bricklayer was paid in 1753 for 'digging out foundation and carrying up a wall for the Dining Room Beaufet', indicating that the shape of the State Dining Room with its great apse was developed at this time. Concealed doors in the apse could be reached from the ground floor by a new staircase and provided easy access for the servants – but they still had to walk a fair distance from the kitchen in the north-east pavilion.

THE MARBLE HALL RECONSIDERED

Of far greater importance were the other two decisions taken during the 1750s, in the execution of the central and most significant element of the house, the Marble Hall (figs. 112 to 114), where the first fundamental change concerned the order of the columns. Kent's drawing for the Hall shows Corinthian columns – highest in the hierarchy of classical orders and therefore to be expected in a space recreating the Tabernacle of Solomon's Temple. But it was the Ionic order that was actually used. Closer inspection of the building, particularly of the roof space above the Hall (fig. 115), indicates that Brettingham must have miscalculated the height of the structure needed for the Marble Hall's

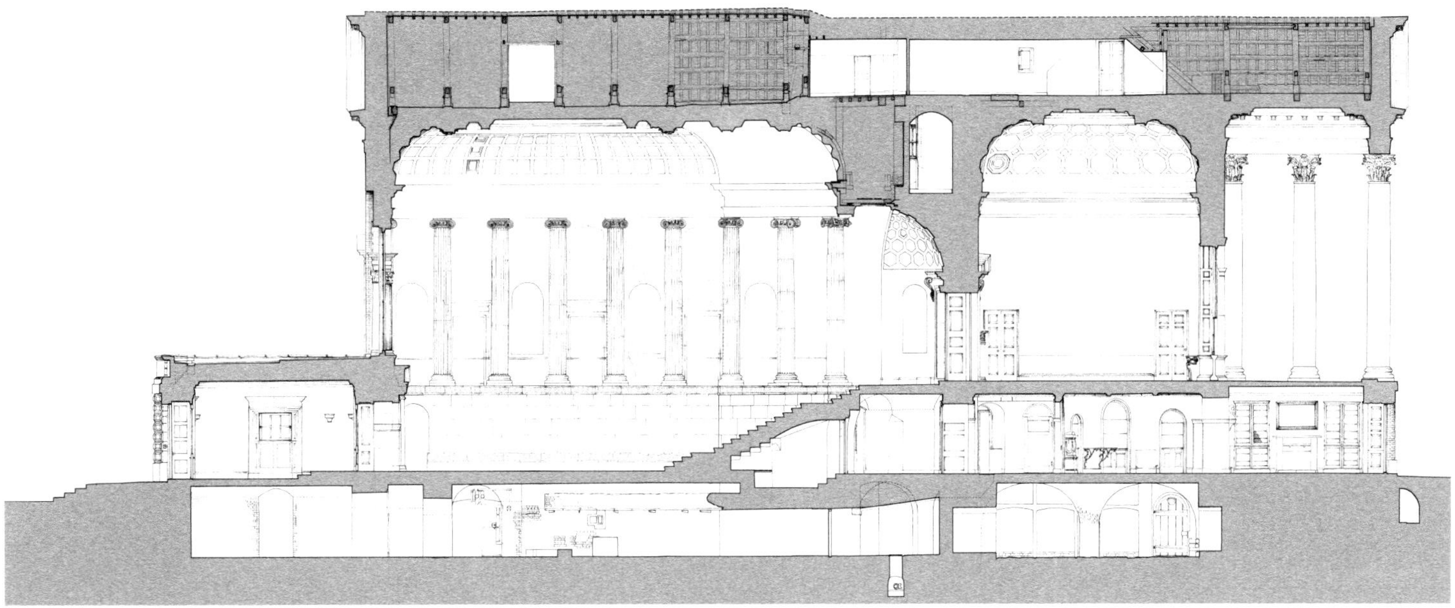

Fig. 113. Holkham, section through the Hall and Saloon, measured drawing, 2005, showing also the basement and the Victorian porch, and the actual situation in the roof spaces: the different levels in the roof illustrate that the southern half of the body of the house was built first and the northern half added afterwards.

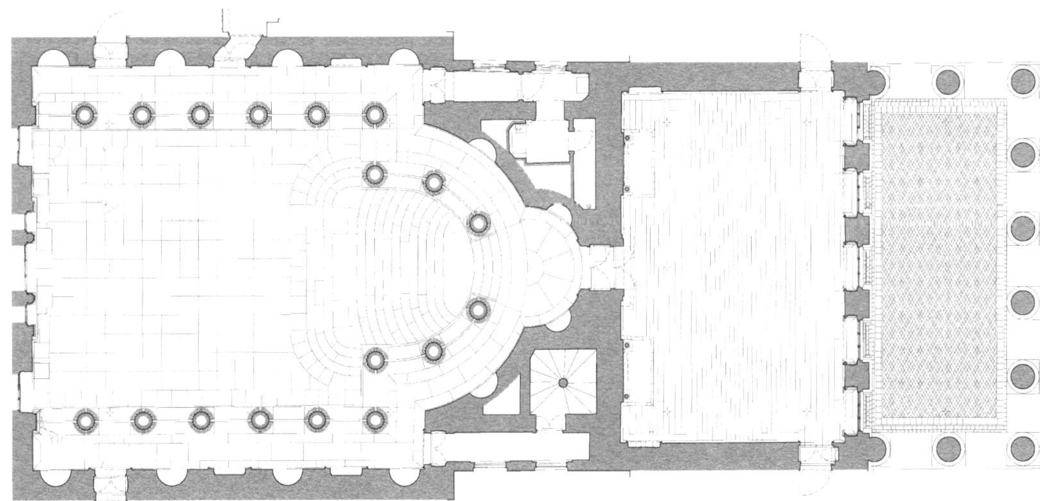

Fig. 114. Plan of the central part of the body of the house, with Marble Hall, Saloon and portico, measured drawing, 2005.

vaulted ceiling. As the whole structure containing the Hall was already completed by 1752 (providing a building site protected from the elements), the miscalculation could not be corrected by creating additional headroom, but only by lowering the height of the room that was to be constructed inside. Switching from the Corinthian to the Ionic order was an ingenious solution, since Ionic capitals take up considerably less headroom than Corinthian ones.

The building accounts allow us to follow the building stages (fig. 116) in some detail. The shell of the body of the house, including the space that was to become the Marble Hall, was completed and roofed by 1752. Work on

Fig. 115. Unused recessed bases for beams in the space above the Marble Hall are the result of planning changes made during the execution of the building.

the interior of the Hall began in 1756, and by 1757 the interior partitions of the huge, empty brick box enclosing the Marble Hall had been built up to main floor level. Walls at ground level separated the Hall's interior from the passages surrounding it. But then John Elliott, the bricklayer, was paid for 'pulling down part of the Wall and Arch at the Entrance of the Great Hall'. Lord Leicester, seeing the room taking shape, must have ordered this momentous change on the basis of what he could visualise on the spot. Plans were redrawn immediately, one main floor plan by Brettingham showing the new scheme for the room (fig. 117).

Comparison with earlier drawings highlights the fundamental effect of the change. The wall Elliott pulled down was the inner wall on the north or entrance front of the Hall. Its removal altered the whole character of the room. The first change was quickly reinforced by a second one. Brettingham's redrawn plan still showed the horseshoe-shaped stairs framing the colossal statue of Jupiter that had been the room's dominating feature from the earliest stages, but then the stairs were redesigned without the pedestal and figure. From a square room, centralised and static, the Hall was now transformed into an oblong, directional and far more dynamic space drawing the visitor up the stairs and into the Saloon (fig. 3 and pl. 8).

Whilst Elliott the bricklayer was pulling down the northern wall, Lillie the carpenter was busy 'altering the Modell of the Stairs and Columns in the Great Hall', as we see from bills of March 1757. Thus Jupiter never achieved centre stage. During the nineteenth century he dominated the orangery (fig. 150); today his body languishes in the game larder, whereas the head is on display in the Smoking Room underneath the portico (fig. 149).

The last days of June 1757 saw the arrival of a group of specialised marble masons who over the next two years would create the splendid temple-like structure that has been admired ever since.[160] The alabaster arrived by ship, and they fashioned it into bases and columns. The capitals, however, arrived ready-made. The columns probably contain load-bearing cores of wood clad with segments of alabaster. On these wooden posts rests the weight of the architrave and the magnificent coffered vault, a hollow shell shaped out of wooden laths covered in stucco (fig. 124). The original colour scheme of the hall, with pink-white wall surfaces,[161] must have beautifully augmented the effect of the marbled alabaster.

Apart from the dramatic impact that the alterations had on the shape and appearance of the Marble Hall, we must also consider the effect on the iconology of the room. On the basis of the existing room alone and without the evidence of the early drawings, who would suspect that the Hall was meant to represent the cube-shaped Tabernacle of Solomon's Temple? This idea, so dominant in Thomas Coke's mind in the 1720s and so central to the concept of Holkham Hall, had now become far less legible than before – an indication, perhaps, that the Masonic fervour of his early manhood had cooled in middle age.

The removal of the inner north wall of the Marble Hall had far-reaching consequences. In Holkham I, later clarified in Kent's drawing (fig. 95), the colonnade on top of the wall

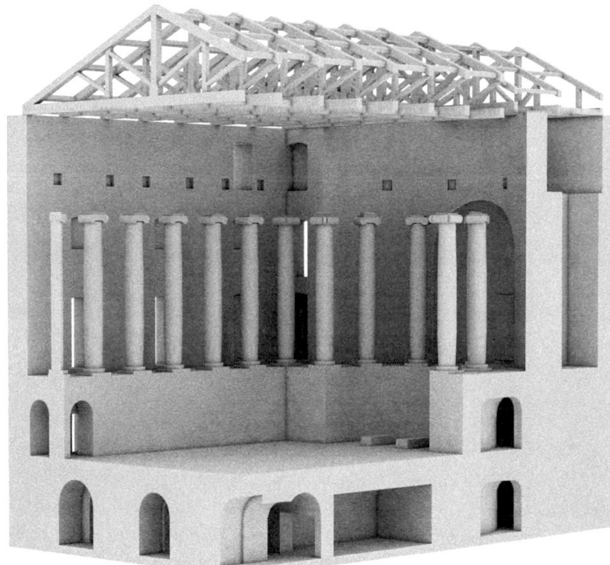

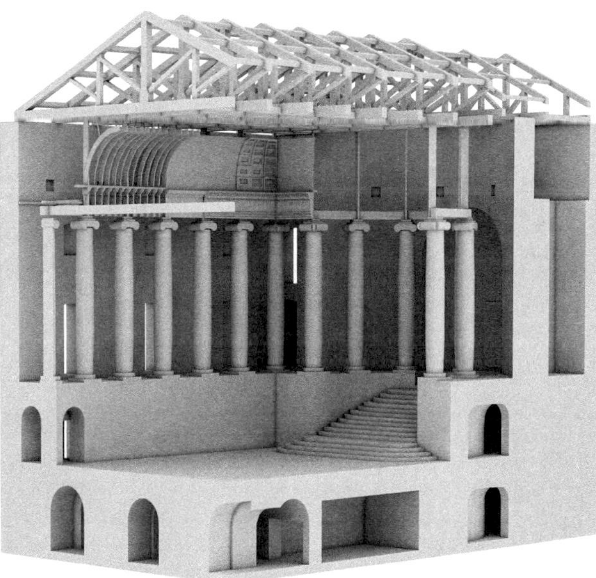

Fig. 116. Visualisation of the construction phases of the Marble Hall, starting from basement level and showing how the inner north wall at ground floor level was first built and then (in 1757) demolished, changing the room from a static space to a directed and dynamic one.

passed along the north front, framing the large Venetian window. The 1757 change meant that the Ionic order now had to connect to the northern wall. According to the rules of classical architecture, this could not be achieved without a pilaster at the point of connection – and the opening between the pilaster and the first column had to be of the same width as the distance between all the other columns. A detail from Brettingham's floor plan highlights the problem arising from this situation (fig. 118): the first columns on both sides of the Marble Hall would interfere badly with the enfilade, the unbroken vista through doorways all in a line behind the northern façade. In baroque or Palladian

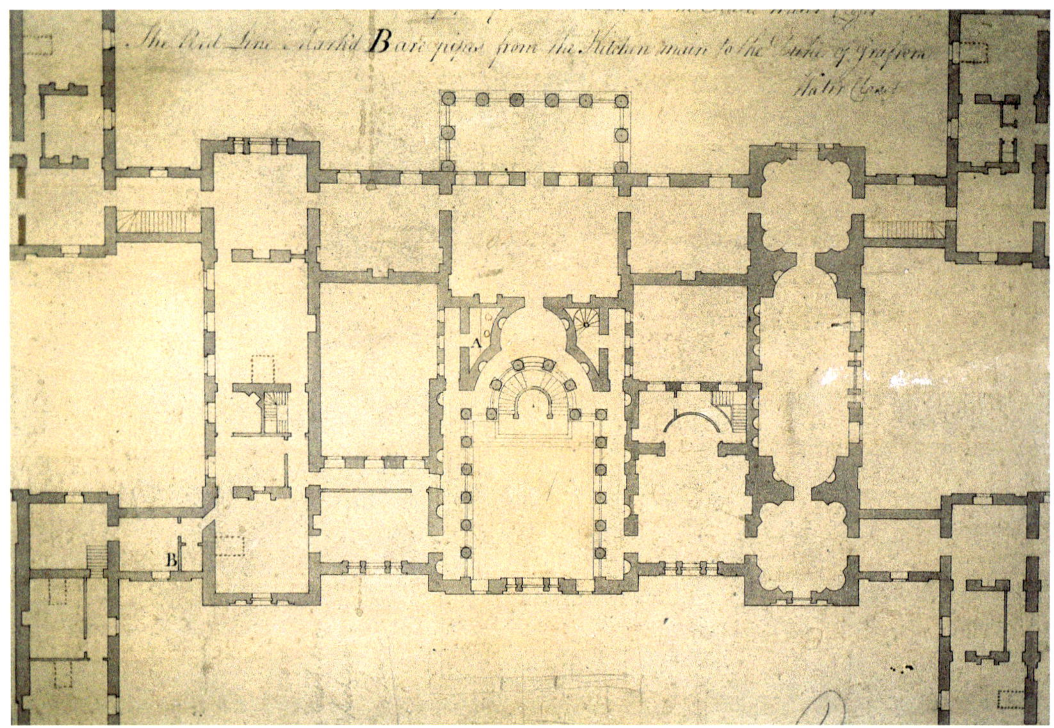

Fig. 117. Holkham II, main floor plan drawn by Matthew Brettingham in 1757 and showing the first stage of the dramatic change in the Marble Hall. The inner north wall has been removed, but the horseshoe-shaped staircase to the Saloon is still there.

Fig. 118. Detail of fig. 117, highlighting the irregularities caused by the changes in the Marble Hall: the northernmost columns are now interfering with the northern enfilade.

terms, this simply could not be tolerated; the enfilade had to be clear at all costs. At this advanced state, moving all the door openings by the necessary eight inches to fit the new place of the columns was impossible, as it would have broken up the interior geometry of the affected rooms.

A way had to be found to effect the necessary shift of the first columns on each side, and this could be achieved only by counteracting the original movement (on plan) of the columns. Just as the pilaster had 'pushed' the columns southwards, so now the colonnade had to be pushed, or rather compressed, in the opposite direction. The southern wall and the columns standing on it had to be brought forward, towards the north. This also helped to create an elongated, deeper apse instead of the semicircular solution in Kent's drawing.

The effect of the correction was just sufficient to push the first columns clear of the door openings behind them, but a closer look at the situation reveals that it was not enough to frame the door symmetrically (fig. 119). Indeed, the gaps between the columns vary slightly, indicating that it was all-important to move the columns clear of the enfilade.

Fig. 119. Detail of the measured drawing, fig. 113, showing that Brettingham's efforts to deal with the problems of the plan changes in the Marble Hall were not completely successful: the door to the Brown (North) State Dressing Room is not perfectly aligned behind the columns.

Fig. 120. The railings of the Marble Hall.

LADY MARGARET TAKES OVER

Despite the remarkable progress made after 1753, Thomas Coke was not to see his great house finished. At the time of his death on 20 April 1759, the exterior shell of the house was finished, but the interiors were yet to be completed. Although the majority of rooms on the principal floor of the *corps de logis* had their decoration, furniture and works of art in place, the State Bedrooms were incomplete, with other items purchased but waiting to be installed. Both Strangers' Wing and the Chapel were yet to be finished inside, and in fact were little more than masonry boxes. Auxiliary buildings such as the countinghouse and stables were yet to be begun.

Coke surprised many contemporaries by leaving the house to his widow, Lady Margaret Coke, Countess of Leicester and Baroness Clifford, 'to be used, occupied, held, and enjoyed during her life'.[162] He also made her a co-trustee charged with finishing Holkham. She and the other trustees took over the management of the building project immediately after Lord Leicester's death. Their first act was to sack Matthew Brettingham and then appoint as his successor the carver James Miller, who had been working on the site since 1748. It is unclear what prompted Lady Margaret to take this step; however, given that the majority of the construction work had been completed by this date, coupled with the fact that Brettingham was increasingly occupied with other projects, it does not seem an unreasonable decision.[163]

The work Margaret carried out on the interiors at Holkham complements the work done whilst her husband was alive. Although she clearly wanted to maintain fidelity to his vision, she did not allow herself to be overly constrained by his memory.

Her approach to completing Holkham is perhaps best shown by the Marble Hall. This significant room was unfinished at the time of Coke's death, though work was sufficiently advanced that it could be completed as he had intended. It appears that Lady Margaret deviated from her husband's plans in only one respect, by introducing metal railings between the columns (fig. 120), rather than the balustrade that both Kent and Brettingham showed in their

Fig. 121. The arrangement of altar pictures of the Chapel, with Guido Reni's *Assumption of the Virgin* in the centre.

drawings. This 'Pattern rail to go between the Columns in the Gt. Hall' was carved in 1761, and the iron rails fixed in 1764.[164]

It has been noted that the railing does not sit well in the room, as it is the only un-Vitruvian element. It is, however, a direct copy of the one in William Kent's famous staircase at 44 Berkeley Square. It is also an interesting choice of inspiration, given the strong female patron – Lady Isabella Finch – for whom 44 Berkeley Square was designed. It seems plausible that Lady Margaret chose these railings as a model because of Kent's influence and that she, perhaps more than her husband, was influenced by Kent's style.

When studying the decoration in Family Wing, the difference in the taste of husband and wife becomes apparent. The first three rooms in Family Wing – Thomas Coke's ante-room and dressing room and the Long Library – were all furnished sparsely. Inventory evidence describes them as filled with mahogany furniture and leather-covered chairs; the ceilings are all described as being by Kent, though the ante-room and dressing room are extremely simple designs; the chimneypieces in these rooms – also described as being by Kent – are strikingly austere, especially that in the Long Library.[165] We know from existing Kent designs that the Long Library in particular was pared back from the decoration proposed by Kent: his painted ceiling lunettes were never executed, busts were introduced above the bookcases in place of cartouches, and the chimneypiece was executed to a much simpler design, one which closely matches those introduced in the ante-room and Thomas Coke's dressing room (fig. 194 and pl. 55).

By contrast, the couple's bedroom and Lady Leicester's dressing room were much more elaborately decorated, with highly sculptural fireplaces – the design for Lady Leicester's dressing room surviving in Kent's hand – and complex

Fig. 122. A drawing showing the many different shapes and sizes of bricks needed for the rusticated front of the ground floor.

Fig. 123. Detail of original brickwork and pointing of the ground floor.

ceiling designs.[166] Archival letters suggest that it was Coke who determined the decorative scheme in this wing, but given the contrasting style of his and his wife's rooms, it seems possible that Lady Margaret may have had some input into the decoration. If this is the case, it also seems plausible that Lady Margaret would return to the work of Kent – who had worked with her husband, who was known to her and whose work she apparently liked – to complete the house after Coke's death.

The final significant interior at Holkham that Lady Margaret oversaw was the Chapel, which had not been started at the time of Coke's death. Here, Lady Margaret introduced an entirely new and more decorative design provided by James Miller (pl. 51).[167] One of Lady Margaret's alterations was to have the altar redesigned to accommodate three paintings instead of the original one (fig. 121). Reni's *Assumption of the Virgin* was still to remain at the centre, but now flanked by a pair of paintings of St Cecilia and St Anne, commissioned from the contemporary artist Giovanni Cipriani. Margaret paid £40 for the pair of paintings, which are signed by the artist and dated 1764. The inclusion of St Anne, the patron saint of mothers, is a poignant tribute to the many children she had lost. Margaret introduced further paintings along the south wall, replacing the three niches indicated in the earlier design, and closed up the projected ground-floor windows with a wall of alabaster, creating a space which is uniformly lit at first-floor level, the light filtering down to those who sit in the pews below.[168] Of the couple, she was by far the more devout, as demonstrated through her independent architectural projects: the restoration of St Withburga's Church and the construction of the Holkham Almshouses (fig. 228). It seems she felt especially capable of putting her stamp on this room, perhaps knowing it was of little interest to her husband.

On the whole, Lady Margaret's contributions harmonise with those of her husband, and it takes an eagle-eyed visitor to distinguish her work from his. Holkham was as much a monument for her as it has been for Coke; for him, it had been the statement of his knowledge, wealth and status; for her, it was a testament to the family she had lost. It is touching, therefore, that it is she who erected the inscription in the Marble Hall (fig. 169):

> THIS SEAT, on an open barren Estate,
> Was planned, planted, built, decorated,
> And inhabited the middle of the XVIIIth Century
> By THO.^{s} COKE EARL of LEICESTER

STRUCTURE AND MATERIALS

The materials used for building Holkham Hall have invited comment from the beginning. In his 1773 *Plans*, the younger Brettingham held forth on the quality and durability of Roman bricks and on the esteem that 'Vitruvius,

Fig. 124. View of the space over the Marble Hall, showing the wood-and-plaster shell of the vaulted ceiling and the apse.

the father of architecture' and the ancient Romans had for brick edifices. He attributed the quality of Roman bricks largely to the earth they used. The Holkham bricks, he informs us, 'resemble the modern yellow brick of the Romans, both in colour and hardness: this similarity was discovered by comparing them with one accidentally sent from Rome in the packing-case of an antique statue.'[169] As Brettingham went on to explain:

> Bath stone, in deference to its fine yellow tinct, was first fixed on for the external surface of the intended structure; but a brick earth was found out in one of the neighbouring villages of Birnham, which, with proper seasoning and tempering, produced an excellent well-shaped brick, approaching nearly to the colour of Bath stone, full as ponderous, and of a much firmer texture.[170]

Corroboration for Lord Lovell's original intention to face the fronts in Bath stone, producing façades resembling those at Houghton and Wanstead, is found in various letters he wrote in 1734, informing Brettingham about his dealings with Ralph Allen, owner of the Bath quarries. But he soon met with difficulties, since the necessary supply of stone could not be guaranteed. 'I saw Mr Allen yesterday we can get no ships to carry the stone so I am at a very great loss', he wrote on 1 April 1734, and half a year later, with the foundations for the first wing already begun, he wrote 'I sett out for Bath tomorrow but see no likelihood of getting Bath stone.'[171]

If the decision to use brick for the hall's façades had to be taken at short notice, the builders were able to make use of the experience they had gained in building the Temple in Obelisk Wood, a brick structure with a stone portico.[172]

The building accounts for Holkham Hall record countless deliveries of bricks carted down the road from the kiln to the construction site: upwards of 2.7 million bricks between 1734 and 1762, with the yellow bricks priced at £1 per thousand. Today, the eighteenth-century kilns have disappeared, but their nineteenth-century successors remained in use long after World War II, presumably without dramatic changes in technology.

Thomas Coke acquired the Burnham Market Brick Kiln in 1728. Bricks from a seam of red clay were used for garden walls; at the Hall, they were used for the invisible parts of the walls and for the non-public areas, such as the courtyards. But from 1730 onwards a white seam provided clay for yellow bricks:

> Of this earth bricks were formed for the outside walls, and likewise, by means of various moulds, for the rustics of the basement story: Some shaped the Bird's-mouth, or rustic joint; others, the window arches; some the headers, and some the stretchers; and not less than thirty different sizes were required to complete the figure of one single rustic.[173]

In fact, fifteen different brick types were needed for the standard rustics alone, but in addition it took a huge number of different shapes to construct the frames and particularly the lintels of windows and doors in the rustic basement (fig. 122). Altogether, no less than 140 different shapes and sizes of bricks can be found in the building.[174] As a close look at the façades reveals, most of the brickwork has never been in need of repointing: even after more than 250 years, the gaps between the bricks are filled with a material that is hard, white and smooth as marble and decorated with the precise line cut by the bricklayers' trowels (fig. 123).

The solidity of Holkham's construction, with interior walls three feet (0.91 m) thick, is as remarkable as the quality of the decoration and the furnishings. The spaces inside the brick shell were formed by the deft use of laths and plaster: large voids are hidden not only behind the coved ceilings, but in some cases also behind the inner walls of rooms. The spaces above the Statue Gallery, the Tribunes and the Marble Hall provide impressive examples of this technique (fig. 124).

The quality and near perfection displayed throughout the building must be the most remarkable and consistent feature of Holkham's construction. Not only the staterooms and the rooms intended for use by the family, but even the most remote and seemingly unimportant parts of the building were made from excellent materials and executed with uncompromising attention to fine craftsmanship. The house, therefore, is a monument not only to the patron who masterminded the design, but also to the craftsmen who built it.

WEST DRAWING ROOM

Pl. 28

►■◄

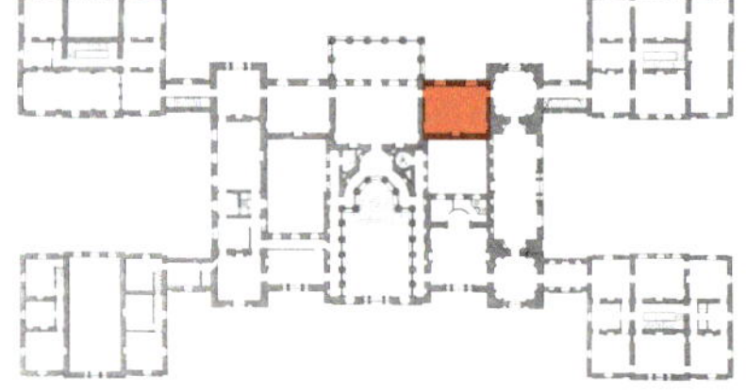

Pl. 29

PIETRI

Edward Coke
Lord Chief Justice

Pl. 30

Pl. 31

Pl. 32

SOUTH DINING ROOM

Pl. 33

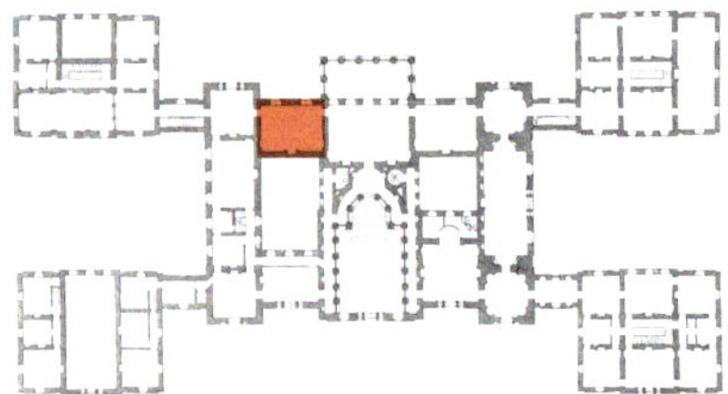

Pl. 34

Pl. 35

Pl. 36

LANDSCAPE ROOM

Pl. 37

►■◄

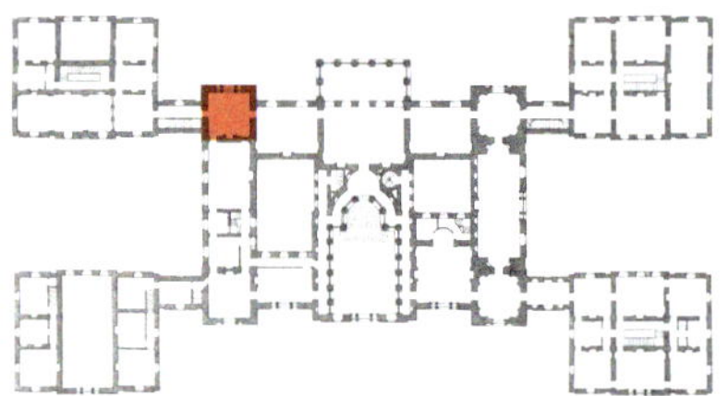

Pl. 38

SALVATOR ROSA

Pl. 39

Pl. 40

GREEN STATE BEDROOM

Pl. 41

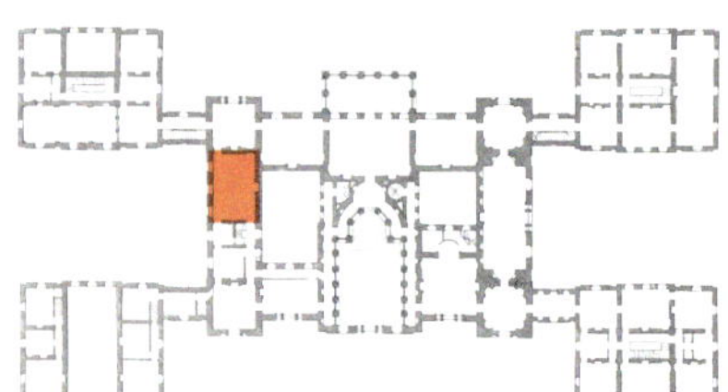

Pl. 42

Pl. 43

Pl. 44

CLOSETS

Pl. 45

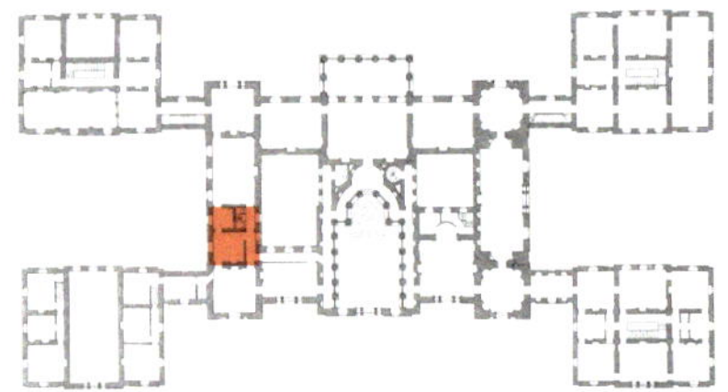

Pl. 46

NORTH STATE BEDROOM

Pl. 47

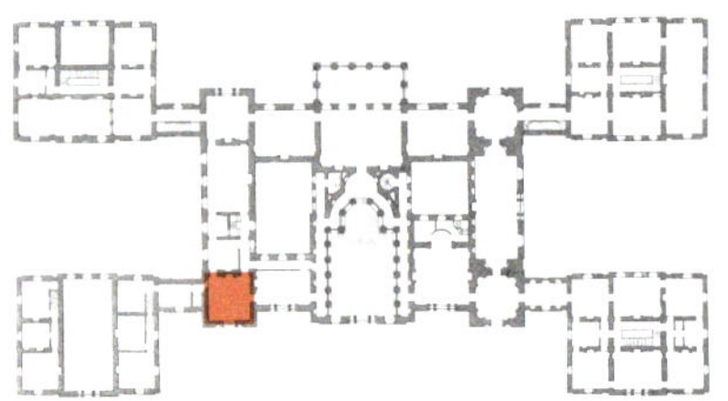

Pl. 48

NORTH STATE SITTING ROOM

Pl. 49

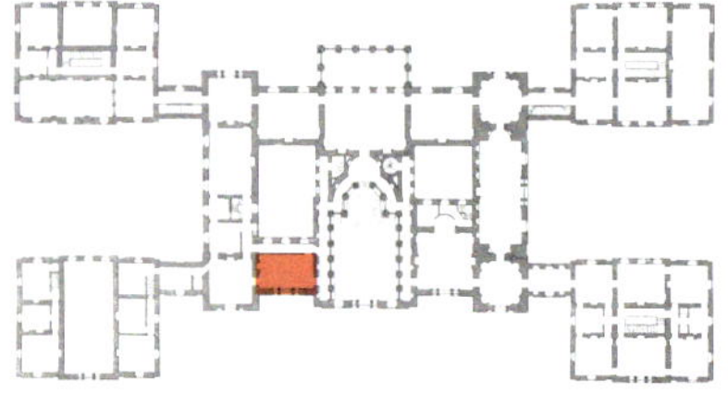

Pl. 50

CHAPEL

Pl. 51

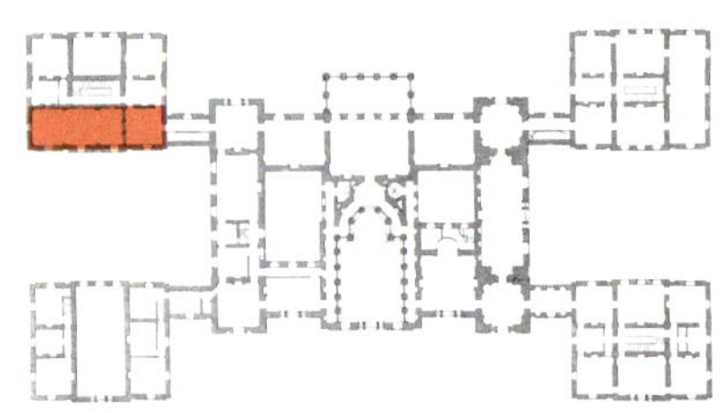

CHAPTER 4

THE ROOMS AND THE COLLECTIONS

OVERLEAF
The Saloon ceiling.

'Now we must think of the inside of the rooms',[175] wrote Thomas Coke to Lord Burlington in November 1736 when the shell of the first and most urgently needed part of his new house, Family Wing, was nearing completion. The remark highlights Coke's approach of developing his great house and all its details step by step as building progressed over years stretching into decades, of taking decisions 'just in time'. Therefore no comprehensive master plan was in place when construction commenced in 1734, and no detailed scheme existed for the interior design, decoration and furnishing of all the great rooms in his country seat. Because of this practice we find three distinct – though superficially quite similar – design themes in the house today. The earliest scheme, in Family Wing, shows the hand of William Kent, who – no doubt under some degree of guidance from the patron – created his personal and distinctive version of Roman magnificence. But when the main body of the house was at last ready to be decorated and furnished from the early 1750s onwards, Kent was no longer alive. Therefore Coke used an alternative approach, which for him may not even have been the second-best option: rather than creating original designs for friezes and ceilings as Kent had done, he relied on the best sources available, namely details from authentic Roman buildings as published in various authoritative works by Messrs Desgodetz, Fréart and others. In his *Plans of Holkham* of 1773, Matthew Brettingham junior scrupulously pointed out all the sources that were used by the learned patron. Then Coke himself died before Strangers' Wing was ready for furnishing, so it fell to his widow, Lady Margaret, to direct the decoration of this final part of the house. Employing competent and experienced craftsmen and apparently also reusing chimneypieces from their London house, she achieved a decorative scheme in harmony with the earlier part, albeit displaying neither the originality of Kent's creation nor the erudition of her husband's rendering of the staterooms.

Holkham's unique interiors can be seen and read as an expression of the builder's personality: they reflect his ambition and his vision. The ambition was to establish the seat of a dynasty, of an aristocratic family founded by Coke himself; the vision was that this seat should epitomise the values associated with ancient Rome. According to the unwritten rules of the times, both the vision and the ambition needed to be expressed and endorsed by the architectural and artistic qualities of the seat, the great house. Its iconography, the visual narratives expressed both outside and inside the building, would be scrutinised; the quality of the artworks and other collections would be eyed and assessed by the builder's critical and sometimes unsympathetic peers. Although he could not really be called nouveau-riche, young Mr Coke was undoubtedly a newcomer in pursuing his aspirations to a far higher status than any of his forebears, including the Chief Justice – and even as Knight of the Bath, as Baron Lovell and ultimately as Earl of Leicester he still had to prove, at every step of the way, his claim to a place amongst the highest in the land.

With this context in mind, the interiors of Holkham Hall can be read, on one level, as a collection of status symbols underpinning Coke's social ambitions. The perfectly baroque state apartment is a case in point: the sequence of rooms from the Saloon, with a build-up of State Ante-Chamber, State Dressing Room, State Bedchamber, State Bedchamber Closet and backstairs would not disgrace the palace of a ruling prince on the Continent. Already an anachronism even in the early 1730s when Thomas Coke planned this prestigious (or even slightly pretentious) apartment, its primary and most exciting function was that of a showcase, allowing Coke to spread out his immense collection of great works of art and arrange the paintings in a clever and intricate way that was simultaneously aesthetically pleasing and intellectually challenging and entertaining. However much he loved his paintings, particularly the Arcadian landscapes by Claude Lorrain and Nicholas Poussin, we may assume that he loved his ancient sculptures even more, and whilst the paintings thrived in the largely baroque environment of the state apartment with its rich textiles, the sculptures needed the more refined and restrained setting provided by the alabaster architecture of the Marble Hall and the painted walls of the State Dining Room and – apex of the whole arrangement – the Statue Gallery (fig. 125 and pls. 20 to 27).

One of Holkham's remarkable achievements is that it integrates two decorative schemes that might be seen as being in competition, even contradiction: one scheme based on emulating ancient Rome, and another based on the essentially baroque standards set by the Sun King's Palace of Versailles (fig. 126). It all comes down to a question of balance: as we have seen in the architecture chapter, Coke played for a while with the idea of a Roman saloon, but shelved the idea. It would have tipped the scales and produced an all too academic construction. As it is, all the details of the architectural decoration in the baroque staterooms are impeccably Roman in provenance, and even the tables and suites of furniture are designed to evoke the interiors of a wealthy Roman's *villa rustica*. But they also work surprisingly well with the rich textures and deep colours of the caffoy and silk hangings and the tapestries that characterise the eastern part of the main house.

Whether Roman or baroque in character – one Palladian principle dominates the rooms on the piano nobile, namely the rigid rule of symmetry. Every door in a wall must have a symmetrically placed counterpart even if the second door, more often than not, is immovable and just there for the visual effect. Field Marshal George Wade experienced the consequences of this rule when he commissioned Lord Burlington to design a house for him in London:[176]

> It seems that Wade had wanted a room in his home sufficiently large to enable him to set up one of Rubens' large cartoons which he had bought in Flanders; but Burlington's classical desire for symmetry at any price made him introduce such a number of doors to balance one another that the wall space was ruthlessly cut up, with the result that the Marshal discovered to his chagrin that he had not a single room in which he could place his precious cartoon.[177]

In acknowledgement of the high regard the Palladians had for this aesthetic principle, the photographs in this book are mostly taken orthogonally rather than viewing a room at an angle.

THE FURNISHING OF HOLKHAM'S GRAND APARTMENT

Holkham's Grand Apartment furniture, introduced in the mid-eighteenth century, is designed and enriched with ornament that is intricately linked to the hall's interior architecture. Like the architecture, the furniture was intended to arouse images of ancient Roman architecture and classical literature in the visitor's mind.

The following description aims to interpret some of the themes that run through the magnificent eighteenth-century rooms. Fortunately, much of the furniture either remains in situ or has been returned to the position for which it was designed. This is also true of the hanging of pictures and the positioning of statues. The original situation is very well documented in inventories from the 1760s and in the detailed descriptions of Matthew Brettingham junior's much enlarged second edition of the *Plans of Holkham*, published in 1773. Wherever useful, the following account

Fig. 125. A view of the Statue Gallery, looking south.

uses the original room names as given by Brettingham. It should be noted, however, that some rooms have changed names over time: a plan (fig. 127) provides some orientation.

'Taste' was an all-pervading issue in the eighteenth century; Holkham's Grand Apartment embodies the taste acquired and refined by Thomas Coke during his years of study in Italy and demonstrates his wisdom in employing Rome-trained architects for the decoration of his house. Holkham shows his devotion to the cardinal art of architecture as well as its successful unification with the other cardinal arts of sculpture and painting. On the coast of Norfolk, Coke created a seaside Roman villa 'worthy of the ancients', one that served to evoke Mount Parnassus, the haunt of Apollo, god of poetry, and his companions, the Muses of artistic inspiration. Coke's enthusiasm for antiquity can already be recognised in a Grand Tour portrait that was executed in 1717, a year before his marriage, by the Italian artist Francesco Trevisani (fig. 7).[178] He is depicted on a canopied seat borne by fabulous winged sphinx monopodiae and supported by embracing nereids. Such water nymphs frame the Renaissance inscription 'Virtus et Fortuna' in the frontispiece to the architect Andrea Palladio's *Quattro Libri Dell'Architectura*, published in 1570. Coke's papers lie on a Roman marble-topped table with a wave-scrolled frame wreathed by Apollo's laurels. A sarcophagus-shaped writing box, with a dome sculpted with figures of Cupid leading Mars to Venus's couch, celebrates 'Love's triumph'. Of course the Englishman has a dog: with his left hand he somewhat absent-mindedly strokes a pug who gazes adoringly up at the sitter. The background of sculptures in niches seems like a vision of the Statue Gallery he was to conceive for Holkham a decade later.

Another Roman painter, Sebastiano Conca, portrayed Coke in the guise of Orpheus, the mythical charmer of trees and animals, referring to Coke's activities in reordering the Holkham landscape and in improving agriculture (fig. 128).

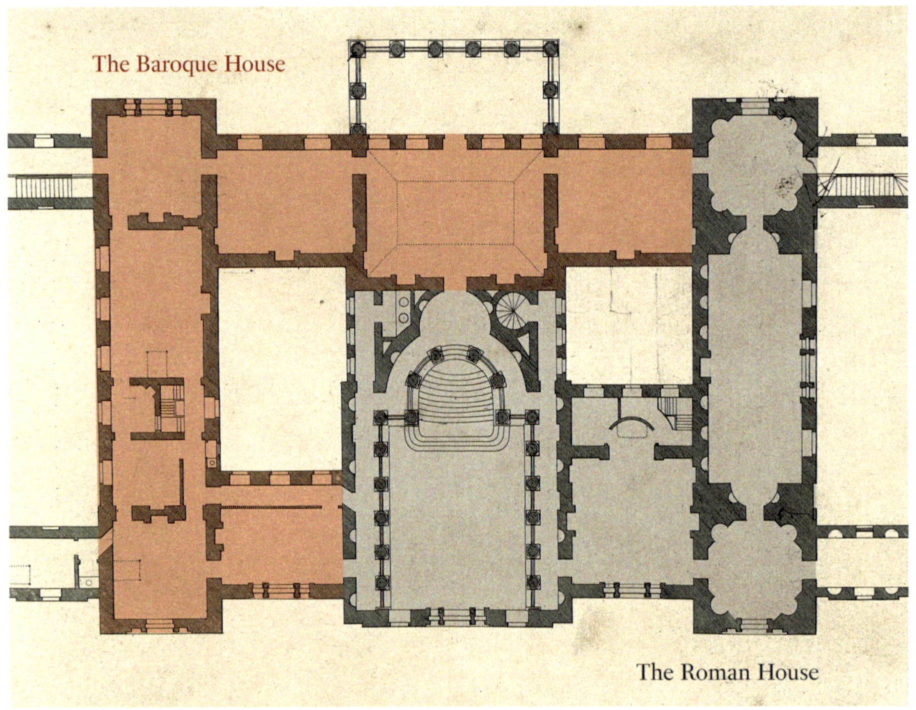

Fig. 126. A plan showing the Roman and the baroque areas of Holkham's Grand Apartment.

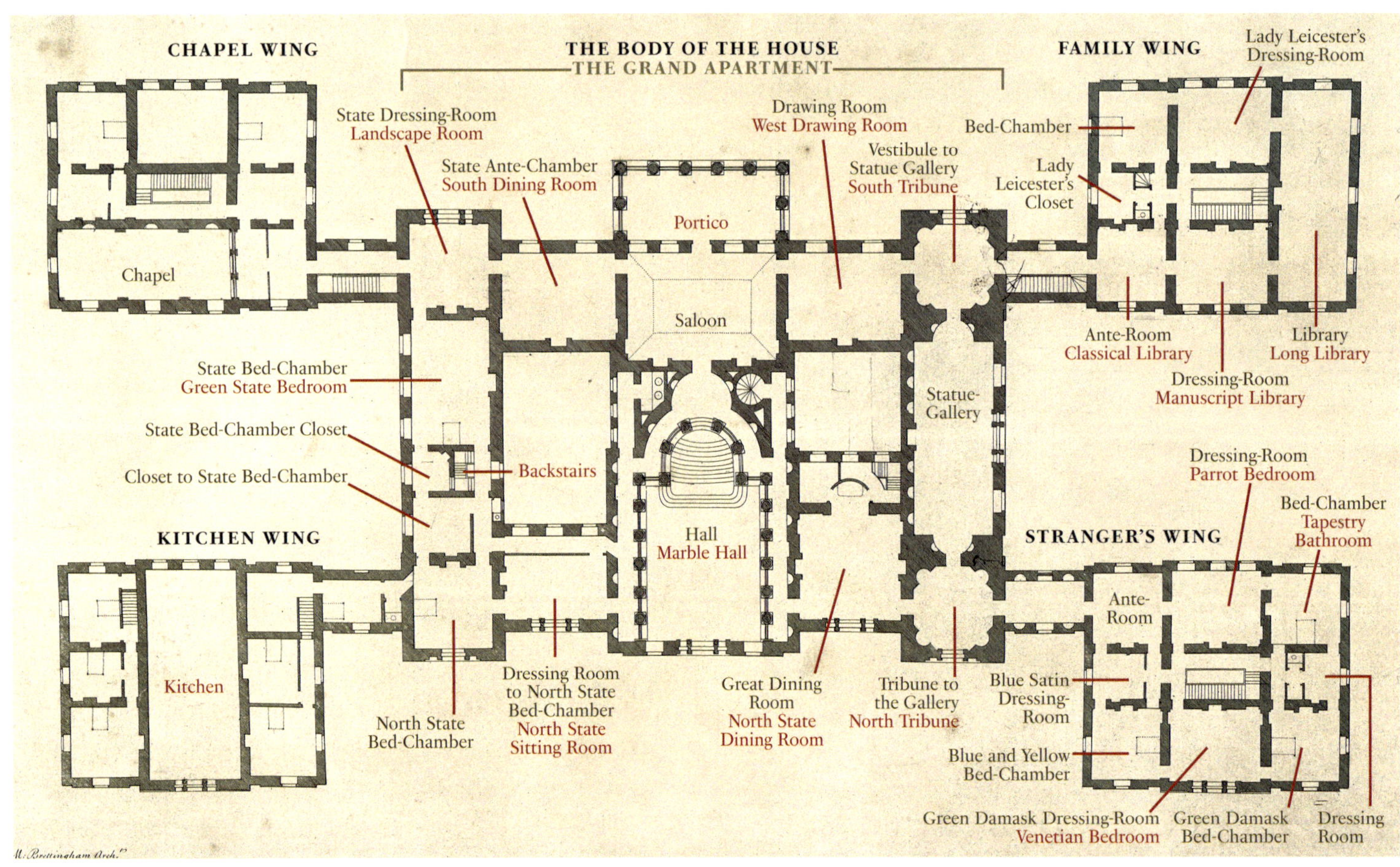

Fig. 127. A plan showing the original room names as well as (in red) some later names used in the text.

Fig. 128. Sebastiano Conca's *Elysian Fields,* commissioned by young Thomas Coke in Rome during his Grand Tour, originally adorned the Green Damask Dressing Room in Strangers' Wing. In 1773, the younger Brettingham characterised it as 'a large Picture full of Figures, amongst which his Lordship is represented in the Character of Orpheus'.

To Coke, garden design, like interior decoration, was a branch of the art of architecture. His embellishment of the estate at Holkham demonstrates the Roman virtue of *pietas* and the honouring of his ancestors, particularly Edward Coke, founder of the family's fortunes, whose legal acumen had contributed to the establishment of the British constitution. Thomas Coke traced a lineage for this ancestor's talent to the Roman law god, the almighty Jupiter. He used the deity's sacred ilex oak to form an avenue leading from the Triumphal Arch through the grounds to Holkham's majestic Marble Hall: a Temple of Jupiter that could serve as a banqueting hall and even, on occasion, a law court.

Three further monuments – an Egyptian obelisk, emblematic of eternity; a domed and pedimented banqueting pavilion, the Temple; and a pedimented seat set on a raised mount – contributed to its paradisiacal air of Arcadia. The façade of the Seat on the Mount was decorated with hermed pilasters of basket-bearing figures personifying the Seasons (figs. 34 and 35). Designed by the Rome-trained artist William Kent and executed by the sculptor Peter Scheemakers, the Seat on the Mount was similar to Kent's 1734 version at George II's villa at Kensington.[179]

Kent's activities in the field of architecture had been fostered from 1719 by Richard Boyle, Earl of Burlington. Amongst Burlington's prized architectural possessions was an album of drawings created by the seventeenth-century court architect Inigo Jones. With the assistance of Kent, nicknamed the 'Signor' on account of his long sojourn at Rome, the Jones drawings provided the basis on which Burlington established 'Roman' ornament as the modern and national style. His enhancement of Jones's reputation as the Palladio of interior architecture and reviver of true Roman ornament was successfully achieved through various publications, such as Kent's *The Designs of Inigo Jones, consisting of Plans and Elevations for Publick and Private Buildings, with Some Additional Designs* (by Lord Burlington and himself), published in two volumes in 1727, and Isaac Ware's *Some Designs of Inigo Jones and Others* in 1731. These

Fig. 129. A section through the main house, looking south, from Brettingham junior's *Plans, Elevations and Sections of Holkham* (1773).

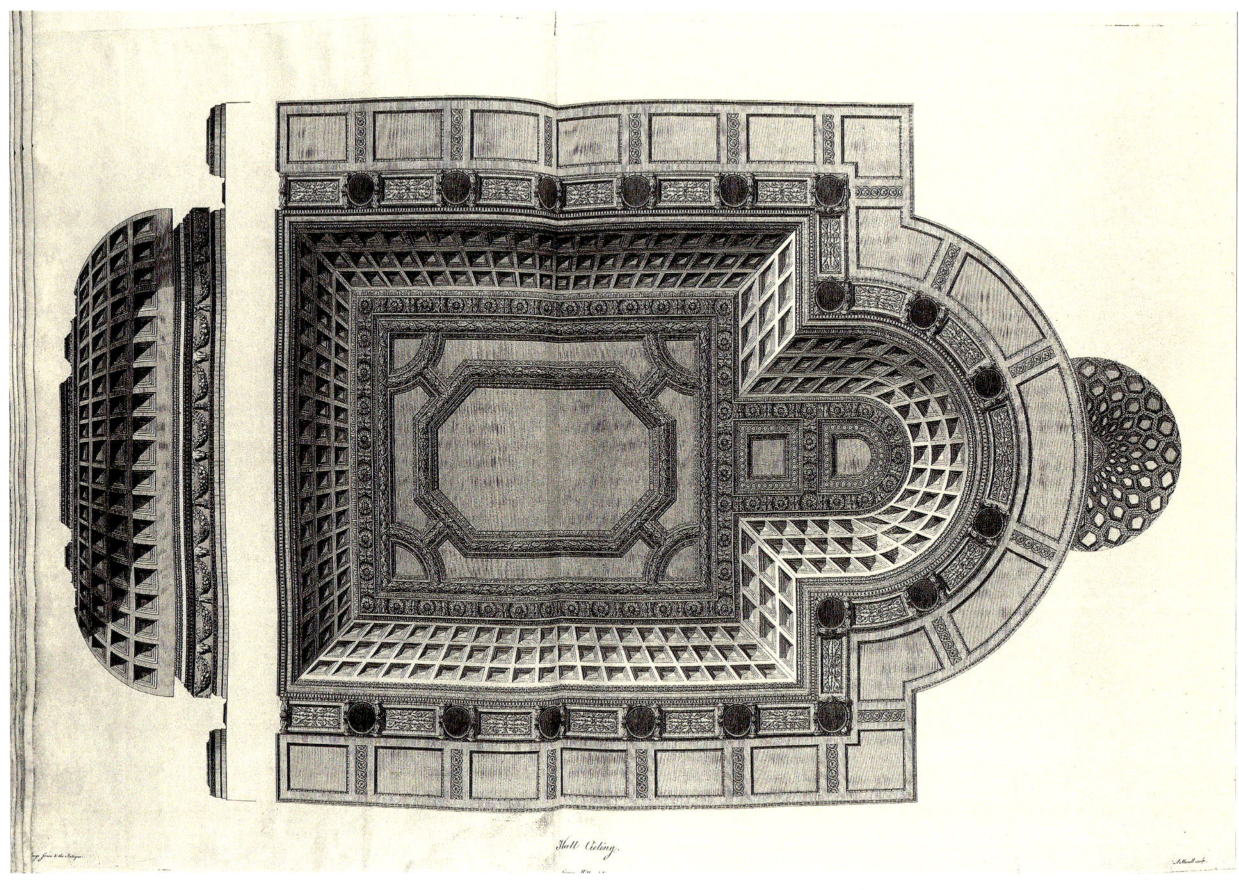

Fig. 130. The ceiling of the Marble Hall (from *Plans*, 1773).

were followed by *Some Designs of Mr. Inigo Jones and Mr. William Kent*, which was issued by John Vardy in 1744. Vardy worked alongside Kent on the Royal Architectural Board of Works for George II and Queen Caroline as well as for their son Frederick, Prince of Wales.

The ornament found in these publications appears throughout Holkham, which itself, in turn, contributed to the modern school of Roman architecture once the elder Brettingham's *Plans, Elevations and Sections of Holkham in Norfolk, the Seat of the late Earl of Leicester* had been published in 1761, shortly after Lord Leicester's death. The second edition of 1773 issued by Brettingham junior contained many more and rather splendid plates (figs. 129 and 130) and took every opportunity to express the elder Brettingham's personal contribution to the embellishment of the house through the acquisition of paintings, sculpture and furniture made on behalf of Lord Leicester during Brettingham's years in Italy from 1747 to 1754.

THE MARBLE HALL

Holkham's Marble Hall, which formed the entrance to the Grand Apartment, was posthumously labelled with a Roman tablet above its temple-pedimented entrance, recording Lord Leicester's achievement in the metamorphosis of his allegedly 'barren estate' (fig. 168). Indeed, the magnificence of Leicester's Ionic-columned and basilica-like banqueting hall hinted at the account of the banquet of the gods in Ovid's *Metamorphoses* or 'Loves of the Gods', especially as it was originally intended that the Hall should be dominated by Jupiter's monumental statue, raised on a stepped altar-dais and proffering a libation *patera*, a shallow bowl (figs. 95 and 150).

Fig. 131. Detail of the columns and the ceiling in the Marble Hall.

In his *Plans*, Brettingham noted that the 'ornaments' of the Hall ceiling cove derived from the Pantheon at Rome, and those of the basilica apse from the Temple of Peace, whereas the Ionic order was copied from the Temple of Fortuna Virilis (figs. 129 to 131). The source for these Roman antiquities was Antoine Desgodetz's *Les Edifices antiques de Rome*, published in 1682.

The bust of the first earl above the door from the Hall to the Saloon, a cast of Roubiliac's marble original for the family monument in Tittleshall Church (fig. 20), was placed there by his widow. The Hall walls were lined with mahogany seats and settees in the form of Ionic-scrolled Roman triclinium couches. The settee pattern, with Jonesian truss-scrolled pilaster feet wrapped with Roman acanthus, almost replicates the 'seats or benches ... of fine mahogany wood' introduced in the late 1720s for neighbouring Houghton Hall, also under Kent's direction.[180] Their composition in turn relates to the seat in Kent's Kensington garden temple and to the Kent patterns for hall and banqueting house seats as illustrated in Vardy's 1744 publication.

Fig. 132. Overdoor ornamentation in the Saloon.

Fig. 133. One of the Saloon side tables with corner posts in the shape of storks.

Fig. 134. One of two identical Roman mosaics on the side tables in the Saloon.

THE SALOON

The Saloon and its temple-porticoed loggia formed the centrepiece of the Grand Apartment overlooking the south front's 'picturesque' gardens. Jupiter's consort, Juno, appropriately presides over this room, which may have served for the remove or dessert when dining, and her bust is displayed above its magnificent entrance (fig. 164). This rosy space is flowered with Roman acanthus leaves raised in bas-relief on crimson caffoy hangings.

In contrast to the masculine severity of the 'vestibulum' hall, the Saloon furnishings are richly polychromed in keeping with the varicoloured Sicilian jasper chimneypieces. The pattern for the ceiling cove derives from Rome's Basilica of Maxentius and is wreathed with 'Venus' wave-scrolled and pearled ribbon-guilloche borders (pl. 16). Sunflowers, sacred to the poetry deity Apollo, feature in the flowered compartments of the ceiling. The stuccoed wall-cornices are wreathed with scrolled *rinceaux* of flowered acanthus leaves issuing from central cartouches. These display the armorial escutcheons of the Coke family, guarded by the family's ostrich and dragon supporters and ensigned with the coronet, received in 1744, when Thomas Coke was created Viscount Coke and Earl of Leicester by George II (cf. family tree). The earldom was also celebrated by introducing Jonesian palm-wreathed coronets in place of the proposed pediments above the doors leading to an enfilade of apartments at both ends of the room (fig. 132). The central door entablature displays Coke ostrich heads emerging from Roman acanthus foliage to garland the scallop-shell badge of Venus, goddess of Love.

Ancient virtue is celebrated at the hearths (pl. 12). Scenes from mythology and Roman history are portrayed in the paintings set above Ionic-columned chimneypieces, with bas-relief tablets garlanded in oak leaves.[181] The picture frames are crowned with fruit baskets, recalling feasts in antiquity, and serve as trophies of peace and plenty. A surviving design for these frames may indicate that Lord Leicester had consulted Vardy over designs for the furnishing of the Grand Apartment.[182]

The Saloon boasts a remarkable pair of buffets or sideboard-tables with outstanding mosaics (fig. 134). Identical sections of a pavement mosaic show frames consisting of a guilloche design composed of multicoloured strands; set against the white ground, a slanted swastika–meander pattern encloses in each space hexagons containing stylised flowers of two alternating types. A section of these mosaics was illustrated by the ambitious and erudite Monsignor Giuseppe Furietti in his *De Musivis vel Pictoriae Mosaicae Artis Origine* (1752). In his book, of which the earl owned a copy, the Italian scholar discussed his excavation of these works at Hadrian's Villa, Tivoli, as well as his working methods of forming such floor mosaics into tabletops. The quality of design and workmanship are consonant with the standard to be expected of the emperor's domicile. The mosaic slabs echo the room's flowered ceiling, while the richly sculpted table frames, with their wave-scrolled ribbons and Venus shells in lambrequined cartouches, harmonise with the room's architecture.

Water reeds, sacred to the Arcadian deity Pan, form the rear supports of the buffets. Storks, emblematic of filial piety, serve as pilasters at the front (fig. 133). This position is usually occupied by Jupiter's eagle, who was in attendance at the 'Banquet of the Gods' and was particularly associated with Ovid's history of Jupiter and his cupbearer Ganymede. Such iconography was promoted by William Kent, who portrayed Roman furniture in illustrations for the English poet Alexander Pope's translation of Homer's *Odyssey*, completed in 1725. The stork, popularised in Aesop's Fables, had become part of the 'modern' ornament featured in pattern books such as Thomas Chippendale's *Gentleman and Cabinet-Maker's Director*, 1754. At Holkham, storks served as guardians of the marble wine cisterns that stood beneath the tables.

THE STATE DINING ROOM

Whilst the tables in the Saloon served as a buffet for the display of gold and silver plate, the principal site for the splendid Leicester plate may well have been the magnificent Roman sideboard–table in the State Dining Room on the north front. This domed room, whose cubic proportions recalled the Egyptian Hall of Antiquity, has its buffet recessed in an apse screened by a triumphal arch with mirrors set into its sides in order to reflect the plate (pl. 18).

Desgodetz's book supplied the pattern both for the apse ceiling, which is stuccoed with flowered mosaics, and for the pilasters, whose golden acanthus scrolls are inspired by those on the Triumphal Arch of the Goldsmiths in Rome. The *Plans* noted that 'the Ceiling of this magnificent Room was for the most part taken from Inigo Jones'. The chimneypieces, 'composed of Sicilian Jasper Trusses and Statuary marble mixed', have tablets inspired by moralistic subjects from Aesop's Fables (see below and figs. 169 to 172). As in the Saloon, these chimneypieces were the work of the sculptor Thomas Carter.

The truss scroll was a favoured element of Inigo Jones's Roman style. Those in the Dining Room derive from a Kent pattern introduced in the parlour at Houghton in 1728.[183] They are echoed in the porphyry console trusses of John Vardy's sideboard–table (figs. 135 and 136). The bowed and serpentined slab of marble was described by Brettingham as being of 'real Egyptian green marble … enriched with gilt metal ornaments', the latter forming a border of acanthus-wrapped reeds. The table frieze is wreathed with a Grecian palm-flowered ribbon-guilloche in golden bronze and is

Fig. 135. Detail of one of the legs of the table in the apse of the State Dining Room.

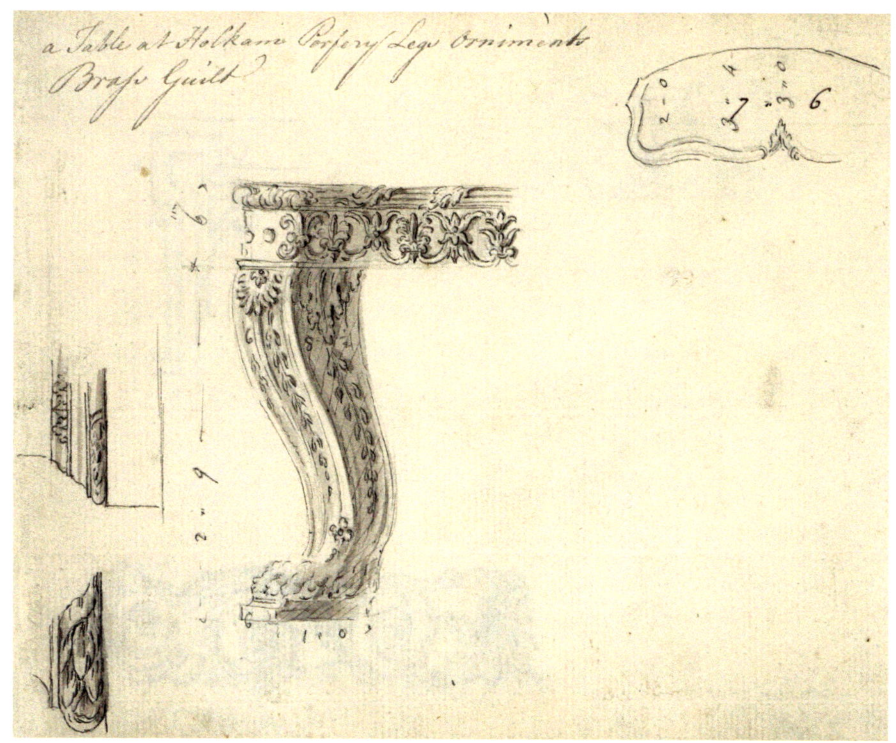

Fig. 136. A drawing by John Vardy with details of the table in the apse of the State Dining Room.

supported on Egyptian red porphyry consoles. These originally formed part of 'an ancient sarcophagus' and are festooned with 'Apollo' laurels issuing from acanthus foliage. Their paw-like feet recall the panthers or lions that, according to the ancient poets, attended the mythical Feast of Bacchus and drew the wine deity's triumphal chariot.

References to Bacchus and Ceres, the harvest deities, in grand or state apartments are used to evoke the well-known Roman adage 'Sine Cerere et Baccho friget Venus' ('Without Ceres [food] and Bacchus [wine], Venus [love] will grow cold'). A surviving drawing in Vardy's hand (fig. 136) may indicate that Vardy also designed this sideboard–table, whilst the carving, as Brettingham records, was executed by Carter.

Standing in front of the table, as part of the sideboard furnishings, is a 'large Bason of Mount-Edgecumbe Red Granite' in the form of a fluted *krater* (wine vase). It is recorded as having been executed from a granite block presented to the Earl of Leicester by the Earl of Mount Edgecumbe of Mount Edgecumbe House, Cornwall. Roman flutes and acanthus enrich the arch-crested frames and truss-scrolled legs of the mahogany parlour chairs, which were upholstered in red Morocco leather. These chairs lined the walls and were only moved to the centre of the room when in use, as were the folding-leaf dining tables which were brought out from a room concealed behind the apse.

THE STATUE GALLERY

Adjoining the Great Dining Room and occupying the Grand Apartment's west front is the Gallery, the great 'chambre d'assembly' or room of entertainment, whose walls are lined with statues. The flowered coffering in the basilica niches is taken from the Temple of Venus in Rome. The niches are set at either end of the Gallery and open through to high-ceilinged octagonal rooms, called Tribunes (pls. 20 and 27).

Pride of place above the hearth is given to a statue of Apollo, which is displayed in a temple-pedimented and laurel-crowned frame (pl. 25). The pilaster trusses of the veined statuary marble chimneypiece are festooned with bacchic veils. The tablet of golden Siena marble is guarded on either side by bacchic lion heads emerging from Roman acanthus. The pattern is taken from Vardy's engraving of a

Fig. 137. The ceiling of the (West) Drawing Room, after a design by Inigo Jones.

Jones chimneypiece design for Wilton House in Wiltshire.[184] It was executed by the sculptor Joseph Pickford, who had trained under Lord Burlington's protégé, the Italian sculptor G. B. Guelphi. As in the Dining Room, the Gallery is furnished with Jonesian scrolled 'console' wall brackets, which serve for the display of marble busts.

Sideboard–tables with 'alabastro peccorella' slabs stood in front of the window piers. Brettingham, who praised them as 'very beautiful' in his *Plans*, had acquired the slabs from the celebrated Roman sculptor and antiquarian Bartolomeo Cavaceppi. The mahogany table frames are supported by Jupiter's eagle claws emerging from truss-scrolled and acanthus-wrapped legs. The mahogany seat furniture, consisting of a set of easy chairs (or 'elbow-chairs') and settees, is upholstered in blue 'Turkey' leather padded with tufted ties and edged with large round-headed brass nails. The chair frames, serpentined and voluted in the 'picturesque' French fashion of George II's reign, are embellished with golden acanthus scrolls and embossed cartouches. They were invoiced in 1757 by the Soho cabinetmakers and upholsterers Messrs Saunders and Bradshaw, who also supplied twelve chairs for the Tribunes. Their frames matched those of the Dining Room chairs, but were partly gilded and upholstered in blue 'Turkey' leather. Originally the room had oilcloth on the floor[185] – a kind of linoleum probably decorated with a Roman mosaic pattern – and white damask curtains at the windows.[186]

The niches in the North Tribune were furnished with large statues on pedestals, while the South Tribune, or Vestibule, was 'fitted up with four Library Book-Cases ... that contain a small collection of Books, for the use of Company' (pl. 27). Originally, the central room of the Gallery also contained presses (large cupboards) built into the end walls, flanking the apses on either side.[187] They were integrated into the dado and must have housed Lord Leicester's admirable collection of old master drawings. The presses must have been removed in the early nineteenth century and the drawings relocated in new presses fitted into the lower part of the niches in the South Tribune.

In 1756, the court cabinetmaker Benjamin Goodison had supplied two card tables, whose legs were carved *en suite* with the 'easy' chairs and whose frames were inlaid with 'Greek-key' ribbon-guilloches fretted in holly.

THE WEST DRAWING ROOM

The Grand Apartment's Drawing Room, to the west of the Saloon, has walls hung in 'Crimson flowered Genoa Velvet' and seats upholstered *en suite* (pls. 28 to 32). The stuccoed frieze, based on Desgodetz's illustration of the Temple of Antoninus and Faustina in Rome, is decorated with Roman candelabra alternating with *kraters* guarded by griffins – mythical eagle-winged lions sacred to Apollo. The ceiling, inspired by a Jones pattern, is divided into compartments, with the beam soffits displaying festive heads of bacchic nymphs garlanded with fruit and flowers (fig. 137). An escutcheon in the frieze of the chimneypiece is similarly flowered, as are the pilasters, whose trusses are supported by the heads of bacchic lions. Executed by Pickford in statuary marble, the chimneypiece's design derives from one invented by Jones for St Giles's House, Dorset, and was illustrated by Vardy.[188] A richly carved, gilt wood frame, crowned with a Venus shell, was provided for the overmantel painting of the 'Madonna in Glory' by Pietro di Pietri (pl. 29). This was another Brettingham purchase, as was the serpentined and brass-banded alabaster slab he provided for the sideboard-table in the facing window-pier and praised as 'an exquisite Table of Alabastro Palombaro'.

Another shell appears as a cartouche on the gilt wood table beneath a wave-scrolled frieze and is accompanied by foliage issuing from the volute-scrolls of the legs (fig. 138) The latter are ornamented with 'Venus' dolphin scales, together with libation *paterae* tied beneath foliage wrapping their trussed and taper-hermed pilasters, which terminate in lion paws. Attention to detail is a vital element in understanding such furniture. The shell motif is associated with the birth of Venus, since it served as her triumphal chariot, which was drawn by dolphins, here represented by imbricated scales on the table legs. The table is likely to have been supplied in 1757 by Goodison, together with an accompanying set of seat furniture. The chair legs are carved *en suite* with those of the table, but terminate in voluted scrolls instead of lion paws.

Fig. 138. The table in the West Drawing Room.

The concept of the Triumph of Venus and nature's abundance was evidenced by a Kent design of the 1730s for an earlier suite of seat furniture, recorded by Brettingham in Lady Leicester's Apartment in Family Wing. On this suite conjoined cornucopiae form their crestings, while the heads and paws of bacchic lions support the arms. Kent's design can be traced back to Jones's design for a chimneypiece at

Fig. 139. The table in the South Dining Room or State Ante-Chamber.

Wilton and relates to his own design of 1731 for a cornucopia-enriched parlour table at Houghton.[189]

A flower-festooned and mirror-bordered pier glass, described by Brettingham as 'magnificent', continues the room's festive theme (pl. 31). A palm-wreathed shell crowns its arched and reeded cornice and is flanked by 'tablet'-cornered and wave-scrolled pediments. This large mirror is not a single sheet but is made up of several glass panels ranged around an oval and flower-wreathed compartment. Brettingham identified the manufacturer as the London carver and gilder James Whittle, whose celebrated partnership with his son-in-law, Samuel Norman, was established in 1755.

This firm is also likely to have made the four mirrors or candle-branch sconces that hang between the arched windows of the Saloon. Each mirror consists of two oval-shaped sections joined by acanthus foliage and crowned by shells. Even more shells embellish the 'picturesque' pier-table frames, which are raised on single console pilasters and support serpentined alabaster slabs.

THE SOUTH DINING ROOM

To the east of the Saloon is the State Ante-Chamber of the state apartment (pls. 32 to 36). Its wall hangings and seat furniture match those of the West Drawing Room, and its frieze is similarly embellished with Roman candelabra and sacred urns, guarded in this instance by seated, rather than standing, griffins. The ceiling, with an elliptical central compartment, is likewise inspired by a Jones design, but instead of garlands of fruit and flowers, its beam soffits are festooned with bacchic 'Vine-Branches, Leaves and Bunches of Grapes'.[190]

The statuary marble chimneypiece, which is enlivened by a frieze tablet of brilliant lapis lazuli, also derives from a Jones 'idea' published in Kent's *The Designs of Inigo Jones*.[191]

The trusses of its taper-hermed pilasters are supported by youths, whose drapery mirrors that on the bust of a vestal priestess, which stands on the chimneypiece beside a bust of the younger Empress Faustina (pl. 36).

The pier glass, the frame of which was executed by the Norwich carver James Miller, who succeeded the elder Brettingham as surveyor of Holkham in 1759, replicates that in the Grand Drawing Room. It is accompanied by a sideboard–table whose serpentined marble slab of *giallo antico* has a bronze border of acanthus-wrapped reeds similar to that on the table in the Grand Drawing Room. The green-veined Egyptian marble frieze displays the same palm-flowered guilloche as the one on the Great Dining Room's sideboard. In place of bacchic lion paws, it is supported by the Coke ostrich and golden truss-scrolled pilasters (fig. 139). Coke ostriches also appear as caryatic supporters in the goldsmith Nicholas Sprimont's design of about 1744 for a silver tureen, which is likely to have been made when Thomas Coke, Lord Lovell was created Earl of Leicester.[192]

THE LANDSCAPE ROOM

The State Dressing Room in the south-east corner of the Great Apartment, also known as the Landscape Room, has 'Crimson Genoa damask' wall hangings (pls. 37 to 40). Although its compartmented ceiling has beams enriched with a pearled ribbon-guilloche in the Jonesian manner, it actually derives from Desgodetz's illustration of the architrave in the Hadrianic Basilica of Antoninus in Rome.[193] The chimneypiece is inspired by Vardy's illustration of Jones's design for a chimneypiece for King Charles II's Palace at Greenwich.[194] The frieze is polychromed with tablets of green *verde antico* marble and has an acanthus-wrapped cartouche in the centre. Veil-draped busts of vestals are supported on its acanthus-wrapped, truss-scrolled and herm-tapered pilasters.

THE GREEN STATE BEDROOM

Since Jupiter and Juno were cast as the presiding deities of the Hall and Saloon, it was only appropriate that they feature above the hearth of the State Bedchamber (pls. 41 to 43). The painting of *Jupiter Caressing Juno,* a subject inspired by Homer, was commissioned for the room from Gavin Hamilton (fig. 192). The chimneypiece, inspired by a Kent pattern,[195] was executed by Carter in statuary marble on a ground of Siena marble. Its oak-garlanded tablet serves as a love trophy, with Venus's billing doves nesting in Roman acanthus. The chimneypiece pilasters are composed of caryatic herms of basket-bearing nymphs, whose features are modelled on the younger Empress Faustina.

The pilasters also recall those of Kent's Kensington garden seat as engraved by Vardy, discussed earlier.[196] This room's richly flowered decoration is primarily intended to evoke the Roman concept of the Golden Age or *ver perpetuum*, of everlasting spring and eternal youth. The seasons are personified in the overdoor paintings of small boys wreathed in flower garlands and executed by the Italian artist Francesco Zuccarelli (fig. 140). Large gilded rosettes flower the ceiling in compartments wreathed by

Fig. 140. One of the overdoor paintings in the State Bedroom, by Zuccarelli.

Fig. 141. The original couch bed, placed temporarily underneath the canopy of the state bed.

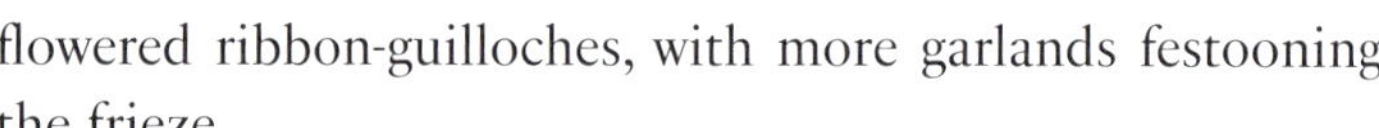

flowered ribbon-guilloches, with more garlands festooning the frieze.

The walls, including the window piers, are hung with colourful floral-bordered tapestries. Three of these are seventeenth-century Flemish tapestries representing three of the four continents then known. A matching fourth tapestry, *The Continent of Asia,* was woven at Saunders's Soho workshops to a design by Zuccarelli. The artist, who arrived in London in 1752, stayed at Holkham while he was working on his designs.[197] As well as executing the overdoor paintings, he also designed two narrow tapestries of youthful shepherds, personifying Sleep and Vigilance, to hang on either side of the Leicester state bed. At an earlier stage of planning, this bed was to be recessed, in the French manner, behind a screen of columns. However, this scheme was abandoned in favour of a stately canopied couch that on occasion could metamorphose into an unfolding bedstead (fig. 141). Its domed canopy is serpentined in a Cupid's-bow form and wreathed by Pan's reeds, while its Ionic-scrolled and triumphal-arched pediments are crowned by scalloped and coronet-ensigned cartouches. These bear the Leicester conjoined 'L' cipher woven in golden thread. The canopy displays richly foliated pineapples at the angles, in place of the usual stately plumes of feathers, and was almost certainly designed by Vardy. Brettingham described it as 'a flowered Genoa Velvet Bed, of three colours'.[198] The window curtains and their pelmets were designed *en suite* with the bed canopy. They all have richly fringed hangings of red, white and green velvet, and were supplied by Saunders. The frames of the couch, and accompanying armchairs and four stools, correspond to those in the Ante-Chamber. The two pier tables comprise serpentined alabaster slabs with reeded and ribbon-wreathed bronze borders. The supporting table frames are wreathed with a flowered ribbon-guilloche and their single-console pilasters are carved *en suite* with the chair legs.

The Green State Bedchamber's Closet, which is entered by a door to the right of the bed, adjoins the closet belonging to North State Bedchamber (pls. 45 and 46). These much more intimate rooms with their smaller and particularly precious paintings and drawings can also be accessed directly and discreetly from the backstairs.

A BAROQUE STATE APARTMENT IN A COUNTRY HOUSE?

Holkham's state apartment deserves a moment of reflection. It repeats the established pattern of a baroque state apartment, which typically starts with a *salle des gardes* or a saloon and then progresses through at least two antechambers, their decoration and works of art becoming progressively richer until one reaches the State Bedroom. This still fairly public room is then augmented by a much more intimate closet or cabinet, decorated with smaller but particularly precious paintings. The closet can be reached by backstairs, allowing important visitors to bypass the public route and come to the master of the house unseen.

Though not invented at Versailles, the idea and form of such a state apartment created as the setting of an elaborate court ritual goes back to the palace of the French king Louis XIV. So impressive and dominating was this model that ruling princes on the Continent, at least through the first half of the eighteenth century, felt compelled to install a similar sequence of rooms in their new or rebuilt palaces as an indispensable symbol of their power and exalted status.

But why does Holkham, of all places, have such a state apartment? What is its function, its purpose? Contemporary visitors from the Continent would have been somewhat bemused by an English country squire and commoner – even if he was eventually raised to the peerage – arrogating to himself the hallowed symbols and trappings of a ruling prince. The imagery in Holkham's State Bedchamber is a case in point: the four continents of the tapestries and the four seasons of the overdoors stand for an absolute monarch's claim to all-embracing power, with Hamilton's *Jupiter Caressing Juno* above the fireplace equating the Leicesters to the divine couple ruling Olympus.

Can Coke have been serious? After all, as John Summerson has put it succinctly, the 'second Whig generation [to which Burlington and Coke belonged] had strong beliefs and strong dislikes, conspicuous among the latter being the Stuart dynasty, the Roman Church, and most things foreign',[199] and a baroque state apartment stood for just those *bêtes noires*.

The explanation most likely involves several layers, some of them serious, some perhaps less so. On the most serious level, possessing a state apartment underlined Coke's ambition to establish an aristocratic dynasty that could hold its own with the greatest families of the realm. But one may perhaps detect an ironic twist, an element of commodification or domestication in the way the august symbols of an absolute ruler have trickled down to the level of a country gentleman. There is also the aesthetic level. Even a

Fig. 142. Relief on the fireplace of the North State Bedroom.

prominent and active member of the Whig oligarchy, particularly one who had travelled extensively on the Continent, might well have come to admire and enjoy the sheer gorgeousness of baroque rituals and their settings, just as a non-believer might still enjoy the pomp and pageantry of a full Catholic mass simply as a beautifully orchestrated spectacle. And beyond this, there is no denying that the richly decorated rooms of the state apartment, and their hierarchic progression in quality, provided Coke with the perfect setting for arranging and hanging his pictures in the most advantageous way.

THE NORTH STATE BEDCHAMBER AND SITTING ROOM

The second State Bedchamber would generally have been approached from the Saloon, via the column-screened corridor overlooking the Hall. Its Dressing Room, now Sitting Room (pls. 49 and 50), which served as a reception or 'withdrawing' room for this Bedchamber, was hung in a blue Genoa damask. The ceiling pattern derives from one of Jones's 'Roman' designs, and the palm-flowered frieze repeats the 'Grecian' style as used on the sideboard in the Grand Dining Room. This interest in Grecian ornament had been promoted since the 1730s by the Society of Dilettanti, a group of connoisseurs of which the first earl was a member. One of the paintings in this room was Procaccini's historical composition portraying *Numa Pompilius Giving Laws to Rome*, now lost. The first earl appeared in this painting portrayed as a Roman senator, perhaps intended to imply the family's ancient ancestry.

The North State Bedchamber (pls. 47 and 48) completes the rooms of the Grand Apartment. It was hung with beautiful seventeenth-century tapestries celebrating the seasons. The marble slab of the pier table was acquired by Brettingham, who described it as a 'curious antique Mosaic' from Hadrian's Villa at Tivoli. The chimneypiece of antique 'Fior di Persica' marble was sculpted by Carter. Its pilasters represent 'Instruments of the Roman Sacrifice ... copied from a very fine ancient Fragment in the Garden of the Villa Medici' which in antiquity alluded to sacrifices at Love's altar. Its tablet portraying 'the Birth of the Poet Lucan' was 'out of Montfaucon' (fig. 142), referring to Bernard de Montfaucon, whose *L'Antiquité expliqué et representé en figures* (Paris 1719–24) was translated into English by David Humphries and issued as *Antiquity Explained and Represented in Sculptures by the Learned Father Montfaucon* in 1731–33. This well-illustrated dictionary provided an excellent guide to the ancient deities and heroes that had been introduced by Lord Leicester and his assistants for the embellishment of Holkham.

PLACEMENT OF SEAT FURNITURE

The current placement of seat furniture against the wall in the Grand Apartment is in keeping with the eighteenth-century system of furnishing. This arrangement frees the centre of the room when not in actual use, and was considered to add to its 'propriety and beauty'. The author Adam Smith condoned this practice in his *Theory of Moral Sentiments* in 1759:

> When a person comes into his chamber, and finds the chairs all standing in the middle of the room, he is angry with his servant, and rather than see them continue in that disorder, perhaps takes the trouble himself to set them all in their places with their backs to the wall.[200]

However, this formal arrangement changed in the early nineteenth century, when all manner of furniture began to be permanently spread around the room. This new pursuit of comfort was worthy of comment by Jane Austen in her novel *Persuasion* (1818). The new fashion for profusion and disorder dismayed an American visitor to England who recorded in 1811 that

> tables, sofas and chairs were studiously dérangé about the fireplaces, and in the middle of the rooms, as if the family had just left them ... Such is the modern fashion of placing furniture, carried to an extreme, as fashions are always, that the apartments of a fashionable house look like an upholsterer's or cabinet-maker's shop.[201]

THE SCULPTURES

The marvellous collection of sculptures at Holkham Hall was the achievement of one man, Thomas Coke, first Earl of Leicester.[202] The marbles include many consummate Roman copies of lost Greek masterpieces, including statues of deities and heroes and superb portraits of eminent Greeks. There is also a notable collection of Roman portraits, both of emperors and private individuals, as well as mosaics, plaster casts and marble copies of ancient figures. The assemblage is remarkable for its size, its exceptional quality and the preservation of the works of art.

Forming the sculpture collection: the Grand Tour

Coke's acquisition of antiquities falls into two distinct phases, widely separated in time by the disaster of the South Sea Bubble.[203] The nucleus of the collection dates from the period of his Grand Tour of Italy (1712–18) in the years before his twenty-first birthday.[204] The second phase of collecting came in Coke's mature years from 1747 onwards, when he was at last able to furnish his new house.

The togatus Lucius Antonius

Among the dozen antiquities he acquired on his Grand Tour were an imposing statue of a man wearing a toga and holding a scroll and sceptre with a *scrinium* (a box with a handle for holding scrolls) at his side – fancifully entitled Lucius Antonius, brother of Marc Antony (fig. 143) – and the elegant statue of the goddess of the hunt, Diana (fig. 144). The Italians had first recognised the importance of both marbles when the learned archaeologist and Commissioner of Antiq-

Fig. 143. Statue of a *togatus* entitled *Lucius Antonius*. The sculpture was once in the saloon of the Congregazione dell'Archiconfraternità della SS. Annunziata in Rome. The restored head is excellent in its features and expression, and its pose is aligned in perfect harmony with the movement of the right arm.

Fig. 144. Statue of Diana. The divine huntress is identified by the quiver at the back with its strap slung slantwise from the right shoulder across the breast, and the (restored) bow in her left hand. There is a small remnant of the original bow near the left hip. Purchased from the house of Ignazio Consiglieri.

uities, Paolo Alessandro Maffei, included them in his 1704 anthology of illustrations with suitably learned descriptive texts of the most famous statues in Rome. Entitled *Raccolta di statue antiche e moderne* and published by Domenico de Rossi (figs. 145 and 146), this was the first eighteenth-century art book whose refined engravings by French artists were designed to appeal to connoisseurs.[205]

The illustrations in the *Raccolta* provide a *terminus ante quem* but nothing else for the additions to both sculptures: the man's gaunt head and arms with attributes; Diana's arms with bow and quiver. Her present head is a later repair, done in England. The male statue is clad in the traditional toga, gathered into a U-form fold, a popular but impractical style of wearing this garment, a style which was fashionable in the first century AD. The top section of the man's head was added separately. This practice of joining, making statuary out of more than one piece of stone, was common from ancient times, but it required time and skill to produce a seam neatly and unobtrusively. Tradition has it that all these additions were executed by the renowned Italian sculptor Gian Lorenzo Bernini, but it was quite common to attribute repairs to famous artists in order to enhance the worth and consequently the price of a work. Although this attribution is not convincing on stylistic grounds, the absence of the Bernini name tag in no way devalues the excellence of the restorations.[206]

Diana

The repaired head of the moon goddess is crowned with a crescent and she is in the act of plucking an arrow from her quiver. Diana was one of Coke's principal acquisitions; its

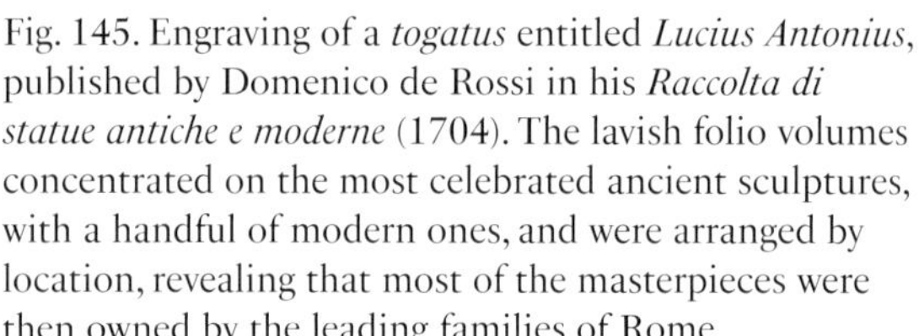

Fig. 145. Engraving of a *togatus* entitled *Lucius Antonius*, published by Domenico de Rossi in his *Raccolta di statue antiche e moderne* (1704). The lavish folio volumes concentrated on the most celebrated ancient sculptures, with a handful of modern ones, and were arranged by location, revealing that most of the masterpieces were then owned by the leading families of Rome.

Fig. 146. Engraving of the statue of Diana, published by Domenico de Rossi in his *Raccolta di statue antiche e moderne* (1704). Paolo Alessandro Maffei believed, as did earlier antiquarians, that, according to Pliny the Elder, Greek statues were nude, whereas Roman works were clothed.

outstanding workmanship is shown by the way that cold stone animates the form under her simple garment. There is a distinction in the treatment of the lower body, with her left half rendered by stiff, vertical pleats, while the right section, following the natural course of the relaxed leg, breaks up the 'column' effect. The circular pedestal with moulded inscription tablet on the straight side is original and indicates that the figure was intended to be viewed as if stepping to her left in pursuit of prey. The upper and lower parts of the body were carved separately, with the seam cleverly concealed by the overfold of the drapery, another example of the method of piecing.

Several myths arose around the purchase of the Diana, notably its export, albeit there is a grain of truth in the legend.[207] There were indeed difficulties in the marble's shipment from Italy, although the tale of the young man's imprisonment and subsequent liberation through the intervention of the Grand Duke of Tuscany is an exaggeration. No doubt this romantic embellishment was circulated as evidence of the determination and derring-do of this young aristocrat hot in pursuit of a priceless treasure. In fact, the proposed shipment of the marble to England did cause a great uproar, for the eighteenth-century connoisseur Alessandro Albani (nephew of the pope and later cardinal) had set his sights on this statue for his collection and appealed to Grand Duke Cosimo III of Tuscany to halt its export. Coke tactfully proposed to return the statue, but Albani, satisfied with this young man's deferential offer and, more importantly, using it as a diplomatic ploy to prevent difficulties in relations between Rome and Britain, refrained from opposing Coke's

Fig. 147. The statue of Diana between Bacchus (left) and Venus (right).

►■◄

Fig. 148. Kent's *trompe l'œil* mural of Thomas Coke's statue of Diana in the King's Staircase at Kensington Palace, c. 1725.

relocation of the work to England. However, this controversial export provoked severe restrictions on later transfers abroad of works of art from Italian states.

Lord Leicester's continuing pride in this statue and his satisfaction in acquiring it is clearly manifested by Andrea Casali's portrait of 1757 (fig. 16). Standing in the Statue Gallery with the Diana in the background, Leicester proudly points to his other valued possession, his coronet. The marble's prestige was further enhanced when William Kent, the prominent all-round artist, included a painted copy of it among figures recreating the court of George I on a wall at the top landing of the King's Grand Staircase at Kensington Palace (fig. 148) as part of his improvements there, completed by 1724.

Jupiter

Another sculpture of note was the statue sold to Coke as Jupiter, chief deity of the Roman state religion, seen here in its present condition (fig. 149) and also as originally restored, holding a scroll and *patera* or plate for a sacrifice and topped with a fine but unrelated head of a bearded deity (fig. 151). The torso itself shows a well-modulated musculature; the groin delineations are neatly rendered and the median line is clearly visible. Nudity with such a body associated the man with ideals of superhuman strength and potency, explicit in representations of gods and heroes. In this case the effect is tempered by the voluminous hip-mantle, a statuary formula of classical Greek inspiration. The drapery is distinguished by its garment pleats, sculpted into dashing displays of *chiaroscuro*. The figure is supported by a palm tree, laden with dates, which is linked to the myth of the rebirth of the immortal phoenix and a symbol of victory. The attribute was never associated with Jupiter and indicates that the body originally belonged to an image of a member of a Roman imperial house.

Initially proud of his purchase, Coke intended to place the sculpture as the centrepiece in the apse of the Marble Hall (fig. 95). Later realising that its position would detract from the impact on the visitor of this magnificent entrance to the house, and that its repairs (notably the unsightly seams of the mended legs) were substandard, he subsequently lost interest in the piece and placed it in a less prominent locale in the vestibule beneath the south portico of the house. In the nineteenth century, the archaeologist A. Michaelis found it hidden behind a giant palm tree in the Victorian conservatory. When the conservatory fell into

Fig. 149. Statue entitled *Jupiter.* The larger than life-size body was once an image of a member of the imperial family, but was restored to accommodate the head of a paternal god before it was purchased by Coke. Further repairs, including to the head, were done in London by the English sculptor Joseph Wilton.

Fig. 150. Initially in the vestibule beneath the southern portico, the figure later resided in the Victorian conservatory. When this building lost its roof after World War II, Jupiter's body was moved to the upper storey of the game larder, which is modelled on the Tower of the Winds in Athens.

disrepair following World War II, the head was mounted separately whilst the body of the figure was removed to the game larder. Unfortunately, this lack of appeal resulted in neglect and the loss of some of the marble's restorations.

The head shows a mature man who exudes a powerful and dignified aura (fig. 151). The small eyes are encased by heavy lids, and the thin eyebrows lead directly into the straight nose with a wide and even bridge. This physiognomy was inspired by works of the famous Greek sculptor Phidias, reflecting the time of the original's creation in the aftermath of the Parthenon, namely the second half of the fifth century BC. The deity has a full head of curly hair, with the forehead hair parted in the centre and flatly brushed to the sides over the low and broad forehead. A large moustache is combed down into the luxuriant wavy beard, cleft in the middle. Exactly which god was actually intended to be represented is unknown; by Roman times a general patriarchal formula was applicable for representations of Jupiter, Mars, Hades, Neptune and Asclepius, god of medicine. Since Rome, an all-inclusive nation, eagerly absorbed other cultures under its rule, the blueprint also suited the fusion of Amon, king of the Egyptian deities, with Jupiter.

Fig. 151. Head of a bearded deity entitled *Jupiter*. In 1954 the sculpture was removed from the body and displayed separately. It is far more exquisitely worked than the body to which it was attached. A. Michaelis believed its artistry was so excellent that the marble merited a cast to be made of it and disseminated for study purposes.

Forming the sculpture collection: the later years

The second stage in the formation of the collection, during which most of the marbles were acquired, occurred some thirty years later, between 1747 and 1754, when Lord Leicester was in the middle of building and furnishing the central body of his house at Holkham, having partly recovered from his lost investment in the South Sea Company. The earl made his purchases through the agency of Matthew Brettingham the younger, son of the executive architect of the building, who was sent to Italy to acquire further sculptures for the adornment of the house. Many marbles were procured from the rather shady antiquarian dealer Belisario Amadei; still more were bought from the leading figure in

Fig. 152. Statue of Neptune. According to a very similar example from Caesarea in Mauretania (modern Cherchell) and now in the National Museum in Algiers, the statue should be restored with a hippocampus (a fish-tailed horse) on its advanced right arm. There are remains of a support which reveal that the trident is a correct repair.

the restoration of antiquities, Bartolomeo Cavaceppi. These additional works exerted a key influence on the design of the house and made the sculpture collection one of its main decorative elements.

Neptune

With Brettingham's assistance, Leicester was very successful in the range and quality of his acquisitions. A statue of the master of the seas, Neptune, holding a trident and standing alongside a menacing dolphin, is an image very rare in antiquity (fig. 152). The brawny torso conveys through its crisp modelling a highly decorative effect, and the ribcage creates a dappled surface. The large dolphin sports about in the water, the curves of its body forming an ornamental helix (fig. 153). The deity has masses of curly hair and a beard which nearly overwhelm the small face. With its tousled coiffure that is illustrative of the unruly seas, the head seems appropriate for the statue.

Juno

A beautiful head of a goddess, named *Juno*, is particularly worthy of attention (fig. 154). its large size argues for its original use as a cult statue, the function of other such heads comparable in being over life-size. The whole of the crown, together with the fillet and back of the head, along with the neck, was originally attached to the 'mask'; this procedure of piecing a head from separate parts has already been exemplified by the head of the *togatus* statue and the bodies of both Diana and Jupiter. This marble head may have topped an acrolith, a composite sculpture with stone extremities but using other materials for the clothed parts

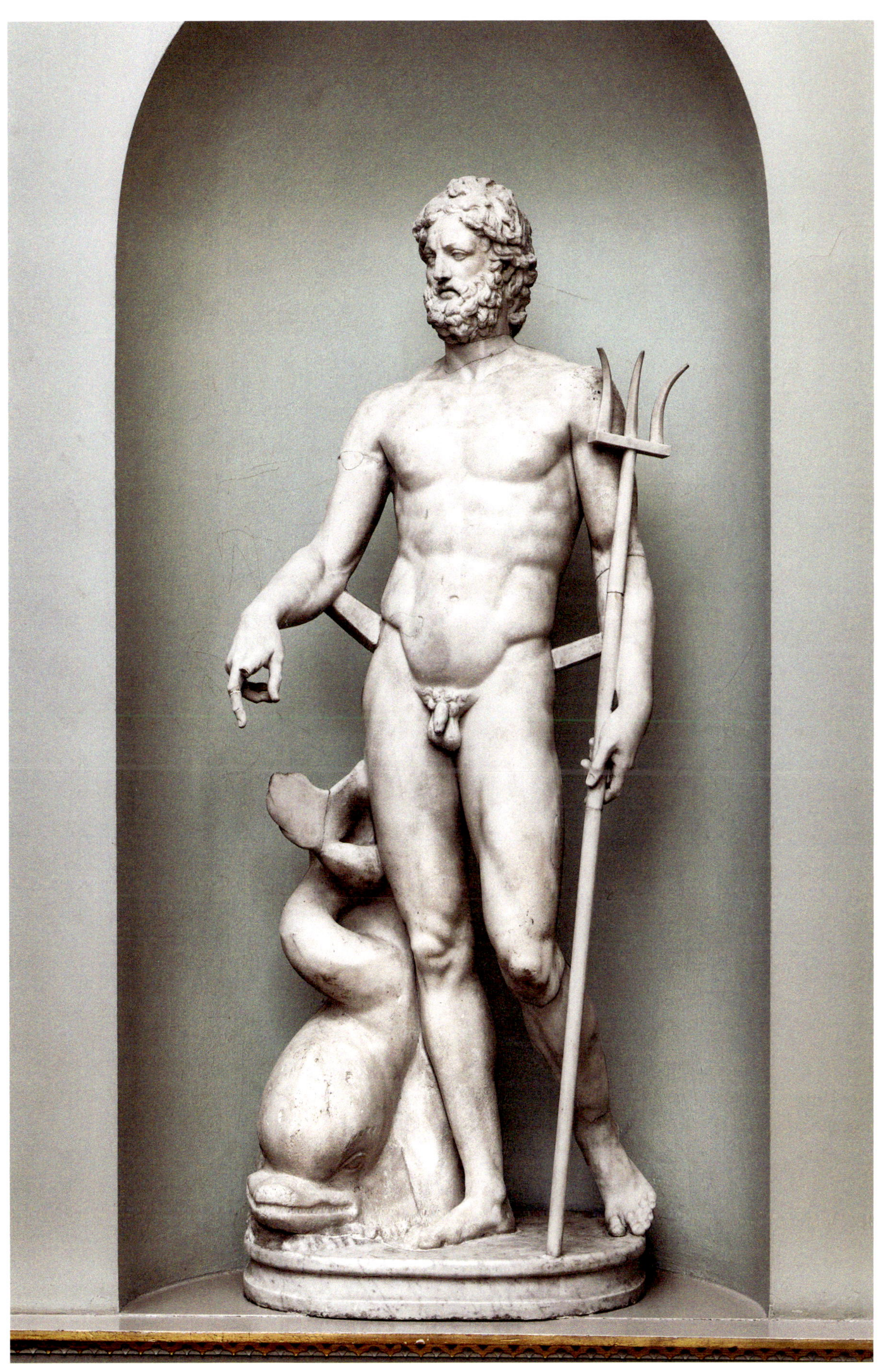

Fig. 153. Detail of Neptune's dolphin. The zigzag-patterned teeth are precisely etched into the stone, endowing the aquatic mammal with a threatening character, eyes and eyebrows aptly carved. The waves are sculpted below the dolphin's mouth and continue on the broken section of the pedestal, showing it to be original to the statue.

of the figure. The head provoked a remarkable controversy some hundred years ago, when Charles Waldstein (known as Sir Charles Walston), a prominent Anglo-American archaeologist, who also competed in the first modern Olympic Games in 1896, attempted to connect it with the decoration of the Parthenon. While this provenance was immediately refuted,[208] the head is in a remarkable state of preservation; this fact, the rarity of such depictions and its superior quality all invest it with considerable importance.

Head of Dea Roma Mounted on a Bust of Rosso Antico

This masterpiece presents the embodiment of Dea Roma, the personification of the city of Rome and more broadly the Roman state (fig. 155). Stunningly idealised yet robust features imprinted on the neutral flesh show a straight broad nose, leading directly into the razor-edged line of the eyebrows and slightly parted full, curving lips. Almond-shaped eyes, a single drill hole marking the tear ducts, are topped with clear-cut upper eyelids; the area just below the bottom lids merges gradually and segues perfectly into the cheeks. The hair is drawn back at the sides over the ears in regular wavy masses and bound into a plait. The pure profile and the refined contrast between the smooth flesh and the corrugated tresses signal very accomplished workmanship. Atop the helmet are the remains of the *lupa romana*, or she-wolf, and twins. The myth makes reference to the founding of Rome, an appropriate attribute for the goddess of the city.[209] *Rosso antico* or *marmor Taenarium* was widely employed for sculptures in antiquity in order to achieve a visual richness of ruby red.[210] The bust has been fashioned into an aegis, decorated with a scale pattern and a gor-

Fig. 154. Head of a goddess entitled *Juno.* Michaelis rightly praised this beautiful head as one of Brettingham's prime purchases. Its excellence later caused Sir Charles Walston to attempt to connect it with the missing head of Aphrodite from the eastern pediment of the Parthenon. Although it is not now thought to be a product of Phidias or his workshop, present verdict holds it to be a most admirable work of Roman art.

Fig. 155. Although Dea Roma appeared in Greek art, on Roman coinage and in the company of emperors on state reliefs, it was not until Hadrian's reign that the goddess was worshipped in the metropolis. In AD 135, the emperor dedicated a temple to Roma Æterna on the Velia Hill, which shows that by mid-second century the deity had evolved into an essential feature of imperial ideology.

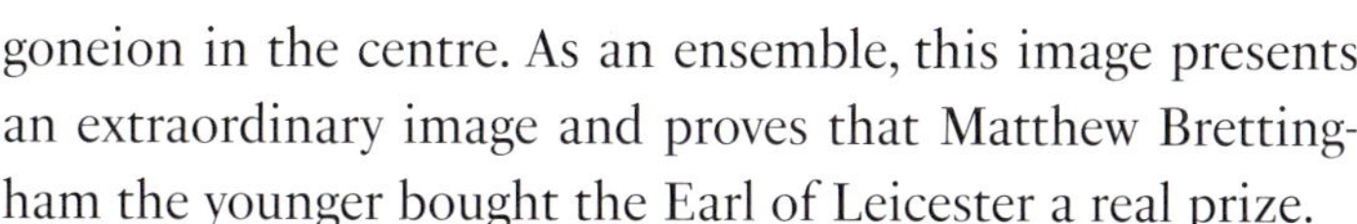

goneion in the centre. As an ensemble, this image presents an extraordinary image and proves that Matthew Brettingham the younger bought the Earl of Leicester a real prize.

Thucydides

Excellent execution, powerful characterisation and splendid condition make the portrait of Thucydides the jewel in the crown of Holkham (fig. 156). The Athenian Thucydides (460–400 BC), the greatest of all ancient Greek historians, is shown here as a man in late middle age with a strong-boned, squarish face and razor-sharp cheekbones. His massive head has a high and wide forehead with deep, receding temples, anticipating the bald patch at the crown. At the root of the broad-bridged nose, wrinkles cause the brow to contract. The bony structures of the brows are superbly carved and topped with pencil-thin eyebrows, while prominent pouches appear beneath the small, heavy-lidded eyes. The bust, draped with a cloak on his left shoulder, is original and Thucydides's left eye is slightly larger than the right, corroborating the fact that his head is turned slightly to his right. The mouth is small. The short-cropped hair is sculpted into sickle-shaped locks and the sideburns and moustache grow

Fig. 156. Portrait of Thucydides entitled *Metrodorus*. There is a plaster cast of the Holkham bust in the Pushkin Museum, Moscow. His *History of the Peloponnesian War* gives us his biography. He fought in the war, contracted the plague and was exiled by the Athenian democracy. Little mention of him is made in fourth-century BC literature. Put simply, Thucydides became unpopular because he was the recorder of an unpopular civil war.

Fig. 157. Portrait of Plato entitled *Lysias*. The philosopher is remembered for many things, including several famous quotes that still ring true today: 'Truth is the beginning of every good to the gods, and every good to man' and 'The first and greatest victory is to conquer yourself; to be conquered by yourself is of all things most shameful and vile'.

down into the compact beard. Thucydides was a contemporary witness to, and active participant in, the struggle between Athens and Sparta. His *History of the Peloponnesian War* was the first recorded political and moral analysis of a nation's war policies, and the work created the idea of recording historical events through eyewitness accounts from the time, thus beginning the concept of contemporary history. Even in the nineteenth century, nodules of soil in which the bust had lain were still embedded in the back of the hair.

Plato

A lively portrayal presents the ancient perception of Plato (fig. 157). The great philosopher is depicted as a mature man with long, full beard and extensive, flowing moustache; his face is riddled with wrinkles. The dome of his head is capped with short, thick curly locks, with longer locks falling onto the brow and swept in a left-to-right movement. Here, his left eye is larger than the right, revealing that originally the Holkham head slightly twisted to its right. In ancient Greek times, heads of philosophers, historians and playwrights commonly topped herms (heads facing in a strictly

Fig. 158. Statue of Marsyas entitled *Faunus*. He wears a crown of stone pine (*Pinus pinea*); according to Apollodorus of Athens, this was the genus of tree on which he was skinned. Antonio Canova, the eighteenth-century Italian sculptor who refused to restore the Elgin marbles, pronounced this Faunus to be 'the finest statue which ever made its escape out of Italy'.

frontal pose and attached to square, lower sections, as exemplified in this post-antique repair). Some scholars posit the attractive idea that the original work, from which this formula is one of numerous Roman quotations (the large number of replicas reveals its importance), was located in his Academy in Athens, ensuring a positive and concrete link between Plato and his school of thought.[211] It may well have been paired with his equally famous teacher Socrates, founder of Western philosophy and among the first moral philosophers of the ethical tradition, as well as with later directors of the school.

Marsyas

Some marbles, amongst them the stunning statue of Marsyas (figs. 158 to 161), came from the renowned collection of Cardinal Alessandro Albani, it being purchased in the state it was found: 'Encrusted over with Tatar of the Earth'.[212] The statue's worth was recognised instantly on its arrival in England, when the renowned and knowledgeable collector Charles Townley, one of the founders of the British Museum, pronounced it 'incomparably the finest male figure that has ever come into this country'.[213] The sculptor's fresh and spirited approach and its excellent state of preservation completely justify Townley's pronouncement. Once again, Leicester got the better of Albani. Marsyas was a woodland creature, half-man, half-goat, and in ancient times was generally referred to as either a *silenos*, who is usually older, or a satyr, who is a youth. The being supports himself on the trunk of a tree, holds a shepherd's crook and sports a pine wreath. His physique is powerfully muscular and the brute's face is a true work of art. The only signs of his true

Fig. 159. The Holkham Marsyas has no tail, and his goat ears are covered by his hair. Only by presenting the wild creature without undue physiognomical exaggeration, therefore as nearly human, could the look of insolence and doubt be so masterfully mingled.

Fig. 160. Detail of the panther skin on Marsyas's back. The pelt is of special interest for its marvellous attention to detail; the front edges have fur clusters, and notches at the back indicate cuts in the skin. The tufted tail end is delicately carved on the support.

character are his goat ears, mostly hidden in his hair, large bristly beard and snubbed nose.

The beast had the hubris to challenge the sun god Apollo to a musical contest. Having won, the deity decreed the insolent creature be flayed alive. Only by viewing the statue in the round can the outcome of the competition be fully grasped, for at its back is an exquisitely carved mask-like panther skin with closed eyes that eerily forebodes Marsyas's fate (fig. 160). The face shows a dignified and thoughtful mien, uncharacteristic of his boorish nature, and in general he seems to be regretting his rash act, becoming aware of his grim destiny (fig. 159).

Narcissus/Meleager

Other outstanding marbles include an important statue of Narcissus, a youth obsessed by his looks, who was transformed by Cavaceppi into the hunter Meleager by the addition of a tree stump support topped with a boar's head, on which the figure heavily leans his arm (fig. 162). The upper part of his head from above his chin has been broken off, but it belongs to the statue; it has suffered less interference by the restorer than the rest of the figure. His short-clipped coiffure is parted into a bracket stylisation at its central parting, and a loose curl is combed before each ear. Nudity equalled heroic status, as with the hip-mantle statue,

Fig. 161. The statue of Marsyas on a rotatable base between Meleager (left) and Neptune (right).

►■◄

Fig. 162. Statue of Meleager. The statue formula is usually assigned to the end of the fifth century BC within the Argive school of the sculptor Polycleitus. Romans had an insatiable demand for Polycleitan replicas and adaptations. The sleek, well-padded forms, enlarged pectoral expanse and swollen nipples are typical of late Hadrianic tastes, and comparisons of the treatment of the hair with portraits of the Emperor Hadrian (AD 117–138) bear out the proposed dating.

Fig. 163. Statue of Venus. According to Brettingham, Cavaceppi restored the statue. The sculptor added the left hand with the vase, an attribute in keeping with the eighteenth-century interpretation of the deity's action as one of disrobing prior to bathing. The rusticated top of the circular pedestal is atypical of ancient workmanship and may be an embellishment by Cavaceppi, like the inverted nipples.

elevating the figure into the realm of the gods; this, together with its melancholic aura, suggests that the statue may have been originally designed for a Greek funerary monument. In Roman times it would have made an appealing garden sculpture.

Venus

A strapping figure of Venus, goddess of love (fig. 163), is remarkable for its superior condition: its head is unbroken from the body. The deity wears a full-length, ungirded tunic, which is fastened on her right shoulder, but has slipped off the other shoulder, baring her breast. Only a few pleats articulate the transparent drapery, showing that the statue is not naked. This 'wet' look suggestively reveals rather than hides the goddess's proverbial charms. She holds up the tip of her cloak, which hangs over her left forearm and originally proffered an apple in her left hand. The long, heavy mantle functions as a solid foil for the diaphanous tunic and it curtains off the figure behind and on either side with the fall of folds. Its present placement in a niche creates a second frame, and this containment concentrates all attention on two seemingly trivial actions. However, the apple and display of Venus's breast are bald statements of fecundity, for she was the goddess of motherhood and care of the young.

Bacchus/Juno

The collection also includes a head of Bacchus, labelled as Juno, depicting the handsome, effeminate god with an abundant and carefully dressed coiffure (fig. 164). The forehead hair is brushed horizontally to either side of the parting and a large section is piled high over the centre of the crown,

Fig. 164. Head of Bacchus entitled *Juno*. The larger than life-size bust shows a distinctly un-antique arrangement of the garments: the buttoned sleeve of the tunic exposes the left breast and over it is a mantle, fastened by two buttons at the right shoulder and bound at the bottom edge by a swathe of drapery.

Fig. 165. Portrait bust of Gordian III. The head is connected to a bust, draped in a *toga contabulata*, a form of dress that was fashionable in the middle of the third century AD, with the section of cloth covering the entire breadth of the chest. The restorer was clearly wide awake on archaeological matters, because he connected the portrait with a chronologically compatible bust type.

dressed into a bundle of curls and bound round the forehead by a ribbon; behind, the hair is formed into a coil at the neck. The feminine image and the coiffure caused the restorer to add a bust of a female with the garment exposing the left breast. The Holkham image personifies the peaceful aspect of the god Bacchus, who was the inventor of viticulture or the tamer of the vine.

Gordianus

A portrait formula, known in numerous copies, was created to celebrate the elevation of Gordianus III to the *imperium* at the tender age of thirteen (fig. 165). His closely cropped hair follows the prevailing military fashion of the first half of the third century AD. The emperor's brow is contracted by two vertical creases above the nose, giving the face a concerned expression. This artistic convention of a contracted brow conveys the *cura* or care that the ruler declared for his subjects and, together with the meditative mien and heavy, lower lids, lends an air of authority and experience to the youthful face – attributes which were meant to reassure the people of his ability to rule, despite his minority. This propaganda tool proved ultimately futile because a member of the élite Roman army overthrew him by appealing to the soldiers, who wanted a man and not a boy as their leader.

Sulla

Among the private portraits is a truly exceptional image of a man, which through its wealth of personal detail and remarkable animation strikes an amazingly individual note that lifts the character well out of the often mundane and mediocre realm of private Roman portraiture (fig. 166). Strikingly, the marble has endured little post-antique interference, having only been polished; also unusual is its preserved ancient bust, albeit heavily mended. The hair is clipped short and the wrinkled brow is contracted at its bridge; a masterfully sculpted eye area presents the sitter with small intense eyes that almost rest on the upper eyelids. Especially remarkable are the firmly pursed, thin lips with a pronounced overbite. The lively turn of the head to his left increases the sense of immediacy and energy. The representation exudes such an air of both brutality and intelligence that we can well understand the reasoning behind its title of *Sulla*, the cruel Roman dictator, who led a military coup against the Republic in order to attain political power through force and purge his opponents.

Fig. 166. Portrait of a man entitled *Sulla*. The bust's fame is attested by an eighteenth-century replica that had been purchased in Rome from the Spanish Cardinal Despuig y Dameto's collection on the island of Majorca. There is also a cast of this head in the National Gallery of Scotland in Edinburgh from the restorer Carlo Albacini's collection of casts of Graeco-Roman portraits. Albacini made many casts from works he restored.

Fig. 167. Portrait of a young lady entitled *Salonina*. According to Brettingham, the marble was found during dredging of the port of Neptuno, a village in Latium (Lazio), near the Tyrrhenian Sea. A replica of this head exists at Petworth House; according to Charles Townley, it was from the collection of the eighteenth-century English antiquary and banker Lyde Browne, who had amassed a vast collection of ancient marbles.

Salonina

A very attractive portrayal, entitled *Salonina* (wife of Emperor Gallienus), presents us with a charming young matron who demurely tilts her head to her left, gazing upwards (fig. 167). Distinctly individualised features include a small, curvaceous mouth, radiating innocence and sweetness from its upturned corners. The forceful chin is emphasised by the deep depression below the lower lip; the nose is slightly hooked. The eyes are large and the eyebrows show separately etched hairs. The centrally parted hair is combed into waves at either side behind her ears, then drawn back, falling on the neck, bound into braids and twisted into a large, flat chignon. The high quality of the marble is revealed in the sculpting of the coiffure: each strand being lightly scored by regular, undulating lines. Although it has been reworked, one can still discern the original, soft modelling of the skin and the fleshy mouth with its blurred contours.

LORD LEICESTER'S ARRANGEMENT OF THE SCULPTURES

In his *Plans of Holkham*, Matthew Brettingham the younger has left detailed descriptions of the rooms from the third quarter of the eighteenth century, which indicate that the placement of the sculptures has remained virtually unchanged for more than two centuries. This fact makes the Holkham collection an incomparable treasure. Apart from the Marble Hall, it was principally the rooms in the western half of the main block, the State Dining Room and the Statue Gallery, consisting of a central room and two adjacent, octagonal Tribunes, that were set aside for the display of the sculpture collection.

A novel and important aspect of the Holkham collection of antiquities lies in Lord Leicester's imaginative placing of his sculptural exhibits and their integration with other works of art, paintings and furniture. Behind every arrangement one can discern his fertile imagination and marvellous sense of humour, but also his erudition. The earl's intention of suggesting multiple meanings by the disposition of his sculptures required a critical mind, historically informed, accustomed to 'reading' artworks and trained in literary judgement. He was fully aware of the power of sculpture to add a distinctive meaning and identity to a setting, and he focused on the rôle that statuary could play in making arcane associations, as well as iconographical connections and contrasts, amply demonstrating the idea of 'wit', that quality of intellect so highly valued in eighteenth-century England.

From Brettingham's correspondence with Leicester we can get a sense of the evolving concept for the exhibition of the marbles. A letter of 3 June 1753 reveals that the earl first intended to place a statue of himself in the central niche of the Statue Gallery. However, he had second thoughts about such a self-aggrandising gesture and so he abandoned the project; he then considered that his cherished Diana would better suit this place of honour, but again he thought better of it. In correspondence of 10 July 1755, he was toying with the idea of installing the Marsyas and his statue of Emperor Septimius Severus in the North Tribune; there was also discussion of purchasing additional statues for the niches of the opposite room, but ultimately the unstable political

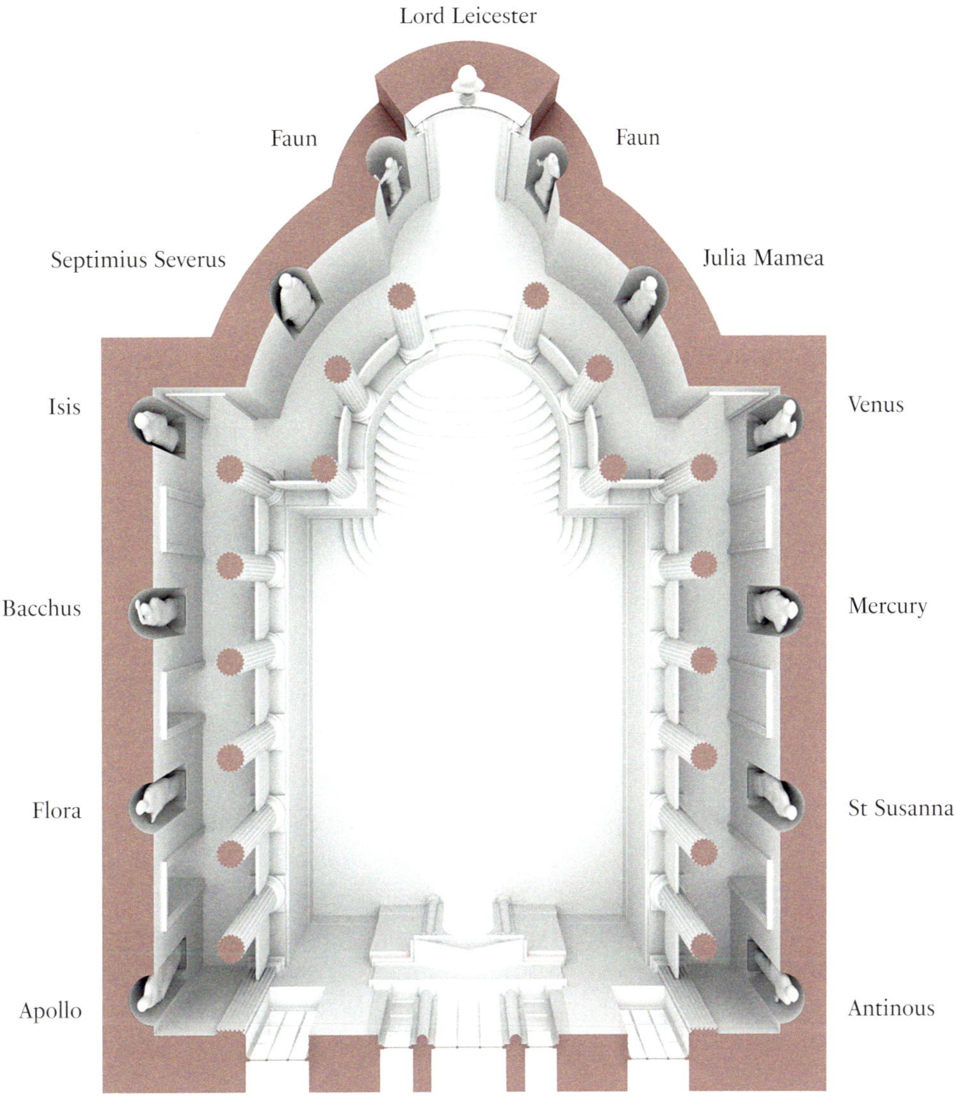

Fig. 168. An overview of the arrangement of sculptures in the Marble Hall.

situation in Europe put further statues out of reach, rendering this plan untenable, so books were installed in lieu of marbles.

In planning the arrangement of the ancient works of art, Leicester was naturally restricted by the contents of his collection, whose purchase had been determined by various factors, but he nevertheless succeeded in creating definite iconographical schemes, and a large selection of casts and marble copies allowed him more latitude in establishing such arrangements. The following description of the rooms containing sculptures, therefore, attempts to follow the way the earl wanted his sculptures specifically and his house generally to be understood, emphasising the layout and context of the works of art, which are crucial to grasping his entire conception behind his building.

THE MARBLE HALL

The sumptuous Marble Hall is the first sight of Holkham Hall's interior (fig. 3 and pls. 8 to 11), making the initial impression on the spectator even more spectacular by the contrast of the passage from the austere exterior with its unprepossessing entrance (the porch is a nineteenth-century addition) into the splendour of the Hall, enhanced by the warm hues of the purple and ivory variegated Derbyshire alabaster of the columns and podium, the latter set off by borders of black marble. Its innovative overall design is loosely based on the Temple of Venus and Roma in the Roman Forum, and other details are quotations from ancient prototypes. The classical spirit of the Hall is perfectly preserved and even strengthened by the statuary.

In the upper ambulatory, twelve niches were provided for statues; only a few of these are antique marbles, the others being plaster casts (fig. 168). Casts, at that time considered legitimate replacements for unobtainable classical originals, had a neutral character, which was enough to convey the essential qualities of a famed work of art. Effect and not authenticity was the determining factor in this case, particularly as the works were partly obscured by the screen of columns. Starting from the apse, along the western wall are arranged plaster replicas of the Callipygian Venus (also known as Venus des Belles Fesses), Mercury (originally a satyr, restored as Mercury), St Susanna (carved by the seventeenth-century Flemish sculptor François Duquesnoy) and Antinous (the handsome, male paramour of Emperor Hadrian; the so-called Capitoline Antinous but actually Mercury), while along the eastern flank (pl. 11) the series of plaster casts begins with Isis, then (a satyr restored as) Bacchus, (a draped female restored as) Flora and finally (a torso restored as) Apollo.[214] The works function in a sharply programmatic way, Lord Leicester having set up a series of connections and contrasts between the figures on either side of the Hall. In the sequence along the walls they alternate in terms of sex, but match the figures on the opposite flank; between the partners there is also a contrast in the poses by the interchange of the engaged or standing leg. Moreover, all the females are clothed and the males are nude.

In a flagrantly lewd pose, the half-dressed Venus confronts Isis, Egyptian goddess of healing and magic, who in contrast stands chastely, fully clad, holding her sacred attributes – a model of propriety. Mercury is placed opposite Bacchus, sporting with a panther. While the latter deity represented the overflowing and intoxicating power of nature, Mercury had more responsibilities assigned to him than any other deity; he was the god of wrestlers, thieves, shopkeepers and tradesmen, literature and eloquence, as well as the messenger of the gods and guider of souls. Although both deities are young men, Mercury, burdened with so many duties, is the very image of sobriety.

The virtuous St Susanna, who chose martyrdom over marriage, stands in stark contrast to Flora, a courtesan who left her ill-gotten gains to the Roman people for the purpose of establishing a festival in her honour, the *Floralia*; extravagant and lascivious, it included games in which courtesans participated. Whereas Flora presided over all that bloomed, the Christian martyr was, inevitably, barren. Likewise, the antithesis between mortal and immortal beauty is the *raison d'être* for the opposition of the statues of Antinous and Apollo. Lord Leicester must have derived some glee from setting a virginal Christian saint between pagan male nudes and injecting a touch of contemporary Christianity into a pantheon of heathens.

Four statues were placed in the apse on either side of the entrance to the Saloon, in the area most visible to the spectator ascending the grand staircase. These include the images of Emperor Septimius Severus and Empress Julia Mamaea – an especially good match, since they represent the beginning and the end of an historical era. Septimius had founded the Severan dynasty, but with the assassination of Mamaea and her son, Alexander Severus, the ruling house ended. The works are also quite similar in size by virtue of their heavy Roman garb, albeit there is a difference in sex and orientation in pose.

Fig. 169. The inscription above the entrance door to the Marble Hall naming Lord Leicester as the creator of Holkham was placed there by his widow.

Two fauns are arranged in the apse; fauns are basically the latinised equivalent of the silens or satyrs of Greek mythology and like their predecessors are also half-human, half-goat and creatures of the countryside. Here, the earl established a distinct dichotomy between the *dignitas* of the rulers of the Roman Empire and the naked, impish creatures of legend. Connected with the worship of Bacchus and fond only of wine and sensual pleasures, they dwelt in forests and fields and represented the vibrant powers of nature. By their insertion into the apse they bring the outside world inside, another theme of the house. They reflect, too, the way the materials and forms of exterior architecture were applied to the Marble Hall's interior.

In the broken pediment above the apse is a plaster cast of Louis-François Roubiliac's portrait of the Earl of Leicester (fig. 20). Here, the owner claims to reign over flora and fauna, symbolised by the fauns, and the civilised world, embodied by the monarchs. The bust most importantly functions as an author portrait for, directly opposite, a plaque above the entrance to the house declares (fig. 169):

THIS SEAT, on an open barren Estate,
Was planned, planted, built, decorated,
And inhabited the middle of the XVIIIth Century
By THO.^{s} COKE EARL of LEICESTER

This proclamation is clearly linked with Leicester's very own representation, for whatever the date of the portrait's installation, it leaves absolutely no doubt as to the authorship of the entire construction: the earl did indeed transform a 'barren estate' by taming primordial nature – rendering the countryside arable and setting in his estate a country house decorated according to his own, very specific tastes.

THE SALOON

From the Marble Hall, the visitor proceeds up the broad staircase to the Saloon. As the main reception room of the house and the centre of the great southern enfilade of rooms, the Saloon is a superb manifestation of Leicester's classical ambitions in several forms of decoration: furniture, paintings, carved chimney tablets and finally the addition of a single classical marble, entitled *Juno* (fig. 164). The earl's use of opposing elements, incorporated in the various pairings of the décor, demonstrates how contrasts can balance one another, resulting in a harmonious universe over which Juno, goddess of the cosmos, presides. Centred in the broken pediment over the main door leading from the Marble Hall and back-to-back with the above-mentioned portrait of the Earl of Leicester, the sculpture establishes a direct association between the 'Queen of the Heavens' and the 'King of the Earth', made manifest in his constructing and ornamenting of Holkham Hall, as well as his establishing bucolic and fertile grounds.

THE STATE DINING ROOM

From the Marble Hall via the State Dining Room to the southern octagon of the Statue Gallery, the overall decoration of the western half of the main block – in marked contrast to the opulent baroque decoration of the rooms on the eastern side – is rigorously Roman in character (fig. 126). Leicester's conscious decision to make a clear distinction between this part of the house and the rest must have been

Fig. 170. Plaque of *The Sow and Her Pigs* in the western fireplace of the State Dining Room. The sow's nose has been broken off since the eighteenth century.

Fig. 172. Plaque of *The Bear and Bee-hives* in the eastern fireplace of the State Dining Room.

Fig. 171. The print from which the relief of *The Sow and Her Pigs* was copied.

Fig. 173. The print from which the relief of *The Bear and Bee-hives* was copied.

intended to emphasise the differences in the precious contents of the rooms, for the centrepiece of the complex was the antiquities collection in the Statue Gallery. This western section of the house served not only as a demonstration of the earl's profound classical learning, but more importantly as a statement of his achievements: his creation as earl, his estate, his legacy.

Dominating the south wall of the State Dining Room are portraits of Emperor Marcus Aurelius and Prince Geta (son of Septimius Severus), placed on either side of the apse (pl. 18). Classical literature holds the key for this pairing, because according to ancient sources, Geta (unlike his older brother, Emperor Caracalla, whose savage passions branded his name with infamy) took a delight in the liberal arts and in the society of learned men and was generally regarded as being upright and honourable, much like his predecessor Marcus, whose name he also bore. Above the two fireplaces, two niches frame the oversized images of Emperor Lucius Verus and Juno (pls. 18 and 19 and fig. 154), creating a distinction between the human and divine realms, for the ruler was the *paterfamilias* of the Roman people and supreme sovereign, whilst the other was the mother of the gods and therefore the foremost female deity. The carved mantelpieces depict two Aesopian Fables (figs. 170 to 173): that of the sow with her litter and the wolf, the other of the bear and the beehive. The room is resplendent with images of earthly and heavenly greatness, and Lord Leicester's insertion of the two small reliefs ingeniously illustrates how the weak could frustrate the designs of the powerful.

THE STATUE GALLERY

The centrepiece of the sculptural collection is the Statue Gallery with its sequence of three rooms: the long middle one and the two octagonal Tribunes (pls. 20 to 27), the latter fitted with four niches each. In the North Tribune, statues adorn the niches, but in the other Tribune, bookcases were installed in place of statuary. In both Tribunes, busts are placed in the broken pediments above the doorways.

The cream of the collection was reserved for display in the central room of the Gallery with its two apsed ends (fig. 73 and pls. 21 to 25). For the first time in England, a gallery was exclusively reserved for the exhibition of sculptures. Lord Leicester's decision to exhibit his marbles without the distraction of other works of art was based on the simple fact that he was the first Englishman in the eighteenth century to have acquired so many important classical sculptures that reflected the prestige and taste of their owner. But the earl went far beyond this general concept by inviting admiration for the intrinsic, aesthetic merit of the works without the distraction of other works of art. This presentation of so many quality marbles in so vast an unembellished space set a standard never truly equalled in the British Isles or anywhere else.

The size and layout of the Gallery set a precedent for Lansdowne House, the London home of another great sculpture collection. It is a curious coincidence that Lansdowne House, as we have seen in Chapter 3, was based on an architectural design developed by Lord Leicester in collaboration with Matthew Brettingham. Leicester could not have foreseen that the house in Berkeley Square he was planning as his town residence was to become home to another man's great sculpture collection.

The choicest statues of divinities and heroes are displayed in two series of three niches flanking either side of the chimney along the eastern wall of the central room with the outer two recesses being smaller than the central niches. Fig. 174 shows the positions of the marbles in the central room. Lord Leicester's overriding consideration with regard to his sculptural displays was visual compatibility, which basically meant similar sizes and erect poses, and understandably the display of classical art within the main room essentially depended on their being considered canonical antiquities, which every person of taste could admire. Yet he went far beyond a bland aesthetic display

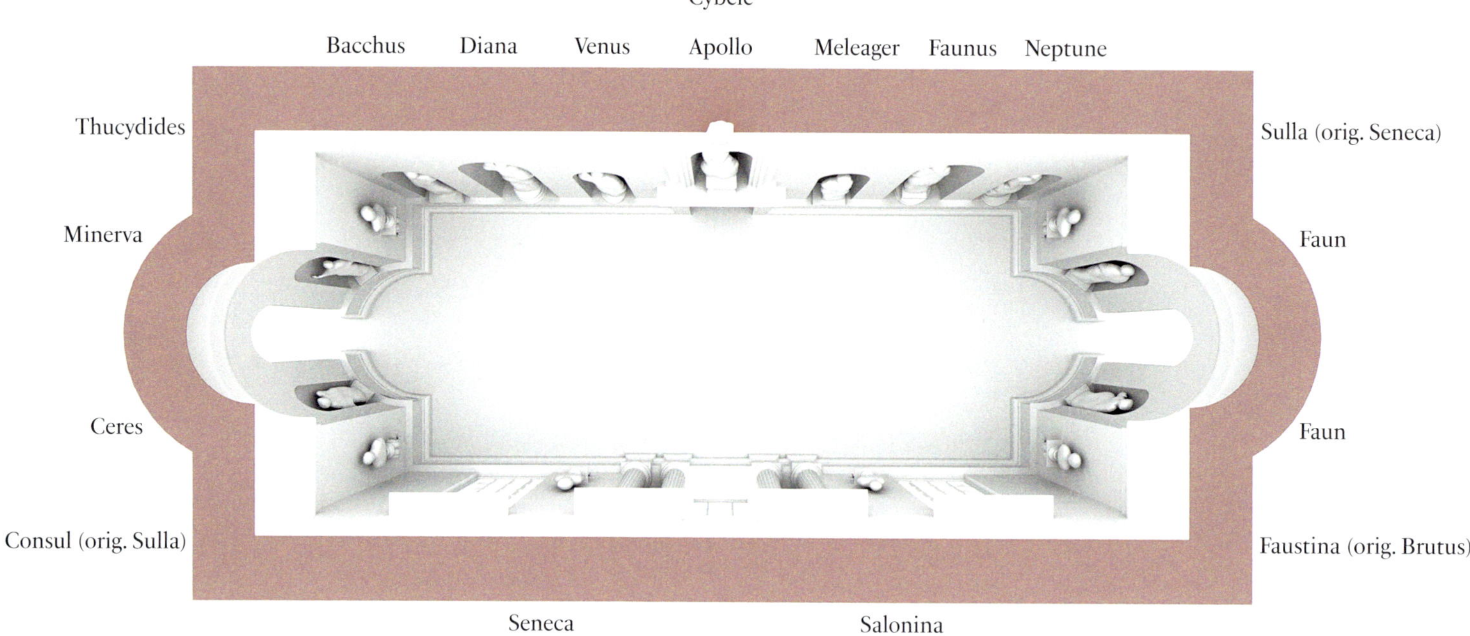

Fig. 174. An overview of the arrangement of sculptures in the Gallery.

characteristic of his time by establishing in their disposition an ingenious programme. All the marbles along the wall, as well as those of the apsed ends, have strong associations with nature and nurture and they function as an ensemble to create an idyllic landscape and thereby celebrate rural beauties and joys. Once again the earl brought the outside world inside, but in this room it is the dominant theme.

Here, as in the Marble Hall, all the males are nude and the females clothed. Leading from the South Tribune into the main room, the two alcove niches contain a pair of fauns, which embody the essence of fertility, growth and abundance of the natural world. Within the principal area are Neptune (fig. 152) and Meleager (fig. 162), who flank Marsyas (figs. 158 to 160). In order to fit into the room's themes of fertility and the countryside, the beast easily assumed the rôle of Faunus, a nature god in Roman mythology who, like Marsyas, was half-human and half-goat. Apollo presides in the niche over the chimneypiece, with the head of Cybele positioned in the broken pediment above (pl. 25). Continuing along the east wall, Venus and Bacchus flank Diana (fig. 147), with Minerva and Ceres standing in the niches of the northern alcove. Here, all the marbles work as an ensemble to create a bucolic setting, echoing the pastoral life beautifully evoked in Virgil's *Eclogues*.

Diana was worshipped as a birth goddess and a bringer of fertility to man and beast alike, as well as the bringer of health to their newly born offspring, but as goddess of the hunt her realm was in the uncultivated forests, where such wild beasts as Faunus (the central marble in the other half of the east wall) roamed, and specifically in Arcadia, where he was the region's own divinity. Faunus's chief preoccupation was to safeguard the fertility of fields and flocks, and he was also a prominent member of Bacchus's entourage. The huntsman Meleager naturally stalked the countryside, whereas Bacchus was the god of fruitfulness and vegetation, specifically the vine, symbolising the sap or lifeblood element in nature. Neptune was the sovereign of the seas, necessary for nature's growth and sustenance, and water-borne Venus, too, was the goddess of fertility through her blatant sexuality as well as her association with dew or moisture, needed for both flora and fauna to flourish. Apollo, as the embodiment of the sun vital to nature's abundance, is consequently positioned above, beaming over Arcadia, and the head entitled Cybele or 'Mother of the Gods', as the protective force at work in nature, naturally reigns over the entire universe.

The theme of nature and its procreative powers draws the two apses together and thematically ties in with the other statues, but here there is an important twist: the fauns of the southern alcove, revered for their connection to rustic landscapes, play a vital rôle in safeguarding forests and fields. As spirits of fruitfulness, they embody the essence of fertility and abundance in the natural world and create a sylvan grove in the southern corner of the room. In the northern apse the reference is to nature tamed, a combination of fertility and utility, made possible through cultivation. Corn was believed to be the gift of Ceres, who was also the goddess of the harvest and in general the inventor of agriculture. Minerva was revered by the ancients for her discovery of the olive and its oil, which she presented as a gift to the Athenians, together with her instructions on methods of cultivating it.

The subject of the harnessing of nature's reproductive function is further underscored in the main room. Minerva is set beside Bacchus, portrayed with a cup and drinking vessel; he taught mankind how to cultivate the vine, invented the winepress and also advised on the means of procuring honey. Venus was the goddess of the gardens and Faunus, a woodland deity of the field and flocks, watched over shepherds, herdsmen and their charges; Apollo was also the protector of flocks and cattle from wolves. Diana with the crescent on her head is the personification of the moon, which in conjunction with the sun regulated matters of planting and harvesting, and Neptune was closely associated with horses (he was called 'Hippios' or Lord of Horses). In its general message, then, the Statue Gallery provides an abridged edition of Virgil's *Georgics*, an agrarian treatise dealing with the tillage of crops, the growing of fruit trees, especially the vine, husbandry and beekeeping.

Into the theme of pastoral delights and the fructifying powers of nature that pervade the room, the earl introduced a wealth of connections and contrasts between the gods and other mythological beings. As the moon goddess, Diana finds her natural counterpart in Venus, the embodiment of the morning and evening stars, and also in Apollo, the sun. Faunus was a wanton and voluptuous creature, very fond of nymphs, whereas Diana was regarded as chaste, though according to ancient literature in her rôle as moon goddess she had a relationship with this rustic beast. Apollo symbolises the male sun and Cybele the female earth. Cybele's position recalls and contrasts with that of Juno in the Saloon and of Leicester in the Marble Hall, for Cybele was the mistress of the cosmos, Juno the queen of the gods and the earl was the king of the earth, after having subdued nature and created a house and grounds evocative of Arcadia.

Four portraits were originally set on consoles on either side of the two apses (the busts along the western wall were later additions). These images from historical reality portray philosophers and politicians haunting the groves of Arcadia and demonstrate the harmonious relations between the imagined ideal life (both philosophy and politics were noble pursuits) and the rhythms of the natural world. They also allude to the application of human knowledge in channelling nature's forces to create bountiful rural bliss. In the Statue Gallery we therefore see a perfect marriage of Virgil's *Georgics* and Book XVIII of Pliny the Elder's *Natural History*, treatises which deal with the improvement of the countryside – exactly as Lord Leicester had transformed the barren lands around Holkham Hall into a productive agrarian estate.

Into the midst of this idyllic setting the earl introduced a dramatic episode, for Diana's motion of plucking an arrow from her quiver is aimed across the space towards Meleager, whose death, according to classical mythology, was a result of the goddess's displeasure. Oeneus, the king of Calydon, had failed to sacrifice to Diana, and in revenge the goddess sent a wild boar to ravage the countryside. The hero, Meleager, and his followers killed the beast, an act symbolised by the creature's head, on which the hero rests his hand.

When Meleager was a boy, the Fates had appeared to his mother, Althaea, foretelling his death as soon as a log burning on the hearth had been consumed by the fire. This event is embodied in the niche above by Apollo, the deity of prophecy, leaning on the tripod entwined with a snake, symbolic of the Delphic oracle. When Althaea heard this news, she extinguished the firebrand and concealed it, but after Meleager killed her brothers in the dispute over the boar's head, she threw the piece of wood onto her brothers' funeral pyre (represented here by the fireplace) and her son then died. The injection of the Meleager episode, a *memento mori*, into an atmosphere brimming with nature's munificence adds an elegiac tone to the ensemble – an impression, however, that is softened by the evocation of nature's cyclical renewal.

INSIDE versus OUTSIDE

The western wall of the main room was left bare save for the windows framed by white damask curtains (pl. 23). This spartan décor thereby focused interest on the outside world by offering undistracted vistas. An account describes the Gallery as 'painted a dead white with ornaments of gilding'.[215] Both the ancient writers Vitruvius and Pliny the Elder discussed the custom of painting walls of Roman villas with diverse renderings of nature and country life, and Italian Renaissance and baroque villas and palaces also employed landscape paintings as extensions or representations of the external gardens, which were important elements of a domicile's surroundings.[216] The same scheme of bringing the outside inside is best seen in the dialogue between the paintings in the Landscape Room and the parkland that can be seen from there through another great Venetian window (pl. 40). The principle of breaking down the barrier between indoors and outdoors is meant to make your interior feel open and green, as if you are outside but have harnessed the elements of nature. By integrating natural features into indoor spaces, it fosters a deep connection between humans and nature.

At Holkham Hall, Leicester continues this tradition of nature tamed, and from this vantage point the spectator looks out onto the idyllic image of the natural world by way of a walled landscape park and lake in the immediate vicinity, and across the lake to the stables and the tended fields in the distance.[217] The outside world is mirrored in and simultaneously contrasts with the interior and its supernatural representation of nature, its fertility and its cultivation by mankind, in this case not, as was customary, by pictorial language but by sculptural means.

For the first and only time, a private collection of ancient marbles of incomparable workmanship and preservation was left, largely by sheer chance, in situ, illustrating the earl's learned meanings with the presentations of his marbles. It is unparalleled in Great Britain or indeed anywhere else.

This extraordinarily original display still allows us to appreciate the amazing imagination and meticulous effort that the Earl of Leicester applied to his sculptural presentations and provides a singular insight into the mind of one of the most fascinating and original individuals of eighteenth-century England.

THE PAINTINGS

Thomas Coke has long been recognised as a great art collector and an outstanding patron of architecture. He built a house for his collection, and he collected for his house. Although the relationship between the sculpture and the architecture at Holkham Hall has been thoroughly analysed, the arrangement of the paintings has not been studied in a similar fashion.[218] Evidently, Lord – and later Lady – Leicester did not apply art historical principles by arranging the works according to school and period, as we are so accustomed to doing today. At the same time, eighteenth-century collectors did not simply display their paintings according to decorative whim, as is often falsely assumed. For there was a third and very important option at the time, which is largely lost to us.

Many of the leading eighteenth-century collections were arranged around the principle of comparison. Paintings from different schools, by different painters and in different genres were put side by side to invite discussion and conversation. The aim was to gain a deeper understanding of each painting's qualities, alongside the character of the painters or schools, and to refine the observer's ability to analyse and enjoy art through comparison. It is for this reason that paintings from different schools were often mixed within the same space – as in the two Drawing Rooms and the State Ante-Chamber at Holkham – or works were collected in one room to invite comparison within a narrower framework – like the examples of seventeenth- and eighteenth-century landscapes in the State Dressing Room. Today's museums often arrange paintings by period and school, a principle that became predominant in the nineteenth century. Mixing the schools was a very different but equally coherent principle that was generally accepted at the time when Thomas Coke acquired his collection and when Holkham Hall was built.

The eighteenth century also took the narrative aspect of an artwork seriously and responded directly to it. Despite the intellectual distance from certain types of classical or Christian mythology and ideology that the Age of Enlightenment developed, the iconography of a painting was still recognised – accepted and used to convey a message, or refuted and ironically played with. Lord Leicester amply applied both approaches – stylistic comparison and (ironic) reaction to the subject – when he furnished his splendid new house.

Paintings commissioned by Thomas Coke himself would most easily convey his desired messages and his aesthetic preferences to viewers, but works acquired on the art market could equally be accommodated. If not, schemes had to be invented to make them fit – or to neutralise their messages. This is where the owner's (or the beholder's) wit came into play. While paintings could be essential for conveying the meaning of a room, an apartment or a collection, the witty

Fig. 175. Peter Paul Rubens, *The Flight of the Holy Family to Egypt.*

Fig. 176. Anthony van Dyck, *Portrait of Albert de Ligne, Prince of Arenberg and Brabançon.*

Fig. 177. Claude Gellée, called le Lorrain, *Apollo Flaying Marsyas.*

display of an art collection could also indicate the owner's view of history through their deliberate choice of models. Artworks could tell the history of their owner quite as much as the history that their creators portrayed. Thomas Coke's collection was a proof of his aesthetic judgement, his taste and his ability to create intelligent contexts. For any collector from the eighteenth-century British upper class, these abilities were a question of status and had to be demonstrated, in particular to their peers. Today we can enjoy these qualities, but they require explanation and translation into the principles of today's museum world.

THOMAS COKE'S COLLECTION

The collection at Holkham is rich in paintings that we consider masterworks today. Many of the Roman baroque painters that Coke collected in great numbers yet with extraordinary quality are today relatively obscure and known mainly to specialists, so it needs to be stressed that they were highly regarded in his lifetime, and many other contemporary works were considered equally important. From the eighteenth to the twenty-first century, taste has changed as much as principles of display. But many works at Holkham are still considered outstanding by today's criteria.

Fig. 178. Claude Gellée, called le Lorrain, *Apollo Guarding the Cattle of Admestus.*

Thomas Coke bought an important large religious work by Rubens, *The Flight of the Holy Family to Egypt* (fig. 175). It is a representative work of Rubens's early career after the artist's return from Italy. Another attraction for Thomas Coke, aside from its quality, may have been that another, slightly earlier version of the composition was kept at Blenheim Palace in the eighteenth century (today at Hartford, Connecticut).

Anthony van Dyck's *Portrait of Albert de Ligne, Prince of Arenberg and Brabançon* is one of only a small number of life-size equestrian portraits that van Dyck painted during his short career (fig. 176). After a prelude when van Dyck stayed at Genoa, he painted the Holkham Hall portrait around 1630, the first of the famous series of his equestrian portraits, culminating in the two large portraits of Charles I. It was painted by van Dyck with important contributions from studio members. Unusually, the noble rider turns his back to the beholder and only his head looks towards us. Van Dyck's composition conveys Arenberg's energy as a soldier and horseman and the speed of the movement. Arenberg started his career successfully in the Spanish army but was imprisoned in 1634 (after van Dyck's portrait was painted) on suspicion of treason. His biography surely added to the interest of the painting for Thomas Coke.

Of the old master paintings at Holkham, the most impressive and important group is the landscapes by Claude Lorrain, who painted the quintessential classical landscapes of the baroque. They present ideal views of Rome and the Campagna, bathed in morning or evening light. With their allusions to places around Rome or to classical mythology, and their atmospheric and emotional qualities, they became extremely popular with an international clientele in Claude's lifetime. In the eighteenth century, a huge proportion of his work was acquired by British collectors. Thomas Coke built up one of the most important groups of his works – paintings and drawings – spanning the whole of Claude's Roman career.

Apollo Flaying Marsyas, hung in the Drawing Room, was bought by Thomas Coke during his Grand Tour (fig. 177). Painted in 1645/46, it stems from Claude's classic period: the deep vista of the landscape is framed by groups of dark trees in the fore- and middleground and lit by the sun from

Fig. 179. Claude Gellée, called le Lorrain, *The Origin of Coral.*

the far distance. In the foreground Apollo is shown flaying Marsyas, but the drama of the story is absorbed by the peaceful and melancholic evening landscape. *Apollo Guarding the Cattle of Admestus* (fig. 178) was painted in the following decade, when Claude's compositions were dominated by strong verticals, like the central trees, and horizontal lines. One can easily feel here how the simple landscape with classical buildings served as a reference point for English gardens such as those at Holkham. In hanging Claude's landscapes next to a large window with a view of the park, the display at Holkham invited this comparison. *The Origin of Coral* (fig. 179) is a late masterwork by Claude and one of his most unusual compositions. It tells an episode from the story of Perseus as narrated by Ovid. The figures are set on the coast in front of a striking rock formation. Its silhouette and a group of large trees on the left frame the composition. Behind stretches the open sea and a distant coastline. The sun in the clouds is reflected in the water.

Another famous Roman work at Holkham Hall was commissioned long after Thomas Coke's death and was acquired from another branch of the family only in 1920. Painted by Pompeo Batoni in 1773–74, it is one of the quintessential portraits of a British Grand Tourist (fig. 180). The sitter was Thomas William Coke, first Earl of Leicester of the second creation, who inherited Holkham Hall in 1776, two years after his return. Batoni surrounded the nineteen-year-old

Fig. 180. Pompeo Batoni, portrait in van Dyck dress of the nineteen-year-old Thomas William Coke ('Coke of Norfolk') on his Grand Tour.

Thomas William with symbols of antique Rome: architectural fragments and the *Ariadne* at the Vatican (at that time thought to represent Cleopatra), in the late eighteenth century one of the most famous and best-known sculptures in all of Rome. While the sculptures and the classical architecture evoked Rome, Thomas William Coke is wearing the so-called van Dyck dress, an updated version of seventeenth-century dress often worn by van Dyck's sitters. This fashion was popular in Britain and often used as a marker of a long aristocratic tradition (not necessarily a correct claim in this

Fig. 181. Luigi Garzi's painting *Cincinnatus at the Plough*, commissioned by Thomas Coke on his Grand Tour, originally hung in the Closet to the Green State Bedroom.

case). The overall scheme also followed van Dyck's full-length portraits. The Roman Batoni thus fused Roman and British traditions in a convincing way. The portrait was commissioned by the Countess of Albany, wife of the Pretender. The portrait was famous among contemporaries because of a presumed affair between the countess and Coke. Holkham also provides an example from the very beginning of the tradition in Trevisani's 1717 portrait of Thomas Coke (fig. 7).

As was the case with his sculpture collection, Thomas Coke amassed his collection of paintings over two distinct periods. He first acquired sculpture and paintings during his Grand Tour in Italy between 1714 and 1717, and then – thirty years later – during the planning and construction of Holkham Hall.[219] Coke spent large sums of money on paintings in Rome. As early as 1714 he bought four small works by Pietro da Cortona and a work by Andrea Procaccini, probably the large painting later hung in the Saloon. Two years later he commissioned additional paintings by Garzi (fig. 181), Chiari and Vanvitelli[220] (fig. 182); in 1716/17, payments were made to Sebastiano Conca for a painting of the *Elysian Fields*, where Coke was depicted as Orpheus (fig. 128). Whilst in Italy, Coke chose subjects from Roman history and mythology, and also acquired typical Grand Tour *vedute* (souvenir views of tourist sights). In his second and much later acquisition campaign, sculpture was bought first: Matthew Brettingham the younger had been in Rome between 1747 and 1754, concentrating initially on acquiring sculptures for Lord Leicester, whereas paintings were mainly bought during the later years of his stay. Obviously, large-scale sculpture had to be taken into account by the architect before the construction of the rooms was finished, while paintings could be more easily fitted into finished interiors. The precedence of sculpture also hints at the relative importance of the two media for Lord Leicester.

The process of arranging the collection went through several distinct phases. Initial ideas about the display of artworks must have been discussed when the construction of Holkham Hall began in 1734. The architectural plans developed considerably during the decades-long construction of Holkham Hall, so that the display of the collections must have been constantly in flux. Letters by Thomas Coke

Fig. 182. The painting of the Colosseum and the Arc of Titus in Rome by Gaspar van Wittel (aka Gaspare Vanvitelli or Occhiali), also commissioned by Coke on his Grand Tour, originally adorned the Closet to the North State Bedroom.

to Brettingham from that early period give an impression of how the installation was decided upon. In 1738, he wrote to the architect: 'Send me also a drawing of the upright sides of the dressing room, wth the dimensions & drawings of the pictures upon them, draw lines as we did sploins [?], wch. we have fix't [...].' And in 1740: 'Send the exact size of the Chimney piece in the bed chamber yt. I may see whither the Frame made for the Picture over it is right. I doubt there is a mistake & yt. that Frame wd. better fit yt. in ye dressing room.'[221]

DISPLAYING THE PAINTINGS

The arrangement of the paintings in Family Wing was apparently reached by trial and error and not completely thought out before the furnishing had begun. The death of the only Leicester heir in 1753 had put new pressure on finishing the house. From this point on, only Holkham Hall would serve as a monument to the family's status, and the house thus acquired new importance. It is quite likely that most of the paintings were given a fixed place only after that date. Hanging the paintings in the state apartments seems to have started only in 1754.[222] Lady Leicester completed her husband's plans after his death in 1759.[223] When analysing these later interiors, it seems likely that Lord Leicester had not developed any overall plan for the furnishing of the entire house that his wife could refer to, even less so for the arrangement of paintings. The final arrangement in the main staterooms, however, was finely honed and carefully thought through.

Despite this circuitous history, the display of the painting collection at Holkham has justifiably been described as 'more carefully thought out than that of any other English house of its generation'.[224] It is not only one of the best-preserved picture displays of the period in England, possibly in all of Europe, but is also extremely well documented. A 1759 inventory of the paintings at Holkham provides a glimpse of the nearly finished house. Brettingham the younger's expanded folio publication of 1773 clearly indicates that the house and its furnishings were 'presentable' to an influential and critical public by this date. One generation later, in 1817, Dawson's guidebook to Holkham followed. Any analysis of Lord Leicester's ideas must be based on these sources. The 1759 inventory supplements the analysis of the house as described by Brettingham and gives us an impression of how the ideas were developed. Even more importantly, it proves which ideas can with certainty be traced back to Lord Leicester himself.

The arrangement at Holkham is of an astounding quality, and at the same time it is typical of the particularly British fashion for placing paintings in precise spots within an architecturally conceived structure and of using frames that were often designed by the architect himself.[225] Brettingham described the paintings in detail, but the cross sections of his publication only delineate walls and frames, the architectural elements of the arrangement focusing on the overall architectural quality of the display.

While Thomas Coke's own art acquisitions in Italy tell us much about his attitude to painting, his political leanings and his experiences in Italy as a young man, the artworks could not have been chosen with their future location or arrangement in mind. This changed completely when the state apartments were progressing during the 1750s, at which time paintings were most likely acquired in order to form or complete distinct groups of artworks or displays on specific walls. These latter acquisitions are particularly evocative when trying to understand the purposeful arrangement of the collection by Lord Leicester – and probably also by his widow.

Still, it was not always easy to successfully integrate paintings acquired on the market. The ideal of 'taste' was powerful and influential enough at the time to judge the collector by his ability to buy the right Rubens – even if other qualities like subject or dimensions did not necessarily fit. Similarly, the acquisition of sculpture was largely determined by the availability and artistic quality of the pieces, even if the personality or the story depicted was also important for the collector. To arrange all these works into a convincing unity posed a great challenge. It helped, though, that an eighteenth-century arrangement was not necessarily as systematic as the earlier, high baroque display, but rather a witty play with given elements.[226] Additional items could be added to complete a story or to spice up an existing idea. Several contradictory layers could happily coexist. To trace the underlying ideas is as difficult as it is entertaining, and as worthwhile as it is risky. For wit is obviously not to be dwelt on for too long. There is always the danger of killing the joke – or worse, of not getting it. This is why one will not find a comprehensive description of the owner's ideas in contemporary sources. Instead, one has to start observing, and guessing, for oneself. Thus it might be good to first look for the cases where Lord (or Lady) Leicester's intentions are immediately apparent. They might well guide us further on our way when exploring the house.

THE LANDSCAPE ROOM

Lord Leicester arranged his famed collection of Claudes, Dughets and other landscape paintings in the State Dressing Room (the 'Landscape Room'), the second ante-room of Lord Leicester's state apartment.[227] Twenty-two paintings are arranged on three walls in a symmetrical fashion. The south

Fig. 183. Claude Joseph Vernet, *Sea Piece.*

window offers the view onto the park (pl. 40). Opposite, Claude Lorrain's large *Queen Esther Approaching the Palace of Ahasuerus* occupies the centre of the north wall and corresponds to the view through the window. Five more paintings are displayed here: Luca Giordano's *Saint John the Baptist Preaching* is prominently displayed above the large Claude, and two landscapes by Orizzonte and two by Gaspard Dughet may be observed on each side. The east and west walls are covered with eight paintings each: the west wall with works by Domenichino, Grimaldi, Dughet, Rosa and Locatelli, while six landscapes by Lorrain and two Vernets are hung on the east wall towards the Chapel (pls. 37 to 39).

The guiding principle seems obvious: a room full of Lorrains and Gaspard Dughets, complemented by the works of Domenichino, Vernet (fig. 183) and others. Presenting a collection of southern landscape paintings, the room is the only one in Holkham where the display principles seem familiar to contemporary eyes. But the intentions were different. A possible model for the display is the Sala dei Paesaggi at the Palazzo Colonna in Rome. Beyond this Roman model, at Holkham one is invited to compare the greatest flowering of the genre in seventeenth-century Rome with its epigones in Italy, such as Locatelli (figs. 184 and 185) and Orizzonte, and in France (Vernet). The Claudes in the lower segments of the three picture walls formed the basis for this idea. Rosa and Giordano, hung higher, developed landscape painting into a more romantic domain (and brought it to Naples), and Locatelli, Orizzonte and Vernet

Figs. 184 and 185. Andrea Locatelli, two paintings both entitled *Landscape with Ruins.*

continued it into the present. Since Vernet studied with Locatelli, teacher and pupil could be compared and put into historical perspective. Lord Leicester wrote to Brettingham in 1755: 'I am glad we have got those Landskips of Lucatelli as they will be wanted over my doors where they'll do very well. However I desire he will also go as far as 200 crowns wch is wt is ask't for the 2 Monsu Vernets, as I sd be glad also to have some Sea pieces.'[228] He was apparently eager to collect the full menu of classic landscape painting, but did not yet have a specific arrangement in mind.

All this seems obvious – but why did the Leicesters add one history painting to this arrangement? Even Matthew Brettingham in his description of Holkham felt motivated to stress the fact that Luca Giordano's *Saint John the Baptist Preaching*, hung in the centre of the north wall's upper row, offered the only example of history painting in the room – not a *paysage historié* (a landscape with a history in it), but a biblical history in the strictest possible sense. The answer might lie in the biography of Saint John the Baptist, who went into the desert to meditate and returned to announce the coming of the Lord. According to the classical tradition, the desert was not necessarily a barren country, but simply lonely – deserted. Quite often, scenes in the desert were set in landscapes that one would, in fact, consider paradisiacal or bucolic. Thus the desert is represented on all three picture walls of the room, in twenty-one landscape paintings of the highest calibre. Grimaldi's *Landscape with Saint John Baptising* on the west wall expands the subject of Giordano's work even further. This idea should not be overemphasised, for most of the landscapes in the room depict scenes from classical mythology and could well serve as proof of the owner's taste and erudition. Both notions were probably intended. Saint John the Baptist could serve as a convincing pun in the last room, which the Leicesters crossed when they passed from their private apartment in Family Wing into the Chapel, marking the point where the classical allusions of the house turned to more devout principles. Within the context of the state apartment, the room united the cream of landscape painting and presented a historic overview of the classical tradition.

THE (WEST) DRAWING ROOM

Three rooms from the Landscape Room, the (West) Drawing Room is another obvious example of Lord Leicester's desire to present his collection in a meaningful and witty context. Unlike the State Dressing Room, where the commentary is placed high up in the centre of one wall with scant regard to the ravishing harmony of the ensemble, one is struck here by how heterogeneous this group of paintings is: in the centre of the north wall is Pietro da Pietri's *Madonna in Gloria*; along both sides are two animal paintings by Hondecoeter and landscapes by Dughet and Claude (pl. 29). In the eighteenth century, van Dyck's equestrian portrait of the *Duke of Arenberg* (now in the Saloon) formed the centre of the west wall (fig. 176), Rubens's *Flight into Egypt* (fig. 175) was displayed on the east wall in 1759; in 1773 Cipriani's *Joseph and the Wife of Potiphar* was added instead.[229] Four landscapes by Orizzonte serve as overdoors (pls. 28 to 31).

Two large animal paintings by Hondecoeter, purchased in 1749 out of a sale of paintings from Robert Walpole's Houghton Hall,[230] adorn the north wall (pl. 29 and figs. 186

Figs. 186 and 187. Two animal paintings by Melchior d'Hondecoeter.

and 187). They were intended and understood as depictions of King William's wars against France and his alliance with England, as well as allusions to his accession to the British throne and the Glorious Revolution. These two depictions of the classic Whig topic, British and Protestant liberty, framed Pietro da Pietri's *Madonna* shown as the Woman of the Apocalypse trampling on an allegory of vice that is also attacked by the Christ Child with a cross, a copy after a Maratta commissioned for Lord Leicester. All three paintings show the struggle between good and evil, between right and wrong, but their combination places them in the most ironic context. The image of Catholic orthodoxy is framed by representations of the Protestant fight against the *roi très catholique* and the English struggle against absolutism. The confrontational theme even resonates in the two landscapes hung below the Hondecoeter paintings.

Dughet's *Stormy Landscape* shows two men in the foreground attacking a snake, and Claude's landscape features *Apollo Flaying Marsyas* (fig. 177), another depiction of revolt, hubris and reinstating the 'right' order. Remarkably enough, this was the only Claude that was not put into the Landscape Room, where all the masterpieces of the genre were otherwise united. Apparently, its message was considered important enough to separate this work from the other Claudes and to complement the rest of the north wall in the Drawing Room. That a sculpture of Marsyas (fig. 158) was on display in the adjoining Statue Gallery might have been an additional reason to hang this painting by Claude in the Drawing Room. Two busts of Roman emperors on the chimneypiece contrasted Marcus Aurelius the philosopher with the evil ruler *par excellence*, Caracalla (pl. 32).

Van Dyck's equestrian portrait of the Duke of Arenberg (fig. 176) might be another political allusion. Albert de Ligne, Duc d'Arenberg, led the Spanish army in Bohemia, Westphalia and the Netherlands. In 1634, he was imprisoned on suspicion of treason against the Spanish government with the Netherlandish nobility. He remained imprisoned until 1642. Van Dyck's painting thus expanded the topic of Hondecoeter's two large allegories. Cipriani's *Joseph and the Wife of Potiphar* (now lost) depicted another example of the right order being violated. In 1759, this space had been occupied by Rubens's *Flight into Egypt* (now in the Saloon), thus setting up a comparison between the two masterpieces of Flemish painting in the collection. Replacing this stylistically obvious counterpart to van Dyck with Cipriani's painting sometime before 1773 sharpened the message of the room.

It is harder to imagine a specific iconographic reason for using four Orizzonte landscapes as overdoors. Angelicoussis suggests that they form a background for the three busts of philosophers over the doors, confronted with a fourth bust of Empress Faustina. Replacing the Rubens with a Cipriani would have strengthened another, equally important objective of the display. Many leading collections of the time in France and the Holy Roman Empire arranged their collections in order to facilitate comparison between artists but primarily between schools. Following this principle, the Drawing Room in the end included works from Italy, France, Flanders and the Netherlands and provided ample opportunity to compare the qualities and the specialisations of these schools (e.g. Italian history painting and Dutch animal paintings). Cipriani's painting added a contemporary work by an artist active in England into this menu for comparison.

Fig. 188. In the Saloon, Andrea Procaccini's *Tarquin Raping Lucretia* was paired with Giuseppe Bartolomeo Chiari's *Perseus Rescuing Andromeda* – both commissioned by young Thomas Coke on his Grand Tour.

PAINTINGS ACROSS THE HOUSE

Rather than examining further rooms individually, it is more illuminating now to look at the entire house to analyse the way the art collection is distributed throughout the state apartments and to determine which sequences of rooms were intended for visitors. The distribution of sculpture versus painting at Holkham is the most obvious feature.

Several very prominent rooms were exclusively devoted to sculpture, first of all the Hall, which served as the triumphal entry into the house. This is not particularly remarkable, as classical vestibules usually exclude painting. The Great Dining Room and the Statue Gallery and its Vestibule in the western wing are also reserved for sculpture. In the remainder of the state apartment rooms, sculptures appear regularly but without a particularly prominent rôle. These are mainly busts or chimneypieces with reliefs. In many rooms they still convey an important message for the arrangement – as in the Drawing Room (see above). Whilst the sculpture can be iconographically significant, paintings or tapestries nevertheless dominate a room.

The sculpture programme is thus mainly associated with public reception spaces: the Great Dining Room, obviously, but also the Statue Gallery, called the 'Chambre d'Assembly' by a guest in 1757. Here, too, the guest wing is linked to the main body of the house through a corridor with five niches for sculpture. Sculpture is also coupled with learning: the octagonal vestibule to the Statue Gallery that served as a library room offers necessary information on the sculpture as well as a splendid view into the Gallery. A tour of the sculpture collection would follow a logical path: the Hall, Great Dining Room, North Tribune, Statue Gallery, South Tribune and then either into the guest apartments or into the private rooms of Lord and Lady Leicester. The western half of the house displays the serene world of antiquity.

A different sequence would lead official visitors from the Hall into the two apartments in the eastern half of the building: either to the state apartment through the central Saloon, the State Ante-Chamber and the State Dressing Room (Landscape Room) into the State Bedchamber and its Closet or – following a similar but shorter route – from the Hall directly into the smaller apartment on the north side sometimes named after the Duke of Grafton, consisting of a dressing room (next to the Marble Hall), a bedroom and a closet. Of these two sequences of rooms, the state apartment seems to offer a far more concise theme. The central Saloon located behind the portico of the south

Fig. 189. Giuseppe Bartolomeo Chiari's *The Continence of Scipio Africanus* was another painting commissioned by young Thomas Coke on his Grand Tour. According to Brettingham junior, 'The Earl himself, then a Youth, is introduced in the Character of Allucius' – the young nobleman to whom Scipio restored his captured bride. The painting has long been gone from Holkham, but briefly reappeared on the market in 1975.

Fig. 190. Amongst the four large historical paintings centring on Roman virtues that originally dominated the Saloon, *Coriolanus in the Camp of the Volsci* by the seventeenth-century painter Pietro da Cortona was the only one that Coke did not need to commission. The drawing by Cortona (in the Kupferstichkabinett in Berlin) closely matches detailed descriptions of the lost painting.

Fig. 191. Guido Reni, *Joseph and the Wife of Potiphar.*

façade featured examples of Roman Republican clemency and of the fight between good and evil.[231] This room fully focused on Rome and emphasised leading modern painters from the immediate circle of Carlo Maratta, who was considered the major painter of his time at this period. Procaccini and Chiari, both prominently displayed in the room, were both Maratta pupils, whilst William Kent was a pupil of Chiari's. Maratta himself was present with two paintings hung as overdoors (as well as in other rooms of the house). Other Roman tendencies were present in the works of Pietro da Cortona and Agostino Scilla.

The message of the Saloon was equally consistent in iconographic terms. Andrea Procaccini's *Tarquin Raping Lucretia* (fig. 188) and Giuseppe Chiari's *Perseus and Andromeda* were hung on the north wall (pl. 12). Paintings by Chiari, *The Continence of Scipio*, and Pietro da Cortona, *Coriolanus in the Camp of the Volsci,* were originally on the side walls. They have gone from Holkham but one of them is recorded in a black-and-white photograph (fig. 189) whereas we can get an idea of the other from a study by Cortona (fig. 190).[232] This room continued the Roman topic from the Marble Hall and presented three subjects from Roman history together with Chiari's *Perseus*: two paintings were examples of Roman clemency, whilst *Tarquin Raping Lucretia* describes the event that triggered the formation of the Roman Republic. But the paintings form one even more logical sequence when seen assembled around the bust of Juno. All four address the rôle and the virtue of women and their dependence on men. The bust of Juno, prominently displayed over the door from the Hall, was to be a pendant to the sculpture of Jupiter, originally intended for the apse of the Hall, thus comparing political and domestic virtue. The room presented at the same time a homage to Lady Leicester in the guise of Juno and to Lord Leicester, the defender of female virtue.

Next to the Saloon on the left lay the State Ante-Chamber, where the arrangement of paintings changed several times.[233] This room was arranged similarly to the Drawing Room in mixing different schools and facilitating comparison between them. The range here was even wider: Venice, Bologna and Rome were present among the Italian schools, and Rubens stood for the Flemish school. Brettingham describes Cortona's *Jacob and Esau* as the centrepiece, framed by Titian's *Venus* and Domenichino's *Loth* – a depiction of fraud surrounded by scenes of the power of love. Reni's *Joseph and the Wife of Potiphar* (fig. 191) on the east wall goes well with the latter theme, whereas the meaning of Rubens's *Flight into Egypt* in this context is unclear. The busts of a vestal virgin and of Empress Faustina on the chimneypiece confronted chaste and unbridled love. In 1759, the focus had been much more on the Old Testament. Luti's *Rebecca*, Sacchi's *Abraham, Hagar and Ismael* and Cipriani's *Joseph and the Wife of Potiphar* had all been replaced in the meantime. It is quite possible that Lord Leicester's original intention was to establish a sequence in which antiquity, Old Testament and New Testament led into the Chapel. But it is also possible that the room was upgraded in artistic quality, for when the Rubens was no longer needed in the South Drawing Room it was brought to the State Ante-Chamber, while Cipriani's *Joseph and the Wife of Potiphar* was at the same time exchanged for Reni's depiction of the same story and Cipriani's painting was moved to

Fig. 192. Gavin Hamilton, *Jupiter Caressing Juno.*

the Drawing Room, where it complemented the iconographic scheme of that room.

The State Ante-Chamber is more easily interpreted as a space where the different schools were compared. Titian and Domenichino flanked Cortona: a baroque and a classicist strand of Roman painting could be compared to Venice. On the side walls Rubens hung opposite Reni, confronting the triumph of colour in Flanders with Bolognese classicism. It is telling that Lord Leicester chose to move Cipriani into the Drawing Room and to add Rubens to the State Ante-Chamber, which provided a strong counterpart and comparison to the Guido Reni and widened the field of comparison.

Through the State Dressing Room (the Landscape Room) one proceeds into the State Bedchamber, where a tapestry cycle with the four continents and allegories of vigilance and sleep surrounded the bed. Gavin Hamilton's *Jupiter Caressing Juno* (fig. 192) struck a subtle balance between high-flown, official bedroom iconography and an ironically absurd comparison between mythological models and contemporary inhabitants.[234]

The tour continued in a very different mood, for the closets were both filled with souvenirs of the Grand Tour: *vedute* and smaller artworks, mainly acquired in Italy, some small-scale jewels of the Italian collection such as the *Battle of Cascina* by Aristotele da Sangallo (a work then considered to be by Raphael) and also Flemish works (pls. 45 and 46). The Duke of Grafton's Apartment equally displayed important paintings in its bedchamber and closet, and tapestries in the dressing room (pls. 47 to 50).

As it has proved impossible to find a similarly conclusive iconography in these rooms, it appears more than likely that the remainder of the collection was hung here when the furnishing of the house was completed. These rooms clearly reflect a more personal choice than the staterooms. Family portraits in the ante-room and in the bedroom of Lady Leicester's apartment somewhat tragically alluded to her rôle as the mother of future generations of the family, as did the sculpture of Isis in her dressing room. It is remarkable that no other family portraits were hung in the main building of Holkham Hall, but rather in Family Wing and Strangers' Wing, where they were meant to impress visitors.

We have so far followed the sequence of the two state apartments in the eastern half of the house, as distinct from the rooms for entertainment in the western half. This is probably the most official way to regard the house and its contents. Other routes were definitely taken and also played an important rôle. The route from Family Wing to the Chapel – the direct way along the enfilade of the south façade – has already been mentioned. This route began in the private apartments in Family Wing that were actually inhabited and served as living quarters rather than as a background for representation. The Library and the vestibule to the Statue Gallery represented the world of learning and also the importance of antiquity to Lord Leicester. The Drawing Room dramatically staged the battle between good and evil, between Whig and Tory, between Protestantism and Catholicism, but also between right and hubris. This conflict was further elaborated on a less political and more general level in the great Saloon. The State Ante-Chamber addressed bodily temptations and sin. Progressing through the desert – the State Dressing Room (Landscape Room) – one entered the Chapel to repent. This sequence can be read as a progression from antiquity through Old to New Testament and redemption, but also as offering two options to fight against the evils of the world: classical philosophy or Christian belief. In which direction should one go? Entering through the Hall, one faced the fight between good and evil in the great Saloon and could then make a choice: either turning right through political conflict into the serene world of ancient philosophy (and nature, as presented in the Statue Gallery), or turning left through sin and repentance into redemption (in the Chapel).

PRINCIPLES AND INTENTIONS

Lord Leicester himself must have had an active rôle in conceiving these schemes. Whilst this arrangement could be seen as conveying its own message, it was equally important as a way of neutralising the Catholic messages of many works in the collection. Typically for British collections, there was a visible tension between the collection of high-quality Italian works and the fundamental distance from their iconography. Framing these works by a new, overarching storyline made it easier to appreciate the collection in a country where any hint of Catholic sympathies had to be avoided.

Equally important for the display was the connoisseurial idea of comparison. The Drawing Room and the State Ante-Chamber in particular offered a display to invite comparison between schools and painters – an option that existed in parallel to the iconographic games described above. Here, Netherlandish painters could be compared to artists from different Italian schools and from France. The pairings of van Dyck with Cipriani and of Rubens with Reni embodied this invitation. Whereas in these rooms the comparison worked between schools, there were also possible comparisons between rooms. The Statue Gallery, the Saloon and the State Dressing Room (Landscape Room) presented different aspects of Rome and the Grand Tour: classical antiquity, modern Roman art and the Roman landscape respectively. Together with the Hall, they provided the classical backbone of a display that included a much broader variety of works and invited a view of van Dyck or Guido Reni in relation to the classical tradition.

Lord Leicester invested great energy in creating a tissue of options, meaning and choice in his country house and his collection, in order to present himself in all his splendour, to prove his taste and his wit, and to impress and entertain his guests. This goal was even more important to him, since his family could not boast of a long, noble ancestry. He is a typical example of the eighteenth-century phenomenon that art collections were often used by upstarts and people of a still uncertain status to demonstrate their acquired rank and importance. The overwhelming quality of the collection and its display, with its network of meanings and allusions, brings us particularly close to the creator of Holkham Hall.

THE ROOMS IN FAMILY WING

When Thomas Coke developed his ideas for a new country seat during the 1720s, its layout greatly resembled that of Robert Walpole's nearby Houghton, a splendid house of parade combining the functions of a private residence with the element of display required for social and even public purposes. At the time, the interiors of Houghton were being completed by William Kent, and one may assume that the main rooms of Holkham I would have been designed in a similar vein. But Coke made the momentous decision of separating public and private functions in his house, allowing him to create a space devoted to his personal interests and to the comforts of the family while at the same time enhancing the formal and representative character of the central body of the house.

This space devoted to personal interests and privacy, today known as Family Wing, was the first part of the house to be built – considerably earlier than the much grander main body. A wing of private rooms for a noble household was a novel concept at the time, and this required the right kind of approach regarding the arrangement of the rooms and their interior decoration. The structure of the wings has already been characterised briefly in Chapter 3, particularly the novel and flexible grid plan with rooms arranged around a central staircase. Like the other pavilions, Family Wing has three habitable levels above the vaulted basement. The main room on the ground floor is the dining room, for less formal use by the family, but there is also a bathroom where Thomas Coke originally hoped to have a piscina in the authentic Roman manner, as he explained in a letter to Brettingham of 14 February 1737/38:

> I w.d not have the floor in the bathing room done any thing to, till I see you for we shall have a trap door in it into the cellar. W.t I mean is I shall have a bath made in the cellar w.ch will rise to that story fit for me to jump into, besides the bath that stands on the floor for a hot bath. but w.n you come to town we shall explain this.[235]

The other ground floor rooms were mostly used by the personal servants – lady's maid, chamber maid, valet, footman and secretary. The small room in the centre of the west side was the guard room into which the covered way led from the old manor house until that was demolished in 1757.[236] The beautifully decorated main floor rooms were for the personal use of the master and the mistress of the house whereas the – still rather attractive – attic rooms were used by their son, Edward. This is also where Lady Mary Coke claimed to have been practically incarcerated until rescued by her mother, the Duchess of Argyll.

On the main floor of Family Wing, Lord and Lady Leicester shared a bedroom in the south-east corner. The bed stood in front of what is now a window that offers a view towards the portico. From the bedroom, Lady Leicester had direct access to her closet and to her large dressing room. To reach his own personal domain, Lord Leicester could either cross the main staircase to his dressing room or the short passage to the ante-room that connected to the Statue Gallery, or he could pass through Lady Leicester's dressing room to enter the Long Library which, to him, was undoubtedly the most important space in the whole building.

As for the interior decoration, what degree of grandeur, of formality was appropriate? Too much would be pompous and oppressive, too little might be embarrassing. To find the right approach, Coke seems to have used a method he had successfully employed in the development of the architectural structure and form of the house: designing by committee, as it has been called, or, in modern parlance, brainstorming with his trusted partners, Lord Burlington and William Kent, on the basis of drafts he had developed with his amanuensis Brettingham. This approach is evident in a letter Coke wrote to Burlington on 26 November 1736: 'I shall ... wait on you with my Port feuill, & make the Signor scold, for now we must think of the inside of the rooms'.[237] The Signor was of course William Kent, and it was he who – no doubt with a certain degree of guidance by the two noblemen – ultimately conceived the decorative scheme for the main rooms of Family Wing. The measurements and proportions of the rooms, the placements of all the openings were already fixed and executed at the time of the letter, but the character and quality of the rooms would be determined by their furnishings – the ceilings, doorframes, friezes and fireplaces. Kent already had a great deal of experience in the field, gained amongst other places at nearby Houghton Hall, and he knew the sources he could draw from, such as the works of Inigo Jones that he himself had published in 1727. And yet his work in the rooms of Holkham's Family Wing is not simply more of the same: in his decorative scheme, Kent achieved an admirable balance between formality and intimacy, hitting the right tone for the private area of a house that was to have a very grand and formal central body.

Fig. 193. Although there must have been many drawings by William Kent for the interiors of Family Wing, the one of the library and this design for a fireplace and overmantel are the only known survivors.

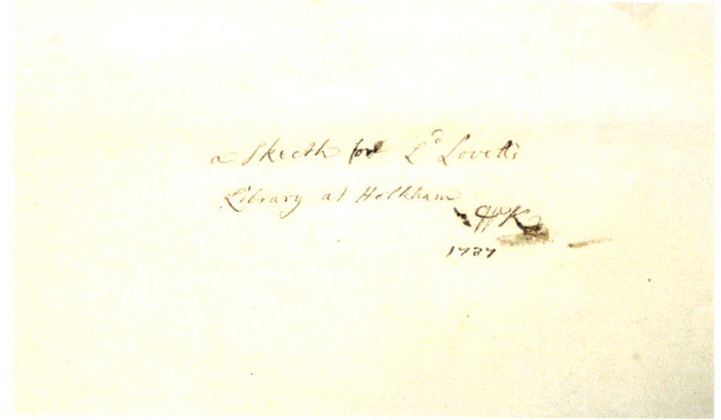

Fig. 194. The back of Kent's drawing is inscribed 'a Sketch for Ld Lovell's Library at Holkham, WK 1737'.

Kent must have made many designs for the rooms, but only two drawings survive in the house. One of them shows a fireplace and overmantel (fig. 193) that can be compared to the one originally in the bedroom but later moved to Lady Leicester's dressing room (pl. 60): the fireplace matches perfectly but there are differences in the picture frame. Not only does the executed piece display Canaletto's *Doge's Palace and St Mark's Place in Venice*, but the frame also extends upwards to contain a much-treasured pastel by Rosalba, *The Maid of the Inn*.

THE LIBRARY

Kent's other surviving drawing for Family Wing is rather more famous. It is even signed and dated, bearing on its verso the inscription 'a Sketch for Ld Lovell's Library at Holkham, WK 1737' (figs. 194 and 195). It shows the long eastern side of the library largely as the room was later published by Brettingham (fig. 196) and as it has survived to the present day (pls. 55 to 58). The symmetrical arrangement of central fireplace and overmantel, the two doorways and the splendid pedimented bookcases are mirrored by the sequence of windows and bookcases on the opposite western wall, and the windows in the long axis provide additional light from south and north. Typically, Kent went somewhat over the top with his suggestion for the decoration of the ceiling, in his design featuring nude figures frolicking between colourful garlands. We also know that Kent was working on a painting for the ceiling of the bedroom which Coke was looking forward to, as he wrote in a letter that it 'pleases me vastly & will show he can paint, for it is very fine'.[238]

In spite of his initial enthusiasm, as with the exterior architecture, Coke had a way of toning down Kent's exuberant creativity to a level fitting in with his own more sober standards and values, as illustrated by the more restrained version of the library ceiling that we see today.

From the inventory drawn up in 1760, we know that Coke furnished his library in a remarkably plain and understated manner. As in the Statue Gallery, a 'painted floorcloth' may have imitated a Roman mosaic floor that would have fitted in with the furniture: a large settee, six large armchairs and a library ladder chair, all covered with black leather, as well as a number of mahogany desks and tables: clearly a place to study books and manuscripts rather than the comfortable sitting room of later generations.

THE BOOKS AND MANUSCRIPTS

Though rather less present in the house in visual terms than the splendidly displayed sculptures and paintings, Thomas Coke's collection of manuscripts and books has always been esteemed on the same level of quality and significance as the works of art he acquired. Indeed, they may even claim some precedence as young Thomas, on his Grand Tour, initially concentrated on buying books and manuscripts before graduating to acquiring, and even commissioning, paintings and eventually sculpture. Today the library encompasses around 10,000 printed books and 550 manuscripts, often with drawings and colourful illuminations (figs. 197 to 200).

Fig. 195. William Kent's design for the east wall of the Long Library, 1737.

Fig. 196. The east wall of the Long Library, as published in an engraving in Brettingham junior's *Plans of Holkham* in 1773.

Fig. 197. Troy burning, an illumination attributed to the 'Master of the Prayer Books' of around 1500, from Ms. 311, a Flemish (Bruges) copy of Virgil's works.

His parents, Edward and Cary, laid the foundation for Thomas's intellectual interests, having put together a considerable library of their own. When they both died in 1707, their books had to be sold to repay part of their debts, but the great interest in learning and reading shown by their firstborn son prompted his guardians to buy back many of them. His mother's translations of classical and Italian authors and travel guides,[239] and his father's history and geography books, diplomatic and travel reports from European and extra-European countries and their books on Roman antiquities,[240] all played a rôle in shaping their son's future interests. Those interests were certainly nurtured and augmented by the influence of Dr Thomas Hobart and his Italian protégé Domenico Ferrari, the governor and Italian tutor chosen by the guardians to accompany Thomas on his extended Grand Tour to Europe on which he embarked, at the age of fifteen, in 1712. Hobart was a bibliophile and collector in his own right and had no difficulty in encouraging his young charge to start collecting books and manuscripts; Ferrari's knowledge of 'the Roman and the modern history of Italy, medals, antiquity's'[241] found a receptive ear in Thomas.

Information about book acquisitions is often vague in the account books covering the Grand Tour.[242] Specific volumes are rarely mentioned by subject, let alone by author or title, or may be identified as manuscripts rather than printed books. Nevertheless, these sparse and scattered notes witness Thomas's gradual intellectual development from a lively and curious teenager to a discerning reader of classical, Renaissance and modern European literature, history and architecture, as well as a sophisticated antiquarian and connoisseur. The subjects of new acquisitions

Fig. 198. A vignette at the beginning of Virgil's *Bucolics*, painted shortly after the copy of the manuscript in 1473 and attributed to the 'Master of Fitzwilliam 268', from Ms. 311.

quickly developed from 'methematick' and horsemanship in 1712–13, to a description of the Cathedral of Pisa (Lucca 1713),[243] progressing to an Italian grammar, François de Salignac de la Mothe-Fénelon's *Les Avantures de Télémaque, fils d'Ulysse* and a copy of Livy's *History of Rome*, all bought in Venice in January 1713/14.

From Venice, Coke's party moved to Rome, where they visited museums and palaces, as well as the Accademia del Disegno, also known as the Accademia di San Luca. Most of the artists from whom Thomas bought or commissioned paintings and drawings were members of the Accademia. Indeed, on 17 May, he had acquired 'a book of picturs found in a Grato' [i.e. Roman *Grotte*], probably Giovan Pietro

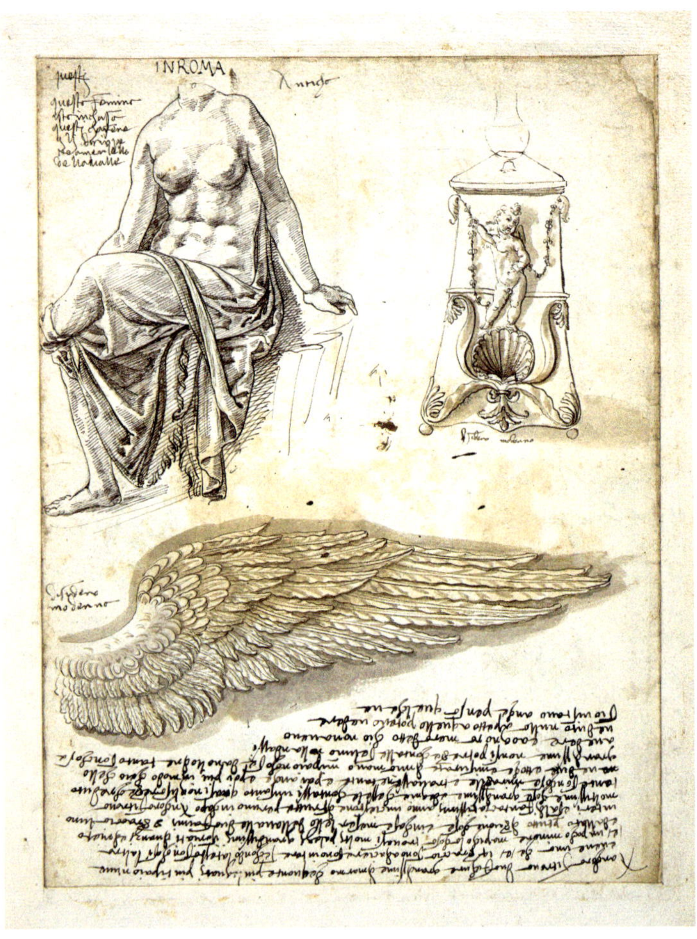

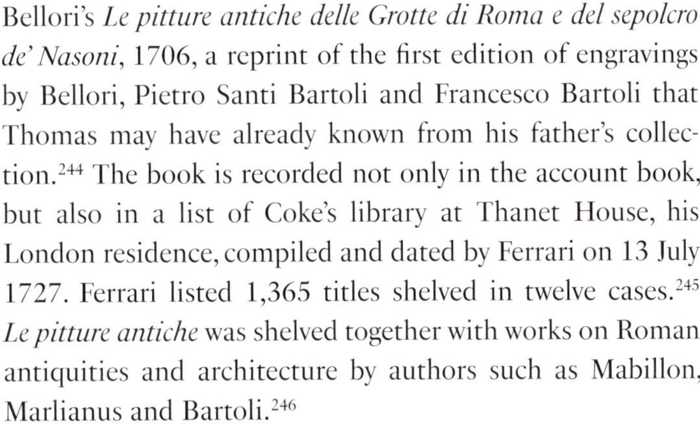

Fig. 199. A sheet of sketches in Ms. 271, an album sold to Thomas Coke as drawings by Raphael.

Fig. 200. Drawing of the Arch of Titus in Ms. 271, sold to Thomas Coke as drawn by Raphael.

Bellori's *Le pitture antiche delle Grotte di Roma e del sepolcro de' Nasoni*, 1706, a reprint of the first edition of engravings by Bellori, Pietro Santi Bartoli and Francesco Bartoli that Thomas may have already known from his father's collection.[244] The book is recorded not only in the account book, but also in a list of Coke's library at Thanet House, his London residence, compiled and dated by Ferrari on 13 July 1727. Ferrari listed 1,365 titles shelved in twelve cases.[245] *Le pitture antiche* was shelved together with works on Roman antiquities and architecture by authors such as Mabillon, Marlianus and Bartoli.[246]

It is not clear, though, when Coke started to purchase ancient codices as well. Could the Livy bought on the same day as Fénelon's *Télémaque* back in Venice in January 1713/14 and described as 'the first parte of Titus Livius', i.e. the First Decade of the *History of Rome* by Livy, be a manuscript rather than a printed book?[247] The only printed edition of the First Decade still at Holkham, a copy of the 1554 Lyon edition by Sebastian Gryphius, bears evidence that it was already in England by the seventeenth century, whereas a possible 1518 edition by Aldus Manutius was sold in the infamous duplicate sale of 1851. But a fifteenth-century manuscript copy of the First Decade is still at Holkham: it was probably produced in the Veneto and may therefore fit the profile. Equally, another fifteenth-century codex of an Italian translation of Plutarch's *Lives*, produced in Central Italy (Rome, Siena or Florence), may be identifiable in a volume listed in the account book[248] as 'book of Plutrach' [*sic*]. If this is the case, the manuscript could have been bought in Rome on 17 May 1714,[249] a few days before Thomas declared 'I am become since my stay at Rome, a perfect virtuoso, & and great lover of pictures' in a letter to Sir John Newton, his maternal grandfather.[250]

Some months later, at the beginning of January 1714/15, while attending the Royal Academy of Turin, Thomas wrote again to his grandfather, letting him know that

T. LIVII BATAVINI HISTORIOGRAPHI [illegible]
PVNICO LIBER PRIMVS INCIPIT

IN PARTE OPERIS
qđ in principio ſu
ſunt reꝝ ſcriptoreſ
um memorabile qu
pturum quod ha
nenſeſ cũ po ro geſ
reſ opibuſ ulle in ſe
lerunt arma neq ı
rium aut roboriſ fuit et haud ignotaſ belli arteſ
primo Punico conſerebant bello et adeo uaria
fuit marſ: ut propiuſ periculo fuerint qui uicerun
maioribuſ certarunt q̃ uiribuſ. Romaniſ indign
cti ultro inferrent arma. Peniſ qđ ſuperbe auar
uictiſ eſſe. fama etiam eſt hannibalem annorum
blandientem patri Hamilcari: ut duceretur in hiſpa
frico bello exercitum eo traiecturuſ ſacrificaret a
ſacriſ iureiurando adactum ſe cum primum poſſe
A ngebant ingentiſ ſpirituſ uirum Sicilia Sardiniaq.
liam nimiſ celeri deſperatione rerum conceſſam. et
Africe fraude Romanoru ſtipendio etiam ſuper

Fig. 201. Initial depicting Hannibal's oath of eternal enmity to Rome in Livy, Ms. 351.2.

LIBRO SECONDO DELLA HISTORIA NATVRALE DI.C.PLINIO SECONDO TRADOCTA DI LINGVA LATINA IN FIORENTINA PER CHRISTOPHORO LANDINO FIORENTINO AL SERENISSIMO FERDINANDO RE DI NAPOLI.

SEL MONDO HA TERMINI ET SE E VNO: CAPITOLO PRIMO.

L MONDO ET QVESTO ELQVALE PER altro nome Anoi piacie chiamare Cielo : elquale intorno gyrando tutte lechoſe chuopre: E giuſta choſa credere che ſia deita etherna & infinita : Ne mai generata: Ne mai da douere perire. Ricerchar lechoſe extrĩſeche di choſtui ne ſapptiene alhuomo: ne comprendere lepuo la congectura delhũana mente. Sacro e & etherno & ſãza miſura. Tutto nel tutto: Anzi eſſo e tutto & e infinito : ma ſimile al finito . Di tutte lechoſe e certo & ſimile a lincerto. Difuori & dentro ogni choſa ĩ ſe Abbraccia. Lui medeſimo e opera della natura : & e eſſa natura. Furore ſãza fallo moſſe alchuni A pẽſare la miſura ſua: & dipoi Ardire exporla. Furono etiam moſſi da furore quegli equali prendendo occaſione di qui innumerabili mondi eſſere affermorono: Onde altrettante nature delle choſe fuſſi neceſſario credere. Et pure ſe in una natura tutti ſi poſaſſino: Sarãno conſtrecti credere che altrettãti ſieno eſoli: Altretante lelune & laltre immenſe & innumerabili ſtelle ſimilmente ſieno multiplicate. Ilperche rimanghono occupati nella medeſima inueſtigatione : non hauendo per queſto trouato el fine che diſiderano. Et ſe pure uoglamo attribuire alla natura: laquale e artefice delluniuerſo che eſſa habbi prodocto lechoſe in infinito: q̃to e piu facile intenderlo in uno mondo ſolo: maxime eſſendo quello ſi grande opera: Furore e per certo: Furore non piccholo Vſcire di quello : Et chome ſe gia lechoſe dentro allui poſte anchora anoi incerte ci ſieno note Inueſtigare quelle difuori: Stimando che chi non ſa lamiſura diſe poſſi conſeguire quella dalchuna altra choſa. O che lamente humana poſſi uedere quello che ilmondo inſe non cape.

DELLA FORMA DEL MONDO. CAPITOLO. II.

EL nome in prima & dipoi il conſenſo di tutti glhuomini equali dicono elmõdo orbe cioe tondo: Dimoſtrano laforma del mõdo eſſere ridocta in tondo pfecto. Ne mãcono glargomenti aprouare queſto medeſimo: perche tale figura da tutte le ſue parti richade in ſe medeſima: & da ſe medeſima puo eſſere ſoſtentata: & in ſe ſi chiude & contiene: ne dalchuna commiſſura o cõgiunctura ha dibiſogno: ne fine o principio in alchuna ſua parte ſente. Preterea al moto elquale ha affare elmondo chome pocho diſotto dimoſtrerremo: Tale figura e aptiſſima. Et finalmente glocchi ne danno uero giudicio: Conciosia che ilconuexo & ilmezo della forma ſpericha da ogni parte ſiuede: Ilche in altra figura non puo addiuenire che nella ſperica cioe tonda.

DEL MOTO SVO. CAPITOLO. III.

EL naſcimẽto & loccaſo del ſole manifeſtamente Cidimoſtrano : che in ſpatio di xxiiii. hore Queſta ſperica machina fa tutta la ſua circulare reuolutione: laquale ethernalmente ſenza alchuno ripoſo & con celerita inenarrabile Gyra. Ne ſi puo facilmẽte intẽdere ſe elſuono: elquale naſcie dellaſſiduo uoltare ditanta machina e ĩmẽſo: & per queſta chagione uincendo elſenſo dellaudito non altrimenti ſi poſſa udire che

Fig. 202. Title page of Pliny's *Historia naturale*, Venice 1476, BN 1985.

during my voyage round Italy I have bought several of the most valuable authors that have written in Italian or about the country, the reason that I incroach as far on your kindness to me . . . is, that if I miss'd the occasion of buying books while I am travelling, I should not be able to find several of the best of them, and it's impossible to buy them to my mind unless I myself am present, & certainly one of the greatest ornaments to a gentleman or to his family is a fine library.[251]

When Coke and Hobart started buying books in bulk – Thomas's library acquisitions on the Grand Tour can be counted in the thousands for rare books and hundreds for manuscripts – their sheer number made it impossible to record all their details (author, title, date, provenance, price, location and date of purchase). By the end of 1715, 'For books' had already become the standard expression used to record the increasingly numerous acquisitions. This simplification of the records and possible stripping of manuscripts and books of their bindings and flyleaves – possibly carried out to avoid the tax on imported bound books imposed by the English government from 1534 to the 1730s – make it almost impossible for us to identify their provenance. As a result, unlike paintings, drawings and sculptures, the date and place of acquisition of most of the volumes is unknown.

The one exception was the momentous purchase of forty-seven medieval manuscripts from the Discalced Augustinians of Lyon as confirmed by Suzanne Reynolds's identification of all these manuscripts in the inventory of

Fig. 203. Sketches of architectural details in Ms. 271, sold to Coke as by Raphael.

Fig. 204. Frontispiece and title page of Thomas Dempster's *De Etruria regali*, published 1723 and naming Thomas Coke as editor.

their *livres manuscripts tres antiques et curieux* (c. 1690).[252] Coke's party spent about twelve days in Lyon between 7 and 18 November 1715, the day on which Jarrett recorded a payment of 161 French livres towards general expenses including the packing of and transport for three boxes of books.[253] Hobart also reported an expense of 431.15 French livres 'For books' in his financial report for November and December 1715.[254]

Most of the codices from Lyon contain patristic and classical texts, Livy in particular represented by seven Italian codices, but also Augustine, Herodotus, Jerome, Priscian, Caesar, Cicero, Ovid, Sallust, Virgil and the *Chroniques des Flandres* made for Margaret of York, third wife of Charles the Bold of Burgundy. Except for ten codices, all these manuscripts are still at Holkham. They all bear the signature 'Thomas Coke' in the lower right corner of their first opening, 'a real statement of intent, an almost ceremonial act signalling the start of his career as a collector of manuscripts', as Suzanne Reynolds puts it.[255]

From then on, the Grand Tour accounts are silent regarding acquisitions of individual manuscripts, so even the date of purchase of the notebook by Leonardo da Vinci that Coke bought around this time, the famous Codex Leicester (now owned by Bill Gates), remains a mystery to this day. We can only assume that the manuscript was in Coke's possession on 13 April 1717, as his servant Jarrett

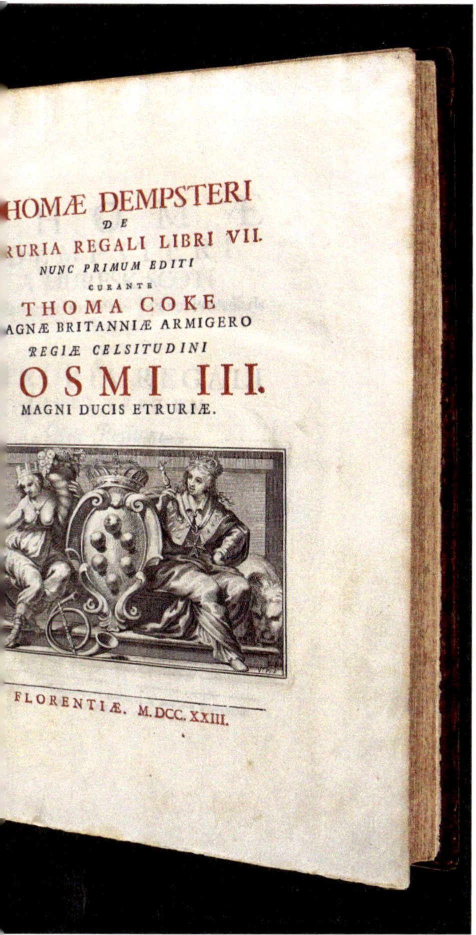

HOMÆ DEMPSTERI
DE
RURIA REGALI LIBRI VII.
NUNC PRIMUM EDITI
CURANTE
THOMA COKE
AGNÆ BRITANNIÆ ARMIGERO
REGIÆ CELSITUDINI
OSMI III.
MAGNI DUCIS ETRURIÆ.

FLORENTIÆ. M.DCC.XXIII.

Fig. 205. Section of the Pantheon in Rome, from Antoine Desgodetz, *Les Edifices antiques de Rome*, Paris, 1682.

recorded that day a payment made in Florence to 'father Danney [i.e. Father Francesco Maria Ducci] for paper to copey out a manuscript 5.4.9 [crowns]'.[256] The codex and its copy – left unfinished due to the death of Father Ducci in 1718 – were eventually brought to England on 21 May 1719: 'Paid to Mr [Andrew] Hay for bringing Pictures from A Broad, Lining, mending & Straining ye same. Carriage Duties at the Custome House. A Hebrew Bible, A Manuscript of Lionardo [*sic*] da Vinci etc. [£]26.05.00'.[257]

One may speculate that some of his manuscripts and their illustrations inspired Thomas in his artistic commissions in Rome and gave him ideas for his future new house at Holkham. Thus, the coffered vaulted ceiling of the temple in the Livy initial (fig. 201) recalls the ceiling of the Marble Hall at Holkham, just as the ceiling of the library at the Benedictine abbey of San Giorgio Maggiore in Venice inspired the cusps above the cases in the ceiling of Holkham Long Library.

A copy of Pliny's *Naturalis historia*, in Italian translation, printed on parchment by Nicolas Jenson at Venice in 1476, was decorated by the Paduan illuminator Giovanni Vendramin with a splendid architectural frontispiece in the typical Mantegnesque antiquarian style that spread from the Veneto to other Italian cultural centres, Florence, Rome and Naples in particular, in the second half of the fifteenth century (fig. 202). Pliny's books were among those that Coke had on display in his library, first at Thanet House and then in the Long Library at Holkham,[258] and one may wonder whether the classical architectural motif of a pronaos providing access to 'Pliny's temple of knowledge' came back to Thomas's mind when William Kent presented him with the drawing of the grand façade of his future mansion. Equally, the manuscript sold to him during his second sojourn in Rome for fifty Roman crowns as 'a book of the drawings of Raphael's', as recorded by Jarrett on 29 August 1716,[259] might have been a source of inspiration (fig. 203).

Fig. 206. Some of the splendidly bound books in the library.

While still in Italy, and probably at Dr Hobart's suggestion, Thomas was busy with a plan to publish an illustrated edition of Livy, based on seven manuscripts he had acquired at Lyon in November 1715 and another seven codices together with several printed editions by the end of his Grand Tour. In the course of his last year in Italy, he entrusted the classicist Anton Maria Salvini (1653–1729) and the philologist Antonio Maria Biscioni (1674–1756) with the task of collating antique manuscripts of the text against two printed editions, and the scholar and antiquarian Filippo Buonarroti (1661–1733) with matching Livy's text with illustrations from antiquarian drawings already in Coke's possession or commissioned by him. Thomas's party left Italy in July 1718, but the correspondence with the Florentine scholars continued.

Shortly after his return to England in May 1718 and marriage to Lady Margaret Tufton, daughter of the Earl of Thanet, on 2 July, Thomas Coke had his books organised in a dedicated library at Thanet House. Dr Hobart continued to act as his librarian, even when abroad, until his death in 1727. While in Florence in the late spring and early summer of 1719, he purchased for Coke the autograph of a history of the Etruscan civilisation by the Scottish historian Thomas Dempster (1579–1625), which at the time was in the possession of Salvini. The sale of the manuscript caused some controversy among the Florentine scholars, but Coke agreed with Buonarroti to entrust the codex to him, with the objective of having Dempster's text corrected and properly edited. He also pledged to fully finance its publication accompanied by a wealth of engravings from Etruscan artefacts and works of art. *De Etruria regali* was published in 1723, its title page naming Thomas Coke as editor (fig. 204).

By 1725 Coke had abandoned the Livy project. Instead, he sent twelve of his manuscripts and Salvini's collation of two others to the Dutch scholar Arnold Drakenborch (1684–1748), who published a full edition of Livy's *Ab urbe condita* in seven volumes between 1738 and 1746. In recognition of his generosity in lending his manuscripts, the author dedicated this edition to Thomas Coke.

In 1727, Domenico Ferrari succeeded Hobart as Coke's librarian. Within the same year, he supplied a catalogue of Thanet House Library. It provides a record for the section on architecture where Palladio's first edition of the *Quattro Libri* (1570) lived on the same shelf as Alberti's *De re aedificatoria* (1485), Scamozzi's *L'idea dell'architettura universale* (1615) and Vignola's *Architettura* (1640);[260] the three volumes of Campbell's *Vitruvius Britannicus* lived next to editions of Vitruvius from 1511 onwards, William Kent's *The Designs of Inigo Jones* (1727) and Alberti's *Della architettura*, published with parallel texts in Italian and English in 1726.[261] Antoine Desgodetz's *Les Edifices antiques de Rome* (1682) (fig. 205) shared a shelf with fundamental works on palaeography by Mabillon and Montfaucon and on the topography of ancient Rome by Marliani.[262] The two volumes of the *Galleria Giustiniana* (1631) and three volumes of Cavalieri's *Antiquarum statuarum urbis Romae*, from two different sets, lived on the same shelf as Kircher's *Obelisci Aegyptiaci* (1666).[263] The latter had been furnished with an elegant binding by John Brindley, binder to Queen Caroline and to Frederick, Prince of Wales. Brindley worked for Coke from about 1723 to about 1728 and then again in the 1740s, binding 485 volumes, mostly in fashionable gilt-tooled red morocco. Scamozzi's and Kent's works were instead bound and stamped with the earl's coronet, therefore after 1744, by Jean Robiquet, a Huguenot regarded as one of the best binders in London at the time who worked for Thomas Coke from the 1730s to the 1760s (fig. 206).

Fig. 207. Title page of Sir Edward Coke's copy of the *Magna charta cum statutis tum antiquis*, published 1576, with his signature and annotations, BN7834.

THE CHIEF JUSTICE'S COLLECTION

Earlier and later family members contributed to the library at Holkham. Sir Edward Coke's rigorous and scholarly collection was legal at the core, mostly English, including a number of his autographs, but equally rich in legal texts and their commentaries from antiquity to his time, often annotated, alongside rhetorical, literary and scientific works in Latin, English and French. His copies of the *Magna Carta and Statutes of England*, both in manuscript and in print, date from about 1300 to the 1600s. The most famous one is certainly a copy of *Magna charta cum statutis tum antiquis, tum recentibus, maxim opere, animo tenendis nunc demum ad unum, tipis aedita*, London, Richard Tottell, 1576, signed

Fig. 208. Portrait of King Edward I in a pocket-size copy of the *Magna Carta* written in the early fourteenth century, Ms. 134.

Fig. 209. King David in prayer in a fifteenth-century Flemish psalter, Ms. 24, fol. 105v.

'Edw Coke' and extensively annotated by him (fig. 207). One of the earliest manuscripts is a pocket-size copy written in the early fourteenth century in Anglo-French, the legal language of the time, and delicately illuminated at the beginning of *Magna Carta* with the portrait of Edward I (fig. 208). Sir Edward's signature features prominently on the front page of most of his manuscripts and books, from the legal texts inherited from his parents to dedication copies from contemporary authors (such as his adversary Sir Francis Bacon), from books acquired or received from other collections (such as Sir Christopher Hatton's library, received with the dowry of his second wife, Lady Elizabeth Hatton, widow of William Hatton, nephew and heir of Sir Christopher) to the catalogue of his own library. He also signed a beautifully illuminated fifteenth-century Flemish psalter, made for the English market, that he had inherited from his mother, Winifred Knightley Coke (1515–1569), daughter of William Knightley (1486–1548), a lawyer who practised in Norwich between about 1495 and 1540, and a student of law herself (fig. 209).

COKE OF NORFOLK'S CONTRIBUTION

Thomas William Coke greatly extended his great-uncle's library by introducing bookcases in the ante-room of Family Wing and Lord Leicester's dressing room. Important works that had been kept in a tower room now found a rather better home in what were henceforth known as the Classical Library and the Manuscript Library – rooms very

Fig. 210. The Roman mosaic above the fireplace in the Long Library was purchased by Thomas William Coke on his Grand Tour.

fittingly dominated by portraits of the two first earls (pls. 52 to 54).

Another important contribution by Coke of Norfolk can be admired in the Long Library. Thomas William Coke may not have had his great-uncle's passionate interest in art, but he acquired a spectacular animal mosaic during his Grand Tour (figs. 210 and 211 and pl. 55).Before he bought it and had it sent to his Norfolk home, the mosaic was last recorded in the late Renaissance Palazzo Mignanelli, now the home of the fashion designer Valentino. Its provenance is attested by a watercolour in Richard Topham's 'Paper Museum' of the early eighteenth century (fig. 212).

T. W. Coke employed this very rare mosaic to provide the key decorative scheme of the Long Library, where it was inset into the central fireplace's elaborate gilt mantel, replacing Griffier's copy of a sea piece by Claude Lorrain. Amidst rocky terrain, dotted with sparse plants, a lion has overwhelmed a leopard. The neutral background provides an effective foil for highlighting the two powerful predators. Such exotic felines were especially appreciated by a Roman clientele. Although the kill is yet to come, the final outcome is in no doubt. A detail, the beasts' tails, artfully signals the outcome of the fight: that of the leopard's droops to the ground, while the lion's flies triumphantly in the air, like a flag. The size of the tesserae is tiny, and in its miniaturist and polychrome techniques the mosaic strove to imitate the effects of a painting. In antiquity, small panels like the Holkham mosaic commonly served as the focal point of decorated floors in private houses.

THE ROOMS IN STRANGERS' WING

Although it was the last part of Holkham to be built, the pavilion for guests, known as Strangers' Wing, was an essential component of the grand country seat conceived by Thomas Coke: the country's élite tended to regularly descend on each other's great houses in large (sometimes very large) groups, and providing hospitality for one's peers was one of the main purposes of a stately home.

Fig. 211. Detail of the mosaic in the Long Library, showing its outstanding quality.

Fig. 212. A watercolour of the mosaic made for Richard Topham's 'Paper Museum' in the early eighteenth century.

Directing the construction of Strangers' Wing was perhaps Lady Margaret's most significant contribution to Holkham. This pavilion was a mere shell at Lord Leicester's death in 1759, and so its decorative features were entirely the dowager's work, often at her own expense. The interiors she created were rich, indeed opulent, with bedrooms hung with tapestry and damask; the ceilings, in common with the rooms in the *corps de logis*, were taken from designs by Inigo Jones. In contrast, the chimneypieces are taken from a number of sources, both known and unknown. Brettingham describes one chimneypiece as being 'an idea of Mr Kent's, done by Pickford'; it can be seen to be a variation of a design by Kent, published by Isaac Ware.[264] The chimneypiece in the ante-room is also a design by Jones; however, this piece has a complicated history, and apparently was commissioned for and originally installed in Family Wing.[265]

Other pieces have no published designer, but Brettingham describes them as being executed by Pickford, which seems improbable given the latter's death in 1760. The marble for six of the eight pieces was supplied in 1761 by William Atkinson,[266] who was the stepson of Joseph Pickford and his business partner for many years; after Pickford's death, he inherited Pickford's stock-in-trade and continued to work at Holkham, being commissioned to complete Coke's monument at Tittleshall.[267] However, it is not clear that Atkinson also carved the chimneypieces. The supply of marble was billed at a total of £70.12s.0d, far short of what one would expect for a finished piece; a second item in the same bill states that he was also paid £637.15s.10½d for 'marble, stone and masons work, which when settled with him will be particularized in the subsequent account', with a handwritten note stating that the work was carried out between February 1760 and June 1764. Sadly, no 'subsequent account' has been found. This much larger figure could encompass the carving of six chimneypieces, though without an itemised bill it is impossible to say for certain.

In essence, Strangers' Wing offers a series of small apartments, each consisting of a bedroom and a dressing room. Brettingham's description of the rooms shows that they were filled with prestigious works of art and mirrored the level of comfort and elegance of the family's pavilion. As in many other great houses, the guest area was also a place to display portraits of the family's ancestors (quite a few of them commissioned posthumously just for this purpose), but also of important relatives and high-ranking friends – the décor and the pictures designed to impress the guests with their hosts' sophistication and their prestigious connections.

Like the private areas of the house, the guest quarters are still being used according to their original purpose and have been regularly updated to offer the level of comfort appropriate for a house like Holkham. This has meant introducing a significant upgrade in domestic technology, the spectacular Tapestry Bathroom next to the Parrot Bedroom providing the best and most amusing example (pl. 72).

FAMILY WING

Pl. 52

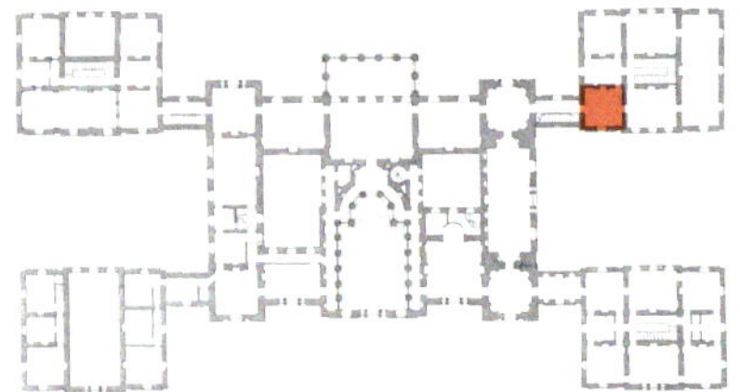

Pl. 53

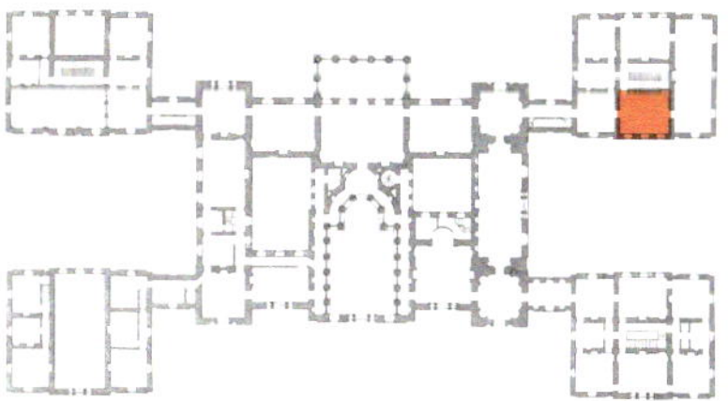

Thomas Coke
1st Earl of Leicester
Son of Edward &
Cary Coke
B 1697
D 1759
TUFTON

Pl. 54

Pl. 55

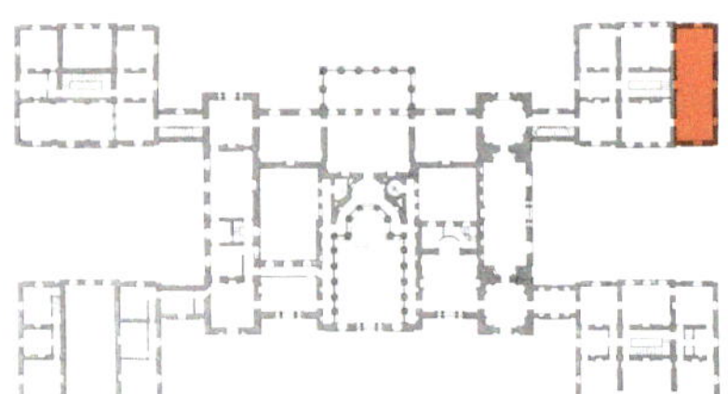

Pl. 56

Pl. 57

Pl. 58

Pl. 59

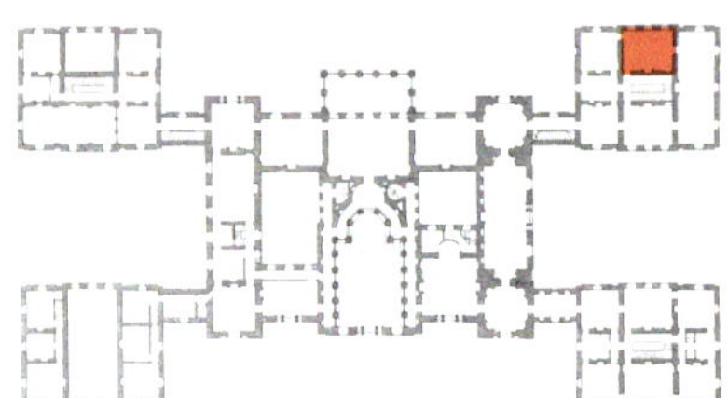

Pl. 60

Pl. 61

DAIRY
SAMSUNG

LESSONS IN CHEMISTRY BONNIE GARMUS
ISABEL ALLENDE
EVERYONE KNOWS YOUR MOTHER IS A WITCH

Pl. 62

Pl. 63

Pl. 64

Pl. 65

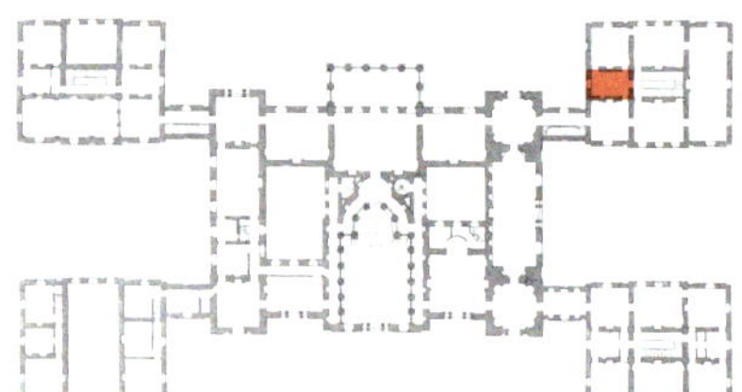

Pl. 66

CHAPTER 5

LIVING AT HOLKHAM

OVERLEAF
Footmen's uniforms in the Earl of Leicester's livery.

Grand buildings from past ages and their often lavishly decorated rooms can offer fascinating and highly satisfying sensory experiences, but anyone studying them for their aesthetic qualities alone runs the risk of missing at least some of their point. As we have seen, Holkham's Grand Apartment was indeed conceived primarily as a deeply sophisticated and many-layered display of a range of narratives, designed to impress, entertain and delight the builder's peers, who would come to visit and stay and who were expected to be impressed by their host's erudition, ambition, taste and wit.

And yet, like all great country houses, Holkham is not a museum, nor has it ever been one. It was a highly functional entity and even its grandest rooms were not there for display and show alone: they were designed to be like the stage for a play, as the setting for social practices and rituals that may seem strange and even incomprehensible to us today but were of extreme importance to people at the time. These rooms only come into their own, they only make sense, when filled with gorgeously and even gaudily dressed-up ladies and gentlemen – the mid-eighteenth century was, after all, the first and only time when 'it became possible ... for a perfectly serious man to attend ceremonies at court in a lavender suit ..., partridge silk stockings, gold buckles, ruffles and lace frills.'[268] They need the smart set of the time, gyrating graciously or making well-bred small talk, attended by footmen elegantly attired in their lord's livery. Therefore it is a good thing that many grand houses have been used as venues for countless costume films and TV series – Wilton, Castle Howard and others for Kubrick's *Barry Lyndon*, Hopetoun for *Outlander*, Highclere for *Downton Abbey* and of course Holkham for *The Duchess*, to name but a few: they bring to life those grand rooms that might otherwise seem brooding and forbidding.

Holkham has known its share of great events, including royal visits such as the reception for the Prince and Princess of Wales in 1865 (fig. 213). Beyond those formal events, a house like Holkham was designed and organised to cater to the needs of an aristocratic family, or rather – not to put too fine a point on it – of one man, the patron and owner of the whole estate. He is at the top of a pyramid, surrounded by his wife and immediate family and supported by layers of upper and lower servants, each fulfilling some essential purpose, all working and living somewhere within the house. Just a couple of generations earlier, the owner's central position would have been immediately visible in the layout of the house – just as the Sun King's bedchamber sits right in the centre of his vast Palace of Versailles. But at some point in time, the notion of privacy was invented, which at Holkham finds its expression in a separate wing for the family and another, similar one for their guests. The other areas of the house accommodated all the various functional areas of a semi-autonomous country house as well as the living quarters of a host of servants.

Contemporary visitors were often very interested in all the functional aspects of a great house. Having discussed the approach to Holkham and its exterior architecture in his *Six Weeks Tour through the Southern Counties of England and Wales*, Arthur Young proceeded to praise

> the inside of the house! ... Aye, my friend, there lies the forte of Holkam [*sic*]; talk not, ye admirers by wholesale, of the fronts – contrivance must have been the characteristic of lord Leicester; for so convenient a house does not exist – so admirably adapted to the English way of living, and so ready to be applied to the grand or the comfortable stile of life.[269]

UPSTAIRS – THE FAMILY AND THEIR GUESTS

The south-eastern part of Holkham's *corps de logis* contains the Grand Apartment one would expect in an early eighteenth-century 'house of parade': an ascending sequence consisting of ante-room, dressing room, bedroom and cabinet, with a back staircase for informal and unobserved access to the inner sanctum. In very formal places, such as the palaces of reigning princes and their ilk, the state apartment became the backdrop for acting out the subtleties of *precedence*, a subject of infinite fascination to all at court. Who had precedence over whom? How far did the owner deign to come forward to receive a guest? How far was a visitor allowed (or, if of superior rank, how far could he be induced) to proceed into an apartment?

The state apartment is a significant new element introduced with Holkham II, the four-pavilion concept developed in the late 1720s. The plans of Holkham I, drawn by Matthew Brettingham in 1726, had provided for two straightforward apartments for the master and the mistress of the house on the main floor, as well as a saloon (which probably doubled as a grand dining room) and a drawing room adjacent to it (fig. 60). There was also a gallery, consisting of three linked rooms, to house the paintings, sculptures and objects of *vertù* collected by Thomas Coke on his Grand Tour, while the adjoining room on the North Front (which became the State Dining Room) was probably intended to be the library.

The introduction of the pavilions signalled a radical change at Holkham (fig. 214). Whilst Holkham I had found a compromise between the formal and the private aspects of

Fig. 213. In 1865, the Prince of Wales (later King Edward VII) and his wife visited Holkham and a ball of honour was given for them in the candlelit Grand Apartment.

the dwelling, Holkham II not only separated those two elements but made each of them clearly visible through their architectural setting. The formal aspect found its perfect expression in a full-blown baroque state apartment, while the desire for privacy was more than satisfied by a secluded wing and by a novel way of arranging the rooms of the gentleman and the lady of the house. Family Wing and Strangers' Wing were, in fact, designed as independent entities, augmenting the house of parade (embodied by the *corps de logis*) with its antithesis, the villa. The main floor plan of Strangers' Wing (fig. 215) illustrates the characteristics of this novel type in its purest form:[270] essentially a rectangle of satisfying and no doubt well-considered proportions, divided by interior walls into a grid of nine compartments. The central compartment houses the staircase, giving direct access to most of the rooms, allowing the servants, whose realm was downstairs, to carry out their jobs efficiently. Each of the rooms encircling the staircase is also linked to its neighbours, thus permitting more intimate perambulation.

Each of the three apartments on the main floor provided a dressing room and a bedroom, but there was also a small room: not an old-style cabinet distinguished by rich décor and valuable works of art, but a closet in the more modern sense of the word. Holkham seems to have been ahead of the game in the introduction of water closets. Thomas Coke's interest in the matter is evident from a passage in a letter he wrote from London in March 1738 to his man on the spot, Matthew Brettingham: 'Remember to make a light out of [my water closet] that is in my dressing room to the stair case.'[271] The 'light' or window in question is still in place and the former water closet, now a drinks cabinet, can be found on the plan (fig. 216). They were furnished in style; '2 Marble Stools for Water Closets' at £9.5s.0d each as well as another at £7.10s.0d were installed in Family Wing in 1741 and others followed later: one in Strangers' Wing, another behind a tapestry door of the Duke of Grafton's bedroom in the *corps de logis*, and a companionable double-seater next to the Hall apse (fig. 214).

As discussed in Chapter 3, the strength of the grid plan lay in its adaptability: by leaving out one or other of the partition walls, and indeed by leaving out sections of the floor, the type was able to provide for larger rooms, such as the Kitchen and the Chapel in their respective pavilions. In Family Wing, the plan was tailored to the needs and priorities of Lord and Lady Leicester and their son. The Library is not only part of the private wing but also its largest space – proof of the regard Lord Leicester had for his books and manuscripts. The arrangements of the rooms in the north-east area of Family Wing indicate that Lord and Lady Leicester shared a bedroom rather than sleeping alone, but each had a dressing room of their own. Lord Coke had the two rooms in the attic; a winter dining room was situated downstairs, in the centre of the south façade.[272]

With the functions of everyday living accommodated in the wings, the *corps de logis* was available for more prestigious uses. According to the building accounts, its two apartments were originally named after the Duke of Cumberland and the Duke of Grafton, respectively – a royal and a well-nigh royal duke, both great friends of Lord Leicester[273] – but like the rest of the main floor rooms, they were used principally for show: possessing a state apartment was the important thing; the actual use was another matter. As we have seen, the works of art in the various rooms were carefully arranged to reflect the personality, the ideas and the ambitions of Lord Leicester.

The room with the most practical use was the State Dining Room, with its particular arrangement of concealed doors in the apse allowing footmen to appear and disappear unobtrusively (fig. 214 and pl. 18). Its decoration, evocative of ancient Rome, linked it harmoniously to the adjoining tripartite gallery, a space that held Lord Leicester's treasured sculptures but doubled – in the words of Admiral Boscawen, who stayed in the house in 1757 – as a 'Chambre d'Assembly . . . elegant to a degree, and when lighted up, quite scenery'.[274]

The admiral's remark gets to the heart of the *raison d'être* for places like Holkham: country houses were designed and built for the purpose of accommodating and entertaining visitors of the same social strata; the arrangement of works of art and of architectural decoration was conceived principally for their benefit.

The qualities and distribution of the various apartments in the house impressed and delighted Arthur Young so much that he exclaimed, 'what of all other circumstances is in Holkam infinitely the most striking, and what renders it so particularly superior to all other great houses – *convenience*'.[275] Like all his contemporaries, Young was well aware of the elementary requirements handed down from Vitruvius via Palladio, the 'three things without which no edifice will deserve to be commended; and these are utility or convenience, duration and beauty'. Whilst duration and beauty are largely self-explanatory, the definition of 'convenience' in the eighteenth-century sense is more complicated.

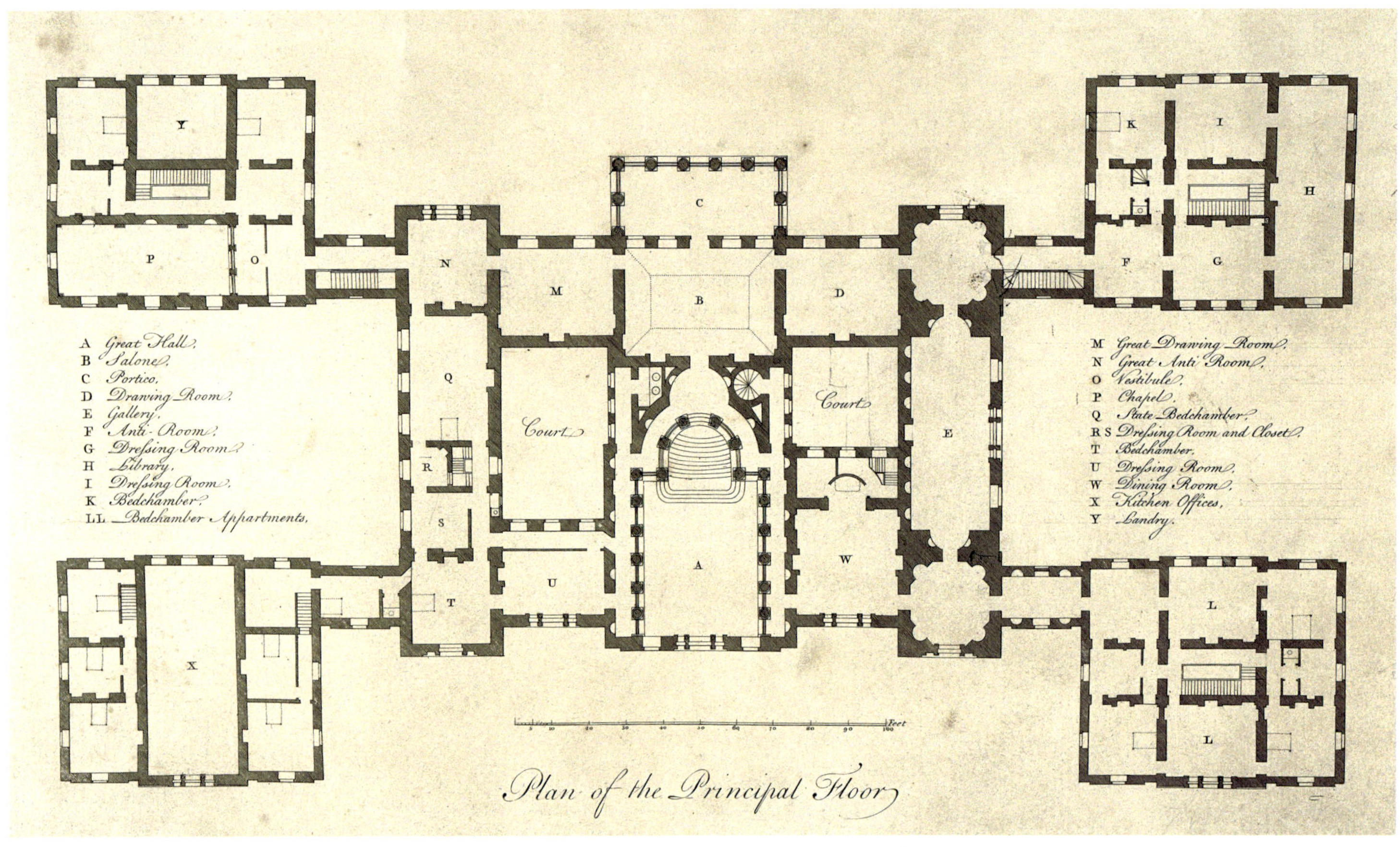

Fig. 214. Plan of Holkham's principal floor as published by Brettingham (1761).

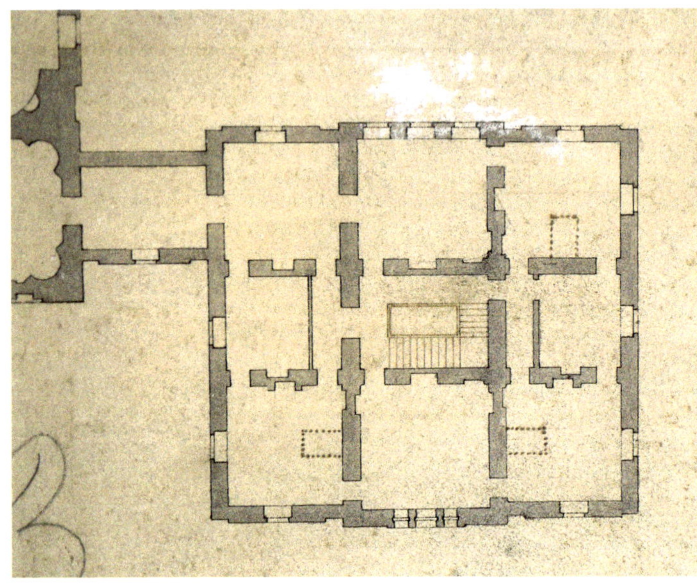

Fig. 215. The main floor of Strangers' Wing in a plan drawn in 1757, showing three guest apartments with their bedrooms and dressing rooms.

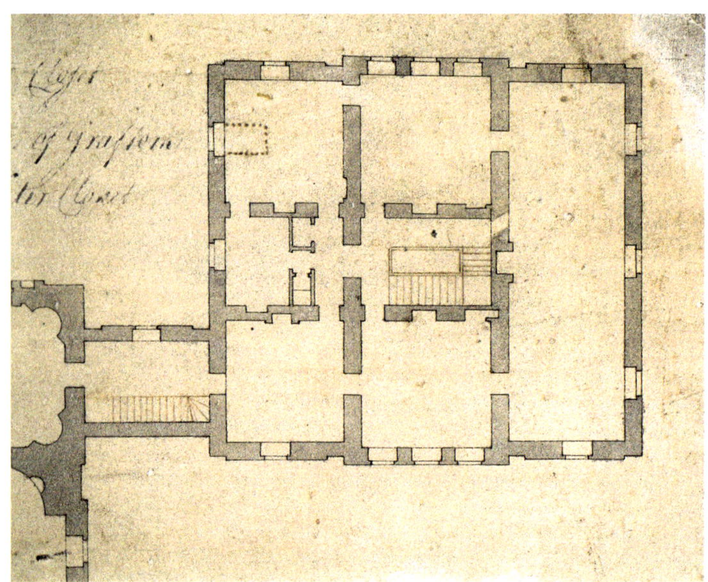

Fig. 216. The main floor of Family Wing in a plan drawn in 1757, showing the bedroom shared by Lord and Lady Leicester and the locations of the up-to-date water closets, one in Lady Leicester's closet next to the bedroom, the other in the corner of Lord Leicester's dressing room.

Convenience, or to use the French term, *convenance*, literally means the 'coming together' of aspects, to achieve something that is fitting or appropriate: the demand that a building and each of its rooms should provide exactly the right size, shape, position and degree of splendour for its particular purpose. By the second half of the century, the term had gradually transmuted into the more modern meaning of usefulness and even comfort. Arthur Young concluded his tour of southern England with a comparison of the houses that impressed him most: Holkham, Houghton, Blenheim, Wilton and Wanstead:

> In point of the beauty of architecture, *Holkham* and *Wanstead* rank first; but which of these have the preference, is a question, which by many would be variously determined. In my opinion, *Holkham* is the most beautiful; for notwithstanding the front of *Wanstead* is *absolutely* uniform, and commanded at one stroke of the eye, advantages *Holkam* does not possess, in consisting of parts, which, though uniform with each other, form not one simple whole; yet there is such a light elegance in the pile; such an airiness, that one would swear it moved; I cannot therefore but prefer it. *Wilton* is so very irregular, that one cannot speak of its architecture in a general stile ... *Houghton* is a magnificent edifice, but heavy; not however to come within a thousand degrees of *Blenheim*; which is a quarry.
>
> Upon the whole, *Holkam* is not only the largest, but undoubtedly the best house.[276]

And yet, living at Holkham has always been a mixed blessing, somewhere between privilege and burden. To be sure, the house is in a league of its own with all its spectacular qualities of the architecture, the interiors and the endlessly fascinating works of art, and its uncounted rooms of all shapes and sizes provide space for any kind of use one can think of.

As a family home it must be quite challenging, being more like a village under one roof than a simple house. And there is, and always has been, the issue of privacy. The first earl addressed this by conceiving the separate pavilions at the corners of the central body of the house, thus separating the residential functions from the more formal ones and creating a family wing and a strangers' wing similar to private villas. The desire for privacy has always clashed with the more public functions of the house. Thus the terraces were created in the 1850s to keep the public from wandering along the south and west sides of the house. With greater frequency of open days and larger numbers of visitors in and around the house, family members can rarely feel completely unobserved. Furthermore, the siting and dimensions of the windows on the ground floor, where there are many private rooms, are determined much more by the requirements of the grand Palladian façade than by the comfort of the inhabitants. From within the rooms, the windows are too small and too far up, letting in not much light whilst impeding the view to the outside.

DOWNSTAIRS – THE SERVANTS AND THEIR LIFE

Houses like Holkham depended on a small army of servants. We know their names and functions, and of course their earnings, from the Domestic Accounts preserved in

Holkham's archives. Even in 1723, long before the new house was built, twenty servants looked after the needs of Mr Coke and Lady Margaret:

Mr Williams	House Steward	£40 p.a.
Edw.d Thomas	Secretary	£30
Abraham Thomas		£20
John Gundamore	Cook	£30
Andrew Griffith	Butler	£12
William Tomley	Porter	£10
James Davids	under Butler & ffootman	£9
Phil: Bender	ffootman	£8
George Roth		£8
William Holland		£7
Richard Chaplin	Coachman	£12
John Large	Postillion	£8
William Bell	Helper in the Stable	£6
Mr.s Smith		£10
Frances Lucas	nursery maid	£5
Doro:	Eales Laundry Maid	
Eliza:	Scotch D.o	
Mary Allen		
Magdalen Roynalt		
Mary Lommon[277]		

In 1755, the establishment in the largely completed new house needed rather more staff, and their wages had risen, too – particularly the cook's, who earned even more than the house steward:

Mander	House Steward	£50 p.a.
Baufre	Cook	£52.10.0
Andree	Valet de Chambre	£20
Birt	Butler	£15
Mitchell	Secretary	£20
Demay	under Cook	£20
James Brianley	Porter	£10
John Butley	Footman	£9
John Williams	"	£9
Daniel Bird	"	£8
John Chinn	"	£9
Robin Custains	"	£9
Andrew Dawson	Menagerie man	£14
Robert Mays	Fisher Man	1s/day
Staniforth	Housekeeper	£20
Mary Staniforth	House maid	£6
Sarah Gir	"	£6
Mary Littlewood	"	£6
Mary Brammer	"	£6
Hanna Bose	Dairy maid	£6
Sarah Hulton	House maid	£6
Rachel Cowley	Laundry Maid	£6
Frances Butcher	Laundry Maid	£6
Anne Framingham	Still House maid	£4
Mary Green	Kitchen maid	£6
Mary Gough	Scullery maid	£4[278]

As in many other houses, the servants' activities mostly took place in a realm of their own, separated from their employers by the proverbial green baize doors. And indeed, Thomas Coke paid particular attention to the design of the house behind the green baize doors, advising Matthew Brettingham to 'Pray take notice of those doors cover'd with green bays', as he sent him on a tour of inspection of other houses,

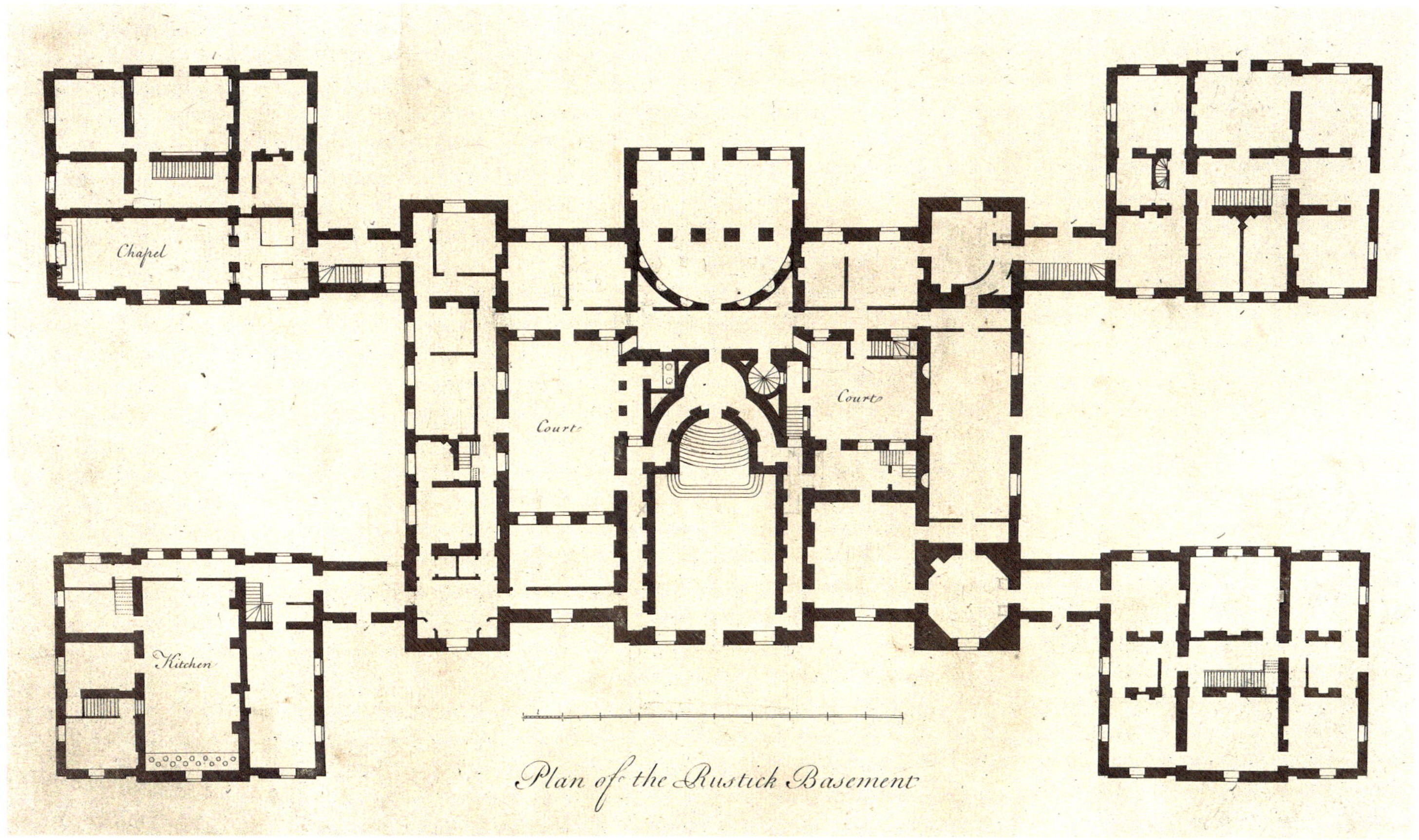

Fig. 217. Plan of Holkham's 'rustick basement' or ground floor, as published by Brettingham (1761).

'and the hinges that make them shut of themselves'.[279] Brettingham's son later confirmed that 'Commodiousness was one of the Earl of Leicester's leading maxims, and this sensible principle is seen in every aspect of the plan.'[280]

The most important feature in this respect was the rusticated basement, which was in practice the ground floor of the house (fig. 217). Brettingham junior explained that its 'peculiar conveniency ... consists in having the upper servants offices, to which the basement story is appropriated, placed under the principal apartments, consequently nearer to the master and his company'. This arrangement avoided placing the servants either in underground basements or in distant wings, and lent itself to a neat progression of domestic departments.[281]

In the south-west or Family Wing, the rooms on the rusticated floor (apart from the 'rustic parlour', or dining room, and Thomas Coke's bathroom) were occupied by personal servants: the lady's maid and a chambermaid (who had direct access by backstairs to the lady's closet above); the valet and secretary in two rather more secluded rooms (beneath the Long Library); and a footman in a small room near the staircase. They were in use by 1738–39, when the servants vacated the three largest to serve as guest rooms, as Coke wanted to bring twelve gentlemen with him to Holkham.[282] These were large pleasant rooms, although their outlook to the west and south would not have been at its best whilst the old hall still stood and building work continued.

As close as possible to Family Wing, at the west end of the south corridor, was the butler's suite of pantry, bedroom and plateroom. From here he had good access both to Family Wing and upstairs to the staterooms at the west end of the main house. The lack of a corresponding staircase near Strangers' Wing, where it would serve no purpose, emphasises the planning behind such features. In his pantry, as well as equipment needed for serving wine and washing cutlery and glasses, he kept those items that might well be called for by the gentlemen, such as backgammon tables, chessboards and pearl and ivory counters. Here, too, he would fill in his books recording stocks of wine and beer: immediately across the corridor were stairs down to his cellars. Beer was piped directly from the brewhouse at the far end of the house. Wine, too, was often bought in bulk and bottled under his direction, using bottles stamped with the ostrich crest and corks supplied by a cork-cutter in King's Lynn.

The other end of the south corridor was the housekeeper's province. She supervised the stillroom, laundry, dairy and housemaids and was also responsible for issuing and recording supplies of tea, sugar, soap and candles. Just around the corner from her bedchamber was the dessert room, where the equipment reveals some of her duties: a press for dried sweetmeats, a pair of wafer irons, a toasting fork and chafing dish, 'tea kettles', coffee and 'jocolot' pots, tin boxes for biscuits and 'a machine for orange butter'. Just beyond it was the breakfast room, where the senior servants gathered for breakfast and probably dessert.

As in the butler's department, the housekeeper's responsibilities extended to the cellars. The maids in the dairy, laundry and stillroom worked on the same level as the wine and beer cellars at the other end of the house, but owing to the peculiarities of Holkham's construction (fig. 108) they were above ground at the east end. The newly completed dairy greatly impressed Mrs Lybbe Powys when she saw it in 1756: 'the neatest place you can imagine, the whole marble'.[283] It probably remained beneath the Chapel Wing until 1915. Laundry maids tended to lead rather more independent lives than the other maids, but this became obvious only when a separate laundry was built in the mid-nineteenth century. Beneath the east side of the main house was the stillroom. Here, there were tubs, a still and an alembic, all for distilling cordials and liqueurs, along with preserving pans, an apple roaster, copper baking plates, moulds for pineapples, fruit and cheese, a mortar and pestle for ice, and, of course, shelves and drawers for the storage of preserves and cordials. The surviving charcoal stoves, set in a large brick stand under the window, are probably original. At a later date, probably in the mid-nineteenth century, a coal-fired brick bread oven was built into a corner; it replaced the original bakehouse off Kitchen Court and remained in use until 1914.

There was one bedchamber on this lower floor, furnished only with a four-poster bed and a grate. This was possibly for one or more laundry maids. Two large rooms in the attic storey of Chapel Wing, each containing three beds, were housemaids' rooms in 1774. When later generations produced numerous children, these rooms became nurseries or family rooms.

Past the housekeeper's dessert room and breakfast room was the house steward's area, situated in the north-east corner. Although lacking the southern aspect of the butler's and housekeeper's quarters, in the eighteenth century his east-facing bedchamber overlooked a flower garden between the wings. It was only in the mid-nineteenth century that his view through to the park was curtailed, first by the new laundry, and later by the bowling alley. Next door, his storeroom also served as his office; he was responsible for accounting for provisions and household disbursements until these duties were transferred to the estate office in the nineteenth century. Around the corner, the Steward's Room itself was the senior servants' dining room. Here, the steward, butler, housekeeper, senior footman and visiting servants of equivalent rank took their dinner, waited on by the Steward's Room's boy. Normally, five or six servants ate here, but it

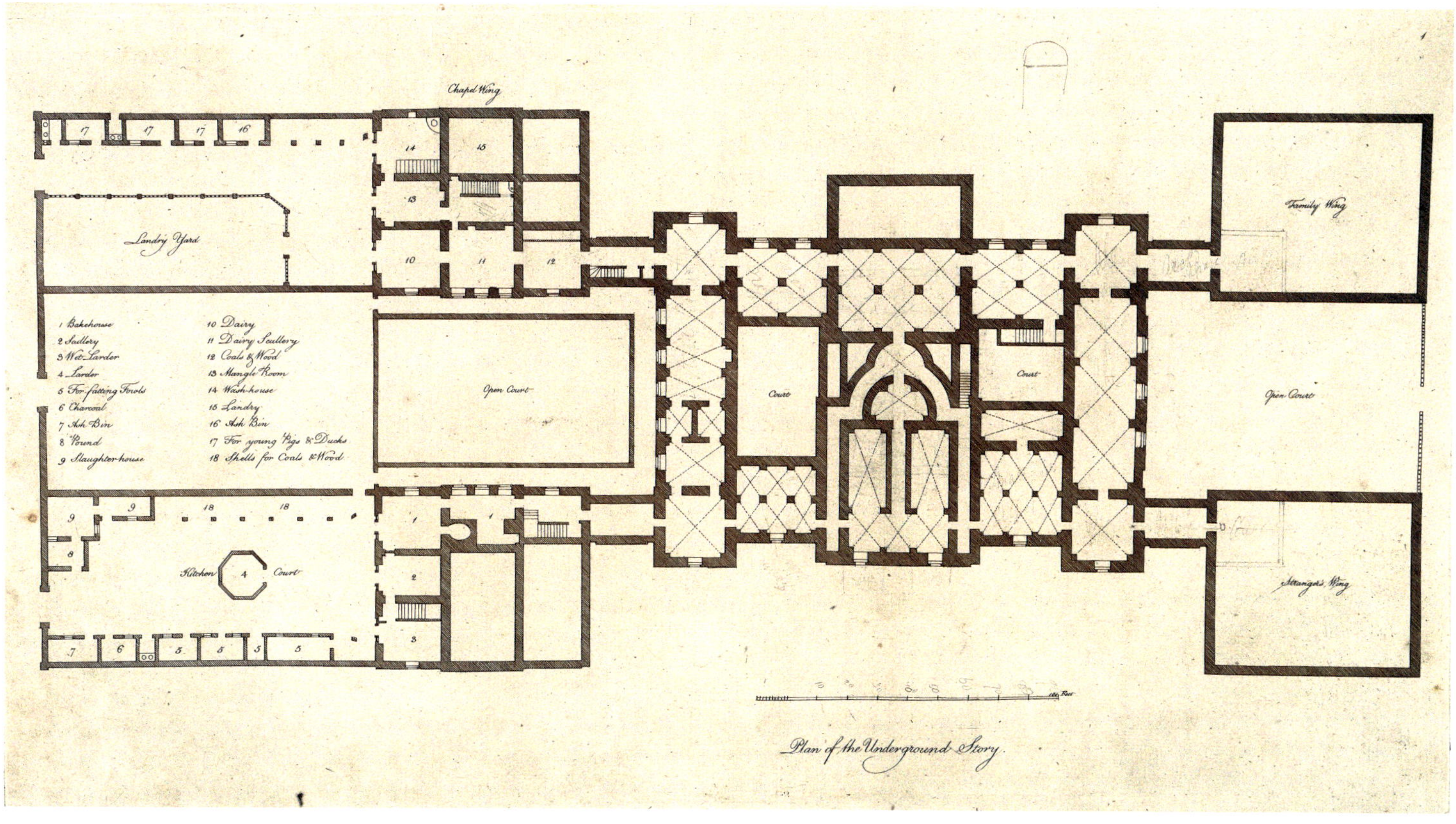

Fig. 218. Plan of Holkham's 'underground story', as published by Brettingham (1761), showing the vaulted basement underneath the main house and detailing all the service areas on the eastern side.

could seat many more if there was a large house party, when extra help would be hired to assist.

The proximity of the butler's, housekeeper's and steward's rooms would probably have been avoided in a house designed in Victorian times, and not without reason, for quite a stir was caused when 'a gentleman of Holkham', who turned out to be T. W. Coke's steward, Francis Crick (formerly his valet), had an affair with the married housekeeper, resulting in both a daughter and a divorce.[284]

Meals in the Steward's Room were probably much hotter than those served in the state dining rooms, for it was close to the Kitchen Wing. The lower servants were even better placed in this respect, providing they did not share their employer's distaste for cooking smells, for they ate in the Servants' Hall, just within Kitchen Wing. They usually numbered between twenty-five and thirty, presided over by the house porter. On special occasions they were far outnumbered by visitors' servants. At other times they could be joined by an occasional craftsman, or for a couple of days by thirty coal carters. When the family was away, a skeleton staff (usually the housekeeper, the porter and some of the maids) received 'board wages'; at such times, the Servants' Hall was deserted and they probably cooked and ate in the housekeeper's rooms.

Stairs next to the Servants' Hall led up to a suite of rooms at the top of the wing, above the kitchen and Servants' Hall. At least three or four rooms, plus a 'gallery', were occupied by footmen or other male servants. In the eighteenth century, all the beds were four-posters, with blue and white checked hangings, and only one of the rooms contained more than one bed. The gallery was apparently a shared room where the footmen powdered their hair and stored their clothes. Off the lower landing, one of the rooms was subdivided in the early twentieth century to provide a bathroom: once a week, with the men out of the way, the kitchen maids were allowed here to take a bath.[285]

Beyond the Servants' Hall, the rest of Kitchen Wing was strictly the preserve of the cook and kitchen maids. Although footmen went as far as the kitchen door, they received the food through hatches, and even in the twentieth century the kitchen and scullery maids rarely left this area. The kitchen was impressive: 'such an amazing large and good kitchen I

Fig. 219. The bell system for calling servants from the various rooms used by family and guests, situated in the service corridor on the south side, next to the portico room.

never saw, everything in it so nice and clever', wrote Mrs Lybbe Powys in 1756. In a random sample year, 1861, the cook and three kitchen maids prepared 18,669 dinners, an average of about 50 each day.[286] This cook was a woman, paid £40 a year; a male French cook appointed a few years later was paid £125. Above the side rooms (pastry room, scullery and larder) were the cook's and kitchen maids' bedrooms, forming a distinct unit, now a staff flat. There had to be a certain amount of flexibility in the allocation of rooms, however, depending on whether a male or female cook was employed at any one time.

At the bottom of Kitchen Wing, in the cellar floor but at ground level (fig. 218), were the lower kitchen (used only at particularly busy times), lower scullery, salting and fish larders, and the exit to the Kitchen Court. In 1756, as the wing neared completion, Thomas Coke spent much time 'setting out' the Kitchen Court with Brettingham senior.[287] Here, there were a pound and a slaughter house, rooms for 'fatting fowls', and sheds for charcoal, wood, coal and ash. The corresponding Laundry Court, outside the Chapel Wing, included a 'bleach ground' or drying yard, and sheds for young pigs and ducks, which, as one visitor noted, gave 'not so good a prospect as it deserves' to the state apartment at that end of the house.[288]

The house porter, responsible for answering all doorbells and locking external doors, had a room near the door in the corridor building linking the body of the house to Kitchen Wing. Higher-ranking visitors would arrive at the central door into the Marble Hall, from where they could be shown more directly to Strangers' Wing. Visitors' servants were accommodated either next to their employers on the top 'attic' floor of Strangers' Wing, or on the upper floors of the east side of the house (later called Nelson Wing). The room above the Landscape Room, for example, was occupied early in the twentieth century by visitors' valets. It is difficult to identify these rooms in inventories, but their large size marks them out as dormitory rooms.

Unusually for such a house, the main service corridors were heated. In 1865, as the house porter noted in his book, the passages and working areas were lit by gas for the first time: possibly a mixed blessing, as it was not considered clean enough for the family and staterooms, which were lit by candles and lamps until the early twentieth century. The rustic basement was shared with only one or two reception rooms, particularly the Portico Room in the centre of the south front, where eighteenth-century visitors waited for the housekeeper to conduct them on the tour of the house, and which in Victorian times became the Billiards Room and then the Smoking Room. Elsewhere, however, it was essential for servants to go about their work unseen: a corridor runs round the outside of the Marble Hall at this level and, on the first floor, service passages lie hidden behind the staterooms.

Fig. 220. Fallow deer, introduced by the second earl in the 1840s, populate the park.

Domestic organisation depended on routine and discipline within each separate department – butler's, housekeeper's and cook's – but a communication system was crucial, not least to enable family and guests to summon servants. There was a partially wired bell system, an advance on traditional bell ropes, installed between 1756 and 1758, and by the turn of the century there was a system of wires and cranks of the type which enabled all main rooms to be connected to a central bell board. In the mid-1840s, a new bell system was installed at a cost of £812.12s.0d (fig. 219).[289] In many houses, the bell board was outside the Servants' Hall, but at Holkham there are two generations of boards on either side of the main south corridor, conveniently situated between the butler's pantry and the housekeeper's quarters.

Although the second Earl of Leicester, eager to modernise the hall in the mid-nineteenth century, built a new laundry, brewhouse and water supply, he felt no need to improve on the arrangement of the house servants' areas. As his family grew, bedrooms that had been occupied by servants proved perfectly suitable for a nursery, schoolroom or guests, even if this meant that the lower servants had to share rooms more often than in the eighteenth century. The dairy and laundry functioned well into the twentieth century; the kitchen, and occasionally the spit, were used until 1939; within living memory, meals were taken in the Servants' Hall and the Steward's Room, and the butler's pantry is still in use. As the number of servants declined after 1914, many of their rooms were sufficiently light, spacious and conveniently situated to be assimilated into Family and Chapel Wings as family rooms, and elsewhere to become staff flats, offices (including the Archives), guest rooms or workshops. Thomas Coke's insistence on 'commodiousness' has stood the greatest test of time: proving its ability to adapt to changing circumstances.

Fig. 221. Pie, Bobs, Pickles, Duke and Jeanie, the family dogs in 1914: a Labrador retriever cross, a chihuahua, a Plummer's or Parson's Jack Russell terrier, a retriever and a small, probably badly behaved terrier cross, something like West Highland and Jack Russell. Doubtless a highly entertaining group.

COUNTRY HOUSE ACTIVITIES AND THE RÔLE OF ANIMALS

The land surrounding a country house has always been of decisive significance on many levels. Traditionally, its agricultural use generated the income that enabled a landowner to build and maintain a great house, fill it with works of art and lead a refined lifestyle. But, as discussed in Chapter 2, the landscape fulfilled other purposes beyond agriculture and forestry. It could be shaped and used in ways that allowed many forms of entertainment, particularly sports such as hunting and shooting – a learned guest, Edward Spelman, fondly recalled outdoor exploits at Holkham in 1742, referring to times 'when we were Fox-hunters'. Hunting and shooting involved animals, not just the prey such as foxes, partridges and pheasants, but also horses and dogs. In the mid-nineteenth century, the second earl introduced fallow deer, who are still thriving in the park (fig. 220).

Dogs have always been important at Holkham, as is documented in many paintings where they make their presence felt (figs. 6, 7, 8 and 9). Lady Margaret, the first countess, was known to have a menagerie of small dogs, including her favourites, Minny and Cæsar.[290]

Their much later successors Pie, Bobs, Pickles, Duke and Jeanie, peering somewhat uncomfortably from a photograph dated 1914 (fig. 221), do not look like working dogs, but there can be no doubt that they were much loved. A dog cemetery in the arboretum records the names, dates and characters of more recent canine members of the household: 'Teazle 1987–2000, The matriarch to all our labradors', 'Rocket 1986–1998, A faithful spaniel', 'Zulu

Fig. 222. One of the markers in the dog cemetery in the arboretum, for a Labrador called Zulu, fondly remembered as 'a sinful dog, but a great character'.

1989–2004, A sinful dog, but a great character' (fig. 222), 'Jupiter, Irish Terrier, May 2008–Jan. 2020, Dad & Juno's dog'. On the mound overlooking the house from the south-west, Swazi, another faithful spaniel (who is in fact buried right there), gazes adoringly at her master, the seventh earl, whose bronze figure sits there on a bench (fig. 223). The current leader of the pack at Holkham is one Bilbo, a basset hound, whose authoritative voice and mien belie his short stature (fig. 224).

Fig. 223. The seventh Earl of Leicester and his spaniel Swazi on a bench next to their own bronze likenesses, a gift from his wife, Lady Sarah, for his 65th birthday in 2001. The dog is in fact buried at this spot.

Fig. 224. Bilbo, the current leader of the dogs at Holkham.

OPEN TO THE PUBLIC

Visiting country houses, sometimes travelling considerable distances to do so, was a favourite pastime of the eighteenth-century nobility. Lord Leicester and his friends regularly visited other estates, mainly out of interest in architecture and connoisseurship. But calling on friends and acquaintances was one thing; the advent of tourism was quite another, as perfect strangers would arrive at the door, not to visit the family, but to view a great house, its contents and setting, as a form of entertainment.

Holkham Hall was a tourist attraction well before it was finished. From the very beginning, it was a hospitable place and it is symptomatic that most of the detailed information we have about early sightseers comes from Holkham's wine books. In these accounts, the servants recorded whom they had served refreshments from the cellars, together with the amount and the type of wine dispensed. This civilised custom was much appreciated by the visitors, particularly because hospitality and kindness were far from being the norm, at least in Norfolk. Sir George Lyttelton, writing to the architect Sanderson Miller in 1758, was not only full of praise for Holkham's aesthetic delights but also recorded that 'I was not offered the least refreshment, but a glass of wine at Lord Leicester's, at any House I visited in the whole county'.[291] Some were even more fortunate. Mrs Lybbe Powys, visiting the house in 1756, recorded that her party

> had a Breakfast at Holkham, in ye genteelest taste with all kinds of cakes and Fruit placed undesired in an appartment we were to go thro'; which as ye family were from home I thought was very clever in the House keeper, for one is so often ask'd by people whether one *chuses* chocolate which forbidding word at once puts (as intended) a Negative on the Question.[292]

The wine books are preserved from summer 1748 onwards, and groups of visitors crop up constantly in their pages. On 10 June 1748, 'Mrs Powditch & Company to see the house and gardens' were refreshed with 'Lisbon' – a red or white fortified wine. 'Mr Warner & Company to See the House & Gardens' on 23 June, 'Three Gentlemen to see ye House' on 12 July, 'Mr Gibbs, Mr Able and Several Tennants with Their Wives to See the House & Gardens' on 15 July and 'Lord Carr, Sr Wm Gage and Sir John Burle with Eight more in Company to See ye House' on 23 July completed the round of visitors that summer (the latter being served with Calcavella, a sweet wine, also from Portugal).

They all came to look at a construction site in full swing. Family Wing had been inhabited since 1740, and some (perhaps not all) visitors were admitted to see the private rooms,[293] but the main block of the house was far from finished. It rose to full height on its southern side, with the first tower completed in 1748 and the second tower following in 1749, but the northern half was lagging behind. No doubt the well-dressed ladies and gentlemen preferred to gaze at the proceedings from a safe distance, avoiding the perils of the building site. The Seat on the Mount, some distance to the south-west of the building, offered an ideal vantage point over both house and pleasure ground; 'the most picturesque spot about the place', as a visitor commented in 1750.[294]

Whilst there was no official entrance fee, we may assume that the servants at Holkham did quite well out of the visitors' generosity. As early as 1747, Horace Walpole had written to a friend that

> Lord Bath and his Countess and his son have been making a tour: at Lord Leicester's they forgot to give anything to the servants that showed the house; upon recollection – and deliberation, they sent back a man and horse six miles with – half a crown! What loads of money they are saving for the French!

If giving half a crown – two shillings and sixpence, with roughly the purchasing power of fifteen pounds in current money – brought the cutting wit of Horace Walpole down on one's head, then obviously the titled visitors were expected to be rather more open-handed.

During the 1750s, the influx of 'Company to see the House' increased steadily; in the summer months, every other day or so a group of visitors was offered either Lisbon or Port. Sometimes two or three 'Companys' arrived in one day, and as soon as the main block was roofed and at least a few rooms furnished, people flocked to Holkham to gawp and to comment.

Most of them were full of praise for what they saw. In diaries and letters they recorded their impressions for their own amusement or for their friends' information. The plantations and the grounds were admired, but not without reservations. Admiral Boscawen commented on the former: 'I can't say good ones, they will be something in time.'[295]

The outside was praised as 'magnificent' and 'a most beautiful building', but the interiors overwhelmed the visitors to the extent that they struggled for adequate words. For the Marchioness Grey, who visited in 1750, 'no praise could be too high for this house', and Lady Hervey in 1765 had 'neither time nor words to attempt a description of Holkham, where the utmost magnificence and elegance is blended with all the conveniences imaginable'.

Whilst most visitors tended to reiterate more or less the same polite comments and judgements, Lady Beauchamp Proctor left a very personal account of a visit in 1764, showing she was anything but overawed by the works of art on display. Some made her blush, such as the

> fine statues, I suppose all brought from Rome, but it was impossible to examine them, they were all so slenderly cloath'd, indeed they were quite indecent, but when there was drapery we ventured to criticize, & some were very beautifull, ... but I was sorry to see my Lord had employ'd some modern bunglers, to add noses, fingers, arms &c which has made most of them appear out of proportion, ... a Juno for example, with a finger that would have suited an Atlas, Noses that gave one strange Ideas, and there was a Jupiter, below stair, whose new turned arms must have been copied from the Colossus.[296]

Fig. 225. Visitors and guests ambulate on the lawn outside Holkham's south front in the 1830s.

She also commented on the Marble Hall, which she called 'superb, I beleive [*sic*] the grandest thing of the sort in England', but she also related that

> 'tis the fashion to condemn the Hall, & not without some reason, for to look down the steps from the Salloon, it does certainly appear like a cold bath'.[297]

After Lord Leicester's death in 1759, the Dowager continued the tradition of allowing access to the house. As Mrs Poyntz wrote to her daughter, Lady Spencer, after praising Lady Leicester for her deeds of charity: 'Holkham is really worth your seeing: Tuesday is the day they show the house, Thursday is her publick day, and it is her delight to show the House' – to friends and acquaintances who would 'find an elegant good dinner, for she is very well served, and there is no fuss'.[298]

Arthur Young, author of *A Six Weeks Tour through the Southern Counties of England and Wales*, published in 1768, was in a sense the first travel journalist to present Holkham Hall to an interested and growing public. He did this well, with a great deal of precise information and sound judgement, and his octavo booklet (together with the younger Brettingham's edition of the large-scale *Plans of Holkham*) provided the material reiterated in many future guidebooks.

Young scrutinised the house and its contents very closely, noting even the damaged nose of the sow (fig. 170) depicted in the tablet of the right-hand marble chimneypiece in the State Dining Room – a victim of tourism, 'broke off by a too common misapplication of sense, feeling instead of seeing'.[299]

Visiting Holkham gradually took on a new and different character in the late 1760s and early 1770s (fig. 225). In September 1772, Lady Beauchamp Proctor revisited Holkham six years after her first visit and found the place positively awash with visitors:

> when we came to the House the Servant told us we could not see it for an hour at least as there was a party going round ... we were obliged to submit to be shut up with Jupiter Ammon [in the Smoking Room beneath the Saloon] and a whole tribe of people, 'till the Housekeeper was ready to attend us, nothing

> could be more disagreeable than this situation, we all stared at one another, and not a Creature opened their mouths, some of the Masters amused themselves with trying to throw their Hats upon the Heads of the Busts, whilst the Misses scrutinized one anothers dress, . . . at length the long wished for time arrived. The Good woman appeared, and we rushed on her like a swarm of Bees, we went the usual round, all but the wing My Lord and Lady used to inhabit themselves, this was new doing up, I dragged them all into the atticks, for which I beleive none of them thankd me, especially one poor woman very big with Child, I wanted to look at the Sea, but it was so hazy we could not distinguish it from a cloud . . .; when we came down, the party vanished, but we were conducted a second time to Mr Jupiter, where we were poured libations of Chocolate, on his altar, that is we had some set out in great form in the Leicester style.[300]

With this huge interest in the house it is not surprising that the first proper house guide was printed soon afterwards: *A Description of Holkham House, in Norfolk; With a Particular of the Pictures, Statues, Bustoes, and other Marbles therein.* 'Published by Permission of the Hon. Wenman Coke' by a Norwich bookseller in 1775, it listed the works of art and their authors in the various rooms, and was condemned a few years later by the visitor Craven Ord for its 'confused and incorrect manner, and not much of service'. Lord Leicester's nephew Wenman Coke, who had inherited the house and estate upon the Dowager's death in February 1775, kept up the custom she had established: the *Norfolk Tour* reprint of 1775 stated that Holkham 'can be seen any day of the week, except Sunday, by noblemen and foreigners, but on Tuesday only by other people'.

Country-house visiting became popular again with the end of the long war on the Continent, and a comprehensive and informative guidebook appeared at last in 1817: *The Stranger's Guide to Holkham, Containing a Description of the Paintings, Statues &c., of Holkham House, In the County of Norfolk, The Magnificent Seat and Residence of T. W. Coke, Esq., M. P. . . . Printed, Published and Sold by J. Dawson, Burnham.* Later visitors were provided with ingenious hand-held picture guides. A pair of such guides to the Saloon and the (West) Drawing Room, dated 1853, are rare survivors of the visual aids that visitors were offered in the second earl's time (figs. 226 and 227).

The 1817 guide provided visitors with clear instructions for their tour: they were to congregate in the vestibule under the portico and Saloon, to wait for 'the Person who shews the House'. Their guide would take them first to the Marble Hall, then up to the main floor, thus denying them direct access to the Saloon from the Marble Hall, which would have been the 'correct' progress according to the builder (who had, of course, thought in terms of baroque representation). Instead, they followed a roundabout course from the Hall via the State Dining Room to the Strangers' Wing, thence through the Statue Gallery to a circuit of the Family Wing. From here they proceeded along the south front enfilade, admiring the rooms of the Grand Apartment, to the Chapel, doubling back through the State Bedroom to the Marble Hall: a sequence that is in effect identical to the one that Holkham's visitors still follow today.

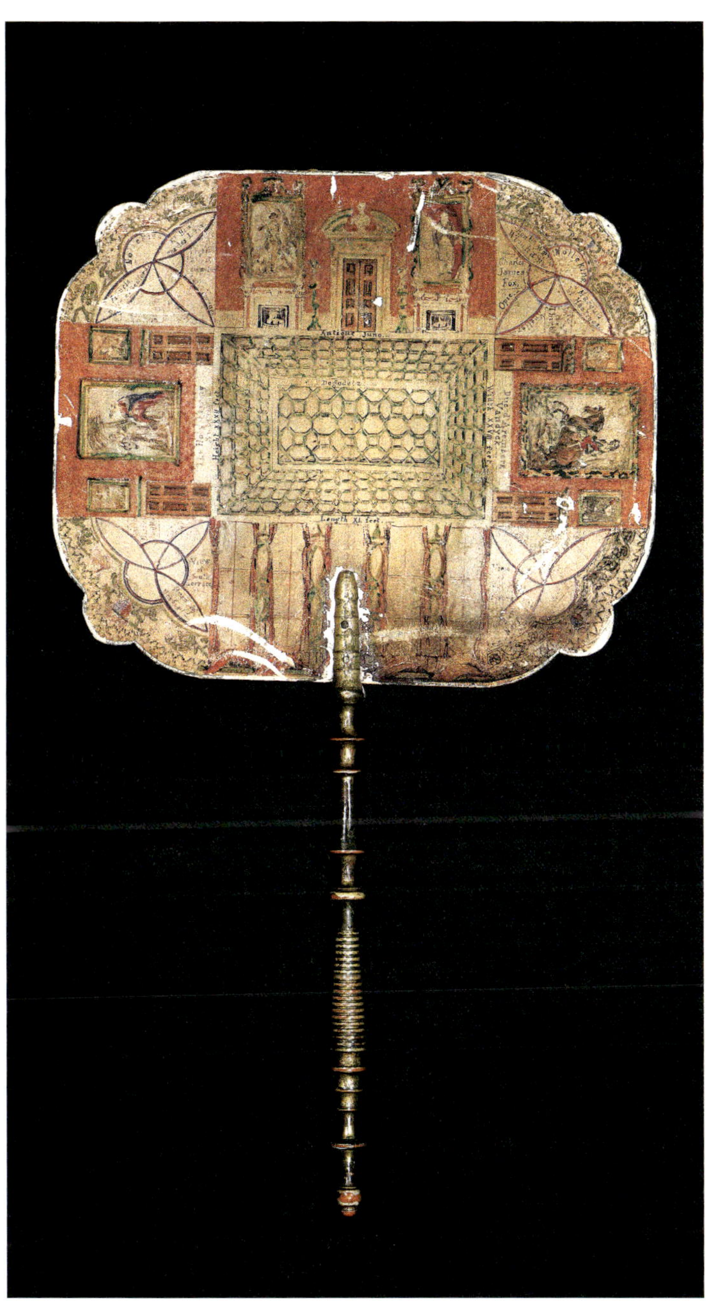

Fig. 226. A handheld picture guide to the paintings and details of the Saloon, 1853.

Fig. 227. A handheld picture guide to the paintings and details of the West Drawing Room, dated March 1853.

STRANGERS' WING

Pl. 67

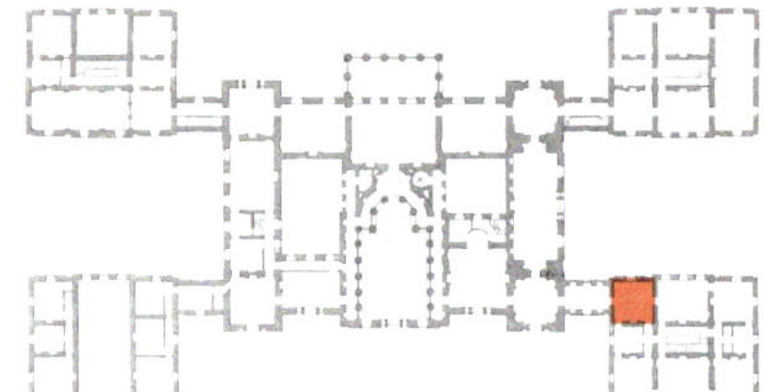

Pl. 68

Pl. 69

CASALI

Pl. 70

Pl. 71

Pl. 72

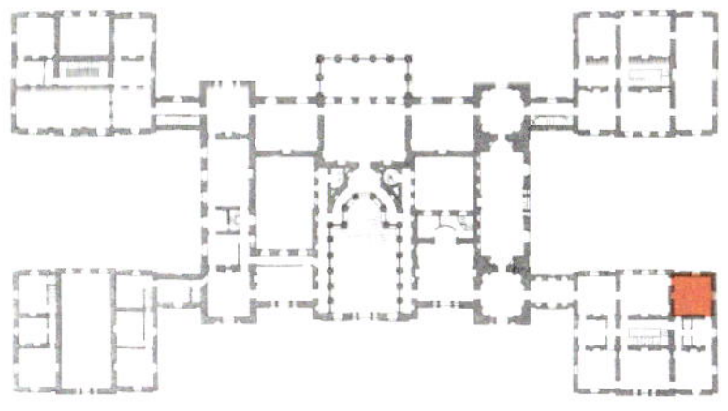

Pl. 73

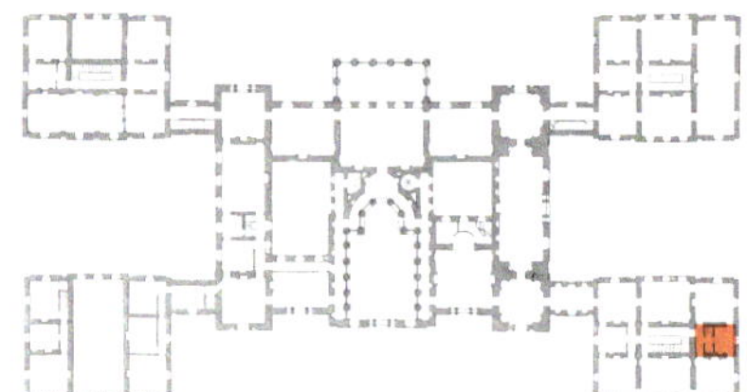

Pl. 74

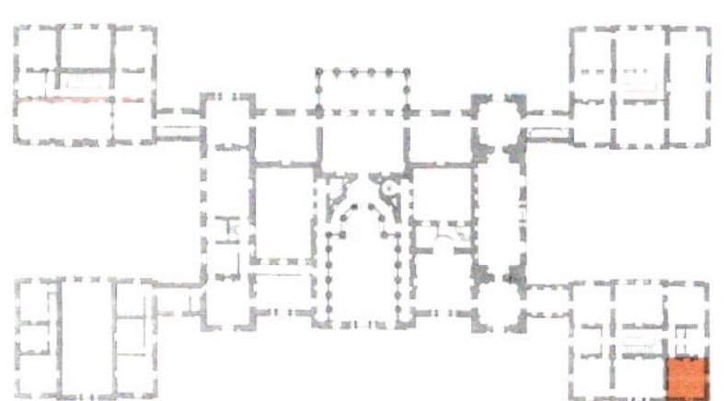

Pl. 75

2
Mary, Princess of Orange
Daughter to King Charles

Pl. 76

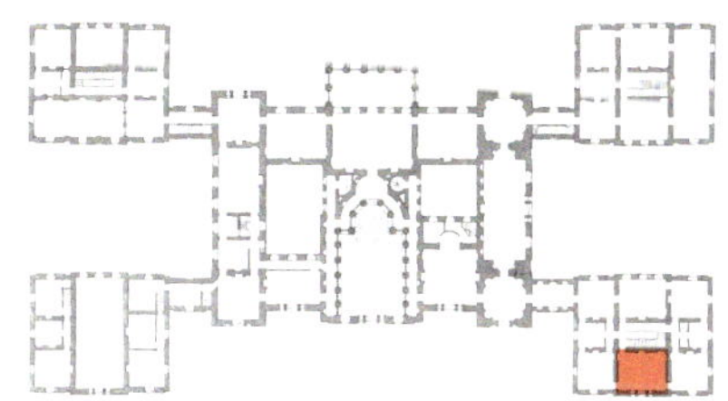

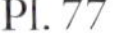

Pl. 77

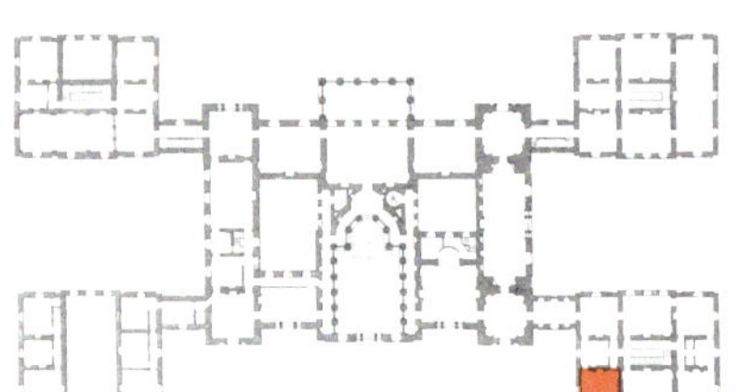

Pl. 78

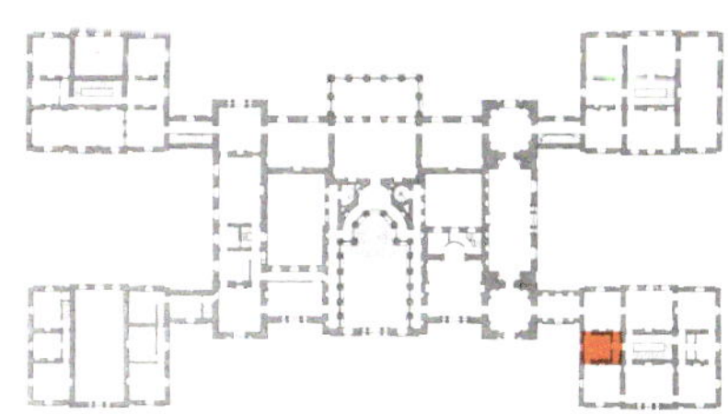

CHAPTER 6

HOLKHAM – PAST, PRESENT AND FUTURE

OVERLEAF
Bronze figures of the seventh Earl of Leicester and his dog on a bench overlooking the south front of the Hall.

Conceiving and creating Holkham – the richly furnished house within its designed landscape – was primarily the achievement of Thomas Coke, first Earl of Leicester of the first creation, together with his friends and his wife. But that was two and a half centuries ago. During those years, and particularly during the twentieth century, hundreds of great houses and estates have disappeared from the face of the earth, their contents auctioned off or even destroyed: in many cases it took only one profligate or unlucky generation to bring a country estate to the ground. Holkham has survived to the present day, and indeed is thriving, because all the owners since the builder – one countess and eight earls – have treated the estate, the house and its contents responsibly, seeing themselves as caretakers for future generations.

A key factor in the preservation of the house almost unaltered has been the longevity of its owners. After Lady Margaret, who completed the house, and Thomas Coke's nephew Wenman Coke, who owned it for only a year before he died, Holkham had three consecutive owners who each lived to a biblical age: Thomas William Coke, later to become the first Earl of Leicester of the second creation, inherited in 1776 at the age of twenty-two and died in 1842, aged eighty-eight. His son, the second earl, inherited at the age of twenty and died in 1909, in his eighty-seventh year. And the third earl died in the early years of World War II at the age of ninety-three. So these three owners together spanned nearly two centuries, and whilst some of them introduced a few changes upon inheriting, in their later years they tended to keep things as they were.

A look at each of the builder's successors will allow us to get an understanding of their individual attitudes to the house and estate and of the variable economic and political tides they faced, from times of great wealth and splendour in the mid-nineteenth century through the darkest times during and after World War II and until the present day. As for the future, it is fascinating to see how Holkham's long history as a place of agricultural reform has become a source of strength and inspiration in a quest to reinvent sustainable agriculture based on traditional methods and values – providing a model that will hopefully be emulated by other great agricultural estates.

MARGARET, COUNTESS OF LEICESTER

Following the death of her husband, Lady Margaret (1700–1775) oversaw the completion of Holkham and became the finished house's first châtelaine (figs. 15, 21 and 59). Her contribution to the architecture of the house has already been discussed, but she had an equally important rôle in the decoration of the mansion: in particular, the arrangement of her husband's art collection. Though the painting hang had been settled in certain rooms – most notably the Landscape Room – at the time of Coke's death, many of the staterooms were yet to receive any pictures. Alongside works acquired by Coke for Holkham, which had been placed in storage waiting for the building work to be completed, Lady Margaret also had to accommodate works transferred from Thanet House and paintings arriving from Italy.[301] Using these works, she completed schemes in the South Dining Room and both State Bedroom Suites, and she installed paintings in the newly completed Strangers' Wing.

The way she arranged her husband's art collection in Strangers' Wing is particularly interesting, her underlying purpose appearing to be the glorification of her husband's legacy, whether through family, personal or intellectual merits. The ante-room was hung with a series of portraits of the Coke family, commissioned by her husband from the Italian painter Andrea Casali (pls. 67 to 69). They were ordered sometime before November 1758, when payment of £300 is recorded.[302] One closet was decorated with a vast array of old master drawings, including two of the most important pieces collected by Thomas Coke – Raphael's *La Belle Jardinière* and Sangallo's *Battle of Cascina*. She also hung Sebastiano Conca's *Elysian Fields*, again commissioned by Thomas Coke, in the green damask dressing room (fig. 128).[303]

The choice of paintings in these rooms is an interesting one. Throughout the body of the house, the paintings were chosen and hung with a specific scheme in mind, one based on complementary pairs, and they served to highlight Thomas Coke's learning and erudition. However, in Strangers' Wing, the paintings are used to highlight the grandeur of his family, his taste and his wealth. The inclusion of the Conca is a corollary to this – the work, which clearly depicts the master of the house as one of the characters, underlines the importance of the Coke family by making sure their presence was felt even in the guests' private quarters. By depicting Coke as Orpheus, the painting also alludes to Coke as an artist (Orpheus himself was famous as a musician, with an ability to charm all living things) while likening the hospitality received at Holkham to that offered in classical mythology.

Lady Margaret arranged the residue of the painting collection and was also responsible for displaying part of her husband's collection of antiques and statues. Although the largest displays of sculpture – focused on the Marble Hall, North Dining Room, North Tribune and Statue Gallery – had been settled by the time of Thomas Coke's death, there were still a number of works to be housed, not least those rehomed from Russell Street. This handful of works – including the small statue of Isis that Brettingham had worked so hard to export from Italy – were incorporated throughout the staterooms, blending into schemes already settled by Coke.[304] She also arranged a number of works sent on by Brettingham in the 1750s, displaying them in the

Fig. 228. The almshouses flanking the northern entrance to Holkham Park, built and endowed by Lady Margaret in 1755–59.

room under the portico.[305] This scheme included a number of plaster casts of famous Roman statues, displayed in niches; the antique marble heads of several philosophers; and three items collected by her husband on his Grand Tour, the ill-fated statue of Jupiter and two Roman funerary urns.

Lady Margaret also took an interest in the care of her husband's book and manuscript collection. She constructed new libraries in the attics to house those works formerly kept in London. Inventory evidence shows that two tower rooms – on the north and south of the house – plus the corridor between them were converted from bedchambers to libraries, and she also commissioned librarians to produce a three-volume catalogue of these spaces.[306] The twentieth-century librarian C. W. James writes that Lady Margaret lent a number of valuable manuscripts to scholars and interested parties such as Dr Ferdinando Warner, Dr Benjamin Kennicott and Philip Yorke, the second Lord Hardwicke.[307]

Margaret was clearly proud of the house, and worked to protect and promote it. In common with contemporaries, she understood the damage that light and dust can cause to objects, and provided the costly fabrics and marble tables with covers and leather cases. Even with such careful curation, in the 1770s she found herself replacing some of the fabrics: the yellow damask that had decorated her rooms in Chapel Wing was deemed 'so ragged' that it was replaced with more of the same, whilst the original green damask of her rooms in Family Wing was 'too bad to be removed' and instead covered with new blue moraine.[308]

Under her tenure, the house was open to the general public on a Tuesday. Visitors on this day would be guided by the housekeeper. She also kept a 'publick' day – for those who could claim a connection to her – on a Thursday, and is described by visitors as delighting in showing the house and for providing 'an elegant good dinner'.[309]

Fig. 229. Armorial window in the Church of St Withburga commemorating Lady Margaret's repairs to the church.

Interestingly, Matthew Brettingham junior's *Plans of Holkham*, published in 1773, was dedicated to Lady Margaret. This volume was a reissue of the work published by his father in 1761, which had conveniently erased any mention of William Kent. The younger Brettingham's version of the work corrected this omission, contained amended versions of the plans – notably including an illustration of the Chapel as executed by Lady Margaret – and a full description of the painting hang. The dedication to this work suggests that it was commissioned by Lady Margaret herself, with Brettingham writing:

> Your affection for the memory and zeal for the honour of the Earl of Leicester are not more conspicuous in the completion of that noble edifice than in the publication of these designs, which are accurately delineated from it at your command.[310]

In the wider estate, Margaret made a couple of notable interventions. It was she who commissioned the construction of the almshouses which today form part of the north entrance to the park. In 1755, with a grant from her husband, she purchased land to build and endow the almshouses; they were completed in 1759 and are still in use today.[311] Originally forming a three-sided courtyard, there was accommodation for six residents. Unlike Holkham itself, these are designed in a picturesque Gothick idiom, with steeply pitched roof (possibly originally thatched) and Tudor-arched doorways (fig. 228).

She also undertook repairs to St Withburga's Church, starting in spring 1767. The work included repairs to the internal and external walls, windows and roof; laying a new floor; stuccoing the interior; commissioning new pews, pulpit, desks, communion table, rails, font, communion plate, linen and service books; restoring the monuments; and fitting up the vestry.[312] Completed in spring 1768, it was estimated to have cost Lady Margaret £1,100.[313] This restoration is commemorated in an armorial window, commissioned by Lady Margaret from the renowned glass painter William Peckitt (fig. 229).[314] It is interesting that Lady Margaret's two independent architectural commissions focus on good works and religion; and both support the assurance with which she altered the Chapel interior within Holkham itself.

Under Lady Margaret's tenure, the leading landscape designer Capability Brown worked at Holkham. He was paid fifty guineas a year from 1762 to 1764, along with travelling expenses to Holkham, and he oversaw work to 'level and slope the ground on the west, north, and east fronts'.[315] The extent of his influence on the landscape, however, has been difficult to determine because of the many broader and more lasting changes wrought by subsequent generations.

Fig. 230. Thomas Gainsborough's portrait dated 1778 shows Coke of Norfolk as a country gentleman.

For Lady Margaret, looking after Holkham also meant caring for the next generation. Although there was clearly no love lost between her and her brief successor, Wenman Coke,[316] she did take an interest in Wenman's son, Thomas William, the future Coke of Norfolk. In 1771, Lady Margaret contacted Thomas William with an offer of £500 to undertake a Grand Tour rather than continue from Eton to university. After he accepted this offer, he was invited to Holkham, where he spent a month in her company; if Stirling's account is to be believed, he was little impressed with her formal style of hospitality, but did note her generosity and eagerness to establish for him the trappings of his position as heir to Holkham.[317]

THE FIRST EARL OF THE SECOND CREATION (Coke of Norfolk)

Thomas William Coke, grandson of the builder's sister Ann, was twenty-two when he inherited Holkham. When he died at eighty-eight, he had become a public figure who is still remembered under the name Coke of Norfolk (fig. 230). Known also as the 'Great Commoner' (before he finally accepted a peerage from the new queen, Victoria, in 1837) or 'King Tom' because of his dominant rôle in Norfolk and beyond, he had been politically active for decades, often at odds with King and Government, notably over such issues as American independence (which he supported). Nearer home, he left his mark on the Holkham landscape through a wide range of agricultural improvements and through greatly extending the park.

There has always been an element of propaganda about the quality and productivity of the land around Holkham. Thomas Coke the builder claimed to have found 'an open barren estate' and turned it into Arcadia, and yet a generation later people joked that one would find there two rabbits fighting over one blade of grass. In truth the soil, though not brilliant, was productive enough even in the Chief Justice's time, and each generation was quite successful in improving the land. For example, long before Thomas William, Thomas the builder had introduced the Norfolk four-course system of crop rotation on his farmland, emulating his neighbour 'Turnip' Townshend at Raynham. This system, rotating wheat, turnips, barley and clover, is regarded as a key element of the British Agricultural Revolution. Therefore, in some ways Thomas William was merely continuing and intensifying his great-uncle's efforts in improving the land and reforming agricultural practices. But there is no doubt that he introduced great and lasting improvements not only to the soil and the crops, but also in the husbandry of sheep and cattle, experimenting successfully with new breeds.

His success and influence as an agricultural reformer were celebrated, three years after his death, by a remarkable monument erected in the grounds of Holkham, mirroring the Obelisk on the southern side of the house. Paid for by subscription to which over a thousand people contributed, it featured a tall column standing on a pedestal decorated with figures of livestock and reliefs illustrating Coke's achievements and principles. Work began in 1845, with £674.19s.9d (almost £50,000 today) spent on celebrating the laying of the foundation stone (fig. 231).[318]

As in the case of his predecessor, Thomas William's activities in improving the agricultural values of his estate may well have been fuelled by need: the inheritance had come with huge debts caused not least by the great house Thomas Coke had created. Those debts may, however, have had a positive effect in preventing, for several decades, any dramatic intervention to the house, any adaptation to changes in taste so usual in other places where a new generation took over and had money on their hands. By the time Coke of Norfolk had recovered the family fortunes, Holkham was already regarded as historic and had become immune to rash changes.

Changes were, however, effected to the setting of the house. William Kent's charming pleasure ground and pond on the south front had disappeared by the end of the century, with the expense of grass now going up unbroken to the south front. And the house was certainly spruced up externally as well. Soon after inheriting, Coke had the window sashes gilded and, from 1790 onwards, considerable sums of money were spent on 'whitewashing the mansion',[319] giving the house a brilliant exterior aspect. The regular expense on limewashing in the decades around 1800 and the renewal of the gilding on the sashes in 1808 were the only major investment in the house before 1815, when 'the new library at Holkham' with carved and gilt bookcases was installed.

Money was also spent on maintenance. There was always adequate provision for good housekeeping. Numerous account books show regular expenditure on the renewal of upholstery, on 'organising the library' and bookbinding, and on repairs to drains, stones, windows, ceilings, stairs, roofs and chimneys. Entries such as this from January 1793 are commonplace: 'Settled & paid Mr Wilder his Bill in full, for cleaning Pictures, at 1 Guinea per Day – £206.4s.0d.'[320]

Clearly the house needed to look its best for the social events it was now regularly used for. Holkham became famed for its hospitality. Large numbers of people came regularly to sometimes quite enormous dinners and balls: 500 guests to a ball in 1788, and even 700 at the last of Coke's famous sheep-shearing dinners in 1821. These latter events, all-male congregations of large numbers of agricultural gentlemen, must have been rather boisterous affairs if we believe Arthur Young, who commented in 1806: 'The Norfolk farmers are rich and profligate; coarse oaths and profanities salute the ear at every turn; and the gentlemen and the great, when they are without ladies are too apt to be as bad as the mob and many of them much worse'.[321]

Fig. 231. A relief from the monument on the north side of the house, erected for Coke of Norfolk soon after his death in 1842, with the earl on the right.

For many years, Coke's first wife, Jane Dutton, whom he had married in 1775, was instrumental in her rôle as hostess. After her death in 1800, her three daughters successively took over this part. But then Coke remarried in 1822, at the age of sixty-eight: rather extraordinarily marrying his eighteen-year-old goddaughter Lady Anne Keppel. Originally he had meant her to marry his nephew William – his heir presumptive, as Coke's three daughters could not inherit. When William refused, Coke is said to have exclaimed: 'By God, if you won't marry her, I will marry her myself!'[322] Lady Anne was to bear Thomas William five more children – not only a son and heir, at last, but three more sons and one daughter. With these new young children as well as the numerous grandchildren from his first three daughters, Holkham became very much a family home.

THE SECOND EARL

When Thomas William Coke died in 1842 at the age of eighty-eight, history repeated itself in a number of ways. Once again a very young man – another Thomas William, just twenty years of age – inherited the house and estate. He, too, was to be married twice, and he, too, fathered a great number of children: eleven children with his first wife, Juliana (fig. 232), and seven more with his second wife. Georgiana, the last child, was born when he was seventy-two. At one point he rather crossly asked a footman who all these children were that were playing so noisily on the terraces, only to be told, 'They are yours, my Lord'. And he reached nearly the same great age, dying in 1909 at the age of eighty-seven. But, unlike his father, he inherited an estate practically free of debt and also free of any legal restrictions as there was, in his case, no entailment: he was free to sell or buy land and to leave his estate to whomever he wished.

Directly after their marriage in the spring of 1843, the rich and lively couple embarked on an extensive programme of reshaping and modernising Holkham, inside and outside. Quite sensibly, their first concern was the heating of the house: a modern 'Heating Apparatus' was installed at very short notice, costing the princely sum of £1,200. The fitting of the 'Apparatus' (a central-heating system with pipes and iron grids for the circulation of hot air throughout the main parts of the house) required major structural work: large amounts were laid out on stonemasons' work, on

Fig. 232. Lady Juliana, the second earl's first wife, with her daughter Lady Anne and her son Thomas William, the future third earl, c. 1870.

ironmongery (£647.16s.7d) and iron casting, on carpenters, blacksmiths and bricklayers.[323]

All through the rest of the 1840s, extensive refurbishment and redecoration went on in all parts of the house, carried out by the London firm of Dowbiggin's. Substantial sums were expended on interior decoration, tapestry, furniture and richly embroidered cloths. Many of the decorative items were purchased in London and brought to Holkham by boat or by train. The atmosphere of the rooms changed considerably – the Victorian curtains, plants and knick-knacks providing quite a contrast to the Palladian rigour.

The second earl's era was perhaps the only time when the treasures in the house and notably the builder's creation were less than respected, even treated with something approaching disdain. Whilst in 1845 the earl could – though only barely – be dissuaded from getting rid of the Chief Justice's law library as 'a heap of rubbish', he certainly had his way with the pictures: portraits of family and friends were now given prominent places in the staterooms, thus radically altering the original scheme, whilst some of the replaced paintings were sold off.[324]

A letter from Lady Elizabeth Spencer Stanhope, the second earl's much older sister from the first marriage, sent from Holkham in 1847 gives a rare insight:

> I will now begin to describe the improvements … Fancy Anna Maria's astonishment at going into the hall and seeing the balustrade on one side vanished, and all the plaister casts descended from their niches and placed between each pillar, looking, as Collyer says, like Madame Tussaud's exhibition, with the large Apollo at the bottom of the steps and Chantrey's bust of my father and old Lord Leicester on each side. This is by way of experiment, but I will not answer for its not being carried into effect – such is the rage for innovation.

Fig. 233. Although a marvel of Victorian technology, the plate-glass windows put in by the second earl disfigured the original well-balanced façade and were gradually replaced in a programme initiated by the fifth earl.

This somewhat bizarre experiment was not judged to be entirely successful and the figures were returned to their niches.

Even greater changes were effected around the house. The second earl's most spectacular achievement, the terraces around the house, have already been discussed (in Chapter 2). He also changed the exterior aspect of the house by two well-intentioned though somewhat intrusive features. One was the addition of the porch to the main entrance on the North Front. The original direct entrance to the Marble Hall, although dramatic in its contrast between the unassuming doorway and the grandeur of the room behind it, offered no defence against cold winds from the North Sea. Several alternative versions were drawn by the architects S. S. Teulon and William Burn before one version by the latter was chosen and executed in 1855. Faithfully copying the detailing and brick material of the original house, it manages to be no more intrusive than necessary.

The other major change concerned the windows. Victorian technology had become able to produce plate glass of remarkable size, and it seems the earl was quite keen on a demonstrative act of modernisation. Thus the original sash windows with their rather more delicate structure were replaced by plate-glass windows in the 1850s, with the window openings in the Saloon even extended in order to install a row of five French windows, giving dramatic access to the portico. Whilst no doubt representing a remarkable technological achievement, the historical photographs leave little doubt that these plate-glass windows were a disaster from an aesthetic point of view (fig. 233): Holkham's grand but rather severe and monumental façades need the softening effect provided by the multiple bars of the Palladian sash windows and indeed the irregularities of pre-industrial glass. It is interesting to note, however, that John Carmichael received £121.4s.8d in 1854 'for painting and gilding (the) mansion windows',[325] thus recreating the external gilding of the original sash windows. The modernised house was used for many glamorous parties, notably during the 1860s, with regular visits by the Prince and Princess of Wales coming over from nearby Sandringham, laying the foundation for a lasting amicable relationship with future generations of the royal family.

In 1866, the railway line along the coast was extended from Heacham to Holkham and a station was built that contained a special waiting room for the family.

The second earl was a countryman through and through; out and about on most days he was at Holkham.[326] Secure in the knowledge that the estate, developed and improved as it was by his two predecessors, produced more than enough in rent money to finance even a generous lifestyle, he tended to continue along the established ways of managing the lands. But he did have his ear to the ground: when a lasting agricultural depression led to a sustained drop in estate income from the late 1870s onwards, he managed to cushion the losses with highly successful international investments – the first owner of Holkham to do so since Thomas Coke's disastrous experience with the stock market in the early 1720s.

Fig. 234. The third Earl of Leicester, c. 1900.

THE THIRD EARL

Succeeding to the earldom at the age of 61, the third earl (1848–1941, fig. 234) looked back on a long military career in the Scots Guards, thus establishing a tradition followed by most of his successors including the present, eighth earl. Until that moment, his position seemed somewhat precarious – with no entailment hampering his father's freedom of action, he could only be sure of eventually inheriting the earldom but not necessarily all of the property. And indeed, though Holkham seemed in good shape financially at the time of the second earl's demise, massive death duties were going to take a huge bite out of this, as would the generous legacies he had arranged for his numerous offspring. (So numerous were they, and so prolific too, that the seventh earl felt he couldn't go to a garden party anywhere in the

English-speaking world without someone approaching him with the words 'by the way, we are related' – words that would send him into an instant coma.)

Upon inheriting in January 1909, the new earl and his wife Alice lost no time in giving the house a thorough refresher. A letter written in October that year by their son, Viscount Coke, to his wife manages to give the impression that the house was emerging from a deep gloom of decay:

> The house is really making great headway; the long gallery is finished, all the scaffolding is down, and it really looks a dream of beauty; the statues are wonderful, and the whole effect and blending of the shades of cream and green are perfect.[327]

The staterooms were redecorated and refurnished, wall hangings replaced or repaired and paint and wood surfaces renewed. In the private rooms, the antiquated interiors were overhauled and new objects introduced throughout: fashionable electric lamps, shades, carpets, tapestries and wallpapers were bought in London. The scarlet curtains and the rug in the Landscape Room survived long enough to give an idea of this particular phase (fig. 235). Two London firms, Cowtan's and Lenygon's, had been brought in to carry out this massive task. Over the following years they were paid enormous sums for 'repairs and alterations at the mansion'.[328]

Electric lighting was installed, supplied from a private generating plant housed in an extension to the stables. Surviving plans document the fitting of bathrooms, water closets and heating systems throughout the building. The advent of electricity saw the replacement of the original mechanical system for summoning servants, a long row of bells in the Smoking Room corridor in the basement, by a new and much smaller signal board; happily, both systems are still there, although disconnected. More technical improvements were made to the house in 1912, when Cowtan & Sons received £466.0s.6d for 'installing Cold Storage & Ice making plant', and an extra £14.3s.0d for a 'magic cleaner & attachments'.[329]

Not only was the house renewed, but the new owners – though already middle-aged – seemed to breathe new life into it with their remarkable hospitality. Thirty-five indoor servants bustled about, their ranks swelled at times by the numerous servants accompanying the guests of great house parties: those attending a four-day royal visit in August 1913 'all brought maids, loaders and valets and the day they left there were three special trains to take them away'.[330]

World War I did not greatly affect the house and grounds, unlike the situation at some other country estates; there was a temporary convalescent home for officers at Model Farm and an army camp near the church. But the family suffered a great personal loss as The Hon. Arthur George Coke was killed at Gallipoli in 1915. He was the younger brother of Viscount Coke (later the fourth earl) and the present earl's great-grandfather (fig. 236).

Regardless of falling income from the estate coupled with rising taxation during the interwar years, the ageing third earl seemed determined to keep up what he felt to be the fitting lifestyle, with white-tie dinners in the State Dining Room, bachelor shooting parties and other social events, facilitated by numerous staff. Right up to the outbreak of World War II, the agent had to keep up a losing struggle, hoping to persuade the earl to reduce expenses and to stop borrowing from the bank.

Fig. 235. The Landscape Room with its Edwardian curtains and rug as depicted in the 1986 house guide.

Fig. 236. The third earl's sons, Thomas William (1880–1949), who became the fourth earl, and Arthur (1882–1915), killed in action at Gallipoli.

During the war, the earl and the family continued to live in Family Wing. The staterooms in the central block were kept under dust covers, while the east side of the house and the offices around the adjoining courtyard were used by the army. Like many people at the time, the earl assumed that Holkham, close to the coast, would be on the front line in the event of an invasion, and he was actually looking forward to it.[331] Believing that the Germans would then use the house as a headquarters, 'melodramatic plans were conceived for local activists to blow up the Marble Hall as the Nazi officials marched up the Grand Staircase. Lord Leicester, who had served in Egypt in 1882, and Suakin in 1885, and in the Boer War, remarked that every 'man, woman and child in Norfolk is looking forward to killing at least two Germans'.[332]

THE FOURTH EARL

Like his father, Thomas William Coke (1880–1949) joined the Scots Guards, serving during the Boer War and in World War I. In 1905 he married Marion Trefusis and they had two sons and three daughters. The third earl had reached the remarkable age of ninety-three years, so Tom (as he was known in the family) was already in his sixties when he inherited Holkham and the earldom in November 1941, during the darkest phase of World War II. Compared to many other country houses that never recovered from damage and decay caused by military use and requisition, Holkham did not suffer too much during the war, but large parts of the grounds and the house were used for military purposes,

Fig. 237. A portrait bust of the fifth earl in the Long Library, amongst mementoes of the royal family, with a picture of the present earl on the right.

whereas some other parts were shut down. Kitchen Wing and the stables area east of the house were occupied and used by a unit of the Royal Engineers. Their heavy vehicles were parked at fixed positions in the yard, with the names they had given to their lorries or armoured cars stencilled on the brick wall. Some of those names, such as Albemarle and Albacore, are still legible today. Another military group, the Home Guard, had their headquarters in the Temple.

A camp for prisoners of war (POWs) was established on the far side of the lake, near the church, and captured Italian soldiers were the first inmates. The fourth earl's young granddaughters, Anne and Carey, were rather fond of them because they were friendly and waved at the children. (Many decades later, Anne vividly evoked the general feeling of the time in her book, *A Haunting at Holkham*).

Then German POWs arrived, mostly members of the *Afrikakorps*, proving rather more sinister than the Italians. All POWs wore white patches on their clothes so they could be recognised from afar. Holkham's bowler-hatted and rather fierce gamekeepers were more than prepared to shoot them should they try to escape; indeed they were looking forward to it, hoping to be able to note in their game books: 'two brace of pheasant, five ducks, one German'.

Since the beginning of the war, the Norfolk coastline had been fortified and transformed by preparations against the threat of an amphibious landing by German troops, which seemed a particular danger at such a shallow stretch as Holkham Beach. Barbed wire and the carcasses of buses and other vehicles used for target practice by the soldiers and the RAF littered the beach, and many pillboxes can still be spotted further inland.

Few people remained in the house: members of the staff had been called up for military service or were working elsewhere for the war effort. However, unlike his father, the fourth earl was hospitable enough, so his granddaughters lived in the house while their parents were away: Viscount Coke was serving with the Scots Guards in Egypt and his wife, Lady Elizabeth, went there with him.

Unlike most of his predecessors since Thomas, the builder of the house, the fourth earl loved art and particularly music, played the violin at nearly professional level and was keenly interested in photography. He was deeply appreciative of the immense cultural value of the outstanding works of art in the house, and he did his best to look after the treasures. The granddaughters were put to work, helping with their maintenance. Anne had the task of seeing that the Codex Leicester was aired regularly, so every fortnight or so she slowly turned over its pages, licking her fingertips to do so – to the horror of later conservators.

The war ended in 1945, but austerity and problems continued. Holkham was faced with the enormous task of clearing up all the structures from wartime that cluttered the grounds and the beaches, a task that went on for many years. Although there was little money available, the fourth earl embarked on the large task of repairing and modernising the hundreds of cottages belonging to the estate, mostly occupied by members of the staff and their families.

HISTORIC HOWLER

Fig. 238. Lady Elizabeth, the fifth earl's wife.

THE FIFTH EARL

Thomas William (1908–1976), known as Tommy, married Lady Elizabeth Yorke (1912–1985), daughter of the Earl of Hardwicke (figs. 237 and 238), in 1931. They had three daughters, Anne, Carey and Sarah, but no son.

Like his father and grandfather before him, he served as a professional soldier in the Scots Guards. During his military service in North Africa he contracted malaria, subsequently suffering from heart trouble caused by the quinine treatment. His father's death in 1949, just eight years after the third earl, meant that Holkham had to deal with another set of death duties within very few years at a time when the estate was also faced with the continuing task of clearing up the remnants of wartime use in the grounds and on the beach. The disastrous North Sea flood of January 1953 caused enormous damage along the coastline, and amongst other things swept away the railway line and station.

At this time, the detrimental effects of a long period of delayed maintenance to the fabric of the Hall could no longer be overlooked. On the outside of the house, stonework was decaying, with pieces falling down. The interior

Fig. 239. Lady Elizabeth and her eldest daughter, Lady Anne, busy in the pottery they ran very successfully at Holkham.

problems were even more alarming, since dry rot was discovered in parts of the roof structure, necessitating determined structural intervention and replacement. The domestic installations such as heating and electricity were obsolete and largely worn out, requiring a great deal of repair and replacement. Similar repairs were needed at many other buildings in the grounds, such as the Temple, the Triumphal Arch and the Obelisk.

For all these repairs, the fifth earl was able to gain unusually massive grants from a Labour government otherwise not known for sympathy towards owners of stately homes; the 1950s were by far the worst time for country houses ever, with hundreds of them being lost through neglect and demolition.

To finance upkeep of the Hall, it became imperative to generate additional income, and this necessity led to new initiatives. Holkham had always been accessible to visitors, albeit on a fairly limited basis, but the number of open days was now increased, initially to nine afternoons in July and August.

An exciting initiative by Lady Leicester opened a rather different source of income. At some point she had seen a POW producing some pottery in the brickyard, using a self-made turntable and locally found clay, and this inspired her to set up a pottery in the former bowling alley just east of the house. Ignoring unsympathetic remarks from her husband, the earl, along the lines of 'How's it going in the potting shed?' she built up production and a thriving business together with her daughters, Carey being the creative one, whereas Anne showed an unexpected talent for marketing the products as a travelling saleswoman (fig. 239). At its peak, the pottery employed 100 people, becoming the largest light industry enterprise in North Norfolk.

Anne even went as far away as the United States to find buyers for the pottery's products, but her quite successful activities there were curtailed by a telegram saying ANNE YOU MUST COME HOME STOP YOUVE BEEN ASKED TO BE A MAID OF HONOUR AT THE QUEENS CORONATION STOP.[333] Her mother the countess held the office of Lady of the Bedchamber to the Queen from 1953 to 1970, and in 1965 was invested as a

Fig. 240. The seventh Earl of Leicester surveying the landscape from the roof of the house in 2003.

Commander of the Royal Victorian Order (CVO). After the many years of wartime austerity, Holkham saw some grand events again in the 1950s, such as the ball to celebrate Anne's coming out, and later her wedding.

With the most pressing repairs in the house accomplished, the fifth earl eventually initiated a programme of replacing the unsympathetic plate-glass windows introduced by his great-grandfather with copies of the original sash windows and their smaller-scale panes. This activity was continued by his successor, the seventh earl, to be completed by the end of the 1970s. One historic building that could not be kept intact was the Victorian orangery right next to the south front of the house, but it was retained as a roofless shell.

Taking over in 1949 after his father's short tenure, the fifth earl had to navigate Holkham through uncharted waters and through a very difficult time for British country

Fig. 241. Lady Sarah, the seventh earl's wife, with one of the many Labrador puppies she bred over the years.

houses. If it is true that the fourth earl was near despair when he found himself unable to pass Holkham on to the National Trust, there cannot be any doubt that both he and his son would have been the first to rejoice that Holkham remained in the hands of the family and lived to see many more and brighter days.

THE SIXTH AND SEVENTH EARLS

Quite apart from the economic pressure at the time, the 1950s were also a time of great uneasiness at Holkham because the succession seemed insecure. As mentioned earlier, the fifth earl and his wife had three daughters, but no son and heir. His only brother, Flight Lieutenant David Arthur Coke DFC, had been killed in action in 1941 as a fighter pilot flying Hurricanes in North Africa. The nearest male relative, Anthony Lovel Coke, lived far away in South Africa. Born in 1909, he was just one year younger than his cousin, the fifth earl. He had no intention of returning to England, so attention gradually focused on his son Edward, born in 1936, as the likely future head of the family and owner of Holkham (fig. 240). In preparation for this destiny, he came to England at the age of twenty-one, to find himself characterised as 'obviously and extremely South African'.[334] Undaunted by the somewhat doubtful stance of his relatives or by the rôle and status that awaited him, he matured to acquire an easy authority, neither pompous nor distant ('Call me Eddy!'), and gradually took over running Holkham when the fifth earl's health failed. When he inherited the property (though not yet the earldom; that went to his father as sixth earl) in 1976, the general situation of British country houses had just begun to make a turn for the better. An exhibition in the Victoria & Albert Museum, *The Destruction of the Country House, 1875–1975*, documented some of the roughly 1,000 country houses lost in the preceding century, contributing to a sea change in public opinion and in government policies.

In this new climate, more positive for the preservation and continuing use of great country estates, Eddy was able to set the estate and the house on a broader economic basis and on a course that has since been taken up and expanded by his son and successor. At a conference in 1999, he described his position in some detail, feeling that it might have been advantageous not to have grown up at Holkham, therefore having no preconceived ideas on how the estate should be managed. He explained that, when he took over, 80 per cent of the estate's income had come from agriculture, but that figure had fallen to 20 per cent during his tenure – mostly because he had gone for diversifying, for opening other sources of income, both from tourism and from various businesses. The visiting public then generated about a third of the cost of running the house.

As for the house itself, the seventh earl continued and intensified a restoration programme already set in motion by his predecessor. In the early 1970s, the fifth earl had decided to gradually replace the Victorian plate-glass windows that had come in for so much criticism over the century or so of their existence. Reinstating the wooden sash windows on this scale was a huge and long task, but very successful in the end – the final highlight being the replacement of the French windows in the Saloon. Following expert advice, the earl continued inside the house in the same vein. Over time, the suites of furniture originally allocated to specific rooms had become dispersed fairly randomly in the house, and many significant paintings had gone from their original position – some of them sold and lost to the house, but others stored in the spacious attics. Recovering furniture and paintings, restoring them and reinstating them where the builder had wanted them to be, went far in reconstructing the eighteenth-century spirit of the staterooms[335] – albeit at the cost of losing the chintzy Edwardian charm introduced after the third earl inherited.

If so much of the original spirit of Holkham survives despite the many changes it has seen, it is probably due to the respect with which it has been treated by its successive owners. The seventh earl's restoration programme has been particularly successful in this respect, whether replacing unsympathetic Victorian plate-glass windows with Palladian sash windows, returning paintings to their intended positions or re-upholstering furniture to original designs.

At the same time, decisive though rather less visible improvements were made in the domestic technology throughout the house. The heating and electrical systems were renewed, an activity that revealed some rather unsettling situations where unsafe switchboxes might have caused a fire at any time. Rather more low-tech was a programme for the guest beds. The revival of the house by the seventh earl and his second wife, Sarah (fig. 241), involved sometimes great numbers of guests staying in all parts of the house – as Lady Sarah once said, 'I can bed 43 people!' When it gradually dawned on the hosts that some of their guests appeared to move rather stiffly at breakfast, they embarked on the heroic scheme of sleeping themselves in every single guest bed to decide which mattresses needed replacing – a move that earned them their guests' lasting gratitude and admiration.

Before addressing Holkham's present and future, we should discuss an issue that has long been the elephant in the room for heritage conservators visiting the house: How do we feel about the removal of the Victorian and Edwardian layers to the house? From John Ruskin in the nineteenth century to the current Burra Charter, conservation doctrine favours minimal intervention and conservation as found: 'do as much as necessary and as little as possible'. In the case of Holkham, this would have meant retaining both the plate-glass windows on the outside and the curtains and rugs in the staterooms; it would have meant retaining the changes to the picture hang effected by the second earl. In retrospect, this would certainly not have been wrong, as these two essential new layers were significant contributions in their own right, documenting the changes in taste and values of the generations who made Holkham their home.

But the discipline of heritage conservation deals in a specific currency, that of 'cultural significance': its task is to retain and, if possible, to enhance the cultural significance of a place. To do this, one sometimes has to make judgement calls: What do we gain and what do we lose by certain actions? It seems fair to say that the Victorian plate-glass windows constituted an insensitive intervention that went against the grain of the original design concept, upsetting the delicate balance between the large stereometric shapes of the architecture and the far more delicate scale provided by the divisions of the sash windows and the even smaller pattern of the bricks and their pointing. As for the changes inside, the first earl's *Gesamtkunstwerk* – the totality of architecture, furnishings and artworks that he conceived – was such a unique creation of outstanding quality that it seemed nearly imperative to grasp the opportunity of recovering and reinstating it, which was made possible by the fact that most of its original components were still available in the house.

THE EIGHTH EARL

In 2005 the seventh earl retired, moving with his wife to Model Farm, and his son Tom took over the management of the estate. Sharing his father's understanding of his own rôle as a caretaker, with a long-term view towards the survival and flourishing of the estate and its manifold values, the eighth earl (as he became in 2015) has, however, introduced a great deal of change and development, reacting to the challenges and needs of the twenty-first century (fig. 242).

It seems fair to say that the seventh earl very successfully ran the place according to the time-honoured principles of a patron ordering the business side and the external affairs, with his spouse looking after the domestic side as well as hospitality and events. With the eighth earl, one can observe a shift to a more corporate approach. There is still one figure in the driving seat, making the important decisions about aims and directions, but there are also highly qualified departmental heads chosen to oversee and direct the very diverse tasks of the estate and the house. There is the agriculture and forestry, there is the nature conservation, there are the various businesses and the properties, there are the visitors and events, and there is the great house with its wide range of demands regarding the works of art and the cultural assets, the library and the archives. Looking at the successful work done over the last two decades, the eighth earl clearly has been fortunate in finding the right persons for the right jobs, all of them looking after their own segment of the complex machine in which each part supports the whole so as to move in the right direction.

There are still people around who remember the situation in the late 1970s, the years before Eddy Coke, his wife Valeria and their children moved into the house. For a long time there was only a security officer, the legendary Fred Jolly, to hold the fort. He gradually covered the rôle of house administrator as well and even stood in as a curator of sorts, with the equally legendary librarian Dr W. O. Hassall coming in from Oxford at irregular intervals to see to the archives and to deal with researchers. In spite of great improvements during the seventh earl's tenure, the house remained seriously understaffed, with the house administrator and his deputy also doing a curator's job, whereas now there are not only a collections curator, a librarian and an archivist doing their specialist work beside the hall manager and her staff, but there is also an external consultant, Maria de Peverelli, coordinating and guiding policies for all the cultural assets in the house.

Maria's involvement with the Hall began when it became clear that the 'use' of the house had dramatically changed,

Fig. 242. Lord and Lady Leicester in 2024.

and so had the competences needed to address these changes. Taking as the guiding principle of her mission something that the seventh Earl of Leicester said in 2006 – 'Everything we do at Holkham must be for the benefit of the Hall and its amazing collections. It is the centrepiece of the estate' – Maria's first step was to better integrate the care and management of the Hall with that of its collections. Long-delayed but essential tasks such as a digital catalogue of the works of art, assessment of their condition, the drafting of a collections management plan and a long-term conservation strategy – including a closer look at the effects of temperature, relative humidity and light on the contents of the house – have been taken in hand.

Collection management has been brought to a new level of efficiency and expertise, in line with twenty-first century best practice, with protocols, rôles and competences clearly defined. Preserving the collections for future generations, facilitating their long-term care and the transfer of information both internally and externally, reducing the possibility of mistakes and accidents – as well as knowing how to address them – and assisting the trustees in their ever-growing fiduciary responsibilities now form the basis of how Holkham Enterprises as a whole looks at the collections. There is still work to be done, but everyone is on the right track. The real challenge is, and will be, to keep the fine balance between opening the house to the public and trying to make it an independent source of income, while retaining the character and use of a family home, which Holkham has managed to do so well for almost 300 years.

Holkham has been – from its earliest days – a place that welcomed visitors. Over the last twenty years, the range of services offered has been greatly extended beyond the elementary and still central option of viewing the main rooms and enjoying the stunning interiors, the sculptures and the paintings. For example, Holkham has become famous for the brilliant interior decorations that fill the main rooms and the Chapel during the Christmas season. Hospitality is provided by the cafeteria and the shop next to the Hall and by the Outlook Café near Holkham Beach. The Lady Elizabeth Wing in place of the former pottery in the yards east of the house is an attractively designed place to celebrate weddings and to hold other social or business events. The recently restored walled garden has received much acclaim and has also become a successful business venture.

A country house is defined by the land that surrounds it: the landscape formed by man sometimes over many centuries and also sometimes for a great variety of purposes and uses. As discussed in the landscape chapter, at Holkham one can find all possible kinds of designs and uses, from the highly formal and artificial terraces to the extensive and practically untouched nature reserves along the beach, and with everything in between. Perhaps the most exciting and most forward-looking development of recent years at Holkham has been taking place in the field of land use, in the approach to the land in general.

The land has always been expected to generate income, but now there is a sense that there are better ways of doing this than following the generally accepted contemporary methods of farming. Faced with the prospect that those contemporary methods may well lead to the destruction of the soil within a foreseeable time, Holkham, under the aegis of the eighth earl, is pursuing a different long-term policy that may well be seen as a way 'back to the roots', back to the attitude and approach of the two first earls. In the eighteenth and early nineteenth centuries, it was found that rotating the crops in a sequence produced good results and also improved the generally rather poor Norfolk soil. Using a six-crop rotation rather than his ancestors' traditional four-crop rotation, and aiming for a 'zero 'cides' (no pesticides or herbicides) policy by 2030, the eighth earl has been embarking on the ambitious project of exploring how a large and privately run country estate may take a pioneering rôle in finding ways of engaging with the land in a policy of give-and-take, using it profitably but at the same time conserving, regaining and improving its manifold values.

Clearly the attitudes and experiences of four centuries have become the foundation for a policy in which traditional values are rediscovered and adapted to the ideas and values of the twenty-first century. In his fascinating and successful book *Land Healer*,[336] Holkham's conservation director, Jake Fiennes, has outlined this approach in which all parts of the landscape from the perfectly natural to the very formal have their place and use, but so also do the animals – from wild to cultivated, from the wild birds of the nature reserve on the beach to the game birds and the deer in park, not to mention the dogs that have always been important at Holkham.

* * *

Over a period of three hundred years, one countess and nine earls have ruled at Holkham (although one should never underestimate the influence of the earls' spouses). The first first earl, Thomas Coke the builder, conceived and created the whole complex ensemble of landscape, house and collections, and his countess, Lady Margaret, completed the house and consolidated the estate. Thomas's nephew, Wenman, had no chance to leave his imprint, but he was the ancestor of a long line of successors. Amazingly, his son and grandson lived and reigned at Holkham all through the long nineteenth century, from the year of the American Revolution to just before World War I. Coke of Norfolk (for whom the earldom of Leicester was revived) intensified and expanded Holkham's agricultural side and paid off all the debts incurred in creating the estate. His son, the second earl, may have been the most fortunate of the line in the sense that he was able to enjoy the estate's charms throughout his very long tenure without any legal or financial constraints. Inheriting quite late and unable or unwilling to make concessions to dramatic economic changes, the third earl continued a similar lifestyle nearly until his death in 1941.

Then World War II and its aftermath threatened Holkham's existence. The fourth earl had only a few years as head of the estate, and his son the fifth earl found himself responsible for an estate threatened on all sides – by a government inimical to great houses, which were denigrated as elitist and privileged, by brutal taxation and also by the fact that there was no immediate male heir. Holkham pulled through by the skin of its teeth, true to the sentiment illustrated by the family crest: the ostrich eating a horseshoe is meant to convey the idea that the Cokes can stomach anything.[337] Having survived the darkest post-war years when other great country houses were abandoned right and left, Holkham was fortunate in getting the right man at the right time in the person of a distant cousin, Eddy Coke. Initially acting for his father, the sixth earl, who decided to stay in South Africa, Eddy eventually became the seventh earl. He made the best of the improved political circumstances for country houses and was able to put the estate and the house on a stable basis again, filling it also with life and giving it a much higher public profile.

On this basis, his son the eighth and current earl, Tom, has been pursuing an ambitious and clearly very successful course of turning Holkham into an estate that faces the challenges of the twenty-first century. Far from being an outdated and irrelevant fossil of a bygone age, Holkham is shaping up as a beacon for the future, as living proof that not only can we all draw enjoyment from what former generations have created, but we can actually learn from the past in many ways and build upon the wisdom of our more rooted forebears.

ENDNOTES

1 Horace Walpole, *Book of Materials*, 1759, 43, unpublished Ms. See https://libsvcs-1.its.yale.edu/hwcorrespondence/page.asp?vol=34&page=38, accessed 19 June 2024.
2 Summerson 1959, 568.
3 Allen D. Boyer, *Sir Edward Coke and the Elizabethan Age*, New Haven 2003; James 1929.
4 For more details, cf. James 1929, Mortlock 2007.
5 Stirling 1908, 74ff.
6 Parker 1975, Wade Martins 2009.
7 Lees-Milne 1962, 225ff., Moore 1985 and 2014.
8 James 1929, 187.
9 James 1929, 190.
10 Wilson 1984, 25.
11 Cf. James 1929, 211 and a letter of 24 September 1718 to Lord Harley: 'We are told they went to see Blenheim, and that the Duchess of Marlborough, who was there at that time, sent them word they should not see it.' HMC Report on the Mss. of his Grace the Duke of Portland KG, preserved at Welbeck Abbey, vol. VII, London 1901.
12 Holkham Archives [hereafter HA] 1718.
13 Rented from Lady Margaret's father. Lees-Milne 1962, 235.
14 James 1929, 212.
15 According to the Bank of England's Inflation Calculator, https://www.bankofengland.co.uk/monetary-policy/inflation/inflation-calculator, accessed November 2023.
16 Parker 1975, 13.
17 HA A/3, 6ff.
18 Parker 1975, 19.
19 Edward Spelman, *The Expedition of Cyrus*, London 1742.
20 Kent had been involved in what he calls 'an imbroglio' about exporting the statue from Rome in the course of which he had been threatened with banishment from Rome; cf. Wilson 1984, 20.
21 Holkham Account Books A/3, 44. See also Mortlock 2007, 114ff.
22 HMC Manuscripts of the Earl of Egmont, vol. I, 26 January 1729/30.
23 Kenneth Ellis, *The Post Office in the Eighteenth Century*, Oxford 1958.
24 *The Gentleman's Magazine*, October 1753, 493.
25 Christopher Johnson, *Highwayman: The Genuine Lives of C. Johnson, J. Stockdale etc.*, 1753 [British Library 6496.b.19].
26 Clark 1992, 251ff.
27 Ibid., 224.
28 Norwich City Records 13e/5.
29 As a young MP, Coke's son Edward played a prominent rôle in the impeachment of the rebel Lords in 1746, after the Jacobite rising: Stirling 1908, 48. It should also be noted that the tablets on the chimneypieces in the Saloon at Holkham with their allegedly pro-Jacobite meaning were executed in the 1750s, years after the Jacobite rebellion had been dealt with.
30 *The Complete Free Mason or Multa Paucis for Lovers of Secrets*. No place, no date (c. 1763/4), 95 [Bodley G. Pamph. 2789].
31 Strangways 1950, 73.
32 BL Add. Ms. 35,587 fol. 298.
33 Hiskey 1997, letter no. 11.
34 Williams 1822, vol. I, 85ff.
35 Williams 1822, vol. I, 243ff.
36 BL Add. Ms. 27,735 fol. 1.
37 *An Epistle from Lord L--l to Lord C--d*. By Mr P---., London 1740 [BL 162 n. 56].
38 Horace Walpole, *Book of Materials* 1759, 43 (see note 1).
39 Equal to 124 kilograms.
40 Boughton House Archives, 1749.
41 List of Fellows of the Royal Society, 1754 [Bodley, fol. Delta 782]. See also *The Gentleman's Magazine*, 1759, 194.
42 Stirling 1908, 91.
43 Kenneth Poolman, *The Speedwell Voyage: A Tale of Piracy and Mutiny in the Eighteenth Century,* Annapolis 1999.
44 Quoted after James 1929, 236.
45 Coke 1889, I, lx–lxi.
46 Coke 1889, I, lxix.
47 James 1929, 248.
48 Preserved as BL Add. Ms. 32,737, fols. 87, 89.
49 James 1929, 256.
50 Walpole 1937, 34, 111.
51 James 1929, 273.
52 James Lees-Milne interpreted this to mean 'a browbeaten, ineffectual person, the very opposite of what she certainly turned out to be', Lees-Milne 1962, 234.
53 Lees-Milne 1962, 262.
54 James 1929, 261.
55 Stirling 1908, 63.
56 Stirling 1908, 64.
57 HCA 7 (1760).
58 According to the inventory compiled after Lord Leicester's death. Murdoch 2006, 229.
59 Pictures of such an *etui* can be found at http://www.petergh.f2s.com/instruments2.html#etui1, accessed 4 July 2024.
60 Brettingham 1761, Dedication to the Duke of Cumberland. Coke's detailed involvement and guiding rôle in the designing and building of Holkham are discussed in the Architecture chapter.
61 Amongst others by Lees-Milne 1962 and Salmon 2015.
62 One might quote the example of the first Earl of Hopetoun, who knew what he wanted at Hopetoun House in the 1720s: Hopetoun 2020, 109ff.
63 Tipping 1928, 210.
64 'Lord Burlington was so much for Palladio, that he used to run down Michael Angelo. 'Tis true the latter did not follow the rules so much as the former'. Joseph Spence, *Anecdotes, Observations, and Characters of Books and Men*, London 1820, 106.
65 Letter by Robert Adam quoted in John Fleming, *Robert Adam and his Circle in Edinburgh and Rome*, Cambridge 1962, 197.
66 Frank Salmon thinks the picture was produced posthumously (Salmon 2015, 86f.), in which case it would have been commissioned by the widow, Lady

Margaret, wanting to do justice to her husband's architectural achievements.

67 Holkham Archives M/64, map of Holkham by Thomas Clerke, 1590. It was not unusual in Norfolk for parishes to be divided between two or more manors.
68 K. J. Allison, 'The Sheep–Corn Husbandry of Norfolk in the 16th and 17th Centuries', in: *Agricultural History Review*, 1957, 12–30.
69 HA, Holkham Deed 656 (i) 'A particular of all the corne growing within the fields and tythable places of Holkham in the year of our lord 1640 my master's only excepted'; Holkham Deed 679, 'A particular of the corn growing within the fields of Holkham in the year 1643.' On medieval husbandry at Holkham, see W. O. Hassall and J. Beauroy, *Lordship and Landscape in Norfolk, 1250 –1350: The Early Records of Holkham* (Oxford 1993), 50–54.
70 HA, F/LCJ 3.
71 HA, Misc. Deed 3795, grant to George Knightley of wardship of Meriel Wheatley, 12 Mar. 43 Eliz. [1602].
72 HA, Family Deed 3, quoting Proverbs 13:22.
73 HA, Holkham Deed 837, 'Reasons to be presented to the committee against Sir Robert Coke's bill', n.d. [1642].
74 Norfolk Record Office, DN/INV 17/8, probate inventory of Anthony Wheatley, 1601.
75 HA F/JC5, letter addressed to John Coke at 'Holkham Hall', from George Purton, Holt, 22 Feb. 1633/34; F/JC 80, account book of Philip Palgrave 1657–60, 122–9; M/66, map of Holkham *c.* 1730, showing the only surviving plan of the old hall.
76 R. W. Ketton-Cremer, *Norfolk Portraits*, London 1944, 41.
77 HA, Tittleshall Deed 107, inventory, undated [1661] among Godwick Hall papers, recently identified as relating to the Holkham house.
78 HA F/JC (Y)1, vouchers: turkeys are mentioned on 5 August 1661 and *passim*. The seeds in a detailed list cited by James 1929, 130, to indicate the wide range of vegetables grown at Holkham, were, in fact, supplied to Robert Coke's London home, Hampden House, King Street (now Downing Street), which also had a sizeable garden: F/G2 (1), 152.
79 James 1929, 111.
80 Barbara English and John Saville, *Strict Settlement,* Hull 1983, 54–5.
81 For a more complete account of the development of the Holkham landscape, see Williamson 1998, 59–72, 100–04, 210, 245–7.
82 HA, maps 2/1 and 2/2.
83 HA; the main sources for this period are the account books, A/11, A/32–7. The writ of *ad quod damnum* is in the Public Records Office, Kew: PRO c 134/37 (7) M9 (U2).
84 This second phase of works is detailed in HA, A 36–9.
85 HA, map 2/4.
86 HA, map 2/3.
87 B. Cozens-Hardy (ed.), *The Diary of Sylas Neville, 1767–1788,* Oxford 1950, 329.
88 Michaelis 1882, 322 still described it.
89 This phase of the park's development is detailed in Holkham accounts, especially A/45, A/46, A/47, A/Au 41 and A/Au 50, and map 2/5. For the Road Closure Orders, see Norfolk Records Office, NRO C/Sce 1, Book 1, 441–7; C/Sce 1, Book 3, 290–2; and C/Sce 1, Book 1, 505–8.
90 John Sandys' notebook of planting at Holkham, HA.
91 Humphry Repton, 'Red Book for Holkham', 1789; Holkham Hall, library.
92 Illustrated in Hiskey 2016, 296.
93 J. C. Curwen, *General Hints on Agricultural Subjects*, London 1809, 238.
94 HA E/Gar 1.
95 HA A/33 for the years 1727/28.
96 HA A/33, 105.
97 HA A/33, 103.
98 See HA A/36, 53, 72, 80, 88 and 106. Also: HA A/38, 52 and A/45 for the year 1761.
99 HA A/36 and A/39, 105.
100 HA A/35, entries of 10 and 29 July 1731.
101 HA A/36, 63 and HA A/36, 90.
102 HA A/36, 55.
103 Ibid.
104 Hiskey 1997, 154.
105 HA A/36, 47.
106 See also Williamson 1998, 245–7, and Stephen Daniels, *Humphrey Repton: Landscape Gardening and the Geography of Georgian England,* New Haven and London 1999, 81–3.
107 Next to Colen Campbell's Wanstead (built 1713–17, demolished 1824); see Hannah Armstrong, *Wanstead House: East London's Lost Palace*, London 2022.
108 British Library K.Top.31.42b-h, first published in Schmidt 1980, 215.
109 HCA 2.
110 Tavernor 1991, 174.
111 Lincolnshire Archives, Monson 7/13/87. Quoted with the kind permission of the Trustees of the 10th Lord Monson and Lincolnshire Archives.
112 VB I (1715), 5.
113 Summerson 1959, 94, going on to say that 'no previous English house had displayed such spectacular and rational loyalty to Rome.'
114 Used by Campbell for his Wanstead III design, dated 1720 by Summerson 1959, 94.
115 A type of window Burlington copied from one of the Palladio drawings in his possession; Barnard and Clarke 1995, 6 and 10.
116 Harris 1994, cat. no. 13.
117 Burlington employed this feature in his design for Tottenham, but not at Chiswick; it persisted, however, through several later versions of Holkham's façade, in both Brettingham's and Kent's drawings, before it was dropped.
118 Brettingham 1773, vii.
119 Palladio 1570, II.13.
120 Harris 1994, 141, 147.
121 In later years Brettingham used the concept very successfully for grand aristocratic town houses he was commissioned to build in London, such as Norfolk House on St James's Square (built 1748–52, demolished 1938) and Egremont House (built 1756–61) on Piccadilly (now Cambridge House). Coke and Brettingham also used it to develop the plan for Coke's own house project on Berkeley Square (see 'Coke architectus' in Chapter 1).
122 Hiskey 1997, 147. The letter itself bears no date but must have been written in March 1734, as the next letter in the series, dated 1 April 1734, clearly refers to it. Some historians, including Hiskey and Salmon, thought that 'our whole design' and the 'going up steps from the hall' referred to the Holkham II concept in general and to the Marble Hall in particular, not realising that Coke, at this stage, was clearly only talking about the latest designs for the project at hand, i.e. Family Wing. As Coke was in regular personal contact with Burlington – in 1731 alone, several visits to Chiswick are recorded in the Holkham accounts (Hiskey 2017, 95) – the latter would have of course have long been familiar with the Holkham I concept and had no need to comment on it.
123 Weber 2013, 27.
124 Letter quoted in Jourdain 1948, 31. It took until January 1720 for the statue to arrive in London aboard HMS *Superb*.
125 Quoted by Jourdain 1948, 45.
126 Mowl 2006, xixf.
127 Coke to Burlington in 1738/9: 'All respects to your Lord^{p} & to Lady

Burlington . . .; no compliments from me to Signor Cazzo Vestito ['Mr Codpiece' - Kent] who would not come to see me, tho' I had cherry Brandy from France on purpose for him w[ch] he shall pay for.' Tipping 1928, 210.

128 Mowl 2006, 217.

129 Discovered by the late W. O. Hassall, inserted into a copy of Blomefield's *Norfolk* in the library of the Queen's College in Oxford.

130 Cf. Burlington's house for General Wade in London, VB III, pl. 10.

131 Timothy Mowl called it a 'disaster' that Kent designed the pavilions 'in a different style that neither accords nor dramatically clashes with the solemn centrepiece', Mowl 2006, 223.

132 Letter quoted by Tipping 1928, 210.

133 Kent received 3 guineas in 1730 and £30 in 1737 (Hiskey 2016, 92). Artists and architects of the time clearly did not get rich even from a big commission: even Brettingham was only paid £100 per annum for supervising all the building affairs of the house, equalling just £16,000 in today's terms: not beyond the dreams of avarice.

134 Palladio 1570, II.27.

135 Drawn by Stephen Wright and dated 1733, Sir John Soane's Museum, SM 37/4/4; see also Salmon 2013b, figs. 13.21, 13.23–5. It seems reasonable to assume that the idea originated at Holkham and that Kent then used it for his designs.

136 Nearby Houghton provides a good example.

137 VB II, 4.

138 Giacomo Leoni, *The Architecture of L. B. Alberti*, vol. V, London 1726, 99.

139 Michael Vickers, 'The use of the royal cubit in country house design', in: *Looking Forwards: The Country House in Contemporary Research and Conservation*, Cottbus 1999. The exact dimension of the royal, or Salomonic, cubit has always been a matter of debate, so the designers of Holkham may have hesitated before deciding which version to employ in the building. According to precise measurement with modern methods, Holkham's façade extends for 104.15 metres – 341 feet 8 inches. Royal cubits were of immense relevance to Freemasons, as they were the unit employed for Solomon's Temple, and in view of Thomas Coke's prominent rôle in English freemasonry (he was Grand Master in 1731) one would expect to find his new building imbued with Masonic significance as a matter of course. And indeed, whilst closer inspection does not necessarily reveal the royal cubit being significant in every dimension of the house, clear resonances of Solomon's Temple, as interpreted by Freemasons, can be shown in the overall layout. The 200 royal cubits of Holkham's façade conform, in Ezekiel's very detailed vision of the Temple, to the front length of the inner building; the building framing in turn the Tabernacle or inner sanctum.

140 'The inner sanctuary was twenty cubits long, twenty wide and twenty high'; 1 Kings 6:20.

141 1 Kings 7:21.

142 1 Kings 7:29 mentions 'lions, bulls and cherubim' as part of the Temple's decoration: *putti* and bulls' skulls adorn the frieze in Holkham's Marble Hall.

143 In fact, the engraving is 'after an original drawing by (John) Webb dated 1665'; Peter Ward-Jackson, *English Furniture Design of the Eighteenth Century*, London 1958, 32.

144 Horace Walpole, *Anecdotes of Painting in England*, 4 vols., Twickenham 1762–71, vol. IV, 115.

145 Brettingham 1773, v.

146 Salmon 2018, 42.

147 Salmon 2013a, 74.

148 For a detailed rebuttal, cf. Schmidt 2015; see also Salmon 2018.

149 Letter to the Duke of Newcastle quoted in Salmon 2013a, 76 after James 1929, 255.

150 BL Add. Ms. 32,713 fol. 165, Letter to the Duke of Newcastle written from Holkham, 29 September 1747.

151 Packington Hall, Warwickshire – cf. Binney CL 1970 (July 9, 16, 23); Lowther Castle, Westmorland – cf. Colvin 1980.

152 The wing was then connected to the old house by a wooden passage on the basement level.

153 Hiskey 1997, 155.

154 Apart from the fact that comparatively little money was spent on digging and foundation work, the phrase 'digging trenches for the foundations' used in the building accounts for the first activities on the main body of the house in 1741 is telling.

155 'Mylord Leicesters neues Gebäude wird eines der magnifiquesten in Engelland werden, es ist ein groß corps de logis, mit 4 Flügeln, so als Pavillons damit connectirt sind. 1 Pavilon ist fertig, und die Rustick Story vom Hause. . . . Diese Pavillons sind durchaus gewölbet, aber nicht tief versencket' – Hardenberg's travel diary is kept in the Geheimes Preussisches Staatsarchiv in Berlin-Dahlem (information kindly supplied by Bernd Adam).

156 Between April 1759 and February 1760, labourers were paid for 'moving the earth from the foundations of the stables and laying it on the North front of the house to raise the lawn'; from October 1760 to April 1761, they were paid for 'digging, filling and spreading Gravell to make the Terrace on the So front of the House'.

157 The fact that the northern half was joined to the earlier southern half has left its traces in the roof construction, as can be seen in the north–south section.

158 James 1929, 268.

159 HA, C/B Ms 17.

160 A detailed labour book showing what each workman was doing each day between June 1757 and Lord Leicester's death in April 1759 has survived at Holkham.

161 I am grateful to Werner Koch for his analysis of the paint layers in the Marble Hall.

162 DD/FD 56B.

163 Amy Boyington, 'The Countess of Leicester and her contribution to Holkham Hall', *The Georgian Group Journal* 22 (2014), 56.

164 HA A/44, 24.

165 HA H/Inv 4, reproduced in Murdoch 2006, 210. Brettingham 1773, 12f.

166 For a description of the decoration of Family Wing and its links to Kent, see Hardwick-Kulpa 2024.

167 Compared to the designs illustrated in Matthew Brettingham senior, *The Plans, Elevations and Sections of Holkham*, 1761, pls. 14, 15.

168 This change in design can be evidenced by comparing the built structure with the plans published in Brettingham 1761, pls. 14, 15. Of the three paintings, one was brought from Thanet House; one was sent from Italy by Gavin Hamilton, arriving shortly after Thomas Coke's death, and seems to have been temporarily stored, along with the third painting (provenance unknown) in the South Dining Room.

169 Brettingham 1773, x.

170 Ibid.

171 Hiskey 1997, 148ff.

172 W. O. Hassall, 'The Temple at Holkham, Norfolk', in: *Country Life*, 16 May 1968.

173 Brettingham 1773, x.

174 Various brick moulds are preserved at Holkham, but they are most likely nineteenth-century.

175 Letter in Tipping 1928.
176 Published in Campbell VB 3, pl. 10.
177 Beverly Sprague Allen, *Tides in English Taste, 1619–1800*, 2 vols., Cambridge, MA 1937, I.106.
178 Cf. also Clark 1992.
179 Vardy 1744, pl. 38.
180 Cf. Moore 1996, no. 36.
181 Interpreted as crypto-Jacobite symbolism by Clark 1992.
182 Cornforth 2004, 317.
183 Ware 1735, pl. 38.
184 Vardy 1744, pl. 14; Moore 1996, no. 58.
185 HDA 9.
186 Murdoch 2006.
187 Remnants of the presses were discovered in the voids between the solid brick structure and the wood-and-plaster shell of the room by the house carpenter, Ian Barrett, and the administrator, Michael Daley, in 2005.
188 Vardy 1744, pl. 16.
189 Vardy 1744, pls. 12 and 41; Moore 1996, no. 47.
190 Brettingham 1773, 6.
191 Kent 1727, pl. 62.
192 J. Mallett, 'Rococo English porcelain', in: *Apollo*, October 1969, 100–13, fig. 6.
193 Desgodetz 1682, pl. 155.
194 Vardy 1744, pl. 6.
195 Ware 1743, pl. 40.
196 Vardy 1744, pl. 38.
197 HA Holkham Day Book, 'Wine Consumption', shows that Zuccarelli lived at Holkham between December 1756 and November 1757.
198 The same varicoloured Genoese velvet was used on a bed that John Vardy designed in the 1740s for King George II. The Imperial crown was displayed in its triumphal arched cornice, as well as in a trophy above the headboard which celebrated 'Love's Triumph'. The bed, with certain alterations, was listed in Chatsworth, Derbyshire in the 1760s and is now at Hardwick, Derbyshire. Cf. D. Adshead and D. Taylor, and Annabel Westman, *Hardwick Hall*, 2016, figs. 277f.
199 Summerson 1970, 317.
200 Adam Smith, *Theory of Moral Sentiments*, London 1759, IV.I.4.
201 Simond 1817, 285f.
202 This essay is a revised and abbreviated version of E. Angelicoussis, *The Holkham Collection of Classical Sculptures*, Philip von Zabern, Mainz am Rhein, 2001. The most important research on the sculptural collection was originally done by A. Michaelis, *Ancient Marbles in Great Britain*, Forgotten Books, London, 2018, 58ff, 302ff. nos. 1–60.
203 For Coke's ruinous speculation in South Sea stock in 1720 and its financial repercussions, see Hiskey 2016, 85f.
204 For a detailed itinerary of his travels, see Moore 1985, 33ff. and Hiskey 2016, 65ff.
205 F. Haskell and N. Penny, *Taste and the Antique: The Lure of Classical Sculpture 1500–1900*, Yale University Press, New Haven, CT, 1981, 23.
206 Matthew Brettingham the younger alleged the attribution in his *Plans* (1773), 5. See Michaelis's opinion: 'one of the most striking successes [of restorations that] I know', Michaelis 1882, 314 no. 36.
207 For the archival research that discovered what actually occurred, see Bruschetti et al. 2014, 138f., I.15.
208 For the heated exchanges between Walston and G. Dickins, see *Journal of Hellenic Studies* 33, 1913, 276ff.; 34, 1914, 122ff., 312ff.
209 C. Parisi Presicce, *La Lupa di Roma* (Rome: Franco Maria Ricci Editore, 2011).
210 *Rosso antico* was much prized by the ancient Romans. The quarries from which this marble was obtained are situated on the Taenarus promontory of the lower Peloponnese. See L. Lazzarini in M. True (ed.), *Marble: Art Historical and Scientific Perspectives on Ancient Stone*, Symposium J. Paul Getty Museum 1988 (Malibu: The J. Paul Getty Museum, 1990), 237–51.
211 For the locale of the school, see K. Fittschen, 'Eine Stadt für Schaulustige und Müssiggänger', in: *Stadtbild und Burgerbild in Hellenismus*, ed. M. Wörrle and P. Zanker, Colloquium Munich, 1993, *Vestigia* 47 (1995): 60 n. 42. For the proposed layout, ibid., 61.
212 Brettingham 1773, 4.
213 R. Payne Knight, *Specimens of Antient Sculpture, Aegyptian, Etruscan, Greek and Roman*, vol. II, Forgotten Books, London, 2018, pl. 27.
214 All the casts were procured by Matthew Brettingham the younger in Rome. The locations of the casts' originals are as follows. Callipygian Venus: Museo Nazionale, Naples. Mercury: Uffizi, Florence. St Susanna: S. Maria di Loreto, Rome. Antinous: Capitoline Museum, Rome. Isis: Capitoline Museum, Rome. Bacchus: Uffizi, Florence. Flora: Capitoline Museum, Rome. Apollo: Villa Albani, Rome.
215 Hiskey 2016, 219.
216 M. R. Lagerhöf, *Ideal Landscape: Annibale Carracci, Nicolas Poussin and Claude Lorrain*, Yale University Press, New Haven, CT, 1990, 4, 30ff.; D. Cosgrave, *The Palladian Landscape*, Leicester University Press, Leicester, 1993, 107ff. For the decoration of a room with frescoes imitating the views from windows at the Villa Godi-Malinveri, see Cosgrave, 11 and figs. 1, 5.
217 For the original layout of the grounds, see Hiskey 2016, 181ff. Appendix 2, 531f.
218 So far the two most important interpretations of the paintings collection are Schmidt 1980, 81–2 and Russell 1989. Mary Tavener Holmes discusses it in a book on the principles of eighteenth-century paintings displays (with Christoph Martin Vogtherr, forthcoming).
219 On Coke's Grand Tour: Hiskey 2016, 65–77; on the acquisitions in the 1750s, see 227–9.
220 Recte: Caspar van Wittel. (Brettingham 1773, 10 calls him 'Occhiali', as he was also known as Gaspare degli Occhiali, Caspar with Glasses.) His painting of the Colosseum was then in the Closet to North State Bedchamber; it is now in Family Wing.
221 Letters by Lord Leicester to Brettingham (1738 and 1740): Hiskey 1997, 153–5.
222 Cf. Schmidt 1980, 27–36.
223 On work after Lord Leicester's death and Lady Leicester's rôle: Hiskey 2016, 230–41.
224 Russell 1989, 137. Russell stresses almost exclusively the aesthetic quality of the arrangement at Holkham Hall.
225 This architectural approach to placing and framing paintings can also be observed in other countries, such as Italy or Prussia, but the phenomenon is much more important in England.
226 See Gervase Jackson-Stops, 'Mythology and the Country House', in: *The Fashioning and Functioning of the British Country House*, Washington, DC, 1989, Studies in the History of Art 25, Center for Advanced Study in the Visual Arts. Symposium Papers 10, 217–38.
227 HInv 2. 62; HInv 4, 32; Brettingham 1773, 6–8; Cornforth 1991, 168–71.
228 Quoted after Cornforth 1991, 170.
229 HInv 2, 61; HInv 4, 31; Brettingham 1773, 3.
230 Moore 1996, 57.
231 HInv 2, 61; HInv 4, 32; Brettingham 1773, 2–3.
232 Pietro da Cortona, *Bittflehende vor einem römischen Feldherrn (Coriolan)*. Kupferstichkabinett Berlin, 00108496.

The identification is supported not only by Brettingham's characterisation (Brettingham 1773, 2f.) but even more so by a detailed description of 1773: 'Coriolanus. The figure of the old man kneeling before Coriolanus, and hiding his face with his hands, is extremely fine; but the figure of Coriolanus himself without dignity, haughtiness, or any great expression. The wife leading the two children, and smiling on them, forms a figure of no expression.' *The Norfolk Tour*, Norwich 1773², 21f. – Bodley [Gough Adds. Norfolk 8° 36].

233 HInv 2, 62; HInv 4, 32; Brettingham 1773, 6.

234 For this and the following rooms: HInv 2, 62f. (Lady Leicester's state apartment is not yet described); HInv 4, 32f.; Brettingham 1773, 8–12.

235 Hiskey 1997, 152.

236 Hiskey 1997, 149.

237 Letter quoted by Tipping 1928.

238 Hiskey 1997, 154.

239 Giovanni Boccaccio, *The Decameron containing an hundred pleasant novels*, 2 vols., Isaac Jaggard, London 1620; Philemon Holland, *The Roman History Written in Latine by Titus Livius with the supplement of J. Freinshemius and J. Dujatius faithfully done into English*, Churchill Awnsham, London 1686; Maximilien Misson, *A New Voyage to Italy*, London 1695.

240 F. Nardini, *Roma antica*, Rome 1704; Thomas Godwin, *Romanae historiae anthologia*, London 1686; Giovan Pietro Bellori, *Le pitture antiche del sepolcro de Nasoni nella Via Flaminia*, Rome 1680.

241 As described by Hobart in an undated letter from Naples to the Earl of Nottingham, sent after 15 November 1707; see Reynolds, 'Thomas Coke e la storiografia romana', in *Seduzione etrusca*, 81 and n. 17.

242 F/TC 4.

243 F/TC 4, 51; possibly identifiable with the *Theatrum basilicae Pisanae* by Giuseppe Martini, Rome 1705, still at Holkham.

244 F/TC 4, 72. Both editions are still at Holkham: the first bears the bookplate of Edward Coke dated 1701, the second preserves an Italian parchment binding with Coke's arms added.

245 F/TC 3. For a fuller description of Ferrari's catalogue, see Reynolds 2015, 'The Holkham Manuscripts: An Introduction', 13–15.

246 F/TC 3, fol. 80, shelf 142: 'Bartoli. Delle grotte di Roma. It. fo. Roma 1706.' The book is also listed in the Library Inventory commissioned in 1772 by Margaret Countess Dowager of Leicester, Holkham Ms. 769i, fol. 24: 'Library, Architecture, Antiquities, Prints, Drawings, Coins &c, Case 4, shelf 3, Folio'. A different Roman edition of Bartoli, *Antichi sepolcri*, 'con figure, Corio Russico, Rome 1697', is recorded on fol. 15 of the same inventory under the heading 'Architecture, Antiquities, Prints, Coins, Case 3, shelf 3, Folio'.

247 F/TC4, 55.

248 F/TC4, 71, 17 May 1714.

249 Two printed editions of Plutarch's works still at Holkham display annotations, respectively in French and in English, that may reasonably exclude an Italian provenance for them, whereas the record could also have referred to a Venetian edition of 1667, also sold in the Norwich sale of 1851, Lot 117: 'Plutarchi, *Vite*, trad. da L. Domenichi, 2 vols, Venice, 1667, bdg on parchment "neat".'

250 Letter of 24 May 1714. F/G 2/2, 467.

251 F/G 2/2, 463f., Thomas Coke to Sir John Newton, Turin, 3 January 1715.

252 Reynolds 2015, 'The Holkham Manuscripts: An Introduction', 7 n. 52.

253 F/TC4, 128.

254 F/TC6, 13.

255 Reynolds 2015, 'The Holkham Manuscripts: An Introduction', 7. One of them, a fourteenth-century French copy of the *Digestum novum* (Ms. 208), was signed jointly by Thomas Coke and Thomas Hobart, and remained in the possession of the pupil after the death of his old governor in April 1727. Coke inherited a manuscript from Ferrari in 1744, an Italian copy of Statius, dated June 1408 (Ms. 330). He also inherited some of their printed books, twenty-one from Hobart and no fewer than 172 from Ferrari.

256 F/TC4, 199.

257 HA A/5, 67.

258 F/TC 3, fol. 93v, Ms. 769i, fol. 9: [Long] Library, Libri Classici, Case 2, shelf 1.

259 F/TC4, 161.

260 F/TC 3, fols. 82v–83, shelf 128.

261 F/TC 3, fol. 82r–v, shelf 137.

262 F/TC 3, fol. 80r, shelf 142. Campbell's *Vitruvius Britannicus* is no longer at Holkham.

263 F/TC 3, fol. 81r, shelf 134.

264 Brettingham 1773, 16, describes the chimney in the Blue and Yellow Bedchamber, but then illustrates it as being in the Tapestry Bedchamber, pl. 50. It can be seen in the Tapestry Bedchamber (now a bathroom). See Isaac Ware, *Designs of Inigo Jones and Others*, London 1731, pl. 32.

265 Hardwick-Kulpa 2024, 78f.

266 HA A/44, 41.

267 'William Atkinson', *Biographical Dictionary of British Sculptors*, available at https://gunnis.henry-moore.org/henrymoore/sculptor/browserecord.php?-action=browse&-recid=82&from_list=true&x=6, accessed 23 April 2024.

268 Adam Nicolson, *Men of Honour: Trafalgar and the Making of the English Hero*, London 2005, 166.

269 Young 1768, 8.

270 Comparison with Wolterton Hall, a contemporary villa in Norfolk, shows that the type works perfectly well on its own.

271 Hiskey 1997, 153f.

272 According to Philip Yorke, in Godber 1968, 143f.

273 The elder Brettingham dedicated his 1761 edition of the *Plans of Holkham* to the Duke of Cumberland.

274 James 1929, 272f.

275 Young 1768, 13.

276 Young 1768, 278ff.

277 HDA 4, 1723, 229.

278 HDA 4, 1755.

279 HA, C/MB 8, Thomas Coke to Matthew Brettingham, undated [possibly 1737], in Hiskey 1997, 152.

280 Brettingham 1773, vii.

281 Much of the information in the following paragraphs is based on successive inventories: HA, H/Inv 4 (1760), H/Inv 9 (1774).

282 HA, C/MB 11, Coke to Brettingham, undated [1738/39], printed in Hiskey 1997, 154.

283 Climenson 1899, 10.

284 Garry 2012, 226ff.

285 HA, recollections of Mrs J. Rattenbury, *née* Pearce, former kitchen maid, July 2002.

286 Climenson 1899, 10; HA, uncatalogued paper, 'Consumption of Meat in Holkham Hall 1856–81'.

287 HA, C/MB Lord Leicester to Brettingham junior, 3 July 1756.

288 Lady Beauchamp Proctor in 1764; Ms. in Forthampton Court, Glos., partly quoted in Ketton Cremer, *Norfolk Assembly*, 1957.

289 According to Girouard 1978, 219, bell systems began to appear in the 1760s and 1770s, and wires and cranks were introduced in the following decades. HA,

Account Books, A/39, fols. 100r, 107r, 109v; A/47, 212; A/48, 290; A/57, 103.

290 James 1929, 213.

291 Lilian Dickinson and Mary Stanton (eds.), *An Eighteenth-Century Correspondence, being the Letters of Deane Swift – Pitt – the Lyttletons … and others to Sanderson Miller*, London 1910, 396ff.

292 Climenson 1899, 8ff.

293 Philip Yorke in 1750, in Godber 1968, 143f.

294 Philip Yorke, in Godber 1968, 143f.

295 Boscawen visited in 1757; see James 1929, 272f.

296 Ms. in Forthampton Court, Glos., partly quoted in Ketton Cremer, *Norfolk Assembly*, 1957, who condemned her comments, however, as 'lively nonsense'.

297 A judgement echoed in print by Young 1768.

298 Mrs Poyntz wrote in 1766; see James 1929, 294.

299 Young 1768, 12. The nose, incidentally, is still broken.

300 Ms. in Forthampton Court, Glos.

301 Murdoch 2006, 226–9; H/Inv 7, list of 'Pictures brought from Russell Street June 1760' and 'The Account of Pictures sent from Italy to Holkham in November 1759 and May 1760'.

302 HA A/V 6/22 and also A/31, week ending 18 November 1758.

303 Brettingham 1773, 15–18.

304 H/Inv 7, fol. 13v. Lady Margaret rehomed the small statue of Isis in the North State Sitting Room, a pair of eighteenth-century busts of Marcus Aurelius and Caracalla in the South Drawing Room, a relief of Julius Caesar in the Green State Bedroom and an alabaster god 'Canopus' in the ante-room to Family Wing. For a description of Brettingham's difficulties exporting the statue of Isis, see J. Kenworthy-Browne, 'Matthew Brettingham's Rome Account Book, 1747–1754', *Walpole Society* 49 (1983): Appendix 1.

305 Brettingham 1773, 18f.

306 Murdoch 2006, 212f.; H/Inv 9, fols. 9v–10r; Mss. 769 and 749.

307 James 1929, 292f.

308 H/Inv 8 fols. 1 and 25.

309 Mrs Poyntz, quoted in James 1929, 294.

310 Brettingham 1773, iv.

311 HA, Holkham Almshouses Settlement, 5 April 1755.

312 Francis Blomfield continued by Charles Parkin, *An Essay towards a Topographical History of the County of Norfolk*, 1739–75, 809.

313 Lady Llanover (ed.), *The Autobiography and Correspondence of Mary Granville, Mrs Delany*, Second Series, vol. II, London 1862, 60ff.

314 J. T. Brighton, 'William Peckitt's Commission Book', *Walpole Society* 54 (1988), commission no. 153.

315 HA A/44, 37.

316 Wenman had challenged the will which left Holkham to Lady Margaret, and she in turn left a will leaving as much as she could to her sister.

317 Stirling 1908, 94–101.

318 HA A/57, 12 August 1845.

319 HA A/48; A/49 The original building accounts, complete and detailed as they are, give no indication that the house was limewashed when it was first built. On the contrary, as the younger Brettingham reported in his *Plans of Holkham* (1773), bricks (used instead of the more usual ashlar) were to be interpreted as a deliberate reference to ancient Rome; so it would make little sense to camouflage them with limewash. Nor was there any practical need to do so: the bricks and the original pointing are both so near perfect and hard-wearing that even today they show little deterioration. Close inspection of the surfaces indicates that there are still a few traces of the limewashing technique.

320 HA A/47.

321 Wade Martins 1980, 118.

322 Wade Martins 1980, 170.

323 HA A/57, P-M 36, P-M, 106.

324 Cf. Cornforth 1988.

325 HA A/63, 30 January 1854.

326 Hiskey 1997, 353.

327 Hiskey 1997, 490.

328 HA A/99, A/100.

329 HA A/101, 4 April 1912.

330 Hiskey 1997, 492.

331 Hiskey 1997, 504.

332 Robinson 1989, 144.

333 See also Glenconner 2019.

334 Hiskey 2016, 520.

335 Cornforth 1988 and 1991.

336 Fiennes 2022.

337 It is a pun or rebus on the family name. As Holkham's long-time librarian, Dr W. O. Hassall, once explained, the ancients believed ostriches to be capable of digesting iron. 'I digest' is *coquo* in Latin – and furthermore, the Chief Justice was of course famous for his digest of English law in the shape of his four-volume work, *Institutes of the Lawes of England* (1628).

PLATES

* ***Linked to video via the***
HIRMER AUGMENTED REALITY APP

PICTURE CREDITS

Lloyd Birch p. 50/51, fig. 47
bpk Kupferstichkabinett SMB / Jörg P. Anders fig. 190
Bridgeman Art Library figs. 40, 56, 74, 91, 213
British Library figs. 60–65
Chatsworth figs. 71, 72
Frank Dalton figs. 206, 237, p. 290/291
ETH Zurich figs. 93, 116, 122
Eton College fig. 212
Government Art Collection fig. 57
Historic Royal Palaces fig. 148
Holkham Estate fig. 26, 150, 225, 226, 227, 232, 235, 236, 238, 239
Christian Keller figs. 103–106, 113, 119
Lengyel–Toulouse figs. 168, 174
Grahame Mellanby FRSA fig. 242
Queen's College Oxford fig. 83
RIBA figs. 25, 58, 89, 96, 136
Leo Schmidt figs. 28, 35, 43, 48, 49, 87, 102, 108, 115, 120, 126, 127, 131, 135, 169, 194, 220, 223, 224, 228, 229, 231, 240, 241
Sir John Soane's Museum fig. 92
Sotheby's fig. 189

all others: Pete Huggins

ACKNOWLEDGEMENTS

The editors wish to express their gratitude to all those who have made this book possible.

Holkham is a very special place, imbued with a positive spirit. Throughout our many years at Holkham, everybody in and about the house has always been invariably kind, supportive and encouraging, making the work on this book a pure joy. At the risk of overlooking someone, we should like to name – in alphabetical order – Laura Ballantyne Taylor, Chris Betts, Emma Bushell, Aneta Derylak, Lucy Downing, Jake Fiennes, Jon Haggerwood, Laurane Herrieven, Katie Holmes, Belle Hutton, Archie Jennings, Lana Lyakhovych, Ryan Mills, Peter Mitchell, Maria de Peverelli, Lucy Purvis, Fiona Robertson, Alice Robinson, Jack Sharman, Mark Taylor, Niamh Walter, Lisa Wickens and Cecelia Woodhead.

Huge thanks to the Earl and Countess of Leicester for their enthusiastic and unflagging support and for their wonderful hospitality throughout the creation of this book!

Special thanks to Sarah Countess of Leicester for never giving up asking for a reprint of the original book – which turned into a much more ambitious project.

Many colleagues and friends have contributed to the study of Holkham over the years and also to this new book, which is, again, very much a group effort. Some have written passages or whole chapters of the text; others have helped with their specific technical ability or expertise. All the contributors are recorded on the title page, but we should particularly mention Christoph Martin Vogtherr, who restructured and greatly extended his section on Holkham's outstanding paintings. Widening the original circle of contributors, Lady Anne Glenconner, Katherine Hardwick-Kulpa and Laura Nuvoloni have filled in some deplorable gaps in the earlier book. Gerard M-F Hill deserves thanks and admiration for copyediting all the text and for contributing the exemplary index.

We should also like to name Elischa Bischof and Renée Lou Jungo in Zurich and Dominik Lengyel in Cottbus, who provided artwork and images. The photography by Pete Huggins stands out – his new illustrations of the text, his unprecedented series of plates documenting all the decorated rooms in the house and also the videos embedded in the book as a pioneering element of augmented reality. Working with Pete has been a pleasure and a privilege.

Many thanks to Markus Götzinger for his creative and sensitive choice and performance (with some colleagues) of tunes for the soundtracks of the embedded videos.

Joanne Colvin has always been helpful in many organisational matters.

We are also grateful for valuable advice and encouragement received from Tim Leese and from our much-respected colleagues Jeremy Musson and Tim Knox.

It has once more been a privilege and a joy to work with Hirmer in Munich, particularly Cordula Gielen, project director for this book, and graphic designer Sabine Frohmader, who created the layout. Our only sadness is that Thomas Zuhr, Hirmer's CEO who made both the original book and the current one possible through his enthusiastic support and encouragement, did not live to see the final product, as he died quite suddenly, and far too young, in July 2024. He is greatly missed.

Leo Schmidt and Elizabeth Angelicoussis

AUTHORS AND CONTRIBUTORS

Most books on great country houses and their estates are written by a single author. But great houses – and Holkham is a case in point – are complex creations, demanding expertise in many fields: architecture and interior decoration, landscape and garden design, as well as paintings, ancient sculpture, books and illuminated manuscripts.

This book on Holkham is the product of a novel approach. It brought together colleagues, each an expert in their respective field – but rather than writing a series of individual learned articles they set out to produce a joint work, speaking as it were with one voice, so as to do justice to the seamless whole produced by the creator of Holkham, Thomas Coke, in the eighteenth century. Some chapters and sections are written by one person, based on their individual research, but the chapter on the architecture in particular owes much to a research project in which a number of people were involved, generating new insights into the history of the house as a built structure.

The following list of contributors attempts to describe what each person brought to this book.

Elizabeth Angelicoussis FSA (London and Athens) is a classical archaeologist. She published *The Holkham Collection of Classical Sculptures* (2001). As co-editor she was instrumental in shaping the aims and standards of this new and greatly extended edition of the book. Her own contribution is pp. 209–37.

Peter Burman MBE FSA (Edinburgh) is honorary librarian of Hopetoun House. He contributed to Chapter 5.

Polly Feversham is an art historian who looked after Duncombe Park, Yorkshire. As co-editor of the original edition she greatly influenced the overall concept of the publication.

Anne Glenconner grew up at Holkham. She published *Lady in Waiting* (2019) and *A Haunting at Holkham* (2020). Her memories of her parents' and grandparents' time are recorded in pp. 339–44.

Katherine Hardwick-Kulpa was Collections Coordinator at Holkham; she now works at Chatsworth. She wrote pp. 153–5 and 329–32.

John Hardy FSA (London) is an art historian who worked for Christie's. He wrote pp. 192–207.

Uta Hassler is an architect and architectural historian, formerly a professor at ETH Zurich. She contributed to the research on the building history, Chapter 3.

Gerard M-F Hill is based in Cumbria. Apart from copyediting the whole book he contributed the index, pp. 361–67.

Christine Hiskey (Wells-next-the-Sea) is an historian and archivist at Holkham. She is the author of *Holkham: The Social, Architectural and Landscape History of a Great English Country House* (2016). She is also the author of pp. 293–303.

Markus Joachim is an architect and Special Librarian for Architecture at ETH Zurich. He contributed to the research on the building history, Chapter 3.

Christian Keller is an architect based in Gladbeck. He contributed to the research on the building history, Chapter 3.

Axel Klausmeier is an art historian and expert on historic gardens. He is also director of the Berlin Wall Foundation. He wrote pp. 73–75.

Werner Koch is a conservator of paintings and retired professor. He contributed to the research on the building history, Chapter 3.

Silke Langenberg is professor of building history and heritage conservation at ETH Zurich. She contributed to the research on the building history, Chapter 3.

Tom Leicester runs Holkham Estate. He wrote pp. 75–81.

Laura Nuvoloni is Holkham's librarian. She wrote pp. 260–270.

Bernhard Ritter (Braunschweig) is a retired professor of geodesy. He contributed to the research on the building history, Chapter 3.

Leo Schmidt FSA taught architectural conservation at Cottbus University. He wrote the Introduction, most of chapters 1, 3 and 6 as well as the introductory parts of the various chapters.

Christoph Martin Vogtherr is Director General of the Foundation for Prussian Castles and Gardens in Potsdam. He is the author of pp. 237–58.

Tom Williamson is a landscape historian and landscape archaeologist at the University of East Anglia in Norwich. He wrote pp. 53–73.

SELECTED BIBLIOGRAPHY

Angelicoussis, Elizabeth (2001): *The Holkham Collection of Classical Sculptures*, Monumenta Artis Romanae XXX, Mainz am Rhein

Barnard, Toby, and Jane Clark (1995): *Lord Burlington: Architecture, Art and Life*, London

Boyington, Amy (2014): 'The Countess of Leicester and Her Contribution to Holkham Hall', in: *The Georgian Group Journal* 22

Brettingham, Matthew [senior] (1761): *The Plans, Elevations and Sections, of Holkham in Norfolk, The Seat of the late Earl of Leicester*, London

Brettingham, Matthew [junior] (1773): *The Plans, Elevations and Sections, of Holkham in Norfolk, The Seat of the late Earl of Leicester, to which are added, The Ceilings and Chimney Pieces; and also, A Descriptive Account of the Statues, Pictures, and Drawings; Not in the former Edition*, London

Bruschetti, Paolo, et al. (eds) (2014): *Seduzione Etrusca. Dai Segreti di Holkham Hall alle meraviglie del British Museum*, Milan

Campbell, Colen (1715, 1717, 1725): *Vitruvius Britannicus, or The British Architect*, 3 vols., London

Clark, Jane (1992): 'Palladianism and the Divine Right of Kings: Jacobite Iconography', in: *Apollo*, no. 4/1992: 224–49

Climenson, E. J. (ed.) (1899): *Passages from the Diaries of Mrs Lybbe Powys of Hardwick House, Oxon. AD 1756 to 1808*, London

Coke, Lady Mary (1889–96): *The Letters and Journals of Lady Mary Coke,* 4 vols., Bath

Colvin, Howard et al. (eds.) (1980): *Architectural Drawings from Lowther Castle, Westmorland*, London

Cornforth, John (1988): 'Augustan Vision Restored', in: *Country Life*, 4 August

Cornforth, John (1991): 'Subtle Sequence Reconstructed', in: *Country Life*, 13 June

Cornforth, John (2004): *Early Georgian Interiors*, New Haven and London

Desgodetz, Antoine (1682): *Les Edifices antiques de Rome, dessinés et mesurés très exactement*, Paris

Fiennes, Jake (with Tim Ecott) (2022): *Land Healer: How Farming Can Save Britain's Countryside*, London

Fréart de Chambray, Roland (1702): *Parallèle de l'architecture antique avec la moderne*, Paris

Garry, Mary-Anne (2012): *Wealthy Masters – 'Provident and Kind': The Household at Holkham, 1697–1842*, Dereham

Girouard Mark (1978): *Life in the English Country House: A Social and Architectural History*, New Haven and London

Glenconner, Anne (2019): *Lady in Waiting: My Extraordinary Life in the Shadow of the Crown*, London

Glenconner, Anne (2020): *A Haunting at Holkham*, London

Godber, Joyce (1968): *The Marchioness Grey of Wrest Park*, Publications of the Bedfordshire Historical Record Society, vol. XLVII, Bedford

Hardwick-Kulpa, Katherine (2024): 'When Fixtures Aren't Fixed: Tracing William Kent's Fireplace Designs at Holkham Hall', in: *The Georgian Group Journal* 32

Harris, John (1994): *The Palladian Revival: Lord Burlington, His Villa and Garden at Chiswick,* New Haven and London

Hiskey, Christine (1997): 'The Building of Holkham Hall: Newly Discovered Letters', in: *Architectural History* 40: 144–58

Hiskey, Christine (2016): *Holkham: The Social, Architectural and Landscape History of a Great English Country House,* Norwich

Hopetoun, Countess of, Polly Feversham and Leo Schmidt (eds.) (2020): *Hopetoun – Scotland's Finest Stately Home*, Munich

James, Charles Warburton (1929): *Chief Justice Coke, His Family & Descendants at Holkham*, London

Jenkins, Simon (2004): *England's Thousand Best Houses*, London

Jourdain, Margaret (1948): *The Work of William Kent: Artist, Painter, Designer and Landscape Gardener*, London

Kent, William (1727): *The Designs of Inigo Jones*, London

Kenworthy-Browne, John (1983): 'Matthew Brettingham's Rome Account Book, 1747–1754', in: *The Walpole Society* 49, Bath

Lees-Milne, James (1962): *Earls of Creation*, London

Mandler, Peter (1997): *The Fall and Rise of the Stately Home*, New Haven and London

Michaelis, Adolf (1882): *Ancient Marbles in Great Britain*, Cambridge

Moore, Andrew (1985): *Norfolk and the Grand Tour: Eighteenth-Century Travellers Abroad and their Souvenirs,* Norwich

Moore, Andrew (1996): *Houghton Hall: The Prime Minister, The Empress and The Heritage*, London

Moore, Andrew (2014): 'Diventare "un perfetto virtuoso e und grande amante di quadri": Thomas Coke e il suo Grand Tour, 1712–1718', in: Bruschetti 2014

Mortlock, D. P. (2007): *Aristocratic Splendour: Money & the World of Thomas Coke, Earl of Leicester,* Stroud

Mowl, Timothy (2006): *William Kent: Architect, Designer, Opportunist*, London

Murdoch, Tessa (ed.) (2006): *Noble Households: Eighteenth-Century Inventories of Great English Houses; A Tribute to John Cornforth,* Cambridge

Musson, Jeremy (2009): *Up and Down Stairs: The History of the Country House Servant*, London

Palladio, Andrea (1570): *I Quattro Libri Dell'Architettura*, Venice

Parker, R. A. C. (1975): *Coke of Norfolk: A Financial and Agricultural Study, 1707–1842*, Oxford

Parissien, Steven (1994): *Palladian Style*, London

Reynolds, Suzanne (2015): *A Catalogue of the Manuscripts in the Library at Holkham Hall*, vol. 1, *Manuscripts from Italy to 1500 – Part 1: Shelfmarks 1–399*, Turnhout

Robinson, John Martin (1989): *The Country House at War*, London

Russel, Francis (1989): 'The hanging and display of pictures, 1700–1850', in: *The Fashioning and Functioning of the British Country House*, Washington DC, Studies in the History of Art 25 – Center for Advanced Study in the Visual Arts, Symposium Papers 10, 133–53, at p. 137

Salmon, Frank (2013a): '"Our Great Master Kent" and the design of Holkham Hall: A Reassessment', in: *Architectural History* 56: 63–96

Salmon, Frank (2013b): 'Public Commissions', in: Weber 2013

Salmon, Frank (2015): 'Thomas Coke and Holkham from 1718 to 1734: The Early History', in: *The Georgian Group Journal* 22

Salmon, Frank (2018): 'The Peer's "Smooth Piers": William Kent and Thomas Coke at Work Designing Holkham Hall in 1733–34', in: *The Georgian Group Journal* 26

Schmidt, Leo (1980): *Holkham Hall. Studien zur Architektur und Ausstattung*, PhD diss., Freiburg

Schmidt, Leo and John Cornforth (1980): 'Holkham Hall, Norfolk', in: *Country Life*, 24 and 31 January, 7 and 14 February

Schmidt, Leo (2015): 'Holkham Hall: An Architectural "Whodunnit"', in *Architectural History* 58: 83–108

Simond, Louis (1817): *Journal of a Tour and Residence in Great Britain during the Years 1810 and 1811*, 2 vols., Edinburgh and London

Stirling, A. M. W. (1908): *Coke of Norfolk and His Friends,* London and New York

Strangways, Giles, Earl of Ilchester (1950): *Lord Hervey and His Friends, 1726–38,* London

Stutchbury, Howard (1967): *The Architecture of Colen Campbell*, Manchester

Summerson, John (1959): 'The Classical Country House in 18th-Century England', in: *Journal of the Royal Society of Arts* 107, no. 5036, July 1959: 539–87

Summerson, John (1970): *Architecture in Britain 1530 to 1830*, The Pelican History of Art, Harmondsworth

Tavernor, Robert (1991): *Palladio and Palladianism*, London

Tipping, H. Avray (1928): 'Four Unpublished Letters of William Kent in the Possession of Lord Spencer', in: *The Architectural Review*, May 1928: 180–83, and June 1928: 209–11

Vardy, John (1744): *Some Designs of Inigo Jones and W. Kent*, London

Wade Martins, Susanna (1980): *A Great Estate at Work: The Holkham Estate and Its Inhabitants in the Nineteenth Century*, Cambridge

Wade Martins, Susanna (2009): *Coke of Norfolk, 1754–1842: A Biography,* Woodbridge

Walpole, Horace (1937): *Correspondence*, ed. Wilmarth Sheldon Lewis, New Haven and London

Ware, Isaac (1735): *The Plans, Elevations and Sections of Houghton in Norfolk*, London

Ware, Isaac (1743): *Designs of Inigo Jones and Others*, London

Weber, Susan (ed.) (2013): *William Kent: Designing Georgian Britain*, New Haven and London

Williams, Charles Hanbury (1822): *The Works of the Right Honourable Sir Chas. Hanbury Williams, K.B., Ambassador to the Courts of Russia, Saxony, &c. from the Originals in the Possession of his Grandson the Right Hon. The Earl of Essex: with Notes by Horace Walpole, Earl of Orford, In three Volumes, with Portraits,* London

Williamson, Tom (1995): *Polite Landscapes: Gardens and Society in Eighteenth-Century England*, Stroud

Williamson, Tom (1998): *The Archaeology of the Landscape Park: Garden Design in Norfolk, England, c. 1680–1840*, British Archaeological Reports, Oxford

Wilson, Michael (1984): *William Kent: Architect, Designer, Painter, Gardener, 1685–1748*, London

Wilson, Richard, and Alan Mackley (2000): *Creating Paradise: The Building of the English Country House, 1660–1880*, Hambledon and London

Worsley, Giles (1995): *Classical Architecture in Britain: The Heroic Age*, New Haven and London

Young, Arthur (1768): *A Six Weeks Tour through the Southern Counties of England and Wales*, London

INDEX

Note: The earldom of Leicester was first granted in 1107 and has been recreated several times since then. The title granted to Thomas Coke (1697–1759) was the fifth creation, and the title granted to Thomas William Coke (1754–1842) was the seventh creation, but in the context of Holkham Hall these are known as the first and second creations of the title.

Abbreviations

BL	British Library, London
Bodley	Bodleian Library, Oxford
CL	*Country Life*
DD/FD	Holkham Archives, Deeds, Family Deeds
F/G	Holkham Archives, Family Records, General
F/TC	Holkham Archives, Family Records, Thomas Coke
HA	Holkham Archives
HCA	Holkham Archives, Country Accounts
HDA	Holkham Archives, Domestic Accounts
HInv	Holkham Archives, Inventories
HMC	Historical Manuscripts Commission
VB	*Vitruvius Britannicus*

COLOPHON

Editors
Leo Schmidt, Elizabeth Angelicoussis

Authors and Contributors
Peter Burman, Polly Feversham, Anne Glenconner, Katherine Hardwick-Kulpa, John Hardy, Uta Hassler, Gerard M-F Hill, Christine Hiskey, Markus Joachim, Christian Keller, Axel Klausmeier, Werner Koch, Silke Langenberg, Tom Leicester, Laura Nuvoloni, Bernhard Ritter, Christoph Martin Vogtherr, Tom Williamson

Project Direction, Hirmer Publishers
Cordula Gielen

Copyediting
Gerard M-F Hill, Michael Pilewski

Proofreading
James Copeland

Graphic Design and Typesetting
Sabine Frohmader, Hirmer Publishers

Production
Sabine Frohmader, Lucia Ott,
Hirmer Publishers

Prepress
Reproline mediateam GmbH & Co. KG, Unterföhring

Paper
135 g/m² GardaPat Bianka

Typefaces
PSFournier Std, Helvetica Neue

Printing and Binding
Printer Trento S.r.l., Trento

Printed in Italy

Bibliographic information published by the Deutsche Nationalbibliothek
The Deutsche Nationalbibliothek lists this publication in the Deutsche Nationalbibliografie; detailed bibliographic data are available online at https://www.dnb.de.

Hirmer Publishers
Managing Director: Kerstin Ludolph
Bayerstraße 57–59
80335 Munich
Germany

ISBN 978-3-7774-4444-4

www.hirmerpublishers.com
www.hirmerpublishers.co.uk

Cover image: Holkham from the south, photo: Pete Huggins
Back cover image: Holkham, the Landscape Room (see also pl. 39), photo: Pete Huggins
Endpapers: Roman mosaic on a side table in the Saloon (see also fig. 134), photo: Pete Huggins

HIRMER AUGMENTED REALITY APP

Development, Implementation, Editing
Neue Gestaltung GmbH, Berlin

Videos
Pete Huggins

Soundtracks
Markus Götzinger

Music by
Henry Purcell and Georg Philipp Telemann performed by Markus Götzinger (oboe), Betina Müller (mandolin), Nikola Götzinger (cello) and Annegret Bohrig (double bass)

Sound Engineer
Johannes Urban